FRANCIS LEDWIDGE

A Life of the Poet

FRANCIS LEDWIDGE

A Life of the Poet

ALICE CURTAYNE

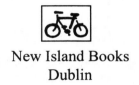

New Island Books
Dublin

Francis Ledwidge: A Life of the Poet
First published in 1972
by Martin Brian & O'Keeffe Ltd

This edition published November 1998
by New Island Books
2 Brookside
Dundrum Road
Dublin 14
Ireland

British Library Cataloguing in Publication Data
A catalogue record for this book is available from the British
Library

ISBN 1 874597 80 4

New Island Books receives financial assistance from The Arts
Council (An Chomhairle Ealaíon), Dublin, Ireland.

Cover design: Jon Berkeley
Printed in Ireland by Colour Books, Ltd.

To the memory of my brother,
Richard Curtayne, Irish Volunteer,
later private in the Irish Guards,
killed in the Battle of the Somme,
15 September 1916

Introduction

Jennifer Johnston

For quite a number of years now I have carried with me, tucked into the back of my diary, a copy of a letter written by my mother's eldest brother to his father. It is dated the tenth of August 1915.

Dear father,

We have been fighting now for four days and I am sorry to say have lost most of the Bn. We were doing fatigues for the first 2 days and only lost about 10 men but yesterday morning about 3 a.m. we were called up to stop a counter attack. In about 2 hours we lost 12 officers and about 450 men. How I got through I shall never understand, the shrapnel and bullets were coming down like hail. Three men were shot while handing me messages. The Colonel also got through all right. Luke had his hand blown off but is all right. Martin got a slight wound in the arm. In the last five nights I have had about 5 hours sleep but still feel fairly fit in body but my heart is broken for all those fellows I liked so much. The water here is very scarce. We get one qt. per day to do everything with, cook, wash, etc. I am at present watching the two divisions which are coming up to relieve us getting the most awful shelling. We are at present much nearer to the enemy than they are, but they are giving us a rest. When they come up we will all attack.

  After yesterday I have a feeling I shall get through this 'job'. I would like to see some of the young lads who are staying at home get a few days of this. If they weren't killed, they would or should die of shame.

I must shut up as I have a great deal to do before this show starts.

Give my love to mother and everybody at home. I hope you are well. So long. I have not had a mail yet.

Thanks ever so much for all you have done for me.

Yours as ever.
Billy

The letter arrived in Dublin after his death on Sunday August 15th, following an attack on a hill at Sulva Bay, taken, temporarily, at bayonet point and at a terrible cost of young men's lives.

I don't know why I carry this letter with me, except perhaps as some kind of warning; a warning against forgetting — or denying might be a better word — a clear and unequivocal happening in our history. The Great War existed. Thousands of Irishmen fought and died or were wounded in body and mind. Thousands of families, like my own, were bereaved. These are historical facts that no one in reality can deny. But what is reality to us? We prefer to see our history in terms of heroes and villains, traitors and patriots; such "Boy's Own" titles help us to forget what we don't want to remember. The truth about the Great War — or the forgotten war as we might call it — is that a very substantial number of men who went to fight in it were, like Francis Ledwidge, both emotionally and practically energised by the belief that the freedom that had for so long been denied to Ireland was at last within sight. They were doing what they believed to be the best thing for Ireland and Ireland's future. Ledwidge put it quite clearly: "I joined the British Army because she stood between Ireland and an enemy common to our civilisation and I would not have her say that she defended us while we did nothing at home but pass resolutions." Others, my uncle included, may not have had such clarity of thought, but by and large their reasons for joining were not ignoble.

When I was a child and growing up that war was still potently remembered. It was in a way more real to me than the war on the edge of which we so precariously perched between 1939-1945. The songs and the stories, the names of the famous Irish regiments were all part of our history; poppies were sold and bought on Remembrance Day, and old photographs of young men in uniform hung on the walls or stood on the mantlepieces of countless homes. Then in the fifties it was as if a door had been slammed and people had instantly forgotten what was behind it; no more sad or heroic stories, the war memorial garden in Inchicore was allowed to fall into a state of total decay. The pictures came off the walls in houses and were locked away as were the medals of the dead or now ageing men. It was as if the men who had fought in that terrible war had committed some crime, some act of treachery that we had to wipe from our memories.

Alice Curtayne's book was first published in the early seventies when our paranoia about those four years of our history was at its height. Her book is, so far, the only biography of the poet and her letters from and interviews with many of his family and companions in both peace and war give a detailed and compassionate picture of his life and death. Without Alice Curtayne's enthusiastic commitment to this young man and his poetry, it is all too possible that the work of Ledwidge might have been allowed to wither away, unread except by a few, simply because he died on the wrong day in a war that people might consider to be the wrong war. Things change though, and we are now more at ease with our past; perhaps less quick to point the damning finger. Maybe this book about such a fine poet and Irishman may help to speed the process of rediscovery. To get back to August 15th, 1915, Ledwidge wrote some days later to a friend at home:

> I am writing this at 7.30 a.m. in my trench 150 yards from the muzzles of Turkish rifles. Over my head, tons of shrapnel are passing every minute. I have many experiences which can only be told not written but the chief one happened on August 15th when you were probably watching "flappers" at Lady Well. We made a big advance that day, when our lines suffered heavily by death. We had to advance over open country towards a hill. How I got there I can't tell, but we did and more than that, we captured the position. When we handed it over to our reinforcements we were a jaded and sorry few. Only two officers were left.

Unlike my uncle, he survived Gallipoli, though his back gave way several months later in Serbia and he spent the best part of a year being shunted from one hospital to another, and then back to the war, this time to the Somme, where Alice Curtayne's own brother was killed, and then to Flanders where on July 31st 1917 Francis Ledwidge was killed, while on road mending duties. "Ledwidge killed. Blown to bits." was what the priest who found him wrote in his diary. "At Confession yesterday and Mass and Holy Communion this morning. R.I.P."

> He shall not hear the bittern cry,
> In the wild sky, where he is lain,
> Nor voices of the sweeter birds
> Above the wailing of the rain
>
> Nor shall he know when loud March blows
> Thro' slanting snows her fanfare shrill,
> Blowing to flame the golden cup
> Of many an upset daffodil
>
> But when the Dark Cow leaves the moor
> And passes poor with greedy weeds,
> Perhaps he'll hear her low at morn
> Lifting her horn in pleasant meads.

Jennifer Johnston

Acknowledgements

MY THANKS are due to H. E. John Cardinal Wright who, on a visit to Slane, originally suggested the idea of this biography by describing the cult of Ledwidge in Boston College, Mass. I could not have undertaken it without the help of: the poet's brother, Joseph, who was patient in dredging up from his memory the answers to my endless questions; the late Dowager Lady Dunsany who was co-operative in conversations and who procured for me the Ledwidge material from the Dunsany papers; Robert A. Christie who wrote out for me all his personal memories; his wife, Oliva and sister-in-law, Carrie, who co-operated with their cordial hospitality; John Shanahan, who allowed me to use the letters preserved by his late mother, *née* Lizzie Healy; Miss Katie Healy and Mrs Farrelly who made available to me other Ledwidge letters; Winifred McGoona, whose hospitality I enjoyed while copying Ledwidge material in her possession; her sister, Daisy and uncle, Patrick Mullen, who gave me the benefit of their personal recollections. Mr T. E. Duffy helped me over a long period, even assisting me to unearth the ledgers in which are recorded the Minutes of the meetings of the Navan Board of Guardians and Rural District Council. I am also indebted to Patrick Vaughey, Mr and Mrs Peter Baxter, John Phelan, John O'Neill, Mrs Cleary, Mrs Loughran (*née* Rita O'Neill), Mrs Ed Farrell, the late Dr Murnane, Tara; H. M. Johnston, M.C.C., Mrs Margaret Conway, Tony Lane, Mrs Clerkin and Miss B. Clerkin, U.D.C., John Ward (The Coalpits), Peter McGovern, Patrick Tiernan; Tom Mac Intyre for obtaining two copies of the now very scarce *The Young Gael*; Messrs Geo. A. O'Gorman, Editor *Drogheda Independent* and J. Davis, Editor *Meath Chronicle* for permission to quote freely from their files; Sigerson Clifford for the use of his unpublished poem; Peter Casey, Paddy Cowley, Henry Gallagher; Oliver D. Gogarty for permission to quote from his father's books and for a photostat copy of a poem; Michael J. Murphy, Mrs Lewis Chase, Washington, D.C., Mr Patrick L. Cooney, Elizabeth Johnston, Manchester Art Galleries, Messrs Constable and Pamela Hinkson for permission to quote from

Katharine Tynan's *Years of the Shadow*, C. E. F. Trench, Patrick J. Sampson and John Sampson, Duleek; Bill Dumbleton, who carried the research to Cairo for me; Laurence Michael Phillips, Jim Bradley, Sam Hughes, Londonderry, for his excellent report of Ledwidge in Ebrington Barracks; Mrs Thomas Dillon; Alan Denson for permission to quote from *Letters from AE*; Patrick Brady and Maire de Paor for allowing me to read their theses on Ledwidge; Thomas Cassidy, Knowth, John Giles, Eileen MacCarvill, Joe Kennedy (*Evening Herald*), Jack Fagan, John Hargrave for permission to quote from *The Suvla Bay Landing*; Terry O'Dea, Mervyn S. Carlyle, May Muriel (Mollie) Quin, Mrs Heather Anderson, Padraic Colum, Mrs D. Vincent; Dr R. C. Simington, Mr Edw. Keane. I am grateful to the Jesuit Fathers, Farm Street, London, and to the Revs M. Marry, Peadar Mac Suibhne, Philip Canon Boyle, Joseph P. Kelly and John Molloy. My thanks are due to the War Office Records Centre in Middlesex and to the staff at the Regimental Headquarters of the Royal Inniskilling Fusiliers in Omagh, especially Major B. J. Mahon, who posted to me books from their library, and his colleague, Colonel G. F. Maxwell, who gave me permission to quote freely from the files of the regimental journal *The Sprig of Shillelagh*; to Captain J. N. Roberts, Captain Cyril Falls and Leslie F. Falls, Lieut.-Col. E. A. G. Atkins, Major Terence Verschoyle, M.C., Major V. H. Scott, M.C., Brigadier G. C. Ballintine, Major T. E. Hastings, M.C., M.D., Major Joseph McLean, Edward King, B.L. (formerly Captain and Acting Major, M.C.), who sent me interesting personal recollections. I am indebted to Captain P. J. Lyne and his friends Sergeant Stanley Adams and Corporal R. J. Thompson who met together to read that part of the manuscript dealing with campaigns in which they had served, and made notes for my assistance; and to Corporal John Dick, who sent me interesting and useful personal memories. I am thankful to the Curator and staff of the National Library of Ireland, the Irish Central Library for Students, and the County Kildare Librarian, Seamus O Conchubair, and his assistants, for their courtesy, interest and help.

Finally, my thanks to Mrs William D. Rowe, Jr, who did research for me in the Library of Congress, Washington, D.C.; Miss V. J. Ledger who did research in England and Mrs Ann O'Connor for typing and correcting the manuscript.

I

'I am of a family who were ever soldiers and poets . . . I have heard my mother say many times that the Ledwidges were once a great people in the land and she has shown with a sweep of her hand green hills and wide valleys where sheep are folded which still bear the marks of dead industry and, once, this was all ours.' Thus Francis Ledwidge wrote of his origins.*

Ledwick, Ledwich and Ledwith are variant forms of his name. Rev. Edward Ledwich, the antiquary (1737–1823), did considerable research into the history of the family. He concluded they were of German origin and had originally settled in Cheshire, England. Thence they came to Ireland with de Burgo in 1200 and were given grants of land in the ancient Kingdom of Meath. The earliest documentary reference records the marriage of Roger de Ledwyc in 1268. The family continue to be listed as landowners down to the end of the reign of Henry VIII. There were estated Ledwiches in Meath and Westmeath in the mid-seventeenth century. The Westmeath Ledwidges, described as 'Irish Papists', were relegated by Cromwell to new homes west of the Shannon. Ledwithstown House near Ballymahon in County Longford indicates to this day where some of them settled.

The fortunes of Francis's branch of the family, curving downwards for generations, were near rock bottom in 1872, the year his parents were married in Slane, County Meath. Patrick Ledwidge, aged thirty-two, was a migrant labourer from another part of the county. His wife, Anne, aged twenty-two, daughter of Nicholas Lynch, was a native of Slane.

It was a love match. Patrick and Anne settled down happily in a two-roomed cottage situated in a cul-de-sac off Chapel Street, known as Cavan Row because the first two houses in it were occupied by families from Cavan. Patrick worked as a farm labourer. His wages

---

* Letter from Frank Ledwidge to Professor Lewis Chase, The Library of Congress, Washington D.C. 20540. Ledwidge Folder, Lewis Chase Papers, Ac. 9468, Box +7.

varied from ten to twelve shillings a week with extra for overtime; he was also given his dinner and perquisites like milk and fuel. Athletic, his prowess as a swimmer is still remembered: 'He could do anything in the water that an otter could.'

The memory of Anne Ledwidge, too, is still vivid in her native village. The older people there describe her in detail: slim, below average height, with dark hair, a sallow complexion, dancing brown eyes, quick in movement, energetic, always good-humoured.

Space soon became a problem for the young couple in their Cavan Row house. Their first child, Patrick, was born within a year; then came Nicholas, who did not survive infancy; followed by Mary, Thomas, Kitty, Michael, Anne.

Early in the 1880's, the Rural District Council for the first time began to build cottages for labourers in Slane and Patrick Ledwidge managed to get his name down for one of them. He was allotted Cottage No. 1116, which was completed on 16 December 1886. It was a happy day for the parents when they were able to move up to Janeville, a quarter of a mile from Slane on the Drogheda road. In addition to its attractive freshness, the house was spacious compared with their first home: three bedrooms, large kitchen, living-room, half an acre of ground at the back for a garden. Even today the sturdy little house still occupies an enviable site, elevated, open and salubrious, with a delightful view of Meath across the valley of the Boyne. Anne Ledwidge was then expecting her eighth child, Francis, who was born on 19 August 1887.

In common with the majority of the dispossessed, Patrick was determined at all costs to have his children educated. Most people in his position believed that conditions were bound to improve; Ireland would rise again; the young people would have to be fitted for the new world. When their eldest son, Patrick, completed classes at the national school, he was accordingly kept on there as monitor, the first step on the road to becoming a teacher. This profession was a hard path in the last decades of the nineteenth century: five years a pupil teacher at a wage of £5 a year; then two years at college for which the student had to pay part of his expenses. Qualified teachers began with a salary of £50 a year.

Tragedy struck the Ledwidge family when the father died suddenly on 13 March 1892 aged fifty-two. The wife whom he had cherished was left in a terrible plight. Her youngest child, Joseph, was an infant of three months. The dream of a well-educated family had to go by the board. The only State assistance then was outdoor relief of a shilling per week per child. Otherwise she was destitute. Her own family and sympathetic neighbours urged her to put the youngest children in a home until at least the older ones were reared, but she shook her head and determined to find work so as to hold on to the house and keep the family together.

Her eldest son's career was the first to be sacrificed; college for Patrick was now out of the question. Nevertheless she insisted on keeping him at school until he qualified for office work. In the meantime she became the wage-earner by doing seasonal casual work for the neighbouring farmers at the current rate of 2/6 a day. It was rude toil. Anne Ledwidge became a slave in the cause of family survival. Helping to make hay and stook corn sounds romantic to city dwellers, but to the field workers whose pace is set by daylight hours and weather changes, it means backache, prickled hands and arms, physical exhaustion. When potato picking, the workers, bending double, followed the horse-plough up and down the drills, or knelt to gather the crop into baskets. Thinning mangolds and turnips was paid for by piecework at about sixpence a drill according to length. Snagging these root crops when grown entailed the added hardship of hands stiffened with cold on frosty mornings. Anne Ledwidge established a parish record for her prowess as a casual worker. When this employment was unavailable in winter, she knitted socks, took in washing, or undertook mending for families. It was the era of neighbourliness and the community helped her along. The farmers who employed her often added to her wages, wheaten flour, milk and other farm produce.

In the scanty leisure mother and children enjoyed together, she often reminded them that they bore a great name and should live up to it. When her second youngest son, Frank, was grown to manhood, he recalled her stories whenever he climbed the hill of Tara:

That old mill, built on the site of the first corn mill ever erected in Ireland, used to belong to my father's people when everybody had their own and those broad acres and leopard-coloured woods, almost as far as Kilcairne, all these were ours one time. . . .

I often asked her of my father (who died when I was four), but was always reproved by her eyes and so I learned to leave that side of her life severely alone. There were four brothers of us and three sisters. I am the second youngest. For these my mother laboured night and day as none of them were strong enough to provide for our own wants. She never complained and even when my eldest brother advanced in strength she persisted in his regular attendance at school until he qualified at book-keeping and left home for Dublin. His position carried a respectable salary.

Anne Ledwidge's hopes were henceforth centred on Patrick, who had manfully taken the place of breadwinner. His contributions enabled her to stay at home and give more care to the youngest children. The girls were sent off to domestic work as soon as they were confirmed.

One day Patrick returned home unwell. Tuberculosis was diagnosed. The disease was at that time endemic in Ireland and as medical knowledge had not yet arrived at a cure, the attitude to it was fatalistic. Patrick became an invalid and died within four years. 'Oh, those four years,' Frank recalled later. 'It was as though God forgot us.' He went on to describe how one day the bailiff and two policemen came to evict the family for arrears of rent on their house, but they were saved at the last moment by the local doctor certifying that Patrick was not fit to be moved. When he died, there was no money to pay for his coffin, 'so the guardians had to put the parish to the expense'.

Resuming his account of the family fortunes, Frank said: 'Mother took to the fields again.' Her staunch character was respected in the neighbourhood and she had no difficulty in finding work. She was consistent in her determination that the children's future should not be sacrificed. As soon as her third son, Michael, was Confirmed, he was sent off to be apprenticed to a Dublin grocer, W. T. Daly, Rathfarnham.

Frank continues:

I was seven years of age when my eldest brother died, and though I had only been to school on occasional days I was able to read the tombstones in a neighbouring graveyard and had written in secret several poems which still survive. About this time I was one day punished in school for crying and that punishment ever afterwards haunted the master like an evil dream, for I was only crying over Goldsmith's *Deserted Village* which an advanced class had been reading aloud. It was in this same school that I wrote my first poem in order to win for the school a half-holiday. It was on a Shrove Tuesday and the usual custom of granting the half holiday had not been announced at play time, so when the master was at his lunch I crept quietly into the school and wrote on a slate a verse to remind him, leaving it on his desk where he must see it. I remember it yet:

Our master is too old for sweets,
Too old for children's play,
Like Aesop's dog what he can't eat
No other people may.

This alluded to the pancakes which are always made on Shrove
Tuesday and are a great treat in rural Ireland. The silly verse accomplished its end. Years afterwards he often spoke to me of that verse
and wished he had the slate to present to somebody who liked the
story.

The master in question was Thomas Madden whose memory is still
so fresh in Slane his ghost might be said to haunt the old school house
(now used as a vocational school), beside the church in Chapel Street.
He taught in Slane for eighteen years. Half a century after his death,
the passionate vitality of his character outshines the memory of con-
temporaries and successors. He was so lame that he had to use both a
crutch and a stick to get around. His eyesight failed badly due—it was
said—to the long hours he spent learning Irish by candlelight in the
winter evenings. Although he wore glasses, he had to hold the print
close up to his eyes.

Madden did not consider education complete without a knowledge
of Irish. Since it was not at that time included in the official curriculum,
he used to bring in the boys half an hour earlier every morning in order
to teach them their native language. One day a travelling man called
at the school, saluting in Irish. The master returned the greeting in the
native tongue, whereupon the visitor burst out into such a voluble
flood of Gaelic that Madden was left wordless and confused. Being
self-taught, his book knowledge of the language was more confident
than his conversational ability. This became a long-standing joke
among the boys, who were secretly jubilant to hear their formidable
master outmatched by a tinker.

Madden was a native of Kilskyre, County Meath. A great reader of
history, he knew the prestige of Slane and its environs in the story of
Ireland. He made liberal use of the cane and varied corporal punishment with biting sarcasm as he tried to raise his pupils' minds to some
level of appreciation. Their region was important before history
began. A vast prehistoric burial ground of increasing international interest today extends between nearby Knowth, Newgrange and Dowth.
A few miles from Slane on the south bank of the river is Rosnaree,
traditional burial place of the third-century Cormac Mac Airt, most

famous of the pre-Christian hero-kings. He is said to have arrived at a knowledge of one God through his own powers of reasoning. He thereupon abandoned the worship of idols, greatly displeasing the Druids, then a powerful priestly caste. Cormac made it known that after his death he wanted to be buried in Rosnaree instead of Brugh na Boinne, where all the pagan kings were interred. But the Druids ignored his wish. Legend says that three times when they were about to cross the Boyne, the funeral procession was halted by the river overflowing its banks. After the third attempt, Cormac's wish was obeyed and he was buried in Rosnaree.

It is the Hill of Slane, however, considered holy ground for fifteen hundred years, that dominates the village. On this height Saint Patrick, according to legend, lit the Paschal fire on Easter Saturday night in the year 432 in defiance of the King then celebrating the spring pagan festival at his court at Tara across the valley. No light was supposed to appear anywhere in his kingdom until the signal was given by a beacon fire on Tara. The rebel fire on Slane was observed with anger. Patrick was summoned to the court where he announced the message of Christianity. His first convert there was Erc, the Chief Poet, who later became Bishop of Slane and whose hermitage is still to be seen, set in a tangle of greenery, in the demesne grounds of the castle.

The Patrician foundation was ruled for centuries by the successors of Erc. After the Viking invasion, it was many times plundered but never destroyed. With the advent of the Anglo-Normans, the Flemings became lords of Slane. They restored the Abbey and brought the Franciscans there early in the sixteenth century. It was suppressed under Henry VIII, but the Flemings were not dispossessed and as they remained Catholics they were able to maintain the Mass in the Abbey, at least intermittently, until the last decade of the seventeenth century.

The view from this historic height explains more eloquently than volumes of history why this ground was so fiercely contested and why Meath is still called 'royal': on every side extending away to the bluish horizon there is a kingly prospect of rich green pastures, varied by the darker green of woods and golden strips of tilled land, through which the Boyne loops its shining way to the sea beyond Drogheda.

Slane figured in the Battle of the Boyne when it was the scene of one of the successive 'last stands' of the Catholic Irish cause. Near that point where a fine bridge now spans the river, King William's army is said to have made a surprise crossing on 12 July 1690, a move that led to the defeat of King James. Nowadays one of the most frequent summer sights on the bridge is a group of visitors rooted to the spot as they gaze upstream to the weir, foaming and cascading, or downstream to the placid riverscape.

The stamp of a benevolent landlord is on Slane. The Conynghams built its terraces of grey stone houses and the unique village square which is in fact a crossroads wide and broad enough to cope with all traffic problems, present or to come. Four handsome, three-storeyed houses are set slantwise at the corners, each flanked by an elegant little carriage-house, and fronted by a green lawn. One of them now has the additional embellishment of two ancient cedars.

Here good relationship between landlord and tenants was traditional. The boys played cricket in the playground, using home-made bats and wickets, but they knew the game and strictly adhered to the rules. Before the Gaelic Athletic Association promoted football and hurling clubs in rural Ireland, there were cricket clubs in villages where the landlord fostered it. Since working men played, it was not in those days a game linked with the ascendancy.

A fever of excitement would descend on the school when the inspector, Mr Dickey, was due for one of his periodic visits. On his arrival in Drogheda, nine miles away, Slane would be alerted. Young Andy Finnegan would be sent at once to keep watch in the Square and report the first appearance of the inspector's sidecar in the distance. Andy would race back to tell the master who, with excited cautions, paraded out the boys in lines. It was not until they had grown to manhood that many of them understood the reason for his frenzy. He lived in terror that his near-blindness would be discovered, resulting in probable dismissal. A teacher was at that time a slave to the inspector. There was no pension scheme then and a married man could save almost nothing from his stipend. This, however, could be increased by a small bonus paid on the pass marks. When Master Madden stormed at his class, 'You'll lose me my result fees,' the boys recognized it as a dire threat.

There were occasional adventures sandwiched into the monotony of school life. One wonderful day, Frank and a companion secured the job of driving a bunch of cattle 'to the shipping at Drogheda'. He was given sixpence as their joint reward and the boys set out light-heartedly on their nine-mile walk. Debating how they would spend the money, they agreed that two clay pipes and a half-ounce of tobacco would be an interesting purchase. The smoking made them sick and irritable. They quarrelled, settled their arguments with their fists and Frank got a black eye.

After shipping the cattle we sallied up the town, giddy, silent and sick, with 3½d deep in our exchequer; we had made friends again while doing a tour of the boat, because there was enmity in the heart of the Mell boys against any lad from the country, and only by our united forces could we hope to pass that quarter unscathed.

With his last halfpenny, he bought a green song-book which he treasured for a long time as a reminder of a great day.

One of Master Madden's devices in teaching the boys composition was to write on a card the name of some historic place in the neighbourhood with a few lines of description underneath. The boys had to expand the short description into a full-length essay. One day Frank got *Slane Castle* on his card and underneath it: 'This castle is built on a straight, steep slope.' Already fascinated with words he dreamily underlined the last three with a blue pencil. The cards were used by a succession of classes and had to be kept clean. Frank was reprimanded.

'What do you mean by underlining these words?'

'To remind myself not to use them,' the boy reluctantly explained.

'Oh, indeed, and why not?'

'Because they don't go right. A slope is an easy kind of slant; if it's steep and straight, it's not a slope.'

'Do you know who you are?' said Madden witheringly. 'You're the boy who knew too much.'

In the Senior School Reader there was a poem called *The Boy Who Knew Too Much*, about a smart lad outwitted by his smarter papa. The class laughed loudly and the name clung to Frank for the remainder of his schooldays. Madden's manner to him acquired a tinge of sarcasm. 'Boy,' he would say, 'you're a genius but an erratic one!' By the time he was preparing for Confirmation, the 'erratic genius' was at the head of the school.

He tells us himself how his taste for books had developed from the green song-book purchased for a ha'penny:

There was a literary society for juveniles run thro' the pages of a Dublin weekly and I soon became a member of this. In all the competitions for which I entered I carried off the prize and soon had a decent library of the books which interest children. Odd halfpennies which I got for some message run for the neighbours accumulated in time and were exchanged for *The Arabian Nights*, *Robinson Crusoe*, *Don Quixote*, and the poems of Keats and Longfellow. My admiration for Longfellow began early and I could recite passages from *The*

Golden Legend at eight years. I loved the series of metaphors in *Hiawatha* beginning:

> Fiercely the red sun descending
> Burned his way along the mountains,

but thought nothing in all the world as wonderful as Shakespeare's fairy song:

> Full fathom five thy father lies
> Of his bones are coral made.

While I was still at school many silly verses left my pen, written either for my own amusement, or the amusement of my companions. Indeed I left many an exercise unfinished hurrying over some thought that shaped itself into rhyme.

I have always been very quiet and bashful and a great mystery in my own place. I avoided the evening play of neighbouring children to find some secret place in a wood by the Boyne and there imagine fairy dances and hunts, fires and feasts. I saw curious shapes in shadows and clouds and loved to watch the change of the leaves and the flowers. I heard voices in the rain and the wind and strange whisperings in the waters. I loved all wandering people and things and several times tried to become part of a gypsy caravan. I read of Troy and Nineveh and the nomads of the east and the mystery of the Sahara. I wrote wander songs for cuckoos and winter songs for the robin. I hated gardens where gaudy flowers were trained in rows but loved the wild things of change and circumstance.

One by one my other brothers and sisters left school for the world until there were left only myself and my youngest brother and mother.

The youngest of the Ledwidge children, Joseph, was Frank's junior by four years. A deep bond of affection united the three who now remained in the old home. Although the older brothers and sisters co-operated loyally in sending their mother whatever money they could spare, none of them was in skilled employment and all their contributions amounted to little. Anne Ledwidge was still working up to the time her two youngest left school. Joe remembers how it weighed on his spirits as a schoolboy to return home to an empty house. Day after day, its loneliness at that hour of mid-afternoon oppressed him. The two boys would have only one idea when they reached home: to find their mother at once. Tired after six or seven hours' exposure to Master Madden's methods, they would stay in the house only while they were cutting a slice of bread, and then rush off to join her wherever she happened to be working. They were glad to help her shorten the job and hasten the moment when she would walk home with them.

Their evenings together were the happiest hours of the day. When their homework was finished, she told them stories, or taught them little songs:

'These stories told at my mother's doorstep in the owl's light,' wrote Frank afterwards, 'were the first things I remember, except, perhaps, the old songs which she sang to me . . . so full of romance, love and sacrifice.

'Meanwhile the years were coming over me with their wisdom and I began to realise that man cannot live by dreams. I had no more to learn in National School at 14, so I strapped up my books and laid them away with the cobwebs and the dust.'

But this is how a fellow poet, Sigerson Clifford, saw that childhood:

I think of you when over Primrose Wood
The rooks fly wing on wing to raid the oats,
And cuckoos on the warm exploding furze
Announce their presence from vainglorious throats.

You are the boy that runs through Driscoll's fields
When morning's dew revives the pale woodbines,
Your bare feet crushing to the cooling leaves
The gold testudo of the dandelions.

And from the fence where fox-gloves fish the bees,
When June's red current flames the streams of air,
I see you bending over Griffin's well
The dust of summer in your dreaming hair.

Is this our Eden where two robins make
A semi-colon on a page of snow?
Is there more music in the blackbird's flute
Than Death will ever show?

II

The land of Bernard Fitzsimons, one of Slane's 'strong farmers', adjoined the Ledwidges' garden. He was a bachelor with an unmarried sister who kept house for him, and both were consistently kind to the young Ledwidges in their fatherless plight. Tom, the eldest boy after Pat's death, was employed by them during all his effective working life. Frank used to do seasonal work for them after school hours and on holidays. Barney Fitzsimons taught him how to plough. There was always a happy, friendly atmosphere in that home.

Frank left school the morning after receiving the sacrament of Confirmation in the spring of 1901. He did not wait until the end of the school year; he was not fourteen until the following August. He went to work full time for Fitzsimons because it was an easy transition from schoolboy to wage-earner. The wages at this period for what was known as 'a farmer's boy' were seven shillings a week with meals.

Thanks to Anne Ledwidge's heroism, the family had survived the critical years. No one but herself knew how she had kept the children fed and clothed and paid the rent for the house. But she never wavered in her determination to lift her sons out of the rut of farm labouring, then rightly considered the most depressed of all occupations. In a contemporary pastoral letter, the Bishop of Kerry described such workers as 'the worst-housed, the worst paid, and the worst-fed class of their kind in any civilised country in the world'. Thirteen years later, a news item in the local paper reports that a deputation had gone from the Meath Labour Union to the Meath Farmers' Association asking for an improvement in the working conditions of labourers. The requests put forward were: a fixed wage of not less than twelve shillings per week; one week's paid annual holiday, half of it to be taken in April and half in October; working hours stabilized from 7 a.m. to 6 p.m. between April and November; and from 8 a.m. to dark from November to April. There is no report that the Meath Farmers agreed.

Nevertheless even such small wages coming into the house would have greatly eased the situation for Anne Ledwidge. But she took the long-term view and was still eager to sacrifice herself so that her sons could look forward to a better future. Michael had settled down at Daly's grocery in Dublin. She believed that shopkeeping offered security and had already made many enquiries about where she could find a similar opening for Frank.

At an early age, the lad was already in demand among the local farmers because he had grown tall and strong. Biddable and hard-working, he got on well with older men, keeping them amused with what they considered his 'outlandish' vocabulary. A little distraction sweetens the day's toil and is an important factor in keeping labouring men contented. Frank had a puckish sense of humour and a facility for making up rhymes about anything under the sun. Whenever a verse came into his head, he would stop in his tracks to scribble it down any-where handy, perhaps on the pier of a gate, a fencing-post, or on a boulder in a field. Time was when his sign manual was scrawled all over Fitzsimons' farm. But the passage of time has effaced the verses except four lines in bold black writing, evidently written with the charred end of a stick, on an inside wall of the cow-byre:

> The bachelors they're goin' to tax,
> Do you think it a shame or a credit?
> 'Tis you young bachelors I ask,
> For they never will tax—Francis Ledwidge.

The verse has been roughly framed in square lines drawn with red ochre, and preserved through more than half a century's re-whitewash-ing of the walls.

During this summer of 1901, when he was emancipated from the national school, Frank also worked part time on the farms of Michael Johnston (Slane) and James Cooney (Mooretown) while his mother explored other possibilities for him. She had occasionally got tempor-ary work in Slane Castle, seat of the Marquis of Conyngham, and was familiar with its domestic quarters. The cook told her she was looking for a trainee houseboy. This seemed a better prospect for Frank and he was sent along.

Every morning when the cook went to Lady Conyngham for in-structions, she took with her a slate on which she jotted down the menus for the day. Returning to the kitchen, she would prop the slate on a shelf to consult it from time to time. This slate fascinated the new boy doing the odd chores and he pored over it each morning, learning off the names of new dishes. He was there only a short time when one morning he mischievously rubbed out the day's orders and substituted a rougher bill of fare, consisting of pig's feet, cabbage, spuds. The cook's sense of humour did not rise to the occasion and Frank was fired. He went back to farm work.

Anne Ledwidge then made enquiries in the neighbouring towns of Navan and Drogheda. She returned one day from the latter town, pleased about her interview with Larry Carpenter, owner of a grocery, bakery and public-house (premises now occupied by Stanley's Garage). Carpenter was popular in Drogheda for his benevolence. Having heard the widow's story, he agreed to take on Frank without payment of the usual apprentice fee. She then set about cleaning up the boy's clothes, pressing and patching, before sending him off like another Dick Whittington to walk the eight miles to the town, carrying his small bundle of effects, her cautions ringing in his ears.

It was the first break from home for the fifteen-year-old boy and he was homesick. Shop assistants at that period worked long hours, the shops remaining open until 11 p.m. or 12 midnight. It was not until 1906 that grocers' assistants succeeded in having shops closed at 10 p.m. on the first five nights of the week. 'The members declared themselves delighted with the shorter hours.' Apprentices had to work four years for food and lodgings only, without pay. As a concession to the widow's son, however, Larry Carpenter allowed Frank home every Saturday afternoon until Sunday evening. This weekly break enabled the lad to get through the first few difficult months.

Drogheda was full of interest to the country boy. In 1902, the watch still paraded the streets at night, announcing the passing hours and reassuring the citizens, 'All's well.' Frank had a great deal to tell his mother and Joe every Saturday night. Joe, then aged eleven and still at school, looked up to his older brother. He remembers accompanying him every Sunday on the return journey to Drogheda as far as Rossin where there is a bridge over the Mattock river.

A few months later, Michael was offered a better job before he had finished his time at Daly's, Rathfarnham. This employer was willing to take on Frank instead and 'allow for' the time spent in Drogheda. Anne Ledwidge thought the exchange would be to Frank's advantage because the eight-mile walk was hard on him in the winter months. She brought him home, tidied up his shabby clothes again, gave him his train fare from Beauparc to Dublin, and put in his pocket the last half-crown in the house. It had been a morning of tears and lamentations. A great bond of affection united the mother and her two remain-

27

ing sons and the parting was painful. When the train left, Anne was probably the saddest of the three. She knew that her second youngest was different from the others, too emotional and sensitive. She wanted to see him toughened up for his own sake so that he could cope better with the world, but she foresaw that life would not be easy for him.

The boy left the train at Amiens Street to make his way to Rathfarnham, at that time a rural suburb. Many times on the journey he had clasped the half-crown in his pocket. It was the first time in his life he had had the spending of so much money, but the thought did nothing to console him. He did not enter an eating-house for food until he was famished, and even then, as he ate, the food did him little good when he thought that the two at home would probably have to go short on his account. On his way through the city to Rathfarnham, he was attracted by a pawnshop window. He imagined the tiepin he was wearing was valuable and finally summoned up courage to go into the shop. But the pawnbroker looked at the pin contemptuously and gave him only a penny for it. Shortly afterwards, he joined a little group listening to a showman demonstrating an electric shock machine. On payment of a penny, one was allowed to hold the handles and whoever could hold on until 100 was registered would win a shilling. It seemed that only strong arms were needed to turn a penny into a shilling. Frank paid a penny several times, but could not hold the handles and lost his money. When he finally arrived at Rathfarnham House, he was sick at heart: his money and his tiepin were gone. Despite his experience of town life in Drogheda and his mother's warnings, he had not been proof against the city's wiles. Moreover, his employer was a dour kind of a man who received him coldly. Already Frank hated the city; he was terribly homesick.

At night when he went to bed, Slane rose up before his mind's eye with such clarity and poignancy that he could not sleep. 'I could not bear brick horizons,' he said afterwards, 'and all my dreams were calling me home.' He thought of the friendly faces and the lighthearted people round the firesides he knew, the games he played every Sunday with Joe and his chums. This parting, he felt, had been a great mistake. As always when he was moved, the lines of a poem tormented him. One night he sat up in bed and began to write a description of his birthplace as he saw it in his mind's eye:

I walk the old frequented ways
That wind around the tangled braes,
I live again the sunny days
Ere I the city knew.

And scenes of old again are born,
The woodbine lassooing the thorn,
And drooping Ruth-like in the corn
The poppies weep the dew.

Above me in their hundred schools
The magpies bend their young to rules
And like an apron full of jewels
The dewy cobweb swings.

And frisking in the stream below
The troutlets make the circles flow,
And the hungry crane doth watch them grow
As a smoker does his rings.

Above me smokes the little town,
With its whitewashed walls and roofs of brown
And its octagon spire toned smoothly down
As the holy minds within.

And wondrous impudently sweet,
Half of him passion, half conceit,
The blackbird calls adown the street
Like the piper of Hamelin.

I hear him, and I feel the lure
Drawing me back to the homely moor,
I'll go and close the mountain's door
On the city's strife and din.

As nostalgic as Yeats's *Innisfree*, it is the first poem of definite promise
he had written. When he finished it, he was excited. Something strange
and inexplicable had happened to him. An outside power had momen-
tarily taken over. The secret elation that filled him made his present
plight intolerable. What was he doing here? He slipped out of bed,

dressed and stole noiselessly downstairs carrying his few possessions. Fortunately he was able to unlock the back door, so he went quietly out and set off on the thirty-mile walk back to Slane. The new job had lasted only a few days. He had not yet reached his sixteenth birthday.

The road from Dublin to Slane is one of the straightest in Ireland. It is said to have been thus planned on the orders of the rakish Prince of Wales who was afterwards King George IV, so that he could more conveniently visit his mistress, Lady Conyngham, in Slane Castle. The granite triangular stones listing the miles for the information of the post-chaise passengers are still nearly all traceable. They gave the boy a mute companionship, their white glimmer reassuring him at regular intervals that the miles were diminishing. Sometimes he lost count when he got sleepy; then he would peer closely to find the next one and go stoutly on.

Apart from his aching legs, it was an interesting night; he watched the changes in the sky before the approach of dawn. Dusty and weary, he sighted Slane on the horizon as the sun was rising. In the distance, advancing along a side road, he also saw two postmen he knew, but he did not want *them* to see him. He felt that everyone knew he had gone off to a fine job in Dublin and it looked too like failure to be back again in a few days. So he sprang over a wall to hide until they had passed. A gamekeeper came up behind and seeing him crouching inside the wall, obviously hiding, accused him of poaching before he was near enough to recognize the lad.

No one was stirring yet in his own house, so he sat down in the garden shed waiting for the back door to open. With the sharpened awareness of motherhood, Anne Ledwidge woke with the conviction that someone was waiting outside. She roused Joe and sent him out to look. There was a joyful reunion between the brothers. Twelve-year-old Joe had been moping without Frank and had no thought other than the joy of having him back again. Their mother, too, received the prodigal with affection and had no blame for him.

Just about the same period, in the spring of 1903, Mr and Mrs David Taylor Carlyle rented a house near Newgrange. Carlyle had been a medical student in Dublin. Half-way through his course his father died, leaving him with an income. The student forthwith abandoned medicine, married and brought his bride to Newgrange. Here they spent an idyllic few years, Carlyle devoting himself mainly to fishing and shooting. Anne Ledwidge heard that they were looking for a boy to help in the garden and yard. She sent Frank to apply for the job. Carlyle's ideas of wages were based on city standards. He took Frank at £21 a year, all found, a sum quite out of line with local rates.

The Carlyles were young and carefree, their personal happiness overflowing upon everyone around them. Among other duties, Frank took care of their shiny new trap drawn by a fast, high-stepping pony. Once a week he drove Carlyle to Drogheda for the shopping, and would wait for him in St Peter's parish church for the return home. A Catholic church before the Reformation, this edifice contains interesting antiquities: Cromwell's soldiers gave its fifteenth-century font rough handling, using it as a horse trough. No one ever visited St Peter's between the services and Frank used to read there while he waited. Too shy to explore it on his own initiative, he would probably never have entered it if it were not for Carlyle's insistence that he should sit somewhere in shelter while he was waiting. Frank grew to love the quiet, elegant interior with its rococco ornamentation around the altar.

Mrs Carlyle remembered how this strange yard-boy used to read and write at the kitchen table at night when his work was done. Sometimes she had difficulty in persuading him to tidy up his books and papers and go to bed. Since Newgrange is only three miles from Slane, he got home whenever he was free. Although he was well aware of the tremendous undercurrent of history in the area, he made no study of it. Part of a vast prehistoric burial-ground known as Brugh na Boinne, Newgrange bears witness to a civilization established here before Christianity. Described as a textbook on megalithic art, its passage-graves are of profound interest to archaeologists. But the pastoral scenes around Newgrange were Frank's delight: a field with a few poppies in it and a blackbird singing on a thornbush made up his sum of happiness. Above all, he loved the Boyne and he thought himself fortunate whenever he had leisure to sit on the bank and just watch the river flowing past.

Three years slipped by and now the Carlyles had two baby boys and were assuming the responsibilities of parenthood. They decided to go back to Dublin so as to be near good schools. There would be no work for Frank in their city house. Once more he was unemployed. It was the year 1906 and he was nineteen. 'I determined never to leave home again,' he said, 'so I took up any old job at all with the local farmers and was happy.'

In the event, however, he worked as a farm labourer for only one more season. In the summer of 1907, roadworkers from Slane were for the first time employed by direct labour. This was thought to be a considerable advance in social justice. Hitherto the roads had been maintained by contractors, usually small farmers who tendered for a few miles of road which they kept in rudimentary repair. The stones were quarried roughly, broken, taken out in horseloads and left in heaps until used to fill up the holes. The contracting farmer with his own horse, and the help of either a son or a servant boy, could get all the work tendered for completed during the year, in the intervals between seasonal farm work. But the Meath Independent Labour Union, functioning since the beginning of this century, considered it unjust that roadwork should be monopolized by small farmers. They had been agitating for a long time for the introduction of direct labour on roads. Demonstrations were organized to back their demand. The change in system would mean an increase of one farthing in the rates and both County and Urban Councils thought this a spendthrift proceeding. But they capitulated when the Labour Union's demand was supported by the United Irish League under John Redmond's leadership.

There was strong competition for road work because the wages were higher than those paid by farmers, 17s. 6d. a week as against 12s. 6d. Road work was carried on for most of the winter and so had not the disadvantage of unemployment near Christmas. A man who could bring his own horse and cart would be paid half as much again as the others. Carried out as described, it was rude toil; the hours were from 8 a.m. to 6 p.m. in summer and until dusk in winter.

Joe Ledwidge had by now left school, too, and was showing exceptional ability in finding work. Their mother had no longer 'to take to the fields'. The home was beginning to have a modest air of prosperity. Frank managed to acquire a bicycle, as the road repairs were often carried out too far away to get to the venue on foot. On the handlebar of the bicycle, he carried a parcel of sandwiches for his midday meal and a can for boiling his tea. If the work was hard and the hours long, it was a healthy life. A contemporary who remembers him in those years describes him as 'tall and athletic, walking with an easy stride; his face tanned from the outdoor life. Under a mop of soft dark hair, his strong features were lit up with a pair of eloquent brown eyes.'

He was contented with his job. It got him out on the roads early and all his life he was an enthusiast for the early morning hours. The work kept him in contact with nature and gave him scope to study it. Even the hedgerows were of inexhaustible interest. Many of the little placenames celebrated in later poems first endeared themselves to him when he was a roadworker.

Numerous friends of his still living in Slane agree that he made a point to be well-groomed when his day's work was finished. He changed every evening into a suit of hand-woven tweed which he favoured long before the revival of Irish industry had made headway. He wore a felt hat turned up in front and carried a walking-stick. His favourite sport was high jumping in which he excelled. When a Gaelic football club was started in Slane, he was one of the first members. Although he does not seem to have qualified for the team, the Slane Blues, he attended all their matches and followed their fortunes with keen interest.

The influence of the Abbey Theatre reached Slane, too, inspiring the young people to found a dramatic class, of which Frank and Joe were enthusiastic members. After only five weeks' practice, they staged *Handy Andy* in which Frank and Joe took leading parts. This was followed by what the local paper described as an uproarious comedy in which Frank took the part of 'A Humourist'.

The following year a new source of employment came to the district. A hundred-year-old, disused copper-mine was rediscovered on the lands of Dollardstown House, Beauparc. The early workings were reopened and enlarged and copper-mining started again. As the wages were higher than for road work, there was a rush of local applicants, including Frank Ledwidge, who was taken on among a hundred men. Since the average life of a copper-mine is rather under than over ten years, rapid exploitation was the management's idea. The miners worked in shifts around the clock. Beyond enlarging the main shaft, little development was done. The mine was subject to flooding from the Boyne and the men working in it got wet to the skin. Several fatal accidents occurred; fall-ins of earth and stones caused numerous cases of serious injury.

Frank was always popular with his fellow workers. A non-stop talker, he entertained them with extempore verse, or stories drawn from his reading. One cold winter day, while the men were gulping hot tea during their lunch break, they grumbled about working conditions and the vile weather. He encouraged them with the reminder that spring was on its way. Then he drew from his pocket a piece of paper on which he had written a poem called *A Song of Spring*. It is to be classed among his *juvenilia*, but the men who listened were not critical; the verses succeeded in changing their mood. Frank slipped the paper back into the pocket of his overcoat which he left in the shed when he went down the mine. One of the men took it and sent it to the *Drog-*

heda Independent. It was published in their following issue, 29 January 1910. Although Frank said afterwards that the joy of having it accepted was 'as fleeting as Jonah's gourd', still the sight of his verse in print acted as a great stimulus. He became a regular contributor to the paper and every succeeding month now saw at least one of his poems in its columns.

Father Edward Smyth, curate in Slane from 1907 to 1911, became a helpful friend, inviting him to his room in the evenings and lending him books. Together they read Frank's poems and Father Smyth suggested improvements. When he was transferred to various other curacies, the friendship continued. He invited Frank on a visit to Mountnugent on Lough Sheelin, and the reunion of the two friends is commemorated in the poem *The Herons*:

> As I was climbing Ardan Mor
> From the shore of Sheelin Lake,
> I met the herons coming down
> Before the waters wake.
>
> And they were talking in their flight
> Of dreamy ways the herons go
> When all the hills are withered up
> Nor any waters flow.

Father Smyth's recreations were boating and swimming for which the river in Slane gave him great scope. But lake waters are treacherous. Shortly after Frank's visit, the priest met his death while diving from his boat, because he was not familiar with the underwater currents in Lough Sheelin.

The stimulus of the Gaelic League reached Slane early in the century. The first branch there petered out to the regret of the young people anxious to learn their native tongue. Ledwidge was deputed by the enthusiasts to write for help to a Navan teacher named Sean MacNamee, recognized as a pioneer in the movement. MacNamee devoted all his free time to forming classes, cycling long distances every evening to teach Irish on a voluntary basis. Thanks to his leadership, he had become greatly in demand as lecturer, debater, teacher and historian. The result of Ledwidge's approach was disconcerting. MacNamee made no direct reply. He was at that time contributing every week to the *Drogheda Independent*, a feature written partly in Irish. In the next issue of the paper his column carried the caustic comment: 'Sleepy Slane is awaking.'

Ledwidge was stung. This surely was no way to answer a simple request for an Irish class to be formed in Slane! He wrote a letter of protest to the paper. The only reply this drew from the Olympian MacNamee was another ironic comment. A formidable controversialist, already renowned for his hard hitting, few would dare to engage in verbal contest with him, but Ledwidge plunged into the fray. At the end of his next letter, he resorted to verse:

> Oh! what a pleasant world 'twould be,
> How smoothly we'd step thro' it,
> If all the fools who mean no harm,
> Could manage not to do it.

This at last got MacNamee into the open. In the next issue of his column he wrote:

On the whole the letter to which I refer is a very good specimen of what can be accomplished by self-advertisement with the aid of a dictionary and if the writer perseveres he may even hope to attract quite a large share of attention. The case is worse when to his deficiencies he adds a desire to mount Parnassus, for then you are never sure of what he'll rhyme into. Notoriety hunters must seek elsewhere for a pretext to air imaginary grievances.

He added that he would not clutter up his column with any further reference to the silly business. MacNamee was known to many acquaintances as 'the briar' or 'the man with the gimlet eyes'. He lives up to his repute in his exchanges with Ledwidge. It is difficult now to understand why he should have reacted like this, but he was by temperament belligerent.

And then peace was made on the football field! Ledwidge's final letter to the paper says:

Speaking for myself and my fellow enthusiasts, I will be very grateful to him if he can suggest a possible way out of the difficulties which I presented to him in the five minutes' chat I had the honour of holding with him after the football on Sunday week; if he is unable to do so I will be content to study the language privately, which I *have* been doing.

No branch of the Gaelic League was started in Slane. Ledwidge continued to wrestle alone with the difficulties of the language.

In leaving him in this isolation, MacNamee inflicted on him a more serious harm than either of them possibly realized. Ledwidge himself was not sure at this period that poetry was to be his vocation. But he was certainly aware of an urgent longing to find expression. He knew in the depths of his being that mighty forces were stirring under the surface of Irish life. He wanted to be in communion with this rebirth and his only access to it was through the Gaelic League. Worse than the disadvantages of no education and poverty is the handicap of isolation from one's fellows, especially in the case of a poet. It is not too much to say that in closing the door of the Gaelic League on him, MacNamee in a sense deprived Ledwidge of his birthright. It was a gesture that had a permanent effect on the young poet's destiny.

Meanwhile the workers at the Beauparc Copper Mine continued to labour in sodden clothes under conditions of increasing discomfort and danger, quarrying the precious metal out of mud and slush. They appealed to Ledwidge to be their spokesman in asking the management to improve the shaft and install better pumps to reduce flooding. He agreed to act for them, was received without sympathy and the request ignored. He then organized a strike and was instantly dismissed; the men returned to work. Labour in rural Ireland at this period had not yet ventured even to raise its head. Two years after this incident, the flooding in the mine became so bad it had to close down for six months while heavier pumps were installed. The yield of copper came to an end in 1914 after only five years' mining.

Ledwidge went back to work on the roads. Local sympathy was with him over the abortive strike and shortly afterwards he was promoted to the job of ganger, or foreman, in the Kells district. His wages were then 24s. a week with overtime too. He was emancipated from shovel and barrow but he now had supervisory duties that entailed cycling forty miles a day. The disadvantage of the promotion was that he had to leave home. He went into lodgings with a Mrs Costello who lived in the Old Barracks, Martry, between Navan and Kells. Although he came back to Janeville nearly every Saturday evening to spend his Sundays at home, he was as grief-stricken about this change in his life as if he were going away for ever. He was now twenty-two, but if he had come of age, he had not yet reached emotional stability, and was just as dependent as ever on the companionship of his mother and brother. This troubled his mother and sometimes, too, even the ever-loyal Joe.

One day Joe brought home a textbook on hypnotism that someone had lent him. The two brothers read it, found that they, too, could exercise hypnotic power and became fascinated by the study. Eventually Frank bought the book for himself by giving up smoking for a time so as to save the price, 18s. 6d. One evening in the hall after the play practice, he told the members of the dramatic class about hypnotism, giving an impromptu demonstration. Selecting a local man named McGuirk, he snapped his fingers and immediately the man fell into a trance from which no one could rouse him. Then Frank told him to fish in the river and McGuirk continued to cast a line assiduously until Frank released him.

Rural people have an exaggerated fear of hypnosis, believing that it emanates from the Devil. One evening, a neighbouring farmer, Captain Deane, asked Ledwidge to lend him a hand with his hay because rain threatened. In the meadow where the cocks were being put up, the talk turned on hypnotism and the men asked Frank to give a demonstration, but none of them would agree to be a 'subject'. Frank picked on Paddy Coyle and began a series of passes and mutterings; but the labourer dropped his fork and ran for his life out of the field. The employer intent on saving his hay was not amused.

The Slane dramatic class continued to get press headlines for many successive seasons. Commenting on 'the powerful drama *Dick Massey's Return*', the *Drogheda Independent* goes on to say:

> The spacious hall was crowded almost to suffocation long before the appointed time for lifting the curtain. Judging from the applause, the class may say the play of Sunday night was the most successful yet held. Mr Francis E. Ledwidge en role Dick Massey was loudly applauded, and when his long harangue on 'English justice'(?) terminated, the house threatened to collapse.

Another glimpse of how Ledwidge used his leisure hours is afforded in his contributions to *The Young Gael*, a manuscript magazine sent out monthly for an annual subscription of one shilling. Circulated by its readers posting it from one to another, it was eventually received back by the editor. I have seen the issues of April and November 1911 of this curious literary journal, both containing early poems by Ledwidge. He was friendly at this period with at least two other contributors, Alice and Katie ffrench of Smarmore, Ardee, who both wrote poetry and who probably introduced him to the journal. Its editor was Frank Mac-Manus, The Manor, Tempo, County Fermanagh, who then went to America and was succeeded by G. J. A. McKitterick, Glenview, Carrickmaclin, Carrickmacross, Monaghan. The sub-editor was Michael Dundon, Ahanish, Borrigone, Limerick, who contributed to the first of the two issues a story in Irish, written in a Gaelic script worthy of the Book of Kells, followed by a free English translation. The number of readers was doubled in 1911. Contributors addressed one another as *Comrade*. In the second of the two issues I have read, Ledwidge apologizes for being such an infrequent contributor, due, he says, to lack of time.

Whether he was at home or in Martry, he continued to work at his poetry. The verses appearing regularly in the *Drogheda Independent* show a steady improvement. He begins to move away from the clichés and the trite phrasing. A poem, *August Night*, published in August 1911, is of special interest because it marks a definite stage of development. He had published an earlier version of this poem in the same paper a year previously. Although both renderings are in the category of juvenilia, the changes are improvements in the choice of words and in scansion, showing that he had begun to acquire technique and had learned to read his verse with a critical eye and ear.

A friend without whose ready encouragement he might never have persevered as a poet in those early years was Matty McGoona, employed in the printing works of *The Irish Peasant* in Navan. Thoughtful and an omnivorous reader, Matty had books, still preserved in his home, which testify to his range of interests.

Through natural ability, passionate interest and wide reading, Matty had become an authority on natural history and astronomy. He studied the life of the wasp and of different species of spiders. His acute observation of nature equalled Ledwidge's but was in fact better informed. An extraordinary enthusiast, when visitors to his home drew him out on one of his favourite subjects, Matty would insist on making them observe a spider; or he would lead them from the warm kitchen at night to name the stars, or to gaze at the giant nebulae.

He was devoted to the revival of Irish culture, fermenting everywhere since the foundation of the Gaelic League. He won a first prize for violin playing at the first Oireachtas held early in the century. After that with skill and passion he played traditional music on the fiddle at *feiseanna* and *ceili* all over the country.

The McGoonas lived in a unique 200-year-old farmhouse, built in the traditional Irish mode on elevated ground beside the monastic ruins of Donaghmore near Navan. Beyond the house was a five-acre fruit farm of cherries and apples, carefully tended by Matty's father to yield good profit by selling the produce off the farm. In the cherry season, the McGoona children would lay out the fruit on broad cabbage leaves on a low wall near the house in readiness for customers who came from Navan for it.

To reach this homestead of unique interest, one turns off the main road on to an uphill boreen edged with ferns and wild flowers leading to a lofty round tower that guards the ancient church ruins and cemetery. Christianity was founded on a rock in Ireland and part of that rock was Donaghmore, traditionally said to have been given to Bishop Cassanus by St Patrick. Change appears never to have touched this pristine foundation. It stands hushed in peace so tangible that visitors find themselves whispering in the roofless church and tiptoeing around the ruins.

Ledwidge was among the many who enjoyed the McGoona's hospitality. Winifred McGoona, one of the younger members of the family, and still living in the old home, told me that he had a special seat at the end of the orchard where he loved to sit when the fruit trees were in blossom. Daisy McGoona, another sister, remembers him coming to the door, always with a sheaf of papers in his hand. She recalls his quickness of movement and his vitality. Matty and he would sit in the orchard, reading aloud to one another and talking until the chill in the night air drove them indoors.

The two friends always spoke of their bicycles as *Pegasus*. The classical name had a special irony in Matty's case because his mount squeaked and rattled. The family would hear its protesting noise as soon as he turned in the boreen. 'You could hear him coming a mile off.' His habit was to fling the bicycle against a ditch before he crossed the yard; he never put it into shelter and never used an oil-can. When reprimanded for this neglect, he said that the rust saved it from being stolen and that its rattle was better than a bell.

After the death of Father Smyth, it was Matty who gave Ledwidge the indispensable stimulus and intellectual interchange. Like all the Gaelic revivalists with a literary bent, Matty was deeply interested in the ancient sagas. He guided Ledwidge in choosing the translations by Standish O'Grady and Lady Gregory. Ledwidge's *Complete Poems* open with the verses *To My Best Friend* and, a few pages later, he again commemorates his friendship with Matty in the poem *To M. McG.*, and near the end of the slender volume he returns to the same theme in *To One Who Comes Now and Then*:

When you come in, it seems a brighter fire
Crackles upon the hearth invitingly,
The household routine which was wont to tire
Grows full of novelty.

And when the shadows muster, and each tree
A moment flutters, full of shutting wings,
You take the fiddle and mysteriously
Wake wonders on the strings.

But the debt Ledwidge owed to Matty is expressed in many of the nature poems, too, and in those based on Celtic mythology.

Although Ledwidge had now made friends beyond his own village and was compelled to work at a distance from it, he was still deeply attached to Slane. A popular personality there was Katie Fleming, owner of Conyngham Arms Hotel, then as now the chief town rendezvous for country people. Katie had no enthusiasm for the hotel business, but she was very sociable and gave her full attention to the bar. When young men dropped in, she settled down to enjoy their company. She liked a game of cards, but she was a bad loser. The boys used to kick one another under the table when they found she had a bad hand and they would manœuvre the game to allow her to win. Victory made Katie sparkle; she would order drinks all round 'on the house'. She bought the first gramophone ever heard in Slane and played it in the bar where it was an additional attraction.

Among the visitors who stayed regularly at the Conyngham Arms was John Cassidy, a sculptor, at this period a middle-aged man whose repute as an artist was well established. He was born in the same parish as Ledwidge and was, too, the son of a farm worker. Cassidy had begun life as a bar-boy in the White Horse Hotel, Drogheda. He spent all his free time drawing. His sketches came to the notice of a prominent townsman, Mr R. B. Davis, who urged the boy to get work in Dublin where he could attend night classes at the Art School. The Cassidys at first thought this a hare-brained idea, but Davis was persistent. He called on the boy's father and talked him into letting the boy have his chance. Young Cassidy gained an art diploma and steadily progressed to a scholarship to Italy, a permanent post at the Manchester Art School and, finally, President of the Manchester Art Gallery.

When this successful son of a local poor man sat down in the bar of the Conyngham Arms, the Slane men gathered round him, hanging on his words. Legends tended to gather around Cassidy. He used to hire a sidecar during his return visits and fill the centre storage space with stocks of food and drink for his parents. He never forgot what he owed to Davis and always called on him, too, enjoying with him a cup of tea and a chat.*

Cassidy had one thing to say to Ledwidge: the poet-to-be would have to find a Davis—in other words, an established writer who could tell him how to proceed. In passing, he mentioned the well-known Meath writer, Lord Dunsany, whom he had met, even promising to introduce the two. But his visit to Slane came to an end before he could do this.

However, he had given Ledwidge a stimulating idea. By this time, the latter had had his poems published by the two County Meath papers and the *Weekly Irish Independent,* and had discovered that none of these papers ever paid for poetry. Local praise was pleasant—he had now had almost a surfeit of it—but he longed to reach a wider public. Cassidy assured him that writers were paid elsewhere; he even knew of men who lived by writing only. How could Ledwidge break out into that world? Where could he offer his wares? He had no idea. He had never met anyone who could tell him.

Dunsany's name was at that time foremost in the literary news. He had already had five books published: *The Gods of Pegana, Time and the Gods, The Sword of Welleran, A Dreamer's Tales, The Book of Wonder.* He had been invited by W. B. Yeats to write a play and had responded with *The Glittering Gate,* produced by the Abbey in 1909. Another of his plays, *King Argimenes and the Unknown Warrior,* was staged by the Abbey Players both in Dublin and London, winning him recognition as one of the leaders in the Irish renaissance. When the idea first came to Ledwidge to appeal for his help, another Dunsany play, *The Gods of the Mountain,* was having a very successful run at the Haymarket Theatre, London, during the summer of 1911. Its text was printed in the December number of *The Irish Review,* a new monthly magazine edited by Padraic Colum.

Early in 1912, Ledwidge sent his principal notebook of poems, both published and unpublished, to Dunsany with a covering letter asking whether there was any merit in the verse. Weeks passed without bringing an acknowledgement and he came to the forlorn conclusion that that hope too had failed. The explanation of the silence, had he but

* Information given by John Cassidy's nephew: Thos. C. Cassidy, Knowth, Slane.

known it, was that Dunsany, an indefatigable traveller, was not in Ireland. He had spent the spring of 1912 in Cannes and was lingering in London, 'wasting June' as he said afterwards, when finally the packet caught up with him. Always disposed to be friendly towards fellow writers, he read the notebook and registered a pleasurable shock of surprise. Over against the published poems, the pathetic note *Unpaid* unfailing appeared. But many of the unpublished poems were better than the printed ones; *Behind the Closed Eye*, for instance, had never appeared. Evidently here was a beginner uncertain how to rate his work. Dunsany wrote a friendly, encouraging letter, warmly greeting Ledwidge as a true poet.

One Saturday evening, when Ledwidge, weary and dusty, arrived home from Martry, the reply was awaiting him. One can see him in the kitchen at Janeville as he slumps heavily into a chair to open the envelope. Then he looked up at his mother and Joe, his brown eyes alive with excitement. Life in a flash had been transformed. The door against which he had been beating had opened, and inside those magic portals a friendly hand reached out to him.

III

Lord Dunsany about this period included among the guests invited to a castle ball Oliver St John Gogarty, a surgeon then prominent among the Dublin literary wits. Before the evening was far advanced, Gogarty felt the need to find a quiet spot out of sight and sound of the dancers and strolled through the rooms in search of such a retreat:

> At last I found a settee in a corner on which sat a tall young man biting a finger-nail. His mouth, which a slight moustache did not conceal, was imperious with a clear line under the cold beauty of eyes and brow. He looked as if he belonged to a race aloof from the pathos of the common concerns of mankind. It was my host, Lord Dunsany.

Edward John Moreton Drax Plunkett, 18th Baron Dunsany, had succeeded to the second oldest title in the Irish peerage. When Ledwidge, aged twenty-five, first met him in the summer of 1912, Dunsany was thirty-four. His education had followed the traditional pattern: Eton and Sandhurst, the Coldstream Guards, in which he had served as second lieutenant in the Boer War. Poet, painter, playwright and a crack shot, he conformed in no way with the traditional Irish idea of a landlord. Sportsman and indefatigable traveller, his adventures as a big-game hunter are recounted in several of his books. Writing was his chief outlet. He spent long hours in a room over the western tower of the castle, evolving his strange tales about a spirit world, or based on an invented mythology in an imaginary country.

In a letter to John Quinn in the spring of that year, AE (George Russell) wrote: 'The most prolific and amusing of Irish writers is now Lord Dunsany. Do you know his queer tales: *The Sword of Welleran, A Dreamer's Tales* and *Time and the Gods*? He is improving and has a great splash of genius in him.'

Nevertheless a literary career had been a difficult, uphill climb for Dunsany. He had made a particularly unfortunate start. Due to wrong advice, he had paid twice over for the publication of his first book; it

43

passed through the hands of two publishers; the second one eventually saw it through the press. It was the last penny he ever spent on the publication of his writing, or to further his sales, but he had had to learn the hard way. Privilege had no part in his success; in fact he found his title 'of the greatest disadvantage'. He sought for just criticism of his work based on its intrinsic merit, without reference to his background, but the fulfilment of this modest ambition eluded him for many years.

His first books were derisively reviewed; his short stories were badly received and he had to steel himself to work without encouragement. On one occasion he sent a play to Herbert Trench and another to Sir Herbert Tree, and then had to spend months on tenterhooks awaiting their replies. He tried to alleviate his daily state of suspense with a quatrain:

> I sit all day upon a bench
> And mutter like the sea,
> Still not a word from Mr Trench
> And not a word from Tree.

When his play *The Gods of the Mountain* was accepted, he was kept for more than a year in a misery of uncertainty before it was produced. Its subsequent success and long run did not efface from his mind the purgatorial period of waiting to see it tried out on the stage.

His trials in the literary life made him sympathetic with other writers, especially beginners. He was generous-minded, a larger-than-life aristocrat. One of his tenaciously held beliefs was that poetry is a sacred art. He explained this viewpoint at a dinner given for him at the Poets' Club in London:

> For what is it to be a poet? It is to see at a glance the glory of the world, to see beauty in all its forms and manifestations, to feel ugliness like a pain, to resent the wrongs of others as bitterly as one's own, to know mankind as others know single men, to know Nature as botanists know a flower, to be thought a fool, to hear at moments the clear voice of God.

When Dunsany finally arrived home that summer of 1912, he lost no time in meeting the young poet. Ledwidge was forthwith given the freedom of the castle, especially the library, either to read there, or to borrow books. The late Dowager Lady Dunsany took up Ledwidge's cause with the same enthusiasm. I asked her what stood out in her memory of the poet's first visits and she told me it was his easy manners. 'The first time he dined with us, he showed no embarrassing shyness. I don't mean in the least that he was bumptious either; he just had natural good manners.'

The first exciting break came when Harold Hodge, editor of *The Saturday Review* and a friend of Dunsany's, accepted one of Ledwidge's poems. The County Meath papers were impressed by this advance.

We learn with pleasure that our poetical contributor, Mr. F. E. Ledwidge, many of whose lyrics have seen the light of day in these columns, has penetrated the sacred arcanum of *The Saturday Review*. We congratulate Mr Ledwidge on the splendid opportunity which has now come to him of cultivating his undoubted poetical talents, and on making the most of the introduction which he has secured to those who are prepared to fittingly requite him for his literary wares.
(*Drogheda Independent*, Sept. 1912)

Later, the *Meath Chronicle* mentioned that *The Saturday Review* had published *Low Moon Land* and obligingly added the information: 'Remuneration received by the author was 6s a line.' There are twenty-eight lines in *Behind the Closed Eye* and Ledwidge must have certainly been overjoyed when his first literary earnings amounted to eight guineas. According to contemporary values it was a large sum of money; seven weeks' wages as a road ganger for a poem he had scribbled out when he was sixteen!

Ledwidge now had the indispensable stimulus. Dunsany wrote many letters in an effort to widen the market for the young man's verse, at the same time showing him how to improve it. He taught Ledwidge all he himself knew about technique. They read the poems together and Dunsany pointed out possible improvements. He selected the best for publication, decided which periodicals were the most likely to accept, and wrote the letters of introduction. With complete faith Ledwidge abided by all the older man's decisions.

In a letter to Dunsany some years later, Ledwidge recalled how much he had been encouraged by those early sessions:

I often think on the beautiful afternoons we used to spend at Dunsany Castle, I listening enraptured to your latest, or wondering whether a comma, or a semi-colon, was the proper stop at some of my lines which you were so soon to see. Then the long ride home with beautiful memories of your appreciation, reciting my latest all

45

the miles until the pedals of my bicycle turned to the rhythm of the piece, delaying me often, for you know I love slow rhythm and short words.

The unusual friendship caused a good deal of local comment. Although the general attitude in Slane was one of suspicion, expressed with headshaking, still Ledwidge soon became a personality. The neighbours looked at him more attentively and in surmise. Anne Ledwidge noticed the changed atmosphere. Where she used to slip in and out of shops with little more than a casual greeting, now people were for ever asking her how Frank was getting on. They would stand around to hear her answer and she had to think up 'news'. She does not seem to have found this too difficult. One day, in the butcher's shop, she was asked the usual question and business was suspended so that everyone could hear the latest. She told them with a laugh:

> The other morning before daylight, I was wakened up by the sound of a window opening. I looked into Frank's room to find that he had gone out the window into the back garden. It was only four clock and there he was, fully dressed, sitting on a bank, writing a description of the sun coming up!

Lord Dunsany was invited in October to give a lecture to the National Literary Society at their Dublin headquarters, 6 St Stephen's Green. He seized the opportunity to introduce Ledwidge to the Society by reading a paper on *A New Poet*. Briefly sketching in the poet's background, he said:

> He knows nothing about technique and far less about grammar, but he has the great ideas and conceptions of the poet, and sees the vast figures, the giant forces, and elemental powers striving amongst the hills.

He then read a number of Ledwidge's poems, descriptive, pastoral and historical. The chairman of that meeting was Dr George Sigerson and among those present were Agnes O'Farrelly, W. O'Leary Curtis, Professor Trench and Padraic Colum.

Colum thought the advent of a new poet deserved to be celebrated. He studied the poem and wrote *An Appreciation*:

> 'Can aught good come out of the County Meath?' one of the speakers asked Lord Dunsany at his lecture on Monday night. They thought that this land of ranches and bullocks did not favour the production of poetry. But Lord Dunsany insisted that Meath was the part of

Ireland most favourable to the production of high-spirited things. Did not the Meath people live under the shadow of Tara? And since they had fought for the good lands, was not the dust of the best of Ireland's kings under their feet?

The unique knowledge which Mr Ledwidge possesses is of the fields of Meath, and this knowledge makes him one of the company of old Irish poets who sang of the deer on the hillside, the badger coming out of its hole, the crane crying over a lake, the blackbird singing in a bush. When he writes of Finn's men, I think he gets the atmosphere that is in the old Fenian poetry.

Francis Ledwidge is lucky in his birthplace, and lucky in his discoverer. Lord Dunsany has made a magnificent attempt to break the decree that a poet may not be famous 'till all the tale of the years is told'.

Padraic Colum told me he remembers having coffee and buns with Ledwidge shortly after the appearance of that article. He recalls the eager brown eyes and the complexion bronzed from an outdoor life. Ledwidge talked enthusiastically of the beauties of Meath. He was surprised that Colum had never visited *Brugh na Boinne*, and invited him to Slane so that he could personally show him over the place. Ledwidge had recently received good payment for a few poems and believed that his future was thereby financially assured. Colum tried to convince Ledwidge that he was foolish to think he could make a living out of poetry, because payment varied so much and was so uncertain, but the young man could not be shaken in his view that, thanks to Dunsany, his financial prospects were rosy.

The *Drogheda Independent* kept local people informed. The editor, Michael A. Casey, was still paternally following Ledwidge's progress:

Our young friend, Mr F. E. Ledwidge, has been getting on. His poetry has won for him a place amongst the sons of genius, and last week his patron, Lord Dunsany, and some other literary celebrities fêted the young Meathman in the capital. His latest contribution to *The Saturday Review* was there read, and the congratulations of his new-found friends extended to the promising young poet. The poem in question styled *All Hallows' Eve* is full of beautiful imagery and phrasing, and quaint and rather creepy conceits.

On 17th February 1913, the Irish Literary Society held an 'Original Night' and invited Ledwidge to contribute. The newspaper report says:

The distinguished young Meath poet recited two new poems of his which won warm encomiums.

Already at Dunsany Castle he had met Oliver St John Gogarty and Thomas MacDonagh. From subsequent letters, we know that he attended a few of AE's famous Sunday evenings, where he met George Roberts, managing director of Maunsel & Co. the Dublin publishers.

Katherine Tynan describes how she met him at a private view of AE's exhibition of paintings. The poet was with Lord Dunsany and she says 'very much under his wing'.

> He had a high-coloured winning face. He was wrapped in a big frieze coat. I can see the eager, gentle face under the dark, soft hair, with the desire to please obvious in it. He was very humble and deferential to an older writer. There was nothing selfconscious about him. He was entirely simple and sincere. While we talked, AE stood by and beamed on us through his glasses.

Of all that Dublin literary coterie, it was probably James Stephens who inspected Ledwidge with the most critical eye. He thought the new poet overdid the countryman act:

> He is only a beginner and must digest his ancestors before we know what he really is like. Meanwhile he has a true singing faculty, and his promise is, I think, greater than that of any young poet now writing. I do not believe, however, that he will ratify this promise by an almighty performance. I don't believe that his thought will equal his faculty for utterance. . . . A man is a mind, and so is a poet, and they are man and poet only to the extent of that. This is the croaking of the crow . . . I do not know Ledwidge at all well. . . . He is what we call here 'a lump of a lad' and he was panoplied in all those devices, or disguises, which a countryman puts on when he meets the men of the town. Country people and children are all play actors.

Brian O'Higgins, the poet, recalled meeting him in 1913:

> I was helping Father Aloysius, O.S.F.C., to edit the *Father Mathew Record*. He called one evening at the office in Church Street and laughingly told me that George Russell (AE) was beginning to dote, for he had given him a second autographed copy of the same book of poems, *Homeward Songs by the Way*. He asked me to take it. . . . It is inscribed 'F. E. Ledwidge, with kind regards from AE'.

The furore turned Ledwidge's head. Aged twenty-five, he had become a celebrity. Now, when he got out of his working clothes in the evening, he took to wearing a white poplin shirt and, instead of a tie, a flowing black silk bow; he grew his hair long; he took to wearing rimless glasses. Being a poet, he felt he had to dress like one (or like the current idea of how a poet dressed). The new look provoked among his friends more derision than approval. Paddy Mullen, a youthful uncle of Matty McGoona, remembers seeing him at this period at a dance in Navan. Mullen was one of the musicians forming the band. A group of girls in one corner were tittering so much that he asked them why; they pointed speechlessly at Ledwidge: he was dancing an eight-hand reel in the centre of the floor and whenever he swung round, his long hair flopped up and down.

But the new horizons opening up did not diminish Ledwidge's interest in his own community. He remained just as vitally committed to Slane. Master Madden died in 1912 and a young teacher named Paddy Healy was appointed principal of the school. Healy lived in the teacher's residence beside the church, where his sister, Katie, kept house for him. He became one of Ledwidge's closest friends. They passed many evenings and most of their Sundays together. They were a convivial pair who liked to frequent pubs where there was good talk.

Peter McGovern told me that he often companioned them on their Sunday outings. He had the reputation of being steadier than either of them and he was considered by the elders of the families to be the man who 'minded' Ledwidge and Healy. They, on their part, knew that they could rely on his discretion. It was always Peter who was questioned afterwards, especially by the women, about where they had been. He invariably said 'Tara', 'Newgrange', or somewhere equally inspiring, whereas in reality they spent most of the time talking in pubs.

Peter was on the local football team, the Slane Blues, whose fortunes Ledwidge still followed with passionate interest, never missing a match. On one occasion, when they played against the Navan Harps, Slane did badly. When the crowd were streaming out of the field, Ledwidge became separated from his companions and afterwards walked up and down the street in search of them. A few of the Navan Harps and their supporters passed him and made a taunting remark about the Slane team. Out shot Ledwidge's fist to send the Navan man sprawling; colleagues rushed at once to the latter's aid and Ledwidge, outnumbered, was borne to the ground. A crowd gathered, among them a few Slane boys who rescued Ledwidge, but not in time to save him from a black eye and a split lip. They were all in bad humour going home that night; 'Weren't you the bloody fool to get into that and make another show of us?' 'They insulted the team,' said Ledwidge hotly, 'what else could I do?' He got no sympathy.

The Vaugheys were among Ledwidge's good friends in Slane: three brothers, Tom, Jemmy and Paddy, a young sister, Ellie, and a cousin, Tessie Wall, who used to live with them while she was attending school. The father of the Vaugheys had died when the children were young; their mother died in the spring of 1908; so it was an unusual home consisting of young people only. Their comfortable house stood on the Hill of Slane, one of the most enviable sites in Ireland. A handsome, slated cottage embowered in trees, it nestled in a little sheltered hollow below the summit of the historic height and some distance from the ruins. In the neighbouring cemetery, tombstones commemorate Vaugheys from the early eighteenth century.

Ellie was slender with delicate colouring and brown hair. She had prominent upper teeth, counted an additional charm because it gave her an attractive lisp. Her gaiety, character and spirit are still remembered in Slane. Mrs Shaw, headmistress of the girls' school, used to keep the pupils back half an hour to learn Irish. But Ellie scampered home at the official time. Next morning, when her studious friends reproached her, she would say, 'I dunno how ye stand all that learning.'

When she left school, she was apprenticed as a milliner to Clarke's drapery, Shop Street, Drogheda. The daily cycle ride was considered too long, so she went to live with relations in Mornington, spending only her Sundays at home. When Ledwidge began to send poems regularly to the *Drogheda Independent* from 1910 onwards, he used to give them to Ellie on Sunday night to hand in at the office next morning to meet the weekly deadline.

In this way she developed a flattering interest in his work. She would report to him snippets of news of the editor and staff, or comments made by people in the shop. Before Ledwidge met Dunsany, Ellie was the poet's only link with his public. After he had secured a patron, she was a sympathetic listener to developments. He was twenty-six, she had just turned twenty when they began to take walks together in the evening. *Thoughts at the Trysting Stile* commemorate this courtship:

> I feel that she will come in blue,
> With yellow on her hair, and two curls strayed

Out of her comb's loose stocks, and I shall steal
Behind and lay my hands upon her eyes,
'Look not, but be my Psyche!'

                And her peal
Of laughter will ring far, and as she tries
For freedom I will call her names of flowers . . .

He revealed to Ellie his poet's heart, trying in halting words to explain his response to the natural beauty of river and valley.

The Broken Tryst describes an evening when he had waited in vain:

                And the blue
Of hiding violets, watching for your face
Listen for you in every dusky place.
Or will you never come, or have you died,
And I in anguish have forgotten all?
And shall the world now end and the heavens fall?

He was in love. During the autumn of 1912 there opened for him a period of enchantment, of heightened living. It was not enough now to see Ellie at week-ends. He discovered reasons for having to see her in Mornington, too. Here where the Boyne enters the sea through a flat, sandy estuary a few miles below Drogheda, there are no scenic highlights, nothing but a few scattered houses and two perpendicular towers locally termed 'the Maidens'. But Mornington has a characteristic, dream-like atmosphere: the crystal-clear water of the river purls in little wavelets against low banks in a misty landscape of greys, blues and buff-coloured sand; the Irish sea on the distant horizon is usually a placid silver streak.

The earliest of Ledwidge's extant letters is dated 22 December 1912 and gives an unexpected glimpse of the poet trying to help his patron. His naïve praise of Dunsany has charm. Considering the relative positions of the two writers in the literary world at the time the letter was written, it is reminiscent of the fable about the mouse and lion. The letter is addressed to Michael A. Casey, editor of the *Drogheda Independent*:

I send you a beautiful story by Lord Dunsany, which tale, along with transcribing it, the author entrusted to me. He told me he would be better pleased if you would send him a proof; it will give him delight to correct any errors which may possibly be made in the printing. On Page 2 of the MS you will find a slip with a sentence

D

thereon which the transcriber failed to put in. I made a mark on the left margin where this sentence belongs. I know you will like the story and give it light.

Though Lord Dunsany was very pleased at the way you printed *Thirteen at Table*, he would much rather see a proof.

There were happy evenings at Donaghmore with the McGoonas. Ledwidge loved the orchard and always sat out there when weather permitted. In the cherry season, when the black cherries were ripe, the trees attracted swarms of wasps. When these were glutted with the wine of the cherries, they would fall to the ground and crawl drunkenly around. Matty would then scoop up a cluster and spread them on the palm of his hand to study them. The McGoona children used to laugh at the blackbirds when, drugged with cherry juice, they became as heavy-winged as the wasps and even slept late in the morning. Later in the year, Ledwidge and Matty would take long walks along the river, returning home about the time when the rest of the family were going to bed. In his favourite seat on the settle at the kitchen hearth, Ledwidge would contentedly relax and describe to Matty all his experience in the literary world. Matty was a sympathetic and judicious listener and would give Ledwidge the benefit of his sage advice. They would talk far into the night.

Sometimes they visited another ceili house nearby on Mrs McGoona's home farm, where an old man named Owen Carroll, crippled with rheumatism, lived with his deaf wife. He played Irish traditional music on bagpipes and the tin whistle. Matty and Tommy McGoona and their uncle, Paddy Mullen, would accompany him on the violin. The neighbours organized dances and card-drives in this house at regular intervals and gave the proceeds to the old couple.

Sometimes a few young men would become absorbed in debating the current political situation and gave the name 'Grattan's Parliament' to their sessions. Presently they found it preferable to move to another house for these discussions so as not to interfere with the music, or the card-playing at Carroll's. Matty sent to the local paper a facetiously solemn account of the move.

A letter from Ledwidge to the *Drogheda Independent* about the Slane football team shows that he had matured to the point of trying to defend them with his pen rather than his fists:

The Slane Football Club have a presentiment that in your next issue will be chronicled their defeat by the Navan Harps at the Mid-League match last Sunday. If points were to be scored by inflicting wounds, the Navan have a few to their credit. They should only be allowed to play football in their bare feet and with blocks on their necks like vicious dogs. When it comes to roughing it, we usually leave the field.

He goes on to protest that although two players were knocked out, the referee allowed the game to continue and therefore the Slane team was entirely justified in quitting the field at half-time. But his intervention did not stop the paper from coming out with a mocking headline *Slane Blues not True Blues*, over a report saying that they walked off the field during the game for no apparent reason.

Dunsany was travelling on a big game hunt in the French Sahara for six weeks in March/April 1913. He described his principal literary activity on his return home:

> I wrote little that summer, but I had the interest and pleasure of collecting another man's poems to make a book. For a memorable event had occurred the year before when I got a letter from a young Irishman enclosing a copy-book full of verses and asking if they were any good. He was Francis Ledwidge. I was astonished by the brilliance of that eye that had looked at the fields of Meath and seen there all the simple birds and flowers, with a vividness that made those pages like a magnifying glass, through which one looked at familiar things seen thus for the first time. I wrote to him greeting him as a true poet, which indeed he was, and his gratitude for that was intense, though quite undeserved; for, as I have said elsewhere, the lark owes nothing to us for knowing that he is a lark. From that time he poured out poems, and was still doing so, and I made a selection from them for his book. These poems were so unexpected and were sent or brought to me so frequently, that they gave me the queer impression that this Irish villager had found some coffer, stored in a golden age, brimful of lyrics and lost long ago.

Ledwidge was excited and stimulated at the prospect of having a volume of his poems published.

Dunsany went to considerable trouble in selecting the best fifty. He did not rely on his own judgment but canvassed help from several literary friends, but chiefly from Professor W. F. Trench, whose major work, *Shakespeare's Hamlet*, was published in June 1913. He succeeded Edward Dowden that year as Professor of English Literature in Trinity

College, Dublin, and held the Chair until his death in 1939. The collaboration between Dunsany and Professor Trench in evaluating Ledwidge's poems continued until the latter's death.*

Dunsany then submitted the final selection to various publishers only to have it rejected by many. Dunsany himself had by this time been published by Elkin Mathews, Heinemann and G. Allen, but apparently none of these was interested in launching Ledwidge. The Irish firm, Maunsell, was among those to whom he applied, but they made such a mean offer, it was refused. Finally, the only publisher who was interested and at the same time willing to pay was Herbert Jenkins, at that time a personality among the London *literati*:

> (He) combined the role of novelist and publisher. His offices were in St James's off Jermyn Street. He had a beautifully furnished room, and would sit in an armchair resting his head on a mauve-coloured cushion which heightened the pallor of his features. On the floor was a thick pile carpet. Jenkins had just made a success as the author of *Bindle*. He was always a very fair paymaster, the kind of man who could never stop working—not so difficult for a bachelor.

But Ledwidge's personal life was shattered when Ellie's attitude to him changed. With some difficulty, she told him their meetings would have to cease. Plainly she herself suffered in telling him this; it had not been an easy decision for her. Although Ledwidge was popular with the Vaugheys, 'a wedding is a different matter' as the local people put it. The young lovers knew that Ledwidge would never be acceptable to her family as a prospective husband. The great barrier to Irish rural marriages was—and still largely is—class consciousness based on property and land values. Sixty years ago, these were the only recognized status symbols. The Vaugheys owned half the Hill of Slane; Ledwidge was a road-ganger with no assets and little prospects. In a practical assessment of this kind, poetry could not be even mentioned.

Ledwidge's poem *Before the Tears* described the first phase of Ellie's withdrawal, when she came to meet him with her elders' admonishments ringing in her ears:

> You looked as sad as an eclipséd moon
> Above the sheaves of harvest, and there lay
> A light lisp on your tongue . . .

His sonnet *The Death of Love* described a farewell in the moonlight:

* Information sent to me by Mr C. E. F. Trench.

> We stood and watched the full-blown moon arise,
> And then I felt her pulse strong in her palm.
> I knew the storm was over and the calm
> Would empty out the sorrow of her eyes.

But there was a last interview early in the day when Ledwidge apparently went to Mornington to plead with her as she was on her way to work. His poem *A Memory* describes this final meeting:

> I feel the warm hand on my shoulder light.
> I hear the music of a voice that words
> The slow time of the feet, I see the white
> Arms slanting, and the dimples fold and fill
> I hear wing-flutters of the early birds,
> I see the tide of morning landward spill,
> The cloaking maidens, hear the voice that tells
> 'You never know' and 'Soon perhaps again',
> With white teeth biting down the inly pain,
> Then sounds of going away and sad farewells,
> A year ago! It seems but yesterday.
> Yesterday! And a hundred years! All one.

When he left Mornington that day, the mind of the rejected lover was in turmoil. What was he to do? He had seen two worlds in an agonizing flash: the region of poetic imagination which was his refuge, and the implacable round of circumstances leagued against it. Would it not be better to abandon poetry and come to terms with reality? But how could he give up his most intimate self and turn into another being? He tried to order his whirling thoughts into *The Coming Poet*:

> 'Is it far to town?' said the poet,
> As he stood 'neath the groaning vane,
> And the warm lights shimmered silver
> On the skirts of the windy rain.
> 'There are those who call me,' he pleaded,
> 'And I'm wet and travel-sore.'
> But nobody spoke from the shelter,
> And he turned from the bolted door.
> And they wait in the town for the poet
> With stones at the gates, and jeers,
> But away on the wolds of distance
> In the blue of a thousand years

He sleeps with the age that knows him,
In the clay of the unborn, dead,
Rest at his weary insteps,
Fame at his crumbled head.

The courtship ceased but he did not accept his dismissal as final. He could not accept it. Ellie still represented the sum of his universe. He would go back to her when he had something to offer. It had not been easy for her to break away; she had been deeply disturbed and he held on to the memory of her unhappiness as a kind of hope. He would insist on seeing her again when he had contrived to get a better job; when he had managed to put some money together; when, when . . . His thoughts went into the poem *A Song*:

I am sad below the depth of words
That nevermore we two shall draw anear.

Had I but wealth of land and bleating flocks
And barnfuls of the yellow harvest yield,
And a large house with climbing hollyhocks
And servant maidens singing in the field,
You'd love me; but I own no roaming herds,
My only wealth is songs of love, for you,
And now that you are lost I may pursue
A sad life deep below the depth of words.

Dunsany noticed the young man's settled mood of melancholy and tried to rouse his spirits, but without success. Ledwidge admitted he could not sleep and that there was a girl involved. Dunsany mentioned it to Gogarty, a frequent visitor to the castle. Later Gogarty sent his host some characteristic doggerel on the subject.

Ledwidge had always been a passionate advocate of Labour, and was one of the founders of the Slane branch of the Meath Labour Union, functioning as early as 1906, and claiming to be the second branch set up in the county. He deserves to be commemorated in Liberty Hall for his action in 1910 at the Beauparc copper mine if for no other reason. Three years before the historic Dublin lock-out, he was leading rural labour, and was abandoned when his following ratted on him. Ledwidge brilliantly harmonized in his own life the writings and teachings of Connolly and Pearse, seeing no conflict between Christianity and socialist, revolutionary principles.

56

When the State Insurance Act became law in 1912, a new type of work had to be undertaken by the County Labour Unions. Their members had to be advised about joining a society approved under the Act and instructed how to fill up the forms so as to get the benefits. The unions welcomed the Act because it alleviated the hardships of unemployment even if it did not prevent it. Ledwidge had been elected to the Committee of Management in 1912. In the spring of 1913 it was decided that the Union members should wear medals (costing 3d each) and Ledwidge designed them. The Union further simplified matters that summer by itself becoming an approved society under the Insurance Commissioners. The following winter they found the resultant work so onerous that they had to appoint a paid secretary and provide him with an office.

At a meeting of the Union on 10 November 1913, two members were named for this post: Francis Ledwidge and James P. Kelly, both of whom had given long voluntary service. Kelly was elected by a majority of one vote. As he was not free to take up the work immediately, he asked Ledwidge to stand-in for a year. Ledwidge then resigned as road-ganger and an office was rented for him in the Square, Navan, at the back of Frank Loughran's.

He was very pleased with this office job. If only it were permanent, he might approach Ellie with a plan. Anyhow it gave him a year which he could use as a stepping-stone to higher grade employment. The changeover at the beginning of winter from road-ganger to clerk eliminated much physical hardship. He would now be under cover for the greater part of his working hours. He could live at home again; the forty miles cycling every day was reduced to fifteen. Every morning now he cycled from Janeville to Navan, carrying his midday lunch on the handle-bars, and returned home in the evening.

Matty encouraged him to learn shorthand. The exercise book recording the poet's struggle with Pitman is still extant. Under one page of symbols repeated over and over again, he wrote 'The efforts of Bruce's spider', at the end of another page he wrote 'Bad luck to Pitman'. Nevertheless he persevered until he was proficient enough to sit for an examination and get a certificate for a speed of 120 words a minute. He also taught himself to use a typewriter. With shorthand and typing, Matty believed that Ledwidge would get a job as a newspaper reporter, possibly indeed with the local paper. Mr Casey, editor of the *Drogheda Independent*, about this time commissioned him to write a series of articles on *The Boyne Valley*. Ledwidge devoted two of the series to Slane.

57

Matty McGoona's father died on 13 November 1913. Ledwidge's visits to Donaghmore ceased for the period of mourning. He wrote to his friend on Christmas Eve:

I apologise in a way for sending this card after your recent affliction. Now I regret saying above for it looks as if I was endeavouring to fold you in Despair's dark cloak forever, knowing as I do that God (our God) wipes sorrow from man's mind as a schoolboy wipes an effigy from a slate. If you possibly can, come to tea this evening. An interesting boy, P. J. Cluskey, whose story is in the *Drogheda Independent*, is coming out in the hopes of meeting you. So come if possible. I will, *we all will be watching you.* I want to see you about writing a thing I know you can write which I guarantee will bring you £5. Happy Christmas to all.

The reference to 'our God' does not mean that Matty and Ledwidge had founded some monotheistic sect of their own. They often discussed the chicanery of men in public life, especially those who made a public display of religious zeal. They rightly believed that religion should direct the whole conduct of man. Like all friends, they conversed in half-phrases that conveyed a great deal to themselves but were incomprehensible to others. 'Our God' was really a reference to the disappointing shortcomings of professedly religious people, especially elderly ones.

In an effort to qualify for better employment when the insurance job came to an end, Ledwidge continued his newspaper series well into 1914. Admittedly penny-a-line writing, many passages are nevertheless of classic permanence. His description of *The Plains of Clonard* is full of poetic currency as though he had taken a handful of shining coins and tossed them together in a bag. He excelled in observation; no eyes were more acutely perceptive of the scene he described. But he was less happy with historical background. Research and marshalling facts held little attraction for him; his sidetracks into history make arid reading.

The 1913 Christmas number of the local paper published a short story of his called *The Dark Sisters of Barristown*, an imaginative tale woven around two thorn trees. These stood as a memorial to two old witches who used to live in the district and who, legend said, used to cast spells on young girls causing them to pine away and die. Ledwidge shows in this story how strongly influenced he was at this period by Dunsany's mystery tales. The story had an unexpected sequel. Three sisters living in Barristown, near Slane, thought they were being pilloried. They protested vehemently to the editor, threatened a libel action against both paper and author, and were placated only with difficulty.

Two of his series of articles were devoted to Trim, one to Bective Abbey and four to Tara. The latter are of special interest as he again refers to Tara as the lost patrimony of the Ledwidges.

He uses landscape as a peg on which to hang his social and political thinking. In one of the Tara articles, he admonishes his own countrymen in a passage, again proving how much he was influenced by Sinn Fein principles and the Labour unrest that erupted in the great social upheaval of 1913. His rhetoric is obviously inspired by the contemporary Labour publications; nevertheless, it has an eerie permanence.

Cast your eyes around the ranches of Meath and see pride in her poverty. The sighing of the unlaboured fields are pronouncing a severe judgement on the air; ay, are sending our able-bodied across the sea in dozens, and to the lunatic asylums in scores. We are the greatest idlers in the world, we Meathians. But we must shortly mend our ways or leave the country, as the dawn of an era of labour is in the sky. We must be prepared to strip off our collars and ties and wear frieze once more, and make a friend of the spade instead of the broken-down aristocrat, or else the rising generation will evacuate us. We must till our fields instead of letting them to the man of cattle, and we must not think our sons and daughters too grand for a trade. It is easy for us now who breathe on the verge of freedom, and have full liberty to air our political feelings, to hold out our hands and say 'Tomorrow it comes'.

IV

Three main topics were discussed in Ireland during the winter of 1913–14: Larkin's strike; Home Rule; the Irish Volunteers.

Employers and Labour engaged in a relentless struggle when 404 principal employers in Dublin combined to break the Irish Transport and General Workers' Union by organizing a lock-out that lasted almost six months. Labour's heroic stand and the consequent suffering of women and children in the festering slums of Dublin publicized their plight.

AE wrote his classic letter *To the Masters of Dublin*:

> Those who have economic power have civic powers also, yet you have not used the power that was yours to right what was wrong in the evil administration of this city. You have allowed the poor to be herded together so that one thinks of certain places in Dublin as of a pestilence. There are twenty thousand rooms, in each of which live entire families, and sometimes more, where no functions of the body can be concealed and delicacy and modesty are creatures that are stifled ere they are born. You determined deliberately in cold anger to starve out one-third of the population of this city, to break the manhood of the men by the sight of the suffering of their wives and the hunger of their children. We read in the Dark Ages of the rack and thumbscrew. But even in the Dark Ages humanity could not endure the sight of such suffering, and it learnt of such misuses of power by slow degrees, through rumour, and when it was certain it razed its Bastilles to their foundations.

The contest ended inconclusively, but nevertheless this was the historic moment when Labour in Ireland stood upright for the first time.

Political unity had been achieved in the belief that Home Rule was as good as law. At a great demonstration in O'Connell Street in 1912, both Padraic Pearse and Eoin MacNeill spoke in its favour. Twenty-seven years previously the first Home Rule Bill had been introduced in the House of Commons by William Gladstone. In January 1913 the

Bill at last passed its third reading by a majority of 110 in a scene of jubilation on the Nationalist benches. The Irish party at Westminster basked in a glow of victory at home: bonfires, lighted tar-barrels, torchlight processions, flags. Nineteen-thirteen was called 'Home Rule Year'. A few weeks later the Bill was thrown out by the House of Lords, but according to new legislation, when a measure had been three times rejected by the Lords, it could be sent over their heads for the King's signature. There were some ominous *ifs*: the Bill was as good as law *if* the Liberal Government kept its promises, or *if* indeed it lasted long enough to keep them. But the Government seemed secure and the majority of the Irish people accepted the leisurely course of the law.

Home Rule was opposed in the north of Ireland. Sir Edward Carson, formerly Attorney-General for Ireland, became leader of the Opposition. The Orange Order pledged its members to refuse to recognize Home Rule and to resist it, if necessary by physical force. The Ulster Volunteers were founded for this purpose.

Although Carson's speeches were tantamount to inciting rebellion and starting a civil war, the Government took no action. In the other three provinces, Sinn Fein was the first voice to cast doubts on the prevailing certainty of victory; to point out the real implication of events in Ulster; to urge less dependence on parliamentary representatives.

At a meeting in the Rotunda, Dublin, on 25 November 1913, the Irish Volunteers were formed by acclamation: some 4,000 people filled the hall and outside was a large overflow. Stewards handed out Volunteer enrolment forms and collected 3,000 signatures. The avowed aim of the Volunteers was 'To secure and maintain the rights and liberties common to the whole people of Ireland'. Eoin MacNeill, Professor of History at University College, Dublin, and Laurence J. Kettle were appointed honorary secretaries. MacNeill being such a well-known Redmondite, his leadership originated the popular belief that the Volunteers were the fighting arm of the Irish Party, just as the Ulster Volunteers were Carson's military strength.

The enthusiasm in the capital for the Irish Volunteers surged through the whole country in the spring. Frank and Joe Ledwidge were among the founders of the Slane corps of which Frank was elected secretary, responsible for correspondence and organization. The Executive in Dublin had no funds during the first few months of their existence. Subscriptions were canvassed from Irish exiles in England and America. Most of the young men who joined the Volunteers in those early days

61

had to dig into their own pockets to pay for a drill instructor and travel, secretarial and organizing expenses. The Ledwidges had by this time a brother and sister living in Manchester and for this reason, at one of the early meetings of the Slane corps, Frank agreed to make a quick trip there to further the cause. With the exception of reading his poems to the Literary Society in Dublin, he had never spoken in public, but now he agreed to give a talk in Manchester for the purpose of founding there a branch of the Volunteers.

This movement now absorbed all Ledwidge's free time. The Slane corps drilled two evenings a week and devoted their Sundays to training, chiefly lengthy route marches to points where they could link up with other units of Volunteers.

The local paper describes the contemporary excitement:

The most remarkable development of the past few weeks in Ireland has been the phenomenal growth of the Irish National Volunteers.

The movement has spread like wild fire. A moderate calculation places the number of men already enrolled at 128,500. And recruiting is going on at the rate of some 2,000 a day. In Ulster, in particular, the increase of the National Volunteer Force is extraordinary. These men are described by competent judges as firstclass fighting material. Many of them are ex-army men, and men like Colonel Moore, formerly of the Connacht Rangers, and Captain White, son of the late Sir George White, the defender of Ladysmith, have placed themselves at their head. All over the country the tramp of the National Volunteers is heard after the day's work is done. *The Times* and other leading Unionist papers in England have already taken serious notice of the movement, and warned all concerned not to make the mistake of despising it. The movement is in sympathy with the Irish Party. It is one of the most extraordinary and portentous Irish movements of our time.

Slane asserted county leadership when it announced a great rally of Meath Volunteers to be held in the village on Lady Day, 15 August.

*　　*　　*

For several years now, Frank and Joe Ledwidge had combined in maintaining a comfortable home for their mother. All the older members of the family were settled elsewhere and able to fend for themselves. Anne Ledwidge found happiness in keeping house for her two youngest sons. She encouraged them to bring in their friends and was always there to dispense hospitality. Her years of hardship were never recalled with resentment. They had left her with an abiding sympathy for the poor and no 'traveller' was ever refused food at her door.

A letter from Frank to Matty McGoona gives a picture of the poet's activities and of life in the Ledwidge home at this period:

Janeville, Slane, 21st January
1914

My dear Mat,

Pardon me for not answering your charming letter and acknowledging your 'Great Thoughts' earlier. I will not venture any excuse, because I have none but the transcendent failing of all poets. I was glad to hear from you but sorry you were not able to come out on Sunday. I hope to satisfy your desire about my 'Ulysses' some time, but I have never done a line to it since. Pegasus is a contrary nag and once he puts his hoof to earth it is only by gentle persuasions he is induced to soar again. For such a long flight as I intended taking over the island of Oxygia where my Ulysses is, it is extremely hard to spur him up when once allowed to rest, and when that disagreeable mood comes over him it is best to allow him his humour, for the simple reason, if I mounted him and spurred him on an involuntary journey he would come down from the sublime to the ridiculous occasionally and every time he descended the critics would put him into pound and abuse me sorely. But I have taken a few short flights on him; and once I saw Gwydion and Math make a wife for Llew out of flowers and birds, and again I saw the last poet of the world dying, and I saw a young queen in a far off land bemoaning the departure of a King who gave her trouble. All these things I have sung about, and will be pleased to read for you when you come next Sunday.

I sincerely hope you have taken that judicious sidestep I cautioned you about. For believe me, Mat, there is a bottomless cliff there through which you will fall into Cimmerian darkness if you are not careful. Travellers in the tropics often see a jewel shining on the wayside and stoop to lift it, but when once their hand touches it, it bursts and the young adder stings them to death, *there is no escape*. A maiden's heart is the same: you may think it a jewel but touch it with the tender words of love, and immediately the reptile bursts forth, and you are lost, lost. Examine it with caution before you stoop as I did and you will perceive the truth of my statement.

Ned McDonnell requests to be remembered to you, he is home with a cold. We were at a very nice party on Sunday night. Don't forget to come on Sunday, and *come early*. Be here for dinner and we will go to the 'Hill' for tea. I have an invitation there and promised to bring you.

Great Thoughts was a literary periodical to which Matty subscribed. The poem *The Wife of Llew* on which Ledwidge was working that winter is based directly on the *Mabinogion*, the collection of fourteenth-century Welsh Romances. These tales had recently been rediscovered and popularized through the translation of Lady Charlotte Guest. It was one of the books currently popular among the Irish writers of the Renaissance. A few years later, Padraic Colum retold the tales in his book *The Island of the Mighty*. Ledwidge's classical allusions show too that he had been reading the *Odyssey*, for which there was also a contemporary wave of enthusiasm due to the writings of W. E. Gladstone, F. A. Paley, R. C. Jebb and Andrew Lang. The extensive use that James Joyce made of the *Odyssey* need not be retold here. Dunsany was concerned that Ledwidge should not only meet his fellow writers, but read what they were reading. It was he who drew Ledwidge's attention to both poetical sources and lent him the books.

Incidentally, one has only to compare the lines that inspired the poet with what he made of them to realize his power and his enormous promise. Here is the relevant passage from the *Mabinogion*:

So they took the blossoms of the oak, and the blossoms of the broom, and the blossoms of the meadow-sweet, and produced from them a maiden, the fairest and most graceful that man ever saw. And they baptized her, and gave her the name of Flower-face.

And here is the poem:

The Wife of Llew

And Gwydion said to Math, when it was Spring:
'Come now and let us make a wife for Llew.'
And so they broke broad boughs yet moist with dew,
And in a shadow made a magic ring:
They took the violet and the meadowsweet
To form her pretty face, and for her feet
They built a mound of daisies on a wing,
And for her voice they made a linnet sing

In the wide poppy blowing for her mouth.
And over all they chanted twenty hours.
And Llew came singing from the azure south.
And bore away his wife of birds and flowers.

Despite Ledwidge's airy pose of wisdom in his letter to Matty, he still found it bitterly hard to adjust his life to the loss of Ellie. He began to take long solitary walks searching for peace of mind:

Then I strayed
Down a green coil of lanes where murmuring wings
Moved up and down like lights upon the sea,
Searching for calm amid untroubled things
Of wood and water.

But he could not find solace even in the serene beauty of river and woodland. Instead it seemed 'the glory is all faded'. She would be for ever part of those scenes because they had enjoyed them together. He would have to get away in order to forget:

I'm wild for wandering to the far-off places
Since one forsook me whom I held most dear.
I want to see new wonders and new faces
Beyond East seas . . .

Hurtful gossip had reached him that Ellie was keeping company with John O'Neill, recalled as one of the most handsome young men in the district, well over six feet in height, who played the fiddle and sang, and was greatly in demand at *ceili* and *feisseanna*. He was employed on the outdoor staff of Townley Hall, an estate four miles from Drogheda (now the 'Kells Ingram Farm', an agricultural school conducted by Trinity College).

Paddy Healy, the schoolmaster, proved a good friend to Ledwidge during that difficult winter. Healy's sister, Mary, was married in January 1914 and Paddy gave a party in his house to celebrate the return of the honeymooners. Ledwidge was among the guests and here he met for the first time Paddy's youngest sister, Lizzie. She was twenty, with expressive grey eyes and striking golden hair; in character she was imperious and self-willed. The Healys followed up the party some days later with a 'scrap dance' in the Parish Hall, Slane, and again invited Ledwidge. Here he met Lizzie for the second time and discovered that they had much in common: she was a reader and had a collection of books, a marvel in the poet's eyes. She sang some of

Moore's melodies for the guests that night and he was delighted to find that she was musical, too. They met again at a dance in Ardee some weeks later, and he wrote to her the following day:

February 9th, 1914

Dear Lizzie,

I hope you got home safely yesterday evening. It must have been pretty hard to cycle to your place, although you could not have been as bad as myself who had to come from Ardee in the teeth of the wind all the time. However, I didn't feel it, as my thoughts were regretting old romances of ancient Babylon, and lamenting the spate of poetry, and you must know, the longest way is very short to the dreamer. I was thinking of other things too, and regretting what nice things I might have said in an opportune moment to someone who has a big heart and a kindly soul. It is always the same with me; when the opportunity has passed I live the drama over again.

I shall not forget for a long time the pleasure I found at the two dances in Slane and wish I could do something in return for the trouble you and your people went to in catering for our delight. When I think of it I feel as lonely as if I had been watching it for an age, and that now it was passed, there was no more to live for. The poem of which I told you in advance is progressing surely, and I shall be glad to send you a copy when it is finished, if you wouldn't mind.

I think you said there were some things of Thomas Moore's you hadn't read. I will leave a copy in Slane for you and you can get it when you come up next week-end. Meanwhile I will be going to Drogheda and if I see anything worth getting I will. But Drogheda is very bad and I may not succeed. I am going to Navan on Lynagh's car on Wednesday. I suppose you won't be out? If so I would see you at Co. Council Hall, Railway Street, about 10.45, or returning from meeting at about 11.15 same place. I would like ever so much to see you sometime and let you know what I say to myself in the fields when I think I am talking to the girl of the big heart and the kindly soul.

Won't you please write to me, as I will be watching a letter from you, because I think of you so often.

He is evidently making a resolute effort here to turn his heart and mind away from Ellie.

Lizzie must have answered quickly because, four days later, he is writing to her again. She had sent him the news that the Farrellys had found a house to rent in Wilkinstown and she was going to live with them. She invited Ledwidge to visit them in their new home and he was grateful for her friendship:

13 February 1914

Thanks ever so much for your charming letter of this morning. I cannot let you know in ink the delightful surprise it was to me: more welcome than the spring which I am watching for since October. I appreciate the compliment you pay me by saying that there was an atom of pleasure in my company. Where I meet people who are like myself, slaves of the book, I can say what I admire but in the conventional company usually met at a dance, unless there is a kindred spirit, my presence is like a pillar of ice in the glow of the room. I certainly shall go to Wilkinstown some day but my reviewal of your library will be only a second consideration, firstly because it's you I want to see and secondly because I know you possess all the old beautiful masters. And dear Lizzie I do want to see you badly, will you ever look at me again if I tell you why? I expect you will be home tomorrow evening for the week-end. Perhaps I would see you for a moment somewhere. I have not yet decided on what date I will go to England, but I shall certainly make it a point to have a long chat with you ere that. This is merely to acknowledge your letter for which I thank you again. If I don't see you tomorrow night, I will drop you a line on Monday. Goodbye and thanks for the happy day you gave me.

The letter reached Lizzie on the feast of St Valentine. On the same day a charming Valentine was delivered at her door—a bunch of violets. There was no note with the fragrant gift, so she immediately assumed that Ledwidge had sent it. The following Saturday she read a poem in the local paper on *Violets*, signed *Inamorato*, and dated *St Valentine's Day*. Ledwidge again, of course! Who else? Overwhelmed by this public tribute, Lizzie tried to rise to the occasion by sending him violets, too, enclosed in her next letter. But her delighted thanks astonished him for he had neither sent her the gift nor written the poem! While he must have felt dashed that he had been a little slow on the poetic draw, he was troubled too, by the news that she had another admirer. As for Lizzie, this comedy of errors rocked the lovers' world.

They met again and Ledwidge thought that they had both got rid of the embarrassment. When he writes to her on 2 March, he has dismissed violets from his mind:

As I told you at Beauparc I have been away from home much of late and only slept about three nights here for the last three weeks. I think I have done with travelling now until I go to England, where I would be now, only a man found an Ogham stone down below near Enniskillen and I was sent with another man from the National University to read it and place it in its chronological position with its sister treasures. I think we succeeded, but it took a lot of hunting up and occasioned the collection of many local legends and a comparison of their relative forms with the matter in hands and a sifting of chaff and wheat.

Janeville. March 9th, '14

Dear Lizzie,

My heart was broken watching that letter from you to know what you would say to me. I would have written earlier but that I thought I might see you Saturday or Sunday.

I am glad that you are not angry with me, but I won't mention love any more, though I can no more help being a lover than I can a poet. Had I my wish I would not desire the blessing of either, for poetry brings me nothing but a desire for better and better work, and love but a few hours pleasure in a place of the fancy—and a few violets that tell me a story to make me jealous. No, I didn't write that poem, and I have been asked that before, and now that you have mentioned it the whole mystery of the thing is expounded. All that remains is to find the name of the donor, and if his initials are V.S., I am acquainted with the whole story. The violets you sent are charming and I shall keep them forever because they will remind me of one who played with princes in the halls of kings and when she became weary angels ministered to her, that was St Elizabeth, and to her I shall pray in future, reminding her how once she thought everything in vain and that now when I am weary of heart I want her comfort.

Yes, I am now as interesting as a new comet and my photograph and three columns of my biography appeared in 27 English papers last Saturday. I would send you one but your people would wonder how you received it.

I am delivering a lecture entitled: *The Irishman Abroad* in Manchester on the 21st. I leave here on the 18th, or perhaps the night of the 17th. I want to see you before I go as I am longing for a chat with you. Could I see you in Slane on Saturday or Sunday next, or had I better go to Wilkinstown on Friday? Dear Lizzie, I very much appreciate your friendship and want to hold it forever. I won't say anything in future that would annoy you and hope you will not tire of me too soon.

The real trouble about the poem attributed to Ledwidge by Lizzie is that it is such a poor effort, most 'unLedwidge-like', not to be rated with even his earliest juvenilia. Opening with the lines:

> Lovely violets! How ye weave your spells
> Round this smitten heart of mine,

it clumps along through sixteen lines of clichés about 'vestal love', 'beauteous maid' and of course 'cerulean hue'. Moreover Lizzie had overlooked the detail that Ledwidge never used a pen name. Truly, for a girl who was a reader, she was not perceptive in her judgment of poetry.

Wilkinstown, where Ledwidge visited her, is a village of unusual charm on the edge of a bog about seven miles north of Navan. It might have been designed for easy gossiping as its houses seem to have come together haphazardly in a sort of conspiratorial huddle and its street has inconsequent angles and curves that invite long pauses for chatting. Beyond this cosy cluster of houses and shops, the road turns north-east to cross a great elevated sprawl of open bog, forming an exhilarating vista closed on the far horizon by the hilly undulations of north Meath and Cavan.

The cottage at that time rented by the Farrellys still stands in the centre of the village, opposite O'Neill's garage. Built in a sheltered corner, typical of Wilkinstown's whimsical building, its gable end fronts the street. An iron gate leads into a small lawn; the three front windows of the cottage look out on this little grassy enclosure. Mary and Willie Farrelly were both teachers and Lizzie kept house for them, but she liked to spend her week-ends with her bachelor brother Paddy in Slane.

A teacher and his family occupy a prominent position in a village where everyone's business is known. The letters exchanged between Lizzie and Ledwidge show that they were in agreement about keeping their friendship a secret from both the Healys and the Farrellys. Lizzie did not confide in her older sisters. Ledwidge could not send her even a newspaper in case they might ask embarrassing questions. The young people had to be cautious about letters, too. The postman in either village would quickly learn to recognize their handwriting and they did not want to be the subject of gossip. All told, the most unobtrusive way to improve acquaintance was to meet in Slane during Ledwidge's casual visits to Paddy Healy.

When Ledwidge was not coping with insurance claims at his desk in the Navan office, he was struggling with his notes for the Manchester lecture. But Lizzie continued to be obsessed with her romantic Valentine. She had found out who had sent her the violets: Vincent Smyth, a few years her junior, son of a schoolmaster in Stackallan. This was a disappointing dénouement. The two families of teachers were intimate from childhood, so romantic sentiments from him would class him in her view as 'a young fool'. But she was still trying to find out who had written the poem on violets published for St Valentine's Day. Surely there was a connection between gift and poem? Her continuing pre-occupation is clear from Ledwidge's next letter to her:

13th March 1914

You couldn't ask too much of me, but since you will be in Slane from Saturday to Tuesday, I will not risk being seen in Wilkinstown on tomorrow as the people are so fond of talking about me now, were I seen, you'd never know where the tale would end. I was in with Paddy and your sister for the last two nights, so when you come I will call up next Sunday night.

The photograph in 'The Telegraph' was very bad and many lies were printed about me, but all this helps to make one famous, and fame is a fulcrum upon which a man may rest and overturn worlds. Yet it can never ease a heart pain.

I don't know anything about the violet poem. I only know that a love-sick youth sent violets to a pretty maiden, but the poem is a coincidence and nothing more.

Yes, the world is full of young fools, Lizzie, and am I not the greatest of them all? But I am not afraid of my laurels when 'Inamorato' writes poetry as I think I can best him any time. But there is a more important thing than poetry in the world. See you Sunday.

The meeting in Paddy's house, however, did not go well. Lizzie was still pouting over the violets. She had wanted to believe that Ledwidge had written the poem to her; that—to her mind—would have been a pleasing solution to the whole mystery. It is probable that Ledwidge was exasperated into saying what he may have hesitated to write:

he would never have written such a bad poem. This did not mend matters.

Then he went to Manchester where he gave the lecture at the John Redmond Club in Hulme. On his return to Slane, he did not resume correspondence with Lizzie. Man-like, he had to admit himself defeated: there seemed to be absolutely no way of appeasing her on the subject of violets.

*   *   *

Meanwhile the help extended by Lord Dunsany to Ledwidge was beginning to bear fruit. Dunsany was abroad most of the winter. Ledwidge wrote to him early in January 1914:

I have been a few days without writing one line, and feeling very miserable when I recollected that the cure for that was a perusal of all your lordship's letters to me, so now I have written the best things of my life in a poem called *Ulysses with Calypso*. I scored inner after inner; of course I went wide of the mark a few times but never wholly off the target. I am as far as 100 lines but not near finished yet. Here are a few of my best. Ulysses weary wandering the seas, and thinking of his queen and son away in far Ithaca was now marooned on the island of Oxygia:

> In the ears
> Of shady hollows and of twisted crags
> Bird song and water song made sweet alloy of sounds

And speaking of whins (furze):

> So full of God
> He thought he entered his beloved land
> Under wide flags that whipped the coloured air.

'Beloved land' is bad. But 'wide flags' and 'whipped', particularly the latter gave me such delight that I smoked an idle hour after getting them.

Herbert Jenkins, as already indicated, had accepted Ledwidge's first volume of poems, *Songs of the Fields*. The proofs arrived and Lord Dunsany on his return wrote the Introduction:

In a wood in which I shoot rabbits I wrote on days on which I was not playing cricket my preface to Ledwidge's first book of poems, expressing the high hopes that I had of this new star among poets, that seemed so fair at its rising.

71

The established writer took considerable trouble with that Preface and Ledwidge was dazzled by the praise. In almost a thousand words, Dunsany felicitated the poet for his 'easy fluency of shapely lines'; he described him as 'a mirror reflecting beautiful fields, or rather a very still lake on a very cloudless evening'. He called Ledwidge 'the poet of the blackbird' (a phrase that has since become tattered through repetition). Dunsany concludes: 'Know that neither in any class, nor in any country, nor in any age, shall you predict the football of Pegasus, who touches the earth where he pleaseth and is bridled by whom he will.' Ledwidge hastened to Matty McGoona with this glowing tribute and when they reached the final flourish, they broke into prolonged laughter because Pegasus is the name they had always given to—their bicycles!

*   *   *

All this time Ledwidge's basic preoccupation was the problem of livelihood when his term of office in Navan came to an end. Disappointment awaited him that summer. When he became proficient in typing and could flourish a certificate to show that he had attained speed in shorthand, his ambition to get on the staff of the Drogheda newspaper was snuffed out by the editor's 'No vacancy'. Ledwidge now realized that he would probably have to emigrate to secure work offering any kind of fair remuneration and permanency.

Then he was elected to the Navan Rural District Council and Board of Guardians. This was no empty honour at that period, but a coveted distinction. It bound Ledwidge still more closely to his own people and his native place. The meetings of these public representatives were usually devoted to considering vaccination defaulters, tenders for repairs to cottages and supplies of bread and other commodities for the workhouse.

The first meeting at which the minutes record Ledwidge's attendance took place on 1 July 1914. It was an occasion when an echo of the public excitement penetrated the council room. A resolution was read from the Edenderry Urban Council protesting against the proposed Arms Proclamation (a legal measure aimed against the Volunteers). Ledwidge spoke in favour of the protest, saying: 'Public opinion is the only weapon we now have and we must wield it unmercifully.' He would have been bound to comment on any reference to the Volunteers as he was at this period giving up all his free time to the Slane Corps.

The successful gun-running at Howth and Kilcoole was hailed as news of real significance. The Howth operation had an unpleasant sequel when British soldiers fired on a crowd at Bachelor's Walk, killing three and wounding eighty. This caused extreme anger all over Ireland and increased the enthusiasm for the Volunteers. Considering all that the Ulster Volunteers had achieved in the way of landing arms (apparently with government connivance), the action taken at Howth and Kilcoole was applauded as proof of the Irish Volunteers' determination.

News that the Archduke Francis Ferdinand and his consort had been assassinated at Sarajevo on 28 June provoked hardly a ripple of interest in rural Ireland. But when Austria-Hungary declared war on Serbia a month later, it was clear to observers of the European situation that a real threat of war had risen darkly on the horizon.

The village in a pastoral hinterland of an island, however, still basked in a charmed circle of carefree tranquillity. It was a golden summer. Lord Dunsany was a keen cricketer who promoted the game locally with great enthusiasm. In the castle grounds between two woods he had a cricket field where at one time or another all the principal cricketers of Ireland had played:

> One often played all the week, including Sundays, but on Sundays it was village cricket played by workmen who had no other day on which to play it. One easily found 22 men to play on Sundays, and a much greater number to watch and have tea in the tent. And they played it well and enjoyed it.

Even when Gaelic football became popular in Slane, cricket retained its popularity. The majority of the players liked both games and amicably practised in the same field. Sometimes when a cricketer was bowled out, he turned at once to football, with the result that sometimes only bowler and batsmen were left at cricket, while those who should have been fielding were playing football instead.

Although Ledwidge did not keep up cricket after he left school, he always enjoyed watching it. He wrote to Dunsany on 1 August:

> You must be tired of the way I change my tune so often. The enclosed may rightly be termed a serenade because I wrote it in the middle of the night, not at another's window, but at my own.
>
> I meant to send your lordship a better copy, but I am tired and couldn't face to type it over again until I know if it is any good.
>
> Aren't you playing cricket next week? I would like very much to see another game.

Meanwhile the European situation became hourly more threatening. On the date the above letter was written, Germany declared war on Russia, and two days later on France. On 4 August, the blow fell when England declared war on Germany.

Ledwidge wrote again to Dunsany on 6 August:

I sprained my ankle on last Sunday jumping at a sports here, and have been very bad all the week. Your lordship knows the sickening sensation of a sprained ankle.

I was in bad humour for poetry. There will be nobody to read us now at all on account of the war; but it will be easy for posterity to remember the dates of our writings, if we live.

P.S. I will probably be called to defend the coasts of Ireland from our common enemy. God send!

Immediately war was declared, Dunsany went to the nearest recruiting centre in Dublin to join up. The officer to whom he reported sent him to the Fifth Battalion of the Royal Inniskilling Fusiliers, then assembling for training in Richmond barracks. With the rank of captain he returned home in uniform on a short leave to put his affairs in order.

Both Dunsany and Ledwidge were positive that while the war lasted, it meant the end of writing. Dunsany was to discover:

Among the many good men amongst whom I lived for the next few years, only one knew me for a writer, and even he must have recognised that the world was no longer a place for the spilling of ink.

Herbert Jenkins decided in the early weeks of the war that he would have to hold up publication of *Songs of the Fields*. In reporting this, the *Meath Chronicle* added: 'The poet thinks it is an affliction averted.' Despite the jest, however, Ledwidge's hopes of making a living out of writing were blasted. His personal dilemma became more acute. Everyone believed that the war meant *real* work for the Volunteers, so that now more than ever he wanted to remain with his comrades. The war, too, heightened his sense of responsibility to the county administration work in which he had become involved.

He discussed his problems with Dunsany who, faithful to his belief that 'poetry is a sacred art', advised him to continue writing whatever happened. He also insisted on settling a weekly allowance on Ledwidge to be paid to him direct from his bank during his absence at the war.

It was the equivalent of Ledwidge's salary from the Meath Labour Union and was intended to tide him over the period between the ending of his job in Navan and finding other employment. Joe Ledwidge told me that Frank acquiesced in this arrangement with extreme reluctance, believing that it solved nothing. But Dunsany's insistence overruled the younger man's objections.

The war lent new significance to the forthcoming Volunteer rally in Slane on 15 August. The gentry of the county had promised to attend this event organized by the people, thus presenting a united front to the threat from the north of Ireland. The Volunteers were now invested with new interest in the eyes of authority, who saw them as first-rate material for army recruitment. All the previous week, as Slane prepared for a huge influx of people into the village, the air became electric with excitement.

Sunday, 15 August, dawned radiantly clear. A crowd estimated at 5,000 began to pour into the village from early morning, and the Volunteers mustered to the number of 2,500, many of them with full equipment. Lady Day in Slane always meant the traditional pilgrimage to the demesne. About a thousand pilgrims usually converged on the Holy Well that day with bottles and cans for the water. Outdoor stalls would be set up where pilgrims might obtain a variety of refreshments, and the vigorous playing of musicians enlivened the pattern. But on the day of the rally, pious people accustomed to making their own of Slane for that day found themselves pushed into the background. Many were unable to get to the village; it was almost impossible to hire any kind of vehicle because of the unprecedented demand.

The Volunteers were reviewed in a large field bedecked with bunting, where stood a grandstand draped with flags. Numerous corps of Volunteers including that of Slane, with Ledwidge among them, were accompanied by pipers' bands whose skirl added gaiety to the gathering. Political innocence and guile met on that field. The Marquis of Conyngham, Viscount Gormanston and Lord Trimleston had by this date joined the Volunteers 'for the defence of our country'. A distinguished group were assembled at the saluting base: Lords Fingal and Dunsany, Colonel Sir N. T. Everard, Doctors Timmon and Byrne of Navan, the two M.P.s, Mr Dean and Mr Patrick White, and a group of fashionable ladies. Lords Fingal and Dunsany inspected the corps and spoke before the proceedings terminated, Dunsany appealing for unity in the present crisis. The bands played *God Save Ireland* and *God Save the King*.

Mr Paddy Cowley of Ardbraccan, who was there that day, told me that when Dunsany concluded his speech, James Quigley, County Surveyor, who was on the platform, stood up impulsively and walked forward. Addressing the Volunteers and lifting his hat, he said: 'Remember, boys, it's Ireland first, Ireland last, and (flinging his hat to the ground to add emphasis) Ireland all the time.' He was cheered with immense fervour.

As the first month of the war slipped by, the newspapers reported that British troops were being withdrawn from Irish garrisons. There were frequent appeals to the people to keep calm. Ledwidge's idea that the Volunteers would now be called upon to defend the shores of Ireland was the currently accepted opinion. According to the local paper:

> If Great Britain needs to withdraw her defensive forces from this country, the Irish Volunteers, in conjunction with their brothers the Ulster Volunteers would be prepared to defend this country from foreign invasion. Today the people of these Kingdoms stand foursquare confronting every enemy who would threaten their rights or seek to infringe their liberties. This is the beginning of the realisation of the dream of Davis, the hope of every patriotic Irishman, that union of Orange and Green which will present to the world the vision of a United Ireland.

This may seem a naive and pious wish to readers with the after-knowledge of sixty years, but to understand Ledwidge's story it is vital to bear in mind the contemporary attitude to the crisis. Colonel Moore, Commander-in-Chief of the Volunteers, said at a later date: 'When I put forward the object of the movement, the one that produced the most intense enthusiasm was the chance of reconciling hostile sections. ... The Volunteers themselves were on strictly non-party lines; it was their boast that they were a national, not a political body.'

The Home Rule Bill was unceremoniously shelved on account of the war. Alongside it on the Statute Book was now another Bill postponing its operation for twelve months, or 'until the end of the war'. These developments were discouraging to ardent Nationalists who had organized the lighting of tar-barrels and the torchlight processions. But the majority of commentators agreed that the war made delay inevitable.

Speaking at Woodenbridge in County Wicklow on 20 September, John Redmond, however, let the cat out of the bag in what was afterwards reckoned a historic pronouncement:

The interests of Ireland, of the whole of Ireland, are at stake in this war . . . undertaken in defence of the highest interests of religion and morality and right. It would be a disgrace forever to our country, a reproach to her manhood, and a denial of the lessons of her history if young Ireland confined their efforts to remaining at home to defend the shores of Ireland from an unlikely invasion, and shrinking from the duty of proving on the field of battle that gallantry and courage which have distinguished their race all through its history. I say to you, therefore, your duty is twofold. I am glad to see such magnificent material for soldiers around me, and I say to you, go on drilling and make yourselves efficient for the work, and then account yourselves as men *not only in Ireland itself, but wherever the firing line extends,* in defence of right, of freedom and religion in this war.

Stripped of its verbiage, this was a recruiting speech and was received as such.

The original members of the provisional committee immediately held a meeting. Five days later, they issued a statement terminating their association with Redmond and the nominees he had forced on them the previous June. This meant that there were now two groups contending for control: Redmond and his supporters, who called their followers the *National Volunteers*: Eoin MacNeill and the original twenty co-founders who retained the name *Irish Volunteers* for their members.

The split was profoundly demoralizing to the rank and file everywhere. Most of the Volunteers had been brought up in the belief that Redmond was Ireland's spokesman. They were shocked at the idea of throwing him aside. They pointed out that MacNeill had been chosen to lead the Volunteers precisely because he was such a well-known supporter of Redmond.

Meetings were held all over Ireland to discuss the division. The behaviour of the Slane Corps was typical. John Ward who was at their meeting told me: 'The whole Hall declared for Redmond with only six men opposing the resolution: the two Ledwidges, Willie Lynch, Owen Briody, John Gallagher and myself.' In affirming loyalty to Redmond, the resolution said:

We view with surprise and disgust the action taken by a minority of self-elected members of the Provisional Committee, and we repudiate the extraordinary document with their signatures.

When Ledwidge walked out of that Hall, the Volunteers to whom for the past nine months he had given his heart, his time and all his spare cash had ceased to exist. Almost the entire Meath Volunteer force declared solidly for Redmond. Drogheda was selected for the new headquarters; the Slane Corps became B Company in the 2nd Battalion of the 11th Brigade. Ledwidge had nothing further to do with it.

The action of the Navan Volunteers too may be cited as characteristic of the confusion that scattered the ranks. They met during the second week of October to consider the Manifesto from the Provisional Committee. Out of a membership of over 400, only 74 attended, of whom 49 declared for Redmond, 23 for MacNeill and 2 were neutral.

During the first weeks of the war public opinion was sanguine that it was going to be a short one. The British Army and Navy were considered invincible and the catch-cry was 'The British will soon finish the Germans'. But events did not take quite the expected course. The British Expeditionary Force landed in France on 16 August and despite their efforts, the Germans had captured Namur, destroyed Louvain and occupied Amiens before the end of the month. Then, in order to step up recruitment, virulent anti-German propaganda began to flood the press: German soldiers were on a ruthless campaign of frightfulness; every day there were reports of murder and rapine. It was worse for civilians than for soldiers: women raped; babies impaled on the swords of Prussian officers, or left alive with their hands cut off; 'appalling official documents' were supposed to be a terrible indictment of the German soldier who became 'the unspeakable Hun'. If the enemy was not defeated quickly and finally, England, dependent on foreign supplies, could not maintain her independence. If she went down, what would happen to Ireland? Public fear was played upon to support the war effort.

Here is a typical poster of the period:

IS IRELAND TO SHARE BELGIUM'S FATE?
Read what the Germans have done to the Churches,
Priests, Women and Children of Belgium.
MEN OF IRELAND
The sanctity of your Churches, the safety of your
Homes, the honour of your Women can only be secured by
DEFEATING THE ENEMY IN BELGIUM

Later, the famous pastoral letter of Cardinal Mercier made it seem a Catholic duty to defend Belgium.

The Navan Rural Council were enthusiastic Nationalists whose ardour was not damped by either the indefinite shelving of the Home Rule Bill, or Redmond's speech at Woodenbridge. At their meeting on 10 October, Mr Owens moved:

That we tender a vote of congratulations to Mr John Redmond, M.P., and the Irish Parliamentary Party in their success in placing Home Rule on the Statute Book. Now a militant organisation had got up in the country and people who had no authority wanted to take control of the Volunteer movement. These dissentients were just the same as the officers of the Curragh; they seceded from the governing body, and he held they were rebels.

Mr Price seconded the resolution.

Mr Ledwidge said he objected altogether to Mr Owens' remarks in reference to the Provisional Committee of the Volunteers. The proper men to follow were the men who started the movement and not Mr Redmond, who, after the movement had been organised, tried to get hold of it. So far as real Home Rule was concerned, they were as far off it today as ever. (*Laughter*)

Mr Price: You said enough.

Mr Owens said the members of the seceding committee in Dublin had no mandate from the Volunteers to become an executive government.

Mr Ledwidge: Yes, they had. I was secretary of a Volunteer corps and we were quite prepared to follow any instructions and did follow those instructions.

Mr Owens: Pending a better organisation.

Mr Ledwidge: Not pending anything; we didn't want better and could not get better men than we had.

Mr Owens: They got no mandate from the country to fall into the position of an executive of the Volunteer movement. The movement was spontaneous.

Mr Ledwidge: It was up to someone to start it.

Mr Owens: The people themselves supported it. I'll give them all credit for entering the movement, but I tar them with the same brush as the officers in the Curragh. The people will support Mr Redmond and his policy to the end.

Mr Ledwidge: You should not tar true patriots with the same stick as you tar the officers.

The resolution was passed.

Mr Ledwidge: I dissent from the resolution. The country will know more about it. I have seen people passing such resolutions unanimously and accepting Mr Redmond's policy, and when the motor cars came next day for them to join the army, I did not see them go.

The Navan Board of Guardians (whose membership was almost identical with that of the Rural Council) took the same point of view. Their chairman, Mr M. J. P. Timmon, J.P., took the same line as Mr Owens and 'congratulated Mr Redmond and the Irish Party on the brilliant success of their efforts'. They envisaged that 'the Orange and Green fighting shoulder to shoulder on the fields of France will come back united never to be separated again, and out of this terrible crisis will arise a united, happy and prosperous Ireland.'

The original Provisional Committee of the Volunteers published a paper called *The Volunteer*. After the split, the majority who followed Redmond sponsored the production of a rival periodical called *The National Volunteer*, the first number of which appeared on 15 October. As was customary, the new publication canvassed the district councils and boards of guardians for advertisements. When this application was read at the meeting of the Navan Guardians on 19 October, the circular provoked an acrimonious argument. One has to read the report to breathe the atmosphere of those days.

Mr Kelly moved that the resolution on the books granting a share of the advertisements to the *Irish Volunteer* be rescinded because the paper was being run in direct opposition to Mr Redmond's policy, and it was now the official organ of the committee of which Mr McNamee was the leader.

Mr Ledwidge: This Board is becoming a name for inconsistency.

Chairman (Michael Johnston, J.P., C.C.): This Board?

Mr Ledwidge: Yes, when one man proposes a thing today and the next day seeks to have it rescinded. I do not see why Mr Kelly should bring that resolution now rescinding his original one that *The Volunteer* should get some of the advertisements of this Board, for the reasons he states, that it is not the official organ of the Provisional Committee . . . I move a direct negative.

Mr Meleady: Mr Kelly did not move a vote of confidence.

Mr Ledwidge: He did.

Mr Meleady: Not today. What is before the Board is the rescinding of the resolution already on the books. I am quite satisfied in saying that I support Mr Kelly. The 60,000 Irishmen fighting in France and Belgium were the men who were best doing their duty to Ireland. Why didn't the Sinn Feiners go out to the Front?

Mr Ledwidge: I do not expect to be seconded. I look at this thing through an X-Rays.

(*Laughter*)

Mr Bowens: The young men of Meath would be better fighting on the fields of France for the future of Ireland. That was his opinion, and he would remark that he was sorry to see there in the town of Navan—and probably in the village of Slane where Mr Ledwidge came from—it was the greatest curse of the country to see the friction caused by the few disgruntled Sinn Feiners—a few Sinn Feiners that followed the tail end of MacNeill's party. There was nothing but strife in the country as long as these people had anything to do with the country. They were always at the wrong end—from Larkin, Healy and back to the Phoenix Park murders. This friction in Dublin was the greatest curse Ireland ever suffered from, and they stood that day a curse to Ireland. On the first day that Mr Redmond got the Home Rule Bill put on the Statute Book, when he said 'God Bless England!' one of the greatest Unionists said, 'God save Ireland!' From that day the people of Ireland and England were united. What was England's difficulty was now Ireland's difficulty, and what was Englands downfall would be also Ireland's. What was England's uprise would be also Ireland's uprise. (*Applause*) He wondered at Mr Ledwidge or any other man calling himself an Irishman to stand up in that room and give expression to what he had said.

Mr Ledwidge: England's uprise has always been Ireland's downfall.

Mr Bowens: No, the days are gone when we had to complain of England. I tell you that these Irish soldiers who today are fighting in Belgium and France and elsewhere are the men who will raise Ireland hereafter. (*Applause*) It is not the men who are talking in this board-room, will they go out—these three or four little Sinn Feiners?

Mr Ledwidge: In the north of Ireland the recruiting sergeants have been saying to the men, 'Go out and fight with anti-papal France.' In the south of Ireland they will say, 'Go out and fight for Catholic Belgium.' The people around Liège and Namur

81

are the greatest Walloons and anti-clerics in the world and they have shown their brutality by their treatment of German prisoners.

Mr Owens: Does anyone believe in the sincerity of the Kaiser when he says that his heart bleeds for these people and the next day he goes and causes even more damage? What was he (Mr Ledwidge)? Was he an Irishman or a pro-German?

Mr Ledwidge: I am an anti-German and an Irishman.

Mr Bowens: You are a pro-German!

Mr Owens: It was on the fields of France that the young men of Ireland should be found if they wished to defeat the Germans, because if the Germans ever landed in Ireland, our lands and property and possessions would be confiscated by the Germans. The Irish people were too few to be divided, and the whole trouble arose from the publications in the *Irish Volunteer*.

Mr Kelly: Objected to Mr Ledwidge's remark that the Board was getting a name for being inconsistent. He thought he should withdraw that. He did not think that the Council was ever inconsistent. It was not he who proposed or seconded that the *Irish Volunteer* get the contract.

Mr Ledwidge: I went even further and told the Council that it was becoming a name for inconsistency.

Chairman: What reason have you for saying that? I think you should withdraw that.

Mr Carty: Yes, he should.

Mr Ledwidge: Every time I attend here something passed at the previous meeting is rescinded.

Mr Owens: At the time the advertisement was given there was no division in the Volunteers.

The resolution was passed, Mr Ledwidge being alone dissenting.

In the conflict between professional patriots and the idealist, Ledwidge had been worsted. He left the boardroom that day an angry man. As he cycled home, his fellow Guardians' laughter at his expense continued to ring in his ears. He saw in his mind their hostile eyes at the previous meeting when he told them *Home Rule is as far away as ever*. The fools! Couldn't they *see* how Ireland was once again the victim of political make-believe? It seemed to be heading towards civil war, and Europe was shaken to the foundations, yet all they did was sit around a table passing pretentious resolutions. The canting old fogeys! When they passed a resolution, they thought they had accomplished something. Who in the world cared about their piffling resolutions?

Well, that was the last of their meetings he would ever attend. To sit there, alone among them, and take their baiting! To be publicly called a coward was a piercing stab. He would have cheerfully sacrificed his life in the Irish Volunteers. He had hoped to defend the Irish coasts with his comrades, a delusion since the split in the ranks. He would show them yet who was a coward. . . .

This was the moment when his isolation assumed tragic dimensions: he had no contact with Sinn Fein, none with the Gaelic League, none with the scattered minority of the Irish Volunteers, to whom he still gave his whole allegiance. He could see no sign that they would ever prevail again; as far as he knew, they had been swept out of public sight by Redmond's supporters parading under the magic name.

As the pedals of his bicycle diminished the distance between Navan and his home, Ledwidge's mind seethed in turmoil. Another trouble weighed on him: Ellie's rejection of him began to look final. The wish to get away, already germinating in his mind for many months, became a compelling urge. Events had brought him to a crossroads and he was forced to make a major decision. Five days later, on 24 October, he enlisted in the Royal Inniskilling Fusiliers at Richmond barracks, Dublin.

Professor Lewis Chase afterwards asked Ledwidge why he had joined the British Army. His considered answer shows that time had not mitigated his contempt for merely passing resolutions.

Some of the people who know me least imagine that I joined the Army because I knew men were struggling for higher ideals and great emprises, and I could not sit idle to watch them make for me a more beautiful world. They are mistaken. I joined the British Army because she stood between Ireland and an enemy common to our civilisation and I would not have her say that she defended us while we did nothing at home but pass resolutions.

V

The compelling reason why Ledwidge had to get away from Slane has been already quoted from his poem *After My Last Song*. Note that the manuscript of these verses is dated June 1914:

> I'm wild for wandering to the far-off places
> Since one forsook me whom I held most dear.

Ellie and her handsome escort, John O'Neill, were frequently seen together. The courtship was said to be serious. Ledwidge could no longer visit the Vaugheys's home because he might encounter the lovers there. A man who has been jilted is always in a plight, but in a small community like Slane, where everyone knew all about one another, the over-sensitive poet found life intolerable. Irishmen have a streak of cruelty in them and it is unlikely that he escaped a few barbs at the pub sessions. Many other convergent factors drove him from Slane: his disillusionment with the Irish Volunteers (he had been leaning on a reed); his isolation; they way his fellow councillors and guardians had harassed him (he wanted to show them who was a coward). His public statement of less than a week previously proved that he was not deceived by the contemporary war propaganda. But later comments show that in one respect he was misled: the commonly held conviction that it was going to be a short war. Army life did not repel him. He had responded eagerly to the physical training and discipline in the Irish Volunteers. If they ever rallied again, he would be more useful to them as a soldier whose drilling had not been interrupted. In addition, the British Army was a welcome distraction, a livelihood, an opportunity for free travel.

He wanted to be part of an 'all-Irish' regiment. The Royal Inniskilling Fusiliers, which Dunsany had joined, came as close to that definition as he could get. Popularly known as the 'Oul' Donegals' from its original formation as the Donegal Militia, it was part of the Tenth Division, more than 70 per cent Irish, described as the first Irish Division ever to take the field in war. Ledwidge also longed to be in touch again with Dunsany. The poet's mind had been in such a turmoil, inspiration had fled; he felt he would never recapture it without the stimulus of literary talk.

One of the legends most difficult to scotch is that Ledwidge enlisted at Dunsany's persuasion. This is not only false; it is a mean partisan invention that diminishes the stature of the two men and casts a squalid light on their friendship. Ledwidge was a man of strong independent views, not easily influenced. His alliance with Dunsany was based on their literary interests. It never deflected him from his allegiance to Labour, to the cause of the common man, to his own village community, or to his patriotic principles. Dunsany, on the other hand, was a man who would never take responsibility for anyone else. His attitude was one of aloof detachment from about everything except writing to which he was passionately committed, so that he found it difficult to handle even his own personal duties.

Paddy Healy was the first to whom Ledwidge wrote from Richmond barracks:

> I was waiting a few days to see how I would like a soldier's life before writing to you.
>
> I am having a royal fine time. I only parade one hour per day, the other six I spend in the quartermaster's store as clerk, for which I receive extra pay and mess with clerks in a place specially allotted to them. For breakfast we get tea, bread, butter, fish sometimes, or steak, always something; for dinner beef, vegetables, and afterwards rice. For tea fish again and usually a pine-apple. You can see I am not so badly off after all. I see Lord Dunsany every day, and in the evenings we meet in his quarters and discuss poetry, the thing that matters.
>
> Dunsany saw to it that I was not sent to Tralee, as an excuse he brought forward the fact of my being an Irish Volunteer and therefore had a certain amount of training. At the recreation rooms on Saturday night next I am giving a reading from some of my embryo books. We will soon be leaving here for the north of Ireland to a shooting range there, and from thence to the seat of war. I look forward to poetry and fame after the war and feel that by joining I am helping to bring about peace and the old sublimity of which the world has been robbed.
>
> Remember me to your sisters and tell Maggie Conlan I will write her a long letter on Sunday. We will have many a good night in

Fleming's yet, Paddy, when I will be able to tell you strange things of strange places and men. If you see 'T.T.' you will tell him how I am. Remember me also to the Hotel Gramophone, Cissy and Miss Fleming.

(Maggie Conlan was a cousin; 'T.T.' was Tom Tully, a regular at the evening sessions in the Conyngham Arms, presided over by Katie Fleming and aided by her gramophone. Cissy Maginn was the barmaid.)

But who wouldn't be in the army? Fish and pineapple for tea and poetry discussions in the evenings. It was a lark, especially as those in the know opined that the war would be over in a matter of months. During the early phase of World War I, even the Irish Volunteers believed that the British Empire was invincible. Ledwidge expressed the common conviction of the day.

A private's pay in the army in 1914 was seven shillings a week; also he was fed, housed, clothed and provided with transport. Higher pay was given for clerical work, meaning an increase to ten or twelve shillings a week at most. Ledwidge, on enlisting, declared his mother a dependent so that she would receive half his monthly pay. At the same time he insisted on terminating the allowance from Dunsany.

*   *   *

However divided local reaction may have been to the step Ledwidge had taken, there was no doubting the fervour with which his fellow Guardians applauded him. At the next meeting of the Navan Board after his enlistment, they were sententious in their approval. They thanked him for 'taking such a patriotic means of proving that he was not what they all thought him—a pro-German.' He was 'a real patriot, the Guardian Angel of Ireland's future', 'his name should be written in gold in a national album, and that album should be placed in an honoured position in the Irish House of Parliament'.

*   *   *

Oliver St John Gogarty heard news of Ledwidge's reactions to army life and, though they were second-hand, passed them on to Dunsany in a letter of 4 November 1914:

Ledwidge, your harper whom you bring with you, met a friend of mine and said that he hoped to preserve some individuality, but three weeks of discipline took it all away.

Certainly the early glamour soon wore off for the new recruit. In a matter of days he was taken out of the office and put into training. He writes to a Slane friend, Bobby Anderson, on 9 November:

My dear Bobby,

I have thought of you many and many a time and the splendid mornings we used to go shooting. This life is a great change to me, and one which somehow I cannot become accustomed to. I have lived too much amongst the fields and the rivers to forget that I am anything else other than 'the Poet of the Blackbird'.

However I am not a bad soldier so far. I have scored 19 out of a possible 20 at the firing range and am in the first drilling platoon and about to move either to France or Egypt in December. We have not a bad time here at all. The only thing we detest is route marching, but even here we are not badly off. We rise at about 7 in the morning although reveille goes at 6. We then get a cup of cocoa and biscuits. When this is swallowed we prepare for parade. We clean ourselves and at 8 o'c the breakfast comes. It is usually tea, bread and butter and fish, sometimes sausages (not German). From 8.30 to 12.15 we are either shooting or skirmishing in the Phoenix Park. We do skirmishing every day either from 8.30 to 12.15 or from 1.45 to 4.15, except days we are on a route march when we don't return until 4 o'clock. When not on a route march we do company drill and gymnasium. We have plenty of time to ourselves and are well looked after. I am glad I joined tho' sometimes homesick, but fame and poetry will come again (D.V.).

To come to things that matter—how are you? And how is your Mother? How is trade and Tessie Wall? Remember me to her. I think I have a postcard somewhere, if so I will send it to her. She is a real good sort. I often fancy myself at your door talking to her about the foolish things of our youth.

I hear the Russians are in Germany. God send they may bring this war to a hasty termination and let me home again. I am drifting far away from Slane, far, far. Remember me to everyone I know. Does W. Corbally still come in the morning and Jack McGuirk for his brown cake? I keep always remembering the little things.

Only a few weeks after enlisting, Ledwidge won a lance-corporal's stripe. The advantage of the promotion was more freedom to visit his Dublin friends in the evening. Privates had to be back in barracks by

10 p.m. unless they had a 'late pass' from their company captain. A lance-corporal was usually free to remain out until midnight.

Far more to Ledwidge's liking than the stripe, however, was that he soon formed an enduring friendship with one of his fellow soldiers, Robert Christie, a native of Belfast, who fortunately survives and who remains to this day the most loyal of Ledwidge's friends. Without his testimony, no account of Ledwidge's army life could have been attempted. Christie ran away from school before his fourteenth birthday and was then an unconscionable time making up his mind about his career: 'I foothered about from pillar to post.' He learned shorthand and typing, then decided to be a dentist. He had almost completed a three-year dental mechanical apprenticeship and was planning to emigrate to Canada when war broke out. 'Then all the fellows I knew were joining up and I joined too. I was in the army before I knew it.' He now lives in retirement in Comber, County Down.

Christie had tried his hand at playwriting and had had a play accepted by the Abbey: a one-act comedy called *The Dark Hour*, set in a farm kitchen in County Down. The *Daily Express* described it as 'genuine comedy, not laboured, no padding. The author has done extremely well'. John Kerrigan played the part of the heartless father. To Christie's disappointment, his play completed its two-week run just the night before he arrived at Richmond barracks from Omagh, so he never saw how the Abbey players performed it.

He told me that he was a sergeant in 'A' Company of the same battalion as Ledwidge, and that his unit was sent from Omagh in September 1914, to complete their training in Richmond barracks, Dublin. The first news he heard was that among the officers was a lord who was also a writer, Dunsany. An army schoolmaster pointed him out to Christie. Later the same man told Christie that Frank Ledwidge, the poet whom Dunsany had befriended, had also arrived in the barracks. Christie made it his business to find him and asked him out to an evening at the Abbey. They saw *The Suburban Grove* by W. F. Casey, then a popular playwright. It was one of the first plays about Dublin life staged by the Abbey and they thought the acting was first-rate. 'We had a grand evening.'

Both of them were short of money. Frank encouraged Christie to send a poem to *The Saturday Review*, even though up to this time Christie had never written poetry. They went to the Y.M.C.A. canteen for some paper and Frank sent off Christie's verses with an introductory letter. Three days later Christie received payment of 10s. 6d. Although this was markedly different from Ledwidge's own rate of six shillings a line, Christie was delighted. They celebrated with another night at the theatre, followed by cheese sandwiches and stout in the sergeant's room.

The friendship between the two steadily developed. Ledwidge confided to Christie that when he first met Dunsany in the barracks, the latter was so annoyed that he almost refused to have any more to do with him. Dunsany had no illusions about army life. He had done his best to ensure that the poet should remain quietly at home, devoting himself to his art. Ledwidge had difficulty in explaining that that, in fact, was a course he was utterly unable to follow. He also gave Christie his love poems to read; they were about a girl named Ellie who had rejected him. Her name, in fact, seemed to be always cropping up when they were discussing fit subjects for special types of verse, or just trying to think out a rhyme.

Ledwidge drew Christie into the circle of his Dublin friends. Amongst the most hospitable of these was the Quin family. Mrs Quin was a native of County Meath, whose maiden name was Keenan. She and her son Jack used to write for the contemporary magazines and newspapers. They first met Ledwidge at a literary gathering in Dublin and Mrs Quin afterwards invited to her home the new poet from her native county.

Father Swayne, formerly parish priest of Kildare, told me that he, too, enjoyed the friendship of the Quins when he was a clerical student in Dublin, and that he met Ledwidge several times in their home. The Quins moved to Ellesmere Avenue early in 1914 and here Father Swayne saw Ledwidge in uniform for the first time:

He was a nice lad, young, enthusiastic, impulsive. There was a certain enthusiasm for the war in those early months but I don't think it was shared by the Quins. Other visitors I remember at their home were Mrs Arthur Griffith and her two Franciscan brothers. Mrs Quin was a niece of Sir Patrick Keenan, resident commissioner of National Education, who had a distinguished career. Her eldest son, David, was in the Education Office. Jack, the second eldest, a striking personality, was a chartered accountant.

Another recollection of those times reached me from Molly Quin, the youngest of the family, who knew Frank Ledwidge very well.

He was a great friend of my brother, Jack. He stayed in our house several times before coming to Richmond Barracks. We enjoyed his visits because he was always in good humour and very jolly. He was good company. I remember that when he was introducing Jack to people, he would always spell out the name 'Q U I—one N', because Jack was particular that it should be spelled with one N. While Ledwidge was training in Richmond Barracks, he came to Sunday dinner with us many times and often brought his friend, Robert Christie, whom I also well remember. My mother was very fond of both of them and invited them to our house as often as they were free to come.

It is clear from all the accounts that the Quins' home was a kind of literary *salon* but with the free-and-easy atmosphere of a country house.

Jack Quin was transferred to a Manchester office a few days after Ledwidge arrived at Richmond barracks. As a parting gift, he gave the poet a small green pocket edition of the New Testament, inscribed:

> To Francis Ledwidge, the greatest soul since Shakespeare this little book of the greatest soul of all is given by his sincere friend and true admirer, J. Keenan-Quin, with the hope that he may safely return.

Ledwidge always carried it in the breast pocket of his uniform.

One winter day he was leafing through the local paper in the orderly room when his eye fell on a brief announcement:

> O'Neill and Vaughey. November 25th, at St Patrick's R.C. Church, Slane, by the Rev. F. Fagan, C.C., Slane, John J. O'Neill, Rossin, to Ellen Mary, (Ellie), only daughter of the late John and Mrs Vaughey, Hill of Slane, Co. Meath.

Until he read those lines with incredulous eyes, he had never really believed in his heart that the understanding between them was shattered for ever. Every time Ellie came into his mind, he remembered how disturbed she had been to break off their affair; despite the rumours, she would not radically change; he would go back to her when he had 'straightened things out'. Until he was confronted with the marriage notice, terrible in its finality, he had not realized how he had been secretly buoyed up with the belief that some day Ellie and himself would regain their lost paradise. Now depression settled down on him like a cloud; he lost his sleep; food tasted like ashes.

In the same week that the announcement appeared, Dunsany (who was aware of Ellie's place in Ledwidge's life), wrote to AE asking permission for Ledwidge to have the occasional use of a room at the Co-operative movement's headquarters, Plunkett House, where the poet might have peace to write.

But the poet-economist, AE, was not helpful. He replied that there was no room vacant for such a purpose, availing himself of the opportunity to tell Dunsany that Ledwidge had borrowed £5 from him the previous September and had not returned it. He mentioned the matter because as 'the mother and father of Ledwidge's soul', he considered that Dunsany should 'know all his protegé's little ways'.

The unpaid debt rankled so much with AE that he told the story also in a letter to J. C. Squire:

> The new Irish poet has gone into the van. I heard vaguely that he had enlisted. I have not seen him for four months but that may be because he borrowed £5 from me on a promise to return it the next day. This singular silence which I have not broken by enquiry has made me think that his verse will lack something or other. However I believe it has been set up and Dunsany had the proofs. The poet is very young but I regret to say he shows this in common with many Irish poets that they borrow money and never mention it again. I would share my possessions with a fellow poet cheerfully but I object to them telling me a little tale about their ship coming in the next day when they might have had what they wanted without straining an imagination better employed in their art.

Dunsany reprimanded Ledwidge and promptly repaid AE. The established writer always sent off the poet's verse; as we have seen in Christie's case, this made a vast difference to payment. The late Dowager Lady Dunsany told me that from this period she kept a small notebook of Ledwidge's accounts. Even during the first year of the war, his receipts from the odd poem placed here and there to advantage amounted to a small fund on which he could draw.

The new recruits in Richmond barracks were given a few days' leave for Christmas; Christie went home; Ledwidge fled to Slane, anxious above all to assuage his homesickness. The long ordeal of Anne Ledwidge's early widowhood had left her with great interior serenity; humble and undemanding, she was good at counting her blessings and saying her prayers. Ledwidge knew that he had only to spend an evening in her company to find peace of mind. As for Joe, he was still the admiring younger brother in whose eyes Frank could do no wrong, an attitude he retains to this day.

It was a winter memorable for its severity. Snow fell in Slane on 15 December and Christmas was ushered in with more snow, then a hard frost followed by rain, conditions that made the roads dangerous. Ledwidge caught cold and could not cycle to Donaghmore to see Matty McGoona; the friends were practically house-bound. The poet's only recreation was sessions in the Conyngham Arms with Paddy Healy.

John Ward told me he remembers meeting Ledwidge in Slane on his first visit home after joining the army. He noticed how he had changed: 'He used to be all fun and good stories, but he had become terribly quiet altogether—not at all the same boy that he used to be.'

It was during this brief visit home that Ledwidge wrote one of his best poems, inspired by the sudden death of a little boy, Jack Tiernan, a neighbour's son who lived near by. The lad used to work for farmers in his free time and was a familiar figure driving in Mr Johnston's cows early in the morning. As Frank wheeled out his bicycle to go to Navan, he usually met Jack passing the gate and they would have some hilarious exchanges. The boy was always ready for a joke and riposted with wit and spirit. This lyric conveys a depth of sorrow in lines of a delicate airy lightness:

A LITTLE BOY IN THE MORNING

He will not come, and still I wait.
He whistles at another gate
Where angels listen. Ah, I know
He will not come, yet if I go
How shall I know he did not pass
Barefooted in the flowery grass?

The moon leans on one silver horn
Above the silhouettes of morn,
And from their nest-sills finches whistle
Or stooping pluck the downy thistle.
How is the morn so gay and fair
Without his whistling in its air?

The world is calling, I must go.
How shall I know he did not pass
Barefooted in the shining grass?

One evening during a visit to Paddy Healy, he met Lizzie again. She was as friendly as ever and did not reproach him for his long silence. She eagerly questioned him about army life and he was flattered by her interest. This girl's friendship had helped him over a painful period of his life a year ago when Ellie had rejected him. Now when he was in a far worse plight because of Ellie's marriage and the knowledge that his real love affair was irrevocably ended, here was Lizzie proffering sympathy again, providentially as it seemed to him.

Back in Richmond barracks, he was still in a tormented frame of mind, consumed with vain regrets. He had almost won Ellie and he had let her go! She had been wretched on that morning of their final parting; *that* was the moment when he should have won her. It had not been after all a question of 'wealth of land and bleating flocks and barnfuls of the yellow harvest yield', because John O'Neill had none of these either and she had married him. He blamed himself bitterly for having hopelessly bungled the crucial moment of his life.

He tried to turn his heart to Lizzie, following the classic example of the rejected lover on the rebound. He wrote to her on 6 January 1915:

> I hope you are back in Wilkinstown again. Since I was home I am watching the days to pass when I could write to you as I promised. I did not like to write to you while you were in Slane: you know why. Of my life in the army since I was speaking to you there is nothing to write. In fact of my life anywhere it is not worth while saying anything. I walk the bye-ways of the world like one pursued by a monstrous fear. Sometimes I think I am wandering towards a life full of sunshine and song and love, but it appears far away yet lures me like the distances of my natal fields.

It is clear from the above that Lizzie cautioned Ledwidge to see that his letters reached her on the days she was in Wilkinstown. The post was delivered after her sister and brother-in-law, both teachers, had set out for school. She did not confide in her family although they were all, as we have seen, on friendly terms with Ledwidge. Her anxiety to keep their correspondence secret is a sad commentary on social life in rural Ireland sixty years ago, the ill effects of which are still with us. Courtship was then considered almost morally suspect. This Jansenistic attitude to 'company-keeping' was preached at missions and was upheld by all elders, clerical and lay. Even crossroad dancing was prohibited in a wave of joyless Puritanism that reached its peak about this period.

Ledwidge managed to snatch another few days at home in the middle of January. The possibility of seeing Lizzie added interest to his visits to Slane, but this time he was not fortunate. His next letter to her is dated 27 January:

I was home a fortnight ago and thought I might see you. When I came back we went away on a long march to the Curragh and are just back. I seize the very first opportunity of writing to you. Dear Lizzie, God bless you for the photograph. You can't ever know how much I prize it. I will always carry it with me until I bring it home again, and then I will work hard to one day ask if I will be worthy of loving you. This is a terrible lot to hope for, but I was ever strong in hope and why not one more effort at the greatest hope of all. . . .

My dear Lizzie, I am just after hearing that I am not for the war. I am sorry in a way as I would like to enter Berlin with the boys I was trained with. It seems that they are going to keep me for clerical work and training recruits and as a reward will make an officer of me. Of course it is as an officer I entered the army and am on the waiting list for my commission. But I will try to get to the front as 'twould be a great experience.

Since Christmas, however, the military discipline had been intensified as Ledwidge soon found when he was again withdrawn from clerical work. He had now neither such easy days, nor as much free time as during his first couple of months in the barracks. Major Bryan Cooper describes the life:

In the New Year, battalion training began, carried out on the occasional bright days that redeemed an abominable winter. Field days, route marches and night operations were the order of the day throughout February, and a second course of musketry was also fired. Though we criticized them bitterly at the time, these Curragh field-days were among the pleasantest of the Division's experiences. By this time the battalions had obtained a corporate existence and it was exhilarating to march out in the morning, one of the eight hundred men, and feel that one's own work had a definite part in the creation of a disciplined whole. The different units had obtained (at their own expense) drums and fifes, and some of them had pipes as well. As we followed the music down the wet winding roads round Kilcullen or the Chair of Kildare, we gained a recollection of the hedges on each side bursting into leaf, and the grey clouds hanging overhead, that was to linger with us during many hot and anxious days.

However, even if army life had become tougher, the war-front was still reassuringly remote.

Ledwidge continued to consult Dunsany about his literary problems. The following letter is undated and appears to have been sent from the orderly room to the officers' quarters:

D Company

Dear Lord Dunsany,

I enclose herewith a copy of the poem which you liked so much and two rather interesting letters concerning it. Doctor Gogarty says 'lain' where it is is bad English and will require turning. I come at once for aid here to you. I have replied to Roberts's letter telling him he can have the poem, but that I don't like it being printed alone. People who do not know me might consider the poem an accident. The least he might do is print three or four, a better anthology has printed three.

Fancy that little thing I wrote here with my pen causing a sensation in the Gogarty school. But I knew it was good when you said so.

P.S. I met Roberts once at AE's on a Sunday night and rather disgusted him by praising Futurist paintings. I remember the terms he offered you for my book.

F.E.L.

George Roberts, a printer, founded the publishing firm of Maunsel's in 1905. As publisher, he drove a hard bargain with writers. He has gone down into publishing history as the man who finally rejected Joyce's *Dubliners* when he had kept the writer waiting for a decision for *five* years.

This letter to Dunsany is an example of the diffidence that dogged Ledwidge all his life. In fact his grasp of English was good and became better as he matured, although he sometimes slipped up in spelling. Ledwidge never fully realized that inspiration and ideas are what count, for the sake of which lesser mortals are willing to correct their expression in English. His insufficient education bothered him too much, and he was unduly dependent on Dunsany for footling corrections.

Ledwidge wrote to Lizzie again in February:

When I come home again, I will do great things, there is very little chance here, and besides I am always so lonesome I can think of nothing but Slane, and the quiet peace of the homeways, and you.

The enclosed verses are from my heart and if you discover faults in the lines pass them over on that account. I must close as it is growing late and I have a roll to call. Write when you can. Remember me to the bog and all the trees around Wilkinstown.

The poem he enclosed was entitled 'To Lizzie'; it afterwards appeared in his second volume of poems under the amended title (using the Irish form of her name) *To Eilis of the Fair Hair*.

Within a week he writes to her again:

When you have a minute to spare, drop me a few lines as I watch and watch for something from the old place every day. I hope the little lad is very well. I saw Larry on duty yesterday. We were sending the Lord Lieutenant away and Larry was just opposite me. I winked at him and he winked back and I made a gesture which he must have understood. I was thinking of Fleming's gramophone and 'The Little Grey Home in the West'.

Larry was Lizzie's brother and a member of the Dublin Metropolitan Police. On his visits back to Slane he was one of the regulars in the Conyngham Arms and enjoyed the gramophone sessions initiated by the amiable Katie Fleming.

Lizzie was pleased with the poem. Ledwidge blossomed out under her tribute:

It is spring now and it must be lovely down in Wilkinstown. Are the birds singing yet? When you hear a blackbird think of me, always remember me when you hear a blackbird!! A very nice lady journalist came to look for information from me yesterday. It seems my poem in the 'Times' (did you see it?) caused a little splash. She was about 20, tall, fair and passing for handsome. She asked me to tea on Sunday, but I am not going. You are very busy I am sure, but whenever you can won't you write me a few lines? I will remember you always.

A week later he writes to Paddy Healy:

I was telling you that I meant to look for a job in the Orderly Room so that when my Commission came I would have a good job. I succeeded so far and have a ripping time. I go to work at 9 in the morning and knock off for the day at four, except there is something to be done in a hurry. I saw Larry once, we were sending the late

1. Francis Ledwidge, aged 25, 1913

2. Ledwidge in Manchester, aged 26, 1914

3. Lord Dunsany when he joined the Royal Inniskilling Fusiliers,
August 1914

4. Dunsany Castle, Co. Meath

5. Ledwidge's home, Janeville, Slane

6. Lizzie Healy
(*Eilis of the Fair Hair*)

7. The Healy family;
standing—Katie,
Paddy, Lizzie;
seated—Mary

8. Ledwidge, holding Mollie Carter, with Christie
in Basingstoke, May 1915

9. Ledwidge with Mollie Carter, *front row*,
in Basingstoke, May 1915

10. Ledwidge in Mudros (after Gallipoli), November 1915

11. Ledwidge's grave in Boesinghe Cemetery

16138 LANCE CPL.
F. E. LEDWIDGE
ROYAL INNISKILLING FUS.
31ST JULY 1917 AGE 26

12. Plaque erected in Slane to Ledwidge's memory

FRANCIS LEDWIDGE
POET
BORN IN SLANE 1887
KILLED IN FRANCE 1917
"HE SHALL NOT HEAR THE BITTERN CRY
IN THE WILD SKY, WHERE HE IS LAID,
NOR VOICES OF THE SWEETER BIRDS
ABOVE THE WAILING OF THE RAIN"

Lord Lieutenant away and Larry was helping us to keep the streets clear; I may tell you it was an easy job as only the idlers and the out of work attended.

I suppose you saw, or heard about my recent poem in the *Irish Times*? But I forgot—you saw it in the hotel on the day I wrote it. There is no immediate news of this Regiment shifting. I don't know what they are going to do with it, they will hardly ever see the war. They are a decent sort and I hope they will not. It is surprising the love one gets for fellows one has roughed it with. I suppose it is the fellow-feeling the poets wrote about. I often think of the jolly nights we spent in the hotel and hope they are not quite done with. How is the landlady? Has she got any new records? Poor Kate, she knows so little of the world!

What do you think of the Germans now? The blockade is doing an awful lot of harm, but I think it will bring destruction to the Huns. The neutral powers can't allow their trade to run the risk of annihilation and must put in a spoke somewhere. But aren't the German submarine officers very clever? I was thinking it was likely that they had a base somewhere, either on the west coast of Ireland, or the east coast of Scotland, as you may be very sure the canals thro' which they came out are very well watched. I don't think the war can last very long now. Do you ever see Tully? How is Navan? Remember me to the pump on the Market Square when next you go there, and the clock over Walshe's. Just now I fancy I see Biddy Finnegan sitting on Noonan's window sill and the thought brings pleasant recollections.

Navan is different now from the picture of it in Ledwidge's mind on that spring day of 1915. Many years ago the pump was removed from the Market Square. The clock, however, still hangs over Walshe's jeweller's shop, recording the time for the townspeople and taken for granted as one of the permanent furnishings of the scene. But when it was first erected, it was considered one of the world's wonders. Noonan's licensed premises is now the Tara Restaurant. The broad window-sill is still there, but sill-sitting isn't what it used to be, the standard of correct behaviour having risen meanwhile. This shop is next door to Loughran's butcher's shop where Frank had his office when he acted as secretary to the Meath Labour Union, and only a few doors from the office of the *Irish Peasant* where Matty McGoona worked as linotype operator. The two friends often relaxed on

Noonan's window-sill during the dinner hour, or before they set off for home in the evenings.

Biddy Finnegan staked a prescriptive right to the same seat. She lived in Barrack Lane and was one of the most formidable characters in Navan. Always wrapped in a black shawl, she had a blistering tongue especially when she had drink taken.

In Ledwidge's next letter to Lizzie, he sent her a lullaby for her little nephew with the comment: 'I think it is pretty good. I mentioned about the crows flying to Slane because I once saw them go that direction from Wilkinstown.'

> Shall I take the rainbow out of the sky
> And the moon from the well in the lane,
> And break them in pieces to coax your eye
> To slumber a wee while again?
> Rock goes the cradle and rock, and rock,
> The mouse has stopped nibbling under the clock
> And the crows have gone home to Slane.
>
> The little lambs came from the hills of brown,
> With pillows of wool for your fair little head,
> And the birds from the bushes flew in with down
> To make you snug in your cradley bed.
> Rock goes the cradle and rock and rock,
> The mouse has stopped nibbling under the clock
> And the birds and the lambs have fled.
>
> There is wind on the bog, it will blow all night
> Upsetting the willows and scattering rain,
> The poor little lambs will be crying with fright
> And the kind little birds in the hedge of the lane.
> Rock goes the cradle, and rock and rock,
> Sleep, little one, sleep, and the wet wind mock,
> Till the crows come back from Slane.

In March orders were issued about packing up and leaving the barracks in good order for the new occupants. But no one knew the date they were leaving, or where they were going. Ledwidge began to prepare for what might be his final visit home. He would have to see Lizzie, of course, but he also urgently wanted to see Matty McGoona, to whom he wrote on 9 March:

I flew in here on Pegasus. You might have known that he would bring me to some outlandish place, for strange are the ways of Pegasus. Ay, he brought me in here and then left me, but I think he will come back for me 'when Peace unfurls her flag of Truce'. I may not be anywhere in the world when he calls again, if he does. But if you do not hear me singing after the war you will know that I have gone across the tide to Keats and the rest of them. It was hard work here all the winter preparing to meet the Kaiser's men and now that Spring is here and all my blackbirds singing we are packing up for the fields of the war. We leave here about the 29th for France.

But how are you this 100 years? I know trouble has lain against you like an incubus and I felt for you many and many a time. I hope you are in good cheer again. I wish you could call a cabinet meeting of Grattan's Parliament and discuss terms of peace with the warring powers. Or has it been abolished and the old members fled? Christ! Matty it's hard thinking on the old times. The pleasant Sundays we used to spend and the hopes we entertained! Their memories follow me like so many Nemeses, and I often feel like a reprobate who has committed his last sin and dare not hope any more for absolution. I am glad we are going to the war, it will cheer me up, it will dispel these thoughts which are at war with me so long. Ellie Vaughey got married! That was a great blow, perhaps the greatest of all. I am going to try for a day home Patrick's Day. If I manage it, could you come to Slane? I want to see you so badly.

How is your Pegasus? And how is the violin? Do you ever play sweet music now? Every time you play 'The Blackbird' think on me. I love that tune and snatches of it sing in my memory an odd time like ghosts haunting an old garden. My memory is no more than an old garden now full of the withered flowers of a dead summer.

Your old affectionate
friend in trouble

In a later letter to Lizzie, he told her:

I must see you before I go to France. I have determined to go. We will not be longer than a few weeks here now, and I must see you before I go. I feel sure that I will return again safely and then, and then! Yes, when the war is over, if I am not shot, I am coming back to Slane. I love it very much because from nowhere else have I ever had such calls to my heart. I love Stanley Hill and all the distances so blue around it. I love the Boyne and the fields through which it sings. I love the peace of it above all.

Slane, Wilkinstown, Donaghmore: his mind revolved around these places where dwelt the people he loved. How could he contrive to see his mother and Joe, Lizzie and Matty in the couple of days' 'compassionate leave' conceded by a flint-hearted army?

> I will train straight to Wilkinstown and perhaps not touch Slane as the time will be short. We are busy getting ready for a move. I could stop a night in Navan or Kells and depart for here next morning. Or maybe I could get a week-end and see you on a Sunday.

He writes again a few days later to tell her about a dream:

> I thought I was out of the army and home again. It was a beautiful day, flowers everywhere, and birds. I could see all the old landmarks so loved by me as I crossed the fields down to the Boyne to meet you. We met at the Mill House. The meeting was by arrangement. You were sitting on the old paling there and singing a song I wrote many years ago. When you saw me coming you raced to meet me, and when we had greeted each other, we walked slowly down by the river, and you were telling me that you missed me while I was away. You said there was a void in your life, a sort of feeling making you hope no more for old aspirations. All our talk was of the past. I wonder why. It was a beautiful dream and when I wakened I was lonesome. I am lonesome all day thinking about it. I write this in a hurry to know if you had any unusual experience. I believe in dreams, and hope my pleasant one was not the news of some misfortune having befallen you. You will let me know.

Far from discerning telepathic significance in Ledwidge's dream, however, Lizzie made it plain that she was out of sympathy. Poetry was acceptable but dreams foolish. The poet had to back-pedal:

> I am very sorry that I surprised you so much with the hasty letter I wrote about my dream. I promise not to do so any more. Looking at it now, it was very foolish of me, but God knows I am always doing things like that and never know how absurd it is until afterwards. It is the hurry to get things off my mind, and this hurry has often made me make mistakes in my life that I will lament forever.

> I will be home for Patrick's Day. Of course I would love to cycle from Slane to Wilkinstown to see you. I won't see you any more

until after the war. We leave about the 29th. I go home Tuesday evening and return Thursday morning.

The letter was followed by a blotched note, undated:

This in a hurry to let you know I am on my way home. I will see you tomorrow (DV) about 3 o'clock. I wrote another note like this in barracks but can't find it. Perhaps someone would post it also.

There was no leave, however, for St Patrick's Day; instead Ledwidge's company was marched off to Dollymount for rifle practice. The poet was now in the grip of a ruthless machine. A postcard followed the note to say that a second plan to go home was also frustrated.

I am extremely sorry to let you know that I will hardly have the pleasure of seeing you this week-end no more than on Patrick's Day. It is a terrible thing to think of but I'm afraid it must be. You see there are only two of us in the Orderly Room who can use a typewriter and while I was away at Dollymount last week firing, the other man went away on leave.

Dear Lizzie, I must tell you about the violets. You don't understand. The mistake must have been mine. I will tell you all about it when I see you.

Violets again! Lizzie was like a petulant child on this subject. Another St Valentine's Day had come and gone. The innocent blossoms had already clouded one spring-time through a misunderstanding; they had caused nearly a year's estrangement; yet the difference had not yet been fully cleared up.

Ledwidge did get away at last and spent a wonderful Sunday in Wilkinstown. Paddy Healy accompanied him from Slane and both were put up for the night by the Farrellys who threw a farewell party for the soldier. He is hardly back in the Orderly Room before he writes to Lizzie:

I am back again in the tents of Mars. I can hardly yet realise that I am really back, but it must be true as I see from my office window three or four hundred men at drill. I am back again indeed, or at least my body is, but my soul is on a little road looking across a gate at a girl standing in a doorway. The road is in the village of Wilkinstown and you are the girl at the door.

I am a thousand times the better of my visit to Wilkinstown. I had the happy realisation of hearing you say you would wait for me until I came back and of taking you in my arms. But although I am so much the better for this I am a lot the worse of it, as now, more than ever I know how much I want you and how much I love you. My love for you is as high as the stars.

We enjoyed the evening immensely, the sport and the company. You must have been pretty sick of us by the time you got us away and I am sure you haven't recovered from the fatigue of the occasion yet. I forgot my stick, the little block which I meant to bring back. If you haven't burned it ere this, hang it up on a nail at the gable of the house until the war is over. It will be an excuse for me to go down again.

The little block was a flat piece of thorn-bush with three stumps of branches growing out of it so that it looked like a three-legged stool. Ledwidge sat on it during the party when there was a temporary shortage of chairs. The Farrellys remember the block they called 'Ledwidge's stool' hanging on the gable wall for years.

Ledwidge wrote to Lizzie's brother-in-law, Willie Farrelly, who was in some degree her guardian, to thank him, too, for the farewell party:

I could have stayed down in Wilkinstown forever, it is so infinitely peaceful, but Pegasus, the wild horse which I have been riding, brought me to this outlandish place to rescue Belgian maidens, English maidens, and surely Irish colleens from the jaws of the bloodthirsty monster even as he brought Perseus to the aid of Andromeda away back in the days of myth.

Many and many a time I think of you in the lap of the quiet bog. You don't know how fortunate you are. I would easily swap twenty years of my life with whatever powers shape our destiny for a home like yours. This may be remedied some day perhaps.

It must be beautiful in the country now. My favourite month, April, is coming. I thought last October I would be home from France by now. I hope at least to be home for Christmas. Everything here points to a removal very early. We, in the offices, are very, very busy. I worked all day on Sunday checking identification discs with men's numbers and making out a casualty form for each man. It was sombre work, but had to be done. We will probably shift in a fortnight or thereabouts. The sooner the better. I am sick of the monotony here. A change anywhere would be welcome. When you see me next I will have long hair and corduroys, perhaps, not khaki anyway.

Poised for flight into the unknown, Ledwidge's mind—as always—was in Meath. On the last day of March he wrote to Lizzie:

There is not a day in the calendar since I came here that I have not thought of everybody in our circle. I am sure it is lovely on the bog now. I would very much like to be walking to Carlonstown via Fletcherstown chapel, you with me of course. The people will be planting potatoes down there now and I am certain there is a scent in the air like a feast of wine. From the desk where I am writing this I see through a window across the soldiers' recreation ground spire on spire of Dublin, and hear the bells of trams and the shout of all its worry and woe, but my thoughts are in Wilkinstown in the little kitchen where I first took you in my arms. I see by a Liverpool paper today that I am at the war for the past fortnight, and according to the *Evening Mail*, I sailed early in March. . . .

I suppose you will spend Easter in Slane. I won't see poor old Slane any more until after the war. I can't rightly say when we leave here. I should say about the 15th.

He wrote to her again on 7 April and on the 13th, by which time he is in a fever because he has not heard from her:

I can't tell you how I feel as post after post comes in and no letter from my dear Lizzie. I met Larry yesterday evening, he was going to the train en route for Slane. I wished that I was going along with him. He told me he had joined King Edward's Horse. I will see him again on Friday evening. We are on tip-toe ready to depart at a minute's notice but something for which we are waiting will not come. The suspense is dreadful. In any case I am sure we will be away this month.

Lizzie's letter arrived at last. She tells Ledwidge she has put up her hair and he is sorry to hear it.

'Who made you do that?' he wants to know. 'I bet it was Mr Farrelly. I suppose he was jibing you. You are no longer a young girl now, you are a young woman. We can't be much longer than a week here now, and I am working like a Trojan, noon and night on documents which will be required at the Front.'

This letter is followed by another dated 21 April:

We are off to the war at the end of this week. Our King and Country need us at last. We leave here about Saturday, or Sunday morning, for Reading, England. The Tenth Division mobilizes there, thence we proceed to some part of the great battle field. It is for you I will fight as you are all I have, or ever will have, worth fighting for. When I come back I will claim you. I may not be long away as immediately the war is over I will be free again.

Ledwidge called on the Quins on 23 April to say good-bye. He found that they had planned a farewell party for the two soldiers. But Bob Christie was unfortunately on duty. It was unthinkable to have the party without him. How could they get him out? Finally Ledwidge rushed off to the nearest post office and sent Christie a telegram:

'Come at once 8 Ellesmere Avenue. Am dying. Frank.'

Apparently the company captain was himself too harassed to question how a dying man could send a telegram; anyhow it worked the trick. Christie describes their last evening with the Quins:

Mrs Quin and Mollie were lovely people and we had memorable times with them. On our last visit there, old Mrs Quin asked Frank to come into her room for a chat; it was the room next that in which the rest of us were sitting. When Frank came out some time later, I noticed that his eyes were wet. He told me to go in as Mrs Quin wished to see me. I went in and that gracious lady said: 'I know, Robert, you are not of our Faith, but if you accept these, God will watch over you.' And she put around my neck a ribbon with several amulets on it. She was a grand old lady whom I always think of with respect for her kindness and for her amusing way of telling stories and jokes. I wore the amulets all the time I was at the Front and indeed still have them.

There was to be one more leave at home before Ledwidge's departure. It was unexpected. He had no chance to notify Lizzie, and, as ill luck would have it, she did not go to Slane that Sunday and he did not see her. In any case his mother claimed all his attention now that the moment for the decisive parting had come. He took Joe aside and made him swear that he would look after their mother and not leave home until he (Frank) got back again. He consoled her—and himself—by repeating that the war would soon be over; he was only going to England; he would be home for Christmas. He might even get home again before his battalion left for the front. He called on the Healys and got news of Lizzie. Katie asked him for a farewell poem and late on

Sunday night he wrote an acrostic for her, running in with it next morning before he took the train. The chief interest of the contrived verses is that he scribbled under them: '27th April 1915—4 hours before setting out for the war. F.E.L.'

Johnny Dick, at that time a corporal in 'B' Company of the Royal Inniskilling Fusiliers left Richmond barracks the same day as Ledwidge and described their departure:

> I will never forget that afternoon. As we marched out of the bar-racks, the gates were packed with people and from that until we arrived at the boat, we marched through solid cheering crowds, all waving to us and wishing us good luck and a safe return. Not only that, but they pressed into our hands and stuffed into our pockets as we passed packets of cigarettes, biscuits, sweets and even bottles of stout. What a send-off they gave us!

John Hargrave, author of *The Suvla Bay Landing*, marched out two days later from a different Dublin barracks and had the same perfervid assurance from the populace that he had chosen the better part. Of course the city slum women in receipt of separation allowances excelled in these demonstrations and believed it their duty to stage them. Even a few dozen of them could put up quite a show:

> What a send-off they gave us when we marched from Portobello Barracks down to the North Wall on April 29th! The whole of Dublin seemed to have turned out. They crowded the streets from the barracks to the dockside. They cheered, they swarmed after us, they broke our ranks—they jostled us, linked arms with us, thrust apples, cigarettes, lucky trinkets, rosaries, scapulars, packets of sweets into our hands.
>
> You'd think we were Cuchullin-heroes one and all, with the old drabs and trulls, and all the young bubsy Biddies from 'the Liberties' (as the backstreet slums were called) slummocking along with us, trying to keep in step with the drums and fifes wheezing and whinge-ing the regimental march of the Royal Army Medical Corps—*Her sweet smile haunts me still*. The high-screaming Irish pipes wailing *The Wearin' o' the Green*; the Connaught Rangers crashing out *Saint Patrick's Day*, and the Leinsters' fife-band swelling-in so sobbing sad with *Come Back to Erin*—and the Faugh-a-Ballaghs swinging to *The Battle of Barrosa* with its defiant yell leaping in the last bar.
>
> All the ships in Dublin Bay sounded their sirens. Even the North

Wall seagulls wheeled and squealed over the quayside. Soon the cheering crowds, the docks, quays, breakwaters, the whole sky-pointing array of steeples and spires, the blue Wicklow hills, and at last the Howth lighthouse drifted astern, dwindled, hazed, shrank to a pencil-line and vanished.

Long after the coast became invisible, a huddle of young Irish soldiers stood on the deck staring into the grey nothingness, silent and disconsolate.

VI

The Tenth Division were conveyed in troop-trains from Liverpool to Hampshire. Here, on a sloping field at Viable's Farm about a mile from Basingstoke, the soldiers set up camp. Spring was well advanced and the weather very good. Ledwidge wrote to Paddy Healy:

> A hurried line to let you know I am thus far. I can't yet say how long we will be here, but I shouldn't think it will be long. The whole Division is here now. It is a lovely place. The camp is a mile from Basingstoke. Basingstoke is a lovely Hampshire town of 11,000 inhabitants. It boasts of a cinema house and many pubs. I haven't been to the former. Remember me to Katie, Lizzie and Mr and Mrs Farrelly. I will write to Wilkinstown tomorrow when I have more time.
>
> I like being under canvas in a beautiful country like this, but my thoughts are in Slane and Wilkinstown and on the little roads about Crocknaharna. Remember me to Stephen Tiernan when you see him. What of 'T.T.'? Has he really joined the khaki crowd?
>
> It consoles me to think that I represent the kind hearts I found in you and your friends at this great war. I will get drunk with you again (D.V.).

In his letter to Lizzie he told her they were mobilizing before going to France; that his silence meant he had counted on seeing her on his last visit home, but was disappointed in that hope. He goes on to say:

> The country around is beautiful. The fields are very nice and green and full of chalk where the banks are broken. The birds sing here too, but my thoughts are in Slane and on the road to the bog. Write to me when you get this and let me know how all are. I hear so little from my home friends.

In Basingstoke, Ledwidge and Christie became inseparable: 'He was no or'nery galoot,' said Christie reflectively. 'Very intelligent, had picked up a lot, spoke like a well-educated man. He did everything with such an air, even if he only walked across a room. He had but to appear on a barrack square for the whole place to come alive.'

'Our tents were set up in a field near the home of a family named Carter,' he went on. 'Frank and I wandered about the roads near the camp, intent on exploring the countryside. On one of these walks, we met and spoke to a little girl aged about five, who told us her name was Mollie Carter. Later we met her father and mother. They invited us in to tea and we became friendly, a friendship that lasted closely all the time we were there. Mrs Carter was insistent that we should have a hot bath every week in her house, followed by tea in the garden. The weather was very hot, so you can imagine what a blessing that was to men under canvas, especially as our tents were swarming with earwigs.

'Lord and Lady Dunsany had rented a house in Basingstoke so as to remain together as long as possible. We saw Dunsany now and again in the camp. He was very friendly and would have been more so, but as you know, bar for actual routine, an officer and other ranks have little chance of communication.

'Our training in this camp consisted chiefly in long route marches all over Hampshire. We fought mock battles that were not anything like the actual thing we were to experience later at the Front. When we were off duty, Frank and I talked endlessly of what we would do when the war was over, and of the plays and poems we were going to write. We planned to collaborate in a play for the Abbey. Our pet character was Corney Noggins and we first thought of him as leaning over a half-door with his pipe in his mouth, talking like a poet about the Kings and Queens of Ireland. If we had written a fraction of the plays we planned, the Abbey would still be playing them. It was only when we got to England and took those peaceful walks among the Hampshire lanes that Frank began to write steadily: *The Place*, *May* and *Evening England* were all written at that time.'

The Dunsanys' first care was to offer Ledwidge the use of a room in their house where he would have peace to write. 'A room away from the barracks' was Dunsany's panacea for all Ledwidge's army difficulties. The increased productivity in Basingstoke noted by Christie could well be due also to the poet having this refuge.

A passage in Major Bryan Cooper's book *The Tenth (Irish) Division in Gallipoli* fills in the details of the everyday routine that kept Ledwidge so fully occupied during the month of May:

They were trained in bombing, bayonet-fighting and musketry. The most salient feature, however, of the Basingstoke period of training was the Divisional marches. Every week the whole division, transport, ambulances and all, would leave camp. The first day would be occupied by a march, and at night the troops either bil-leted or bivouacked. On the next day there were operations. As night fell, the men bivouacked on the ground they were supposed to have won. On the third day we marched home to a tent which seemed luxurious after two nights in the open. The individual officer, or man, gained but little military experience since as a rule the whole time was occupied by long hot dusty marches between the choking overhanging hedges of a stony Hampshire lane.

The everlasting route-marching was detested by the rank and file. One day Christie found himself trudging behind a captain he described as 'a morose critter', whose way of getting the men to step out was con-tinuous yelling and swearing. Christie bore it as long as he could and then dropped out and rejoined the column far back out of earshot of the captain. He was reported for this and the penalty was the loss of a stripe.

Another day the company were resting briefly on the roadside when Ledwidge noticed that they were beside the entrance to a big house. Both he and Christie were white with dust and longing for a cup of tea. They asked permission to call at the house from the sergeant, who said they could try it on but not to be long. As the pair trailed wearily up the imposing drive, they envisaged a lady like Mrs Carter coming to the door. Christie agreed to do all the talking because he had—or so he believed—a winning way with ladies. When they rang the door-bell, it was immediately jerked open by a little gnome of a man in plus-fours who peered at them through thick glasses. The unexpected apparition struck them dumb: the speech they had prepared was for a woman's sympathetic ear. But Ledwidge recovered first, saluted smartly and said: 'Sir, we come to you like the beggars of old, throwing ourselves upon your mercy to entreat you for —a cup of tea.' A smile spread over the man's face and he said, 'Why, yes, certainly.' He was just going out but would tell his housekeeper. He indicated a side door where they were to knock. This time it was opened by a smiling woman who gave them a warm welcome. She sat them at the kitchen table and regaled them with tea, home-made bread and fruit tart. She told them to call whenever they were passing, but in fact they never saw the house again.

Christie found the firing practice a trial. He could never hit the target; whenever he fired he 'got a lancer', meaning that a pennant went up to record a miss. He told me that he couldn't even see the target; all he could do was fire in the general direction where he knew the target was and hope for the best. The fact that he had a vision defect, spherical astigmatism, was not discovered until years later. One day Dunsany was behind Christie watching his poor performance. He bent down to murmur in the ear of the flustered recruit: 'Christie, your pen is mightier than your sword.'

Ledwidge, according to Christie, fitted easily into army life and took the discipline in his stride. He was athletic by inclination and punctilious about his appearance. The Irish Volunteers, too, used the British Infantry Manual, so his training with them stood him in good stead.

Dunsany, on the contrary, despite Sandhurst and his experience in the Boer War, disliked army life and conformed with difficulty. One old soldier described him to me, rushing on to parade with one of his puttees streeling, intent on fixing his monocle. All accounts agree: he was not an orthodox soldier, too mild-mannered, too gentlemanly. His company were devoted to him because he was such a refreshing change from the usual type of officer.

Ledwidge found his time for letter-writing severely curtailed. His next letter to Lizzie is undated, but the postmark is 31 May 1915:

My dear own Lizzie,

It is too bad that I have been so long in answering your welcome letter, but since we came here we have been in a state of great unrest, one day here and three somewhere else, as Paddy can tell you. Basingstoke is a beautiful place in the middle of Hampshire. It is a town not as big as Drogheda but better populated. The country around is beautiful. I have even come across a bog of several acres, on which turf never was cut, full of heather and little pools, white at the bottom with shells. We had dinner there on Whit Monday and Lizzie, as true as God I left my dinner and with a couple of bars of chocolate went into a little copse to dream of the bog far away. You are beautiful, Lizzie, and I must win you for I am lonely without you and always thinking of you in the land of good hearts. God bless and keep you until I return. I never will forget the night myself and Paddy spent in Wilkinstown. I thought then I would be home by now but I seem to be as far away from returning as when I first joined the colours. We expect to be going away soon and are glad as we are tired of the monotony of camp. The weather is frightfully warm here for a month now. Remember me to all. I am sure the bog is lovely now, how I wish I were there! There's the bugle.

Was anyone ever so ingenuous, or so foolishly hopeful? Bearing in mind that one cannot judge events, or the outlook of people involved in them, with the knowledge of fifty years later, still Ledwidge's viewpoint is astonishing. When he joined, he expected a commission and clerical work only; he looked on the army as an avenue to adequately paid work when the war was over; he was completely deceived by the current propaganda that 'the Germans will be finished off in a few months'. How wide of the mark were his confident forecasts: 'I thought then I would be home by now.' 'I don't think the war can last very long now.' 'I thought last October I would be home from France by now. I hope at least to be home for Christmas.' He lives in a world of happy illusion. It is difficult to avoid the conclusion that the poet did not even read the daily papers.

When I mentioned to Christie, Ledwidge's letters to Lizzie, he was astonished. He told me that in all their time together Ledwidge never spoke of anyone but Ellie. Sometimes the poet's continual harking back to an old wound made Christie almost lose patience. In his view, here was a girl who had chucked Ledwidge and married another, so the best thing that the poet could do was forget her. When he tried to say this to Ledwidge, he met a look so charged with grief that he never again referred to it.

One day in June, Dunsany sent for Ledwidge to tell him the good news that the page-proofs of *Songs of the Fields* had just reached him. After ten months' observation of wartime conditions, Herbert Jenkins had at last decided to publish. It was now a year since Dunsany had written the introduction; it was over six months since the galley proofs had been corrected. They sat down together in Basingstoke to scrutinize the final proofs, tested the rhythm, discussed words and punctuation. As they worked, the menace of the present faded out of their minds and they were back again in the good days they had known together in Meath. Jenkins had asked Dunsany to add a few paragraphs to the introduction indicating the changes that had taken place in their fortunes, so he complied:

I wrote this preface in such a different June, that if I sent it out with no addition it would make the book appear to have dropped a long while since out of another world, a world that none of us remembers now, in which there used to be leisure.

Ledwidge came last October into the Fifth Battalion of the Royal Inniskilling Fusiliers, which is one of the divisions of Kitchener's First Army, and soon earned a lance-corporal's stripe.

All his future books lie on the knees of the gods. May they not be the only readers.

Any well-informed spy can probably tell you our movements, so of such things I say nothing.

Basingstoke Camp, June 1915.

Ledwidge's first volume contained fifty poems and was entitled *Songs of the Fields.* The discerning reader who has savoured the quotations does not need to have the imperfections pointed out: the gappy lines in which the metre stumbles, the occasional infelicities in the use of words. *Bound to the Mast* is an imitation of Yeats. In five or six other poems, the influence of Keats is not yet assimilated. The tribute 'To Lord Dunsany' is sentimental and contrived. Genius is here struggling for expression. In this slender little book, inspiration on the whole triumphs over the flaws, and the pure lyric note rises enchantingly from its pages.

Despite Dunsany's commitment and his excellent intentions, he was, unfortunately, not the right man to help the poet perfect his art. I do not want to appear bent on denigration. Dunsany's success has been described. Although neglected as a writer for a long time now, he appears due for a return since two of his early books are about to be re-published in paper-backs. His biography will be written. But his attainment was not in poetry; his verse was uninspired and heavy-footed.

In the meanwhile the war had reached a stalemate. There had been no progress on the Western Front since the battle of the Marne in September 1914. The German Army had been barely checked in its plan to steamroll across France. In three months the Allied losses amounted to nearly a million casualties. The two opposing armies were immobilized. Soldiers home on leave gave harrowing descriptions of the first winter spent in the trenches. It was this deadlock that set the Allies thinking of a diversionary attack on another front.

By 1 November 1914, Turkey had joined the war as Germany's ally. The attack on Turkey through the Dardanelles Straits was finally organized as a military operation with the navy in support. General Sir Ian Hamilton was appointed commander-in-chief of the Gallipoli expedition. By the time Ledwidge reached Basingstoke, six landings had already been made on the peninsula by British, Australian and New Zealand troops. At the cost of 20,000 casualties, 30,000 soldiers had succeeded in getting a foothold on the narrow beaches and holding on. But all they could do was hold on. The Turks occupied fortified positions in the ring of hills dominating the shores. The Allied soldiers with their backs to the sea could not advance inland until they got more guns, more bombs, more ammunition, and above all, more men. On the day Lord Kitchener inspected the Tank Division, the Dardanelles Committee were deliberating about how much help could be spared to Hamilton. A week later, they decided on sending him three divisions, including the Tenth.

Christie told me the first hint they got of their destination was seeing a Connaught Ranger in the next field clowning around with a pith helmet on his head. They grinned at him over the hedge and asked where he got the hat. 'Wot, 'aven't you 'eard? We're goin' to the bleedin' East.' About a week later, there was a great stir in Ledwidge's battalion when they, too, received their issue of tropical kit: open-necked shirts, sand-coloured khaki drill uniforms and pith helmets. There was horseplay in the tents as the young recruits tried on the big mushroom-shaped headgear and imagined themselves in romantic bivouacs under the desert stars.

At first probably no one in the rank and file connected the tropical kit with the Dardanelles because the public in England at that date knew next to nothing about that war front, 3,000 miles away. Hamilton's despatches gave no news. The censor, on Kitchener's instructions, saw that there was no leakage of information. No one had as yet come back from there on leave. It was over a month after the first landings before a single photograph of the terrain appeared in the British press.

Rupert Brooke's death on his way to the Dardanelles was the first episode that gave a romantic air to the expedition. He had died on the Greek island of Skyros from blood poisoning, due to sunstroke, only a few hours before his contingent was due to leave on the last stage of their journey to Gallipoli. Handsome, gifted and heroic, the same age as Ledwidge, twenty-seven, he was the symbolic figure destined to light up the imagination of his time.

The crusading spirit, later known as the 'Gallipoli fever', mounted daily as accounts of Brooke continued to appear. Ledwidge must have been excited at the possibility of following in another poet's footsteps. The region itself had a powerful appeal. Even to think of sailing over the Aegean sea to the land that lives for ever in the Greek classics! The Dardanelles were the Hellespont of antiquity. When Jupiter hurled Vulcan from heaven, the fire-god fell on Lemnos. Jason and the Argonauts landed there; on the same site Agamemnon lit fire-beacons to tell the Queen of the fall of Troy.

The men in Dunsany's company knew from their first acquaintance with him that his heart was not in the army. On the everlasting route marches around Hampshire, his abstracted air and dreamy eye revealed that his thoughts were elsewhere. Christie described a typical episode. One day the Tenth Division fought a mock battle with the Eleventh, when the 'enemy' succeeded in capturing most of the food. Dunsany's company and many, many others were left to face a long march back to camp on empty stomachs. The usual type of officer would have left his men to take their punishment: 'Good enough for the beggars. They have to be licked into shape.' Not so Dunsany. At the first village they reached after their 'defeat', he told the men to fall out and rest. While they were sitting by the roadside, he disappeared. Presently he came back holding in both arms a huge pile of loaves. Christie recalled the triumphant grin over the mountain of bread he was carrying, his face screwed comically to one side as he kept his monocle in place. He had combed the village and bought up all the bread coupons available, four loaves to every ticket. He also managed to get from a farmhouse a huge lump of butter. With this fare, washed down with pints of stout, he fed his men, and what threatened to be an ordeal turned into a picnic.

One evening in June, word flew round the camp that Dunsany had received a telegram from the War Office, ordering him back to Ireland to train recruits in Derry barracks. There was a shortage of officers capable of doing this work; they had to be men with previous army training and war experience. Most of the officers in this category were already at the Western Front. But the order to Derry meant an indefinite spell of dull, grinding routine Dunsany dreaded; he was very depressed.

The men in his company gathered in little mutinous groups and went to his quarters to plead with him to stay. According to Christie:

He came out to them and there was a scene. He kicked up the devil and there were tears in his eyes when he addressed them; he said it was a shock to him to be told he was not going with them after all. What is more, *he meant it*. He went around the camp like a soul in pain and mind you there were some of the others I do believe who would not have minded being left behind. Yes, Dunsany was a good soldier from his men's point of view.

Ledwidge had an ache in his heart. Even though in the army there is the minimum communication between officers and lower ranks, still Dunsany's independent attitude to military life had been a great moral support. He was a link with the old placid life, with poetry, with Meath. When he left for Derry, Ledwidge was lonely.

*   *   *

At tea in the Carters' garden, the two Irish soldiers and their English friends speculated on the exciting adventure looming ahead. Ledwidge promised Mrs Carter he would bring her back a Turkish carpet. He wrote a poem on a battle in toyland for the little girl who had befriended them. Christie, too, wrote a poem on a teddy-bear as a parting gift for Mollie. The pair took their verses to the editor of the local paper, who later published them.

On the night of 18 June, Ledwidge was disturbed by a vivid dream of white birds flying over the Atlantic ocean. He thought he was in Kerry, looking up at the sky and wondering where they were flying. Next day the dream haunted him like a vague presage of disaster. To escape from his mood of apprehension, he wrote a poem:

> Over the border of the dawn
> Far as the blue Atlantic sky,
> The white birds of the sea go on
> In breezefuls, wailing as they fly.
> What lure of light calls them afar
> From sheltered niche and sandy dune
> Built in the changes of the moon
> And yet where all their younglings are?
>
> 'Tis star-set now where Una lies,
> And on the little holy road
> Morn breaks the windows of the ice
> That all night round her dwelling glowed.
> No barking fox, or banshee tale
> With terror filled me in that dream,
> But white birds, whither with your scream?
> And cloudy winds, wherefore your wail?*

* Unpublished poem in the Dunsany papers.

After some hesitation, he called the poem *Caoin*.

While he was writing this, bad news reached him that seemed to confirm the dream and his sadness: Ellie Vaughey had died. He immediately applied for six days' leave and went to Manchester. Ellie married to someone else was a state of affairs to which he had been painfully adjusting his mind since last November. He had been telling himself that, provided she was happy, he might learn to live with the idea. But Ellie dead meant a finality of separation that shattered him.

The O'Neills had settled in Manchester after their marriage. But the Vaugheys decided that Ellie was to be brought home to be buried beside her parents on the Hill of Slane within a few hundred green yards of her birthplace. In condoling with the two families, Ledwidge pieced together a story that broke his heart. The marriage had not been a success. Manchester meant a better livelihood to O'Neill, but to Ellie painful exile. She was a bad housekeeper. Her health declined in the smoky city air. She had a difficult pregnancy and was continually ailing. The roses glowing in her cheeks in the freshness of Slane and Mornington quickly faded, her teeth decayed; she lost her good looks. After seven months she was about to give birth prematurely and had to be rushed to hospital. There a Caesarian section was found necessary. She died during the operation, but the infant daughter lived and was brought home to be reared by a grandmother. After the funeral John O'Neill gave up their home and joined the Irish Guards. He remarried afterwards. When I met him, he was understandably reticent about his brief married life with Ellie.

Ledwidge remembered her gaiety and her capricious ways. Time had played both of them a terrible trick. Less than three years ago she had irradiated his whole life and he had lived from meeting to meeting in that Maytime of unclouded happiness. 'She will come in blue. . . . Her peal of laughter will ring far.' Once more he was plunged in sorrow for his witlessness in remaining apart to nurse his injured pride. He had left her unbefriended, poor little Ellie.

Ellie's death had a curious and permanent effect on him. He felt mystically more close to her than he had ever been while she lived; 19 June became an important date in his life, a kind of spiritual watershed. She began to dominate his thoughts again. In this strange reunion through death, his courtship of Lizzie began to look almost like betrayal, and he ceased to correspond with her.

Back in Basingstoke, he mechanically resumed army routine. Christie recalls an evening after Ledwidge's return from the short leave, concerning which he was utterly silent. They were out walking together, each wrapped in his own thoughts, when Ledwidge suddenly seized Christie's arm and pointed to a blackbird standing on a mossy boulder, fearlessly observing them. He pulled an envelope from his pocket and jotted down the poem that later appeared in *Songs of Peace* under the title *To One Dead*:

A blackbird singing
On a moss-upholstered stone,
Bluebells swinging,
Shadows wildly blown,
A song in the wood,
A ship on the sea.
The song was for you
And the ship was for me.

A blackbird singing
I hear in my troubled mind,
Bluebells swinging
I see in a distant wind
But sorrow and silence
Are the wood's threnody
The silence for you
And the sorrow for me.

It was the first of the many elegies he was to write for Ellie.

*   *   *

On 10 July, in the chilly hours of the pre-dawn, the companies to which Ledwidge and Christie belonged were alerted for departure. After a hasty breakfast, they were ordered to fall in behind their officers for the march to the station. Compared with Dublin, their send-off was subdued. The friendly Carters had managed to find out which companies were on the move that morning. As the two friends marched past their house, Mollie and her mother appeared at a window, waving good-bye; Mollie's father was waiting for them at the station with parting gifts. From Basingstoke they travelled by train to Devonport where their ship, the s.s. *Novian*, was in readiness for departure, the decks already crowded with soldiers sitting on their packs, waiting to be allotted berths. Ledwidge and Christie were among the last to cross the gangplank. The ship was already getting up steam. They, too, sat on their packs and watched as the anchor was weighed and the ship glided out of harbour.

The *Novian* was a coal boat only roughly adapted to carry troops. Although their quarters were overcrowded, the men enjoyed the novelty of a sea voyage, a welcome change after ten weeks of route marching and fighting mock battles. The majority played cards endlessly, others read, smoked, or wrote letters. The sea was calm, even in the Bay of Biscay. It was a voyage without incident.

Ledwidge invariably occupied the same place on deck, sitting with his back to the mast, his constant companion, Christie. In their quarters jam-packed with sweating humanity, these two succeeded in creating around themselves a little world of their own. The empty horizon of sea and sky gave the poet too much scope for reflection. Ellie's death had sent such an abiding undercurrent of grief through his days, he would have welcomed more distraction.

When they had rounded the Straits of Gibraltar and sailed into a warmer zone, the increasing heat made the men's crowded quarters intensely uncomfortable. Their ship had been designed for the North Atlantic, not for the Mediterranean. During the hours of darkness, no gleam of light was allowed on board because of the danger from submarines. The tightly closed apertures made matters worse below deck. The men found sleep impossible. They surged up every night to lie in the open. This did not suit the officers of the watch, who complained that stepping through hundreds of sleeping forms prevented them from doing their rounds.

As the distance from Ireland daily increased, Ledwidge was racked with homesickness. The little places around Slane were for ever passing before his mind's eye: the Mill Wood; Stanley Hill; the foaming white water of the weir; Vaugheys' house embowered in trees on the Hill; the religious solemnity of Donaghmore with its round tower standing up black in the moonlight; the 'woody windings' of the Boyne, where wild cherry, woodbine and furze flourished on the banks. Sometimes he was overwhelmed with fear that he had looked his last on that earthly Paradise.

But his worst pang of memory was his mother's face when he said good-bye to her. Why had it fallen to him of all people to cause her such sorrow just when Joe and himself had steered her into an easier life? The first serious poem he wrote on the voyage was an effort to sublimate his sympathy for his mother and his homesickness:

On the heights of Crocknaharna,
(Oh, the lure of Crocknaharna)
On a morning fair and early
Of a dear remembered May,
There I heard a colleen singing
In the brown rocks and the grey.
She, the pearl of Crocknaharna,
Crocknaharna, Crocknaharna,
Wild with gulls is Crocknaharna
Twenty hundred miles away.

On the heights of Crocknaharna,
(Oh, thy sorrow Crocknaharna)
On an evening dim and misty
Of a cold November day,
There I heard a woman weeping
In the brown rocks and the grey.
Oh, the pearl of Crocknaharna
(Crocknaharna, Crocknaharna),
Black with grief is Crocknaharna,
Twenty hundred miles away.

It was the end of July when the *Novian* dropped anchor at Mitylene, 120 miles from Gallipoli. As the ship drew near the island, it seemed to the watchers on deck that it was making straight for a sheer cliff. They were close to it before they perceived a hidden opening, a narrow, fiord-like passage, just wide enough to admit a big ship. As they steamed slowly along this channel, the soldiers noted that it was lined with guns on either side, but above the guns were lovely olive groves and vineyards. The fiord was the entrance to a hidden land-locked harbour, crowded with the shipping of all the Allied nations, including even a five-funnelled Russian ship, hailed by the men as the *packet of Woodbines*. A swarm of brightly painted native craft immediately bore down on them. Men in rowing-boats laden with melons, grapes and other fruit offered their wares for English coins, or even for an article of clothing, and the trading was brisk and merry.

But no shore leave was allowed. The commander-in-chief, General Sir Ian Hamilton, was hourly awaited to carry out an inspection on board ship. Discipline was rigorously tightened; companies had to remain together, so Christie and Ledwidge were separated. All the soldiers saw of the island's interior was during one hot, dusty route march around the foothills, when they were tantalized by the bunches of grapes ripening in the vineyards. Christie succumbed to temptation, fell out of rank, and gathered a handful. He was reported and lost his remaining stripe.

While they were thus engaged, Hamilton arrived on the H.M.S. *Chatham*. The General's *Gallipoli Diary* affords another glimpse of our men:

> The Irish and Inniskilling Fusiliers had not got back on board ship by the time I was ready for them, so I hurried off by motor launch to a landing in another part of the bay, and walking through a village, caught them resting by their piled arms after a route march. All of these men looked very well and cheery. The villagers were most friendly and had turned out in numbers, bringing presents of flowers and fruit.

There followed another few days' waiting on board for the signal to go forward. The men played cards on the scorching deck and drank 'gallipolis', cocktails of gin and ice. There was an acute shortage of reading, and one out-of-date newspaper on board was passed around endlessly from hand to hand. It was 5 August when word at last reached the *Novian* that a vessel would arrive the following day to convey them to the landing point at Suvla Bay.

Soberly the soldiers assembled on deck for their final briefing. Embarkation orders were: no smoking, whistling, singing or shouting. They were warned about thirst: they must begin at once to learn how to cope with it. Water where they were about to land was in short supply. Each man would be given one and a half pints in his water-bottle, but he was not to drink it until absolutely necessary, and then only a sip at a time.

VII

On the afternoon of 6 August the s.s. *Heroic* arrived in Mitylene and berthed beside the *Novian*. Although the sides and bows of the new-comer had been repainted the same dark grey as the battleships, Christie and many others instantly recognized her as a former passenger steamer that used to ply between Belfast and Liverpool. But the spruce vessel they remembered was now battle-scarred, her bridge and funnels pierced and dinged.

The men had been told to leave behind them on the *Novian* every-thing not essential for their personal needs at the war-front. The order did not prevent them from looking grotesquely overloaded as they filed across the gangway between the two vessels. Every soldier carried in a bulging pack his greatcoat, two blankets and a ground sheet. His haversack was filled with three days' iron rations of tins of bully beef and bags of biscuits. Draped around his neck and packed into his pouch were two hundred rounds of ammunition. He carried on his person two respirators and a full water-bottle. He also had a rifle and bayonet, an entrenching implement, mess-tins, and either a pick, shovel, or camp-kettle. His pockets were stuffed with writing materials and an assortment of personal impedimenta.

The sun poured on the scene out of a brassy sky; underfoot, the decks were scorching. There was scrambling on board the *Heroic* as the men pushed and elbowed for the coveted space in the shade of the lifeboats. The ship weighed anchor again and and began to glide towards the harbour entrance. The men were looking their last on the dreamlike scene: still water reflecting motionless shipping; land like a painted back-drop of hills clothed in olive groves, peaceful farms, little villages twinkling in the sun. Once outside the long, narrow passage into the harbour, they encountered a pleasant breeze that tempered the heat. The sea turned a darker blue, with lively foam-capped waves. When night fell, however, the tropical heat made it impossible to sleep below and the men, pouring with sweat, had to come up again to rest on the closely packed deck where the wind was chilly and the boards sticky with salt dew.

At daybreak the *Heroic* came within sight of the fifty-three-mile long tongue of land that is Gallipoli. The ship dropped anchor well out to sea but opposite Suvla Bay, about one-third of the way up the west coast. They had joined an impressive naval assembly of warships, cruisers, destroyers, troop and hospital ships. Far off to the east, half-shrouded in pearly haze, lay the country of fabulous interest. As the light strengthened, they saw a long strip of golden land with a gently undulating skyline of low hills, rising out of a milky blue sea—a scene disarmingly innocent and beautiful. Suvla Bay is a small, semicircular sandy beach enclosed by two promontories shelving down to the water. Behind this beach the ground rose into hilly country encircling the shore like an amphitheatre.

Suddenly there was an ear-splitting roar as the warships opened a bombardment of the hills and the Turkish guns barked back. The sea was splashed by shrapnel and the waterspouts of shells. The men in most of the transports were told to lie down on deck. The landing had already begun. Six thousand soldiers had arrived from Mitylene that morning. They were being conveyed from the transport ships to the beach in motor-lighters dubbed 'beetles' because they were painted black and had long landing ramps projecting from their bows. These could carry 500 men and were armour-plated against shrapnel and gun-fire. Hour after hour as the sun rose higher, Ledwidge stood in his heavy equipment among the ranks on deck. They watched the con-tinuous flashing of the Turkish guns in the semicircle of heights, an-swering the ear-splitting roar from the warships. But the really awe-some sight was the human element: their fellow-soldiers landing in the midst of the battle. The men away off on the ships could follow the metallic glitter of the bayonets as their comrades raced inland into the rising ground beyond the beach.

The long delay was partly due to an insufficient number of lighters, and partly to a change of plan while the landings were in progress, causing confusion. It was midnight when D Company were at last taken ashore. The 'beetle's' decks were covered with pools of blood because on its return journey it carried the wounded from the beaches to the hospital ships.

Ledwidge and his comrades stepped quietly on to the beach in pitch darkness before the moon came up. The Turkish guns had long since fallen silent and all was quiet. Glad to ease off their heavy loads, they lay down in a little gully and fell asleep. When daylight came, they found that they had spent the night among the wounded of another regiment, close to a clearing-station of sorts. A number of the injured were sheltered under a large tarpaulin propped up at the corners on sticks. But many were lying about in the open, too, and nearly all of them were asking for water. Few of the men just landed had any left in their bottles, as they already finished it on board ship.

They found themselves in a sandy, hilly country, roadless, trackless and, as far as one could see at first glance, empty of human life. The hills that had seemed so alluring from the sea were very different on closer acquaintance: their steep sides were broken up into a maze of dried-up gullies and ravines criss-crossing in all directions in a crazy geological formation that was, in fact, the country's best defence.

Ledwidge's group had no idea which way to turn to find their regiment. Sheltering under an outcrop of rock in a deep gully, they decided to have breakfast, but the moment they spread out their rations the flies swooped. They had to hold the food in one hand and beat off the flies with the other. When they prised open their tins of bully-beef they found the heat had turned it into yellow liquid on top of which the lean bits floated. Thirsty men could not touch it.

It was late morning when D Company linked up at last with their own battalion. The officers conferred in a group and the men could only guess the news from their sober faces. It was not good news: 20,000 men had been landed in a few days with comparatively light casualties, but they had not carried the hills where the Turks were entrenched. It was a repetition of the April landings: they had won a hold on the beaches and no more.

Did any of them suspect that the brave new invasion plan had already collapsed by that day, 8 August? The heights north and south of the bay should already have been taken. The Allied troops at that time outnumbered the Turks by twenty to one. Under competent leadership the invasion should have carried the hills. The true story behind the scene is that 1,500 Turks with only a few howitzers and not even one machine-gun had kept 20,000 soldiers pinned to the beaches; Turkish reinforcements of men and guns were already speeding up behind the hills. As the British command lost precious time deliberating, the opportune moment was lost.

Late in the evening of their first day in Gallipoli, D Company were allotted a trench that the engineers had dug for them the day before. It was situated about half-way between the sea and the summit of a little ridge. The light sandy soil, alternating with rock, made the construction of proper trenches an impossibility. 'Scoopout' would perhaps better describe the sort of shallow hole in which the men took cover. This 'slug-coloured grave' (in Compton MacKenzie's words), was to be Ledwidge's home for two months.

Christie and Ledwidge had hardly seen one another since the companies of the Fifth Battalion had been kept separate in a tightening of discipline. At the landing their companies were on opposite ends of the line.

A torpedo-boat in the sea below Christie's dug-out was engaged full time at condensing water. It circled around and kept up an encouraging exchange of signals. The water was drawn ashore by boat and stored in a sail-bath on the beach. Christie was one of a fatigue party sent down to get the water-bottles refilled, each man carrying four bottles. He spoke to the sailor in charge of the supply, who promptly asked:

'What part of Belfast are ye from?'
'The Antrim Road,' I told him.
He shook my hand and said:
'Ye kin have the bloody ship, Capten an' all. I'm from Sandy Row meself, an' I wish to God I wuz back to't.'
I saw by the twinkle in his eye that he was a comic turn.
'If ye think of askin' for leave, I'll go along with ye,' says I.
'Not a bad idea,' he said. ''Twould be a good chance to tell th'oul woman how much I miss her an' the chip shop!'
He filled all our bottles and assured me that when we met again I wasn't to be shy of speaking to him, as he wasn't a bit stuck up. He told me to come down for as much water as I wanted as long as his ship was there. His parting shot was:
'Go on th' Blues!' and I called back:
'Up Celtic!'
A big grin creased his face as he aimed a mock fighting blow to his jaw. The following morning as I came in from outpost duty, I looked down eagerly for his ship. It was gone and except for a litter of empty boxes and some bedding, that part of the beach was deserted.

Condensing sea-water for the army was found to be too costly and was abandoned after the first few days.

Both Christie's and Ledwidge's companies were in reserve for their first week in Gallipoli. The men were ordered to keep under cover. The natural supply of water came from numerous wells. But the Allied soldiers could not get to them because they were either ringed with landmines, or surrounded by well-concealed snipers. Whenever the Turks drew back from a sector containing a well, they corrupted it by throwing in corpses and dead mules. The Allies had to rely chiefly on water carried from Lemnos island, or even from Alexandria. This was stored in kerosene tins on deck in the midsummer heat. Dirty and brackish at origin, by the time it reached the men, it smelt and tasted of petrol and was stained with rust.

Soldiers who had seen service in India knew a trick or two about survival in a hot climate. One of them told Christie to collect a few smooth pebbles and keep them always moving in his mouth, so as to promote the flow of saliva. He found this such a useful tip that he never suffered from thirst. He passed the word around but few followed his example.

The smell of unburied corpses was another horror of the peninsula because most of the dead had to be left where they fell. Thyme grew abundantly everywhere in the sandy soil and the men were for ever picking handfuls of it to hold to their noses. The scent of thyme to this day brings back to the survivors mind-pictures of Gallipoli.

During that first week dysentery became endemic. All duties had to be carried out under cover of darkness and the soldiers were supposed to sleep during the day. But when the sun was overhead sleep was out of the question. As the sun moved out of the meridian a patch of shade appeared and the men would scuffle to occupy it. The flies would then swarm on their faces. Sometimes they would hear the rich Munster brogue, or clipped northern accents, raised in exasperation in a nearby trench, and then Ireland seemed to be all about them.

On Sunday, 15 August, shortly after dawn, the Fifth Battalion were ordered to prepare for an advance. Christie's A Company and Ledwidge's D Company were in the forefront, A on the slope of the hill and D extending the line down the valley. They were to take Kidney Hill, so named from its shape on the map, rising at the opposite side of an open plain. The rugged hilly ground to be crossed before the open space could be reached made it impossible for the men to keep formation. No orders could be heard in the din of the guns; signals could not be seen; every man was on his own. The Turks on the hills had a perfect view of the open ground on which they rained a curtain of fire. The advance was checked when the commanding officer was killed and two majors wounded. Again and again the rank-and-file rallied in groups to race across the open ground, men falling at every step. After eight hours, the Fifth Battalion had dug in on the line they had gained on the edge of the open plain. Here they received orders from the brigade commander to withdraw and return to the position held at noon.

Captain Adams, who was in command, sent back word that he would collect our wounded before falling back. To have left them would have been to doom them to almost certain death. . . . By midnight over 100 men had been rescued, the soldiers carrying them in on ground sheets. . . . It was nearly four in the morning before the task was completed. Then the survivors of the Battalion fell back to the trench from which they had moved to the attack. In all, 6 officers had been killed, 230 wounded and 78 missing—more than half the total strength of the Battalion on landing at Suvla Bay.

Christie told me:

It was about 2 o'clock on 15 August when the order to 'Fall in' reached my company and we were straightaway marched into battle. We attacked down the side of a gully with scrub bushes as our only shelter. I will not try to tell you of our advance to the Turkish trenches. Bar the whine of the bullets, there's not much to tell. On that open ground, I remember going up into the air—and that was that. When I came to, I found that one of my legs had been hit and I could not get to my feet. I looked around and saw Major Owen lying some distance away, his head covered with blood. I crawled over to him and clumsily tried to improvise a bandage on his wound from my first-aid kit. He asked me to help him get at his water-bottle and, drawing out the stopper, he took a drink. Soon the stretcher-bearers arrived and took him away. They told me that they would come back for me immediately, but they never came back.

It was quite dark when I was picked up. Four men carried me in on a ground sheet and when they put me down, I thanked them. As I said, 'Thanks, boys,' Ledwidge's voice above me yelled, 'Is it *you*, Bob?' He had been holding one of the corners of the sheet. As there were so many wounded, the Medical Corps could not cope with them and he had volunteered to help. Needless to say I was surprised —and pleased—to meet him again. He asked me about my injury and all I could tell him then was that I could not walk. He said, 'See you in the morning,' and darted away to carry in more wounded.

Next morning we were all taken on stretchers to a ridge near the sea to await the R.A.M.C. transport which conveyed us to an improvised hospital. We were kept there some time until we were taken off in a ship. I did not see Ledwidge again before I left Gallipoli.

It was the end of their soldiering together. The bullet that put Christie out of action had severed the sciatic nerve of the left thigh. He was taken to England for an operation to suture the nerve. After fourteen months in hospital he was sent back to Belfast, where he was discharged from the army on crutches. He never recovered the use of his left ankle and still wears a steel to supply the missing lift.

Ledwidge sent Dunsany this account of the engagement:

It is surprising what silly things one thinks of in a big fight. I was lying one side of a low bush on August 15th, pouring lead across a little ridge into the Turks and for four hours my mind was on the silliest things of home. Once I found myself wondering if a cow that I knew to have a disease called 'timber-tongue' had really died. Again a man on my right who was mortally hit said: 'It can't be far off now,' and I began to wonder what it was could not be far off. Then I knew it was death and I kept repeating the dying man's words: 'It can't be far off now.'

But when the Turks began to retreat I realized my position and, standing up, I shouted out the range to the men near me and they fell like grass before a scythe, the enemy. It was Hell! Hell! No man thought he would ever return. Just fancy out of D Company, 250 strong, only 76 returned. By Heavens, you should know the bravery of these men: Cassidy standing on a hill with his cap on top of his rifle shouting at the Turks to come out; stretcher-bearers taking in friend and enemy alike. It was a horrible and a great day. I would not have missed it for worlds.

A week later, Ledwidge wrote to Paddy Healy giving additional details of the battle. The passages deleted by censor, using a thick black pencil, are indicated by brackets. Some of the sentences struck out can be read with a magnifying glass.

News from Slane was the best that could be done for me, and I pray that such messengers as our post-men shall have no less a place than Gabriel.

I am writing this at 7.30 a.m. in my trench 150 yards from the muzzles of Turkish rifles. Over my head (tons of shrapnel are passing every minute). There is not much rifle-fire just now, except a few snipers whom we can't locate. I have many experiences which can only be told, not written, but the chief one happened on August 15th, when you were probably watching 'flappers' at Lady Well. We made a big advance that day (when our lines suffered heavily by death . . .). We had to advance over open country towards a hill (. . .). How we got there I can't tell, but we did, and more than that, we captured the position. When we handed it over to our reinforcements and retired for rest we were a jaded and sorry few. (Only two officers were left out of . . .)

Thank you, dear Paddy, but before I came away I made arrangements in London for tobacco and books. I had a book sent me from Lord Dunsany yesterday. Of course an ounce of 'Carroll's' would be great. Joe sent me some but I didn't get it yet.

I am on the left of Achi Baba above Sedd-el-Bahr. We have French and Australians on our right. The line runs from sea to sea. The weather here is very warm, terrific, but just now there is a breeze.

Tell them all in the Hotel I am well and glad to be here for it is great to be here after all. I saw half the world. I was in Egypt and Greece, saw Italy, Spain and all my dream countries and now I am in Turkey, wanting to be back in Slane again.

On 16 August, the Turks continued to bomb the British lines all day. The Munster Fusiliers, established on a ridge they had captured, retaliated with bombs that were only home-made contraptions consisting of a detonator pushed into a jam-tin, and a fuse lighted with a match. Their officer had sent down an urgent appeal for reinforcements, more bombs, more ammunition. But there was a chilling silence from headquarters.

The silence meant that the army command had broken down. The divisional commander, General Sir Bryan Mahon, piqued over a question of seniority, went off in a huff to Lemnos during the attack of 15 August, and washed his hands of the whole mess. The commander of the Suvla Bay landings was sacked that evening. In nine days, six officers in charge had disappeared, either invalided out, or booted out. A new command was trying to make an assessment of a disastrous situation.

Another assault on the Turkish lines was planned for Sunday, 22 August. The changes in the high command brought about no improvement in the supply of guns, ammunition, or bombs. The leaders now decided to time the attack for that hour in the afternoon when the westering sun was shining direct in the faces of the Turkish gunners, thus hindering their observation. But something freakish happened to the weather that day: the usual early morning mist did not disperse from the hills, but continued to shroud them in a gossamer veil as the day advanced. The fog cleared from the foothills, beaches and sea, on which the sun shone brightly. This meant that the Turks remained concealed, but they had perfect observation of what was happening below.

Hamilton, the commander-in-chief, came over to Suvla that morning from his headquarters on Imbros island some distance from the peninsula. The unusual fog on the hills worried him. He thought it justified postponing the attack, yet he did not give the countermand because 'he did not want to worry the new commander in charge of operations'.

The Fifth Inniskillings were in corps reserve that day and were not sent to the attack, but they suffered severe losses in the ranks from Turkish shell-fire. Father Charles Henry Devas, S.J., chaplain serving in Gallipoli, gave a vivid picture in his unpublished wartime diary of what this second engagement looked like to a non-combatant standing by to help:

Saturday, August 21st

Last night at the foot of the rising ground on the inland side of the dried salt lake that we had marched over, we dug a certain number of pits, like graves, in which we lay, but a good many—both officers and men—lay in the open, but hidden by the clumps of dense shrubs. In the morning no drumming up was allowed, breakfast consisting in theory of biscuits, bully beef and water, but in fact a certain number did drum up and Doherty brought me a cup of tea for which I scolded him, but which I gladly drank. All the morning we crept about or lay still. I heard a good many confessions. At 2.45 p.m. they moved off to the attack. I remained where we had slept with Doctor Wilkinson and his staff. When the attack began, we saw what a bad place we were in for receiving wounded, as bullets whizzed and fell all around us, but we had nowhere else to go. The wounded began to come in very soon, some walking, some carried, and we were all so busy that we did not notice how time was flying and no parties of stretcher-bearers from the Field Ambulance had come to evacuate our wounded. They lay in pitiful row after row, groaning and moaning. As the evening advanced more shells fell in our neighbourhood (I presume the Turk was trying to prevent reinforcements arriving) and these set fire to the bushes. It was a nightmare. Bullets whizzing, shells bursting, fires leaping up on all sides of us, and these rows of helpless wounded men. As there was no one else to do it, I left the wounded and organised parties of men—where they came from no one knew, or who they were—to beat back the fires. In the midst of these labours, Major Taylor's cheery voice rang out: 'Hullo, Padre, where's your advanced dressing-station? We've been hunting for it everywhere.'

The regular evacuation of the wounded now began, but many were killed between us and the beach by shell fire, though we did not know of it till long after. All men of every denomination showed such pleasure at seeing me and clung to me as if they were little children. As Doctor Wilkinson and I knelt on either side of a man, a bullet passed between our heads and killed the orderly at the man's feet. Strange lost men from other regiments burst in upon us with white faces; officers, stretcher bearers, despatch riders passed us asking for directions of units which we could not give.

In the early morning of the 22nd, I lay down and fell asleep at once. I woke about 7 a.m. The wounded were all gone. The doctor and his orderlies were asleep anywhere, just dropped off where they happened to be. Also little groups of men back from the fighting, some sleeping, some drumming up as if nothing had happened.

The assault of 22 August proved to be a more bloody and an even more overwhelming defeat than that of 15 August. Numbers of officers were killed and as only they knew the compass bearing, the rank and file lost their direction. The fierce bush fire that turned the whole battle-front into an inferno added to the confusion. There were 5,300 casualties that day for the gain of one Turkish trench.

September came, bringing stalemate. There were hardly any officers left to give orders. Discipline became slack. The dirt became engrained into the men's bearded faces. Sea bathing was a help on a few limited sectors of the line, but never on West Beach where Ledwidge was, as this area was exposed to the Turkish guns. The moment a man entered the water, a shell followed him, so bathing was forbidden. 'When we were swarming with lice, it was tantalizing to have to look at the sea and not be able to wash in it.' Hollow-cheeked and hollow-eyed, the men developed what they called the Gallipoli stoop from always crouching under cover.

The Turkish snipers took a toll of lives each day. They knew every gully, rock and tree in the land and made the most of this knowledge.

Numbers of them penetrated the Allied lines and were found even on the beaches. They painted their faces green for better camouflage and would crouch under bushes, picking off the Allied soldiers as long as their ammunition lasted. Discovery meant death but these snipers were fanatically brave and eager to give their lives for Turkey. They waged a terrible war of nerves on the invaders.

The nights began to turn cold; the flies vanished. Ledwidge's duties included 'listening-post' every second night. This dangerous and wearisome task consisted of slipping out over the trench parapet after dark, armed with a rifle and fifty rounds, crawling into a hole in no-man's-land, and waiting there until the signal came to retire. Then one wriggled back again through the bushes into the safety of the trench. One night on listening-post, Ledwidge sighted and shot a Turk creeping near the Allied lines.

On 26 September, orders to pack up reached the Tenth Division. As night descended on 30 September, the soldiers assembled at Lala Baba, a little height standing between the Salt Lake and the sea. While darkness shielded their movements, they were transferred with the utmost speed into the beetles that carried them out across the bay to where the s.s. *Sarnia* was anchored in readiness. Ledwidge had looked his last on the peninsula where 19,000 of his comrades in the now shattered Tenth Division had met their death.

In England, the G.H.Q. of the Mediterranean Expeditionary Force was being bitterly criticized. The evacuation of Gallipoli was urged as the only course left. Hamilton was recalled. The new commander-in-chief reappraised the whole situation and advised withdrawal at no matter what loss. All through November, arguments at the War Office were batted back and forth. At the end of that month a deluge of rain followed by snow swept down on Gallipoli, the worst blizzard in forty years. The men were drowned, or perished of cold, as they cowered in the trenches; one-tenth of the total remaining British strength was lost in this storm.

To round off a well-known story: night after night, under cover of darkness, the evacuation was carried out. Layers of blankets were laid along the piers and the men's boots wrapped in sacking to deaden the noise as they crept stealthily to the boats. In the trenches nearest the Turkish lines, self-firing rifles were rigged up to make the enemy think the front lines were still occupied. At daylight, everything on the beaches looked the same to the Turkish sentries on the heights, as troopships and lighters by then had disappeared from the bay. In this way

118,000 men were taken off the peninsula with no casualties. The evacuation was completed early in January 1916, leaving behind enormous quantities of army rations and equipment. The operation is described as one of the most successful retreats in military history.

VIII

Ledwidge and his comrades on the *Sarnia* were landed at daybreak at Mudros, chief port of Lemnos. This island in the Aegean sea, consisting chiefly of bare volcanic hills and sandy beaches, had been lent by Greece to the Allies as a naval and military base. It had no scenic beauty other than the blue sea and the glory of the sky, especially at sunset.

The British Admiralty was delighted with Mudros: a natural harbour three miles wide ringed by low hills, with enough depth to provide harbourage for Allied ships. Apart from that, it was a miserable town of ramshackle houses, shops that were only open-fronted booths grouped around a large church; a sprawl of wooden huts on the wharves, disfiguring encampments on the hills. One of these was a transit hospital and the other a barbed-wire compound for Turkish prisoners.

But the shoddy place was heaven to the men arriving from Gallipoli. Tents were a luxury to sleep in after the shallow trenches. They had water. The cooler weather had disposed of the flies. They were out of range of the peninsula smell. They could stand upright, no longer crouching in hourly danger of their lives. After the Gallipoli fare, they did not complain of the canteen food. The harbour was always crowded with the shipping of the Allied nations, so that soldiers and sailors from all over the world passed through, bringing animation and colour to the streets.

Ledwidge and his companions, however, had not been brought there for the good of their health. When Bulgaria joined the war on Germany's side, Greece and Serbia had appealed to the Allies for help. Before the Fifth Battalion had left Gallipoli, Kitchener and Joffre had agreed that two divisions, one French, one British, should be sent to Serbia. Events developed swiftly. Ledwidge's unit were left in the peace of Mudros only two weeks. On 15 October, they were marched on board the *Aeneas*, bound for Salonika where they landed next day.

Here the poet found himself in a dream country of almost unreal beauty: mountains rising to the sky, capped by streamers of white cloud; dark green cypresses emphasizing the vivid white houses and

the grace of tall minarets. He saw there for the first time Greek mountain troops in white uniforms, long shoes decorated with pompons
and picturesque head-dress.

On disembarking, the battalion formed up and marched to Lembet,
a little village six miles north of Salonika. The Inniskilling Fusiliers
were among the first British troops ever seen in that region and crowds
of natives accompanied them the whole way to Lembet. After a couple
of weeks' training, the unit was transferred fifty miles by train to the
Greco-Serbian frontier, where they set up camp near the Lake Doiran–
Strumnitza road.

While the transport ship was only on its way to Mudros to convey
the Tenth Division to Salonika, the Bulgars attacked Serbia on 10
October. The Serbs fled, destroying their harvest as they retreated.
King Constantine of Greece was an unreliable friend of the Allies. He
decided on neutrality as the safest policy for Greece.

The result was that the Tenth Division found themselves in a country
where practically no food was available and rationing the army became
a problem. All went well for the first few weeks. Autumn in Serbia is
a beautiful season. There was plenty of fish to be had in the camp by
Lake Doiran. The men found a hot spring bubbling out of rock and
enjoyed washing in it. Then they got the order to move about four
miles farther up into the mountains and there the real hardship began.
The weather became much colder, especially at night when the water
froze in the men's bottles. Food became increasingly scarce. A few
soldiers were detailed every day to go out and hunt for it. Sometimes
they came back empty-handed with doleful faces; occasionally they
returned with a few hens tied to their belts. There was no rum issue,
which would have been a help in keeping warm. They were without
cigarettes for six weeks. Once a raiding party came back in triumph
with some rolled leaf tobacco, but as they had no paper to make
cigarettes, their joy was short lived. As November advanced, they were
on starvation rations: one tin of bully beef every day between four
men, and two army biscuits each.

Kennedy, the battalion historian, gives a picture of this mountain
camp:

Our site was very rough, with rock and stunted undergrowth, and
it was thus very difficult to erect our bivouacks. There were two men
in each bivouac, these being formed by two ground sheets with a
great-coat to close the weather end. It can be imagined what it was

134

like on a mountain ridge under the conditions described, the temperature on the 23rd November being 30 degrees below freezing point. We suffered untold hardships . . . from the severe frost and bitterly cold winds. There were hundreds of cases of severe frost bite amongst the troops. The nearest field ambulance was a long distance back and the position of our Battalion was about two miles from the nearest place to which a limbered wagon could get.

He goes on to describe how men who were frostbite cases had their puttees wound round their feet and ankles before being placed on a bare-backed mule, led by its driver to the wagons. Four men at a time were put sitting in these; men shrieked with pain when they jolted off to the point where ambulances could pick them up.

It was on that inaccessible mountain ridge that the greatest event of his literary life befell Ledwidge; an advance copy of *Songs of the Fields* reached him. He was so delighted that the little volume was almost food and warmth to him. He held it incredulously in his hand like a message from another world. His joy was all the keener because of the long, frustrating delay: sixteen months since he had corrected the galleys, four months since the page proofs had been returned.

His first book! To leaf through the pages was to be transported back to Meath: Slane in the spring with the cuckoos calling and the blackbirds singing in the rain. The murmur of the Boyne water in his ears; the little hills and valleys wrapped in bluish mist were before his eyes.

> The hills are crying from the fields to me,
> And calling me with music from a choir
> Of waters in their woods where I can see
> The bloom unfolded on the whins like fire.
> And, as the evening moon climbs ever higher
> And blots away the shadows from the slope,
> They cry to me like things devoid of hope.

The blurb on the dust-jacket described him as 'the scavenger poet', a term that annoyed Ledwidge's friends. Dunsany wrote to the publishers asking for a correction. He pointed out that Ledwidge was at one time foreman of men repairing roads, an employment that could not be described as 'scavenging'. Jenkins replied that the description heightened interest in the poet and helped to sell the book. In other words, publishers have to live. There is no record of what Ledwidge himself thought.

He wrote to Dunsany on 31 October 1915:

Thanks very much for your two letters received a couple of days ago. Yes, I received your cigarettes all right. We had a busy day with the Turks when they came, but that didn't prevent us from smoking them.

So 'Songs of the Fields' are out at last. I suppose the critics are blowing warm and cold over them with the same mouth, like the charcoal burner in Aesop's fable. Jenkins sent me a copy. It is a lovely book and quite a decent size, but my best is not in it. That has to come yet. I feel something great struggling in my soul but it can't come until I return; if I don't return it will never come.

I wish the damn war would end; we are all so sick for the old countries. Still, our hearts are great and we are always ready for anything which may be required of us.

I am writing a poem which I will send you when finished; meanwhile I hope my book sells by thousands. I won't try to thank you for all you have done for me and are doing. You know how grateful I am.

But in fact he got rave notices. *The Times* said he reminded them of Keats and *Truth* affirmed that 'The spring of English poetry has been dry for many a long day, but in *Songs of the Fields* it gushes forth anew in a stream of pure crystal.' *Bookman* said that none of the poets of the New Army had written finer poetry and *The Tatler* welcomed the newcomer: 'His songs have thrilled the beauty-loving world, and have made his name beloved in the hearts of all those to whom Nature is really and truly their mother.' Other laudatory reviews appeared in the *Pall Mall Gazette*, the *Standard, Sphere, Globe, Daily Telegraph* and *Manchester Guardian*. The result was that the first issue was rapidly sold out and a second impression printed.

Dunsany, still in Derry training recruits, was just as elated as Ledwidge at the success of *Songs of the Fields*. He acted as agent and sent press cuttings of the reviews to the poet, who acknowledged them on 13 November:

Thanks very much for your two letters to hand and press cuttings. These were the first I had seen and I am delighted beyond words. I cannot tell you how grateful I am to you for all you have done for me and when you congratulate me on the success of my book, you forget that but for you it could never be, and you leave me with all the glory.

The reviews are better because each critic appreciated different poems, this shows a worthiness from cover to cover, a worthiness I had only hoped for in two or three pieces. None of them have selected the verses Mr Marsh took, this makes the whole book more valuable still. I wish I were back again. But there seems no hope yet of our returning.

The weather is getting bad, the nights in particular. Being in a mountainy country we suffer much from rain and cold. A goodly few of us have rheumatism badly, but the work is still here and the doctor is inexorable. The enclosed poem is one I wrote in a thunder shower in Salonika. There are still great things to come from me and I am full up, but have no time. I will not accept any post, if I return, but what you approve of. I would rather sweep the roads for the people who are so free, and write pure poetry than deceive people for £100 a year in the city. I am called. Thanks very much again and best wishes to you.

Marsh referred to by Ledwidge was Edward Marsh, private secretary to Winston Churchill and associated with him for fifty years. Marsh was at this period the foremost patron of poetry in England. One of the founders of the Poetry Bookshop in London, he befriended many poets: Harold Monro, who ran the bookshop, V. Sackville West, W. H. Davies, Lascelles Abercrombie, John Drinkwater, D. H. Lawrence, J. C. Squire, Rupert Brooke, Siegfried Sassoon, Maurice Baring, Francis Brett Young. Marsh was a generous as well as a practical patron. Between 1911 and 1922 he published five volumes of contemporary poetry under the title *Georgian Poetry*. The second volume (1913–15) contained three of Ledwidge's poems: *A Rainy Day in April, The Lost Ones* and *The Wife of Llew*. To be chosen by Marsh was a distinction; the only other Irish poet he published in those early years was James Stephens. The earlier volumes of Marsh's collections had phenomenal sales. Half the proceeds went to the Poetry Bookshop and the other half was divided among the contributors. Walter de la Mare said that at one period he made more out of what was published in *Georgian Poetry* than out of all his other verse published elsewhere.

The effect of receiving his first volume of poems was a stimulus to Ledwidge in whom the poetic gift had been lying almost dormant. He did not write one line of poetry during his eight weeks in Gallipoli. In Mudros he finished a long poem, 128 lines, written specially for a fellow soldier Cassidy. But when he sent this to Dunsany according to his habit, the latter replied:

Good, in parts very good, but Patrick MacGill could do it. Tells us all about what the Big Bold Man feels at the Raw Red End of All the Earth, and I'm sure we should all feel very grateful for it and feel better men for buying it at 3/6 net, but as a matter of fact it isn't quite what anybody ever felt anywhere, or ever will.

Early in November, Ledwidge writes again to Dunsany:

I am too short of paper to send you copies of some poems I have written, but I will be careful of them until an issue takes place, if one ever does in this awful place. I wish I could get back for a rest and go to France in the spring. I will never hold out all the winter here as I suffer terribly from rheumatism. The nights when not raining are freezing and one wonders which is the worse for the pains.

Of course you understand that we are quite different from what we have been in your day. We are all weak and sick, but we suffered much.

Would there be any chance of getting home for a month? The Doctor will only give one a day's rest, that is no cure for rheumatism when the same day miles of a march have to be done and that night a 'listening post' in some outlandish hollow.

When I get paper I will send you copies of my latest work, meanwhile if you could get a holiday for me I would be so grateful, and so would my mother.

It was not in Dunsany's power as a junior captain to arrange a leave of absence for the poet, who ingenuously overrated the older man's influence in the army.

Reading the old poems in their new book form had a sorrowful effect, too. They brought Ellie back to life again and Ledwidge was delivered up to the old torment. Twelve of the fifty poems in the collection were inspired by her. The sights and sounds of the camp were around him; but in his mind he was back with Ellie in the woods at home on those clear spring evenings when the days begin to lengthen and love was in his heart. Hers was a ghost he could not lay even on that ice-bound mountain ridge of Serbia.

The sudden blizzard that swept down on Gallipoli at the end of November afflicted Serbia, too. The mountains were covered with snow and hundreds of men went down with frostbite in a few hours. Huddled in his bivouac, Ledwidge wrote two poems which he sent to Dunsany a few days later with this explanation.

Remember in reading the enclosed the circumstances under which they were written. *When Love and Beauty Wander Away* was written by Lake Doiran one awful night of thunder and rain. I was thinking of the end of the world as the Bible predicts it and tried to imagine Love and Beauty leaving the world hand in hand, and we who could not yet die, standing on the edge of a great precipice with no song, no love, no memory. At the same place, thinking of another thing, I wrote the *Nocturne*.

Shortly after the storm, the Bulgarians came out in strength against the British and French divisions, who were outnumbered by the well-equipped enemy in front, while behind them was a Greek Army of doubtful sympathy. The Allies had to make a strategic retreat back to Salonika. As the French troops were in great danger, the British had to cover the retreat, which began on 8 December. Progress down the mountain was very slow.

Ledwidge's unit had to march for six days. He afterwards described the experience in a letter to Paddy Healy:

It poured rain on us all the long ninety miles we had to march, and what with sleeping in wet clothes, sweating and cooling down, I got an attack of Barney Fitzimons back. You have read of our retreat. Shall I ever forget it! We should have left the previous evening but just as we had mustered to go we received word that a French Brigade was almost surrounded higher up and we were called to do a flank attack. We did, and extricated the French, but got into a similar condition ourselves by morning. The Bulgars came on like flies and though we mowed down line after line, they persisted with awful doggedness and finally gave us a bayonet charge which secured their victory. We only just had about 200 yards to escape by and we had to hold this until next evening and then dribble out as best we could.

Not only had Ledwidge terminated his correspondence with Lizzie, he does not mention her in his letter to her brother.

Even in his extremity of hunger and exhaustion, the poet's brown eyes were darting around, observing the passing scene. He was composing verses in his head and scribbling them whenever there was a halt for a rest. *The Cobbler of Sara Júl* is an off-beat, escapist kind of poem, the sort of verse that might easily run through a man's head as he trudged along. It commemorates a place where the soldiers made a brief stop.

He sent the poem later to Dunsany with this comment:

Sara Júl (Sari-Gueul) is a village in Serbian Macedonia about half-way between Lake Doiran and Salonika. Like all the Greek villages, Sara Júl is quaint and very beautiful, seen even in the worst conditions of weather as I have seen it. We stood there two days on our retreat, waiting for a train which never came. Sara Júl is one hilly street with the houses built very much out of line. Bread (Oh dear me! Bread! What wouldn't we give for a mouthful of bread!) tins, lanthorns, clothes of all colours are displayed in the windows. Quaint signs creak in the wind and where you see a vine climbing up a house front, underneath you hear my cobbler's hammer. I wonder if people will understand the line: 'Slow steps come fast to the knife and rule.' Of course an old cow walks very slowly and as it grows older it goes the slower and therefore the faster to the tan-yard.*

Ledwidge, on this retreat, marched through country only recently vacated by the Serbs. Once, when a halt was called, he found himself standing on the roadside beside a Serbian girl who was shivering violently. She had lost her family in the mass exodus and was lightly dressed in the clothes she was wearing when she ran from her home. In an impulse of compassion, he put his greatcoat around her shoulders, forgetting that his glasses were in one of the pockets. It was a long time before he was able to get new glasses. The British soldiers passed many groups of dead Serbian soldiers lying where they had fallen and they were glad to exchange the dead men's boots for their own which were worn to flitters. A lift by train had been promised for the last stage of the retreat. But as they marched into the station, the empty train pulled derisively out, a gesture on the part of the train crew to express the black hate in their hearts for the British.

On the last few miles of the march, the men's pace was reduced to a crawl, their legs moving mechanically as though they were sleep-walkers. The rain stopped and the sun shone out on the tents at which they stared unbelievingly. All the soldiers in the camp ran out to look at them, as the unit had been given up for lost. Ledwidge collapsed before he could reach camp. His back had become so painfully in-flamed that he couldn't stand up. An ambulance was sent out for the casualties and they were taken to a hospital near Salonika.

About a week later, he was taken to Egypt and admitted to the Giza Hospital in Cairo. Shortly afterwards he was transferred to the Citadel Hospital at the opposite side of the city, where he arrived just before

* Poem in the Dunsany papers.

New Year 1916. Part of this great fortress, then utilized as a temporary hospital, overlooked from a considerable height the entire city of Cairo, which is built on flat ground around the Nile. As the view is to the west, it was superb at sunset when the minarets of hundreds of mosques flashed in the golden rays. The Giza pyramids could be discerned from the Citadel and even the edge of the desert, veiled in purple haze.

Ledwidge sent a postcard to Paddy Healy couched in terms of a plutocratic tourist, proving that his ordeal had not diminished his sense of humour:

> How on earth are you getting along? I will certainly see you soon as it is getting too warm for a longer stay so far south.

He had already reported his illness to Dunsany, but that letter is lost. He wrote again on 19 January 1916 from the Citadel Hospital:

> Many thanks for your book of writing paper. You will have received my other letter ere this letting you know I was admitted to hospital.
>
> I am getting on first class except for my back which is still painful and very weak. The doctors in Giza hospital recommended me to be sent home but I have heard nothing of it here so far. I write an occasional little thing yet which you will read some day, but I lost a lot of manuscripts in the long retreat from the Balkan front.
>
> Will such evenings as we knew at Dunsany ever be again? I hope so, although for me a lot of the old glamour has passed and my poetry is written for other reasons than at first. When I stand on the balcony here and look down at the city, with all its pinnacles and mosques, as if the Gods were disturbed at a game of chess aeons ago, it seems to me that I have left this world and live along the Yann with the inhabitants of Mandaroon, still wanting to return but unable to find the back door of that little shop, which to me is our doctor's heart.
>
> Lord Clare one time invited Goldsmith to dinner and introduced him to Lord Calmot, who paid little heed to the great man before him. Next night, the poet, relating his experiences to Johnson, Reynolds and the rest, said in an earnest (?) joke: 'Lord Calmot treated me as if I were an ordinary man.' I repeat this jokingly: 'The doctor treats me as an ordinary man.'
>
> Did you ever hear the natives here sing down the streets in the evenings? A friend of mine who knows Arabic very well gave me a translation one evening as we listened and I set it ringing thus:

What time is it, Mr Mahommed?
It's just a little bit after seven,
Where are you going to, Mr Mahommed?
I'm going the long white way to heaven.
And will you come back again, Mr Mahommed?
I'll be back at a little bit after eleven,
If the world doesn't end before.

P.S. Your new seals are charming, particularly the one about the flower of fame. 'Mortal soil' is a wonderful conception. F.E.L.

One of Dunsany's unusual recreations was cutting seals on silver for his own use. Among the many he made was an illustration of Milton's line, 'Fame is no plant that grows on mortal soil' with which he sealed the letter acknowledged above by Ledwidge.

The poet wrote to Paddy Healy the same week:

I hope to pledge you with Johnny Walker in Kate's home of the early black fasts. So Cissy has gone. What a catastrophe. Was it the severe pressure of the recent licensing act caused them to part? Or had Cissy caught the mania for striking? I regret the cause anyhow as Cissy was a useful adjunct to our late hours. You see I am in hospital. I am not wounded, though only God knows how I escaped the fiends of the Bulgars. I saw horrors there that must have made the soul of Dante envious. What really drove me in here was the bad weather we experienced on our retreat. . . .

I am going on well and thankful I am here. I will tell you the whole story when I see you. Meanwhile remember me to Katie and the bog. Thanks for congratulations on my book. It is a great success financially and I think, from the reviews, a great literary success also.

His sick-bed was cheered by the flattering notices of his book, a continual surprise and delight to him. The *Review of Reviews* of December 1915, gave him almost a whole page, the centre taken up with a large photograph: his features are rough-hewn, a big mouth and a wide nose, yet the set of his head and the dark, wavy hair are attractive; he is wearing the handwoven tweeds he favoured, white shirt and knotted in a bow a wide black silk tie, fine-rimmed glasses hooked behind his ears. Excerpts from the long article are typical of the line of publicity favoured by the reviewers:

To start life as a farm labourer and to graduate as a road scavenger is not the usual prelude to a career of distinction, yet this is the record

142

of Francis Ledwidge, a young Irishman . . . His first little volume of verse will win for him many friends. The poet's lines are charged with human feeling, and are sure to make their appeal. We quote two haunting stanzas from 'After My Last Song'.

This was success even by the standards of sixty years later.

He writes to Dunsany on 5 February, still from the Citadel Hospital:

> Thanks for *Georgian Poetry* to hand a few days ago, also for other parcel just received. Mr Marsh is to be congratulated on his selection of verse, but somehow I think he could have got better from *Songs of the Fields*. I am glad to be there all the same. I enclose three small things of many I have written in Greece and Serbia, some of them indeed under shrapnel.
>
> I'm afraid I'm not getting better. My back is very painful and weak and I have a terrific headache. There are Navvy imps in my head. I am going somewhere for sulphur baths, perhaps these will do me good. My dreams are awful things and I hate going asleep because of them. Sometimes I am lying in a coffin in a terrific dream. I will be all right again some time.
>
> I wonder if I might trouble you for a small book of poetry. There is nothing to read here but prose and I have read the few books worth while. Charles Garvice and Nat Gould I have strongly denounced, and many others whose very names are anathema to me.
>
> A 'C. of E.' chaplain who lives here called to see me one day because he had heard of my book. He seemed to be taking a great interest in me and promised me a book of poetry, but suddenly he saw on my chart that I was an R.C. and hurried from me as if I were possessed.
>
> He never came over to me since although he has been in the ward many times. I wonder if God asked our poor chaps were they R.Cs or C. of Es when they went to Him on August 15th.
>
> Thanks again for your thoughtfulness.

He was transferred to another hospital at Helwan, a small town on the outskirts of Cairo, famous for its sulphur springs. Before World War I, health-seeking tourists used to flock there for the baths, at that time a fashionable cure for rheumatism and kindred diseases. During the war, the Grand Hotel was taken over as a hospital for Allied soldiers. Helwan is no longer a health resort. The medical fad has died out, leaving only the rotten-egg smell of the springs that still flow. Otherwise this small town can have changed very little since Ledwidge viewed it. It is largely untouched by the Westernization that Nasser wished on Cairo and most of the people still wear the traditional Arab dress, the graceful galabeyeh. As it lives an outdoor life, its streets are usually crowded with people, bicycles, and carts loaded with vegetables or junk.

Ledwidge wrote to Dunsany on 14 February:

I enclose a few short poems which I ask you to read while I do a better one that is haunting me. You see I have come further south for more heat and sulphur baths as the doctors in the Citadel think these things are what I want mostly. Helwan is close to the lesser pyramids known as the Sakarrah group. There is another Sakarrah thousands of miles away where I wish to be. There are greater wonders at the Sakarrah* of Slane now; for all across the field of that name the half daisies are waiting and watching for the further advance of Spring ere they open fully and hold up cymbals to the music of the rain. 'Oh, to be in Ireland now that Spring is there!' Is there any place like Ireland? Why even the fields have their names and traditions.

Somehow I don't seem to get better of these pains at all. My back is very painful and weak still, but this place may improve it. It is my last chance anyway. I used to think if I had a book published it wouldn't matter how soon I died but now that I have one before the public I want to live to do better. I suppose such aspirations are really the striving of the soul for the greater things beyond its prison walls of the body.

You are so good and obliging that I venture to ask you another favour. Will you send the best of the enclosed somewhere and in advance send my brother £2. I have no means of sending him any money from here and he wants £2 for some particular spring work. He is a student severe on himself and I like him to be able to pursue his studies so I subsidise all his necessities. Jenkins would do this but I thought it better ask you. But you *must* ask the reviews to make the cheque payable to you. His name is Joseph, old address.

I will let you know now I am getting along with the new poem. It will run to some length.

Who would think James Stephens could write such a poem as *The Goat Paths*?

* Also the name of a field on Fitzsimons's farm, probably derived from the Gaelic word *Corha*, a pillared stone.

This letter shows in action the 'accounting' undertaken by Lady Dunsany for Ledwidge since he joined the army.

The following day the poet sent Paddy Healy a coloured postcard of a Cairo street named Sharia-el-Tabbauch:

> Wouldn't this make a beautiful street scene for an oriental play? How are you?

Dunsany was still in Derry and Ledwidge on 8 March tries to comfort him for his state of inactivity:

> I haven't heard from you for a long time. I hope you haven't left Ireland anyway. I am still in bed. The doctors don't seem to do me much good. I had jaundice and divers other complaints. The jaundice left me with a pain in my side which annoys me greatly. Also my back is bad and my right ankle.
>
> It is spring in Ireland. If you love the gods who govern the seasons don't be anxious to leave Ireland now. I know how eager you are for the field, but it will soon be all over. The Turks are beaten, and the struggle at Verdun is Germany's last great effort. By the way I have great respect for the Turks. They fought us a clean fight, and we must admit they are brave soldiers. In my admiration for them I have read 'The Koran'. Mahomet nearly equals you in finding a simile for the moon. You have said: 'When she is old she hobbles away from the hills.' Mahomet says: 'She is twisted and broken like an old palm branch.' I am not able to transcribe some few poems from an old book. This letter is causing me some trouble to write.

Ledwidge writes to him again on 12 March:

> Your letter of February 20th did me more good than all the dirty medicine I have been drinking for the past three months. So you liked the poem about the sheep? So do I, very much. Did you get the Arab poems? I like these also and the ones I now send, particularly *The Cobbler*.
>
> I didn't get your books yet. I am eagerly watching them. I like Matthew Arnold's *The Forsaken Merman* and *The Scholar Gypsy*. But I love Keats. I think poor Keats reaches the top of beauty in *Odes to a Grecian Urn*, *To a Nightingale* and *Autumn*, as well as in several of his beautiful apostrophes in the poem *Endymion*. I like Keats best of all. I remember years ago praying to Keats for aid.
>
> I am still a-bed. The doctor says he thinks there is an abscess com-

ing on my liver. I will not undergo any operation no matter how I fare. Just now I am told I am to be sent to the 27th General Hospital, Abyssia. If you write again, that will be my address.

They send me to doctors who are murdering me. Damn them! If they only knew all I want to do. They don't care. Why won't they send me home where I would get well?

The hospital to which he was now sent—the fifth since his collapse —no longer exists. The doctor who received him there proved to be the most sympathetic Ledwidge had encountered in the army. Every man's good dream of a doctor, he tried to heal not only body sickness, but heart sickness and homesickness, too. Sitting beside Ledwidge's bed for a chat, his eye fell on *Songs of the Fields*, which he promptly borrowed. It transpired that he knew Dunsany's books. No longer now was Ledwidge 'treated as an ordinary man'. This doctor promised to get him transferred to a hospital in England and immediately set about snipping through the red tape that closed the way.

The new friendship transformed Ledwidge from a depressed invalid into a cheerful convalescent as is evident from his letter to Dunsany of 21 March:

As I anticipated they have sent me here from Helwan. I am now much better and hope to be allowed up in a couple of days. The doctor who is attending me is a fine man. He knows all your books and even heard of mine. He has spoken to me about Sime's work and believes as I do that your books have immortalised the fame of Sime.

I send you a copy of a small thing recently written. You will know all about it when you read it, and who it is about, for you will remember my telling you at Basingstoke about someone who died. That was the time I went home and was six days absent. Was it much wonder?

If you listen very carefully by the time you get this letter you will hear that 'wandering voice' as Wordsworth calls the cuckoo. I would like to hear him and will too, in dreams.

I wonder when you were in Africa was it the little things of home which annoyed you? An old broken gate I wot of and a plough in a ditch and other similar neglected things are always in my mind. Did you receive the last poems I sent, the one about the *Cobbler*, etc? I have many more old ones in my haversack and some day soon will transcribe them and send you copies. They are all faded with Balkan rains, but I will remember the lines that are obliterated.

I hope you are enjoying good health, that is worth many castles; still I would sooner write a great poem and die than live out the century unknown.

The reference in the second paragraph is to Ellie whose funeral Ledwidge accompanied from Manchester to Slane. Sime was the artist who illustrated many of Dunsany's early books, the black and white sketches being a perfect complement to the writer's weird tales. The affinity between writer and artist was so complete that on one occasion Dunsany asked Sime to do a set of sketches and then proceeded to write stories to suit them.

The poem enclosed in the letter was *The Resurrection*. Ledwidge's mind was still dwelling fornlornly on Ellie:

> My true love still is all that's fair,
> She is flower and blossom blowing free,
> For all her silence lying there
> She sings a spirit song to me.
>
> New lovers seek her in her bower,
> The rain, the dew, the flying wind,
> And tempt her out to be a flower,
> Which throws a shadow on my mind.

On the last day of March, he sent Dunsany another group of poems enclosed with a note:

I have just a few minutes to get a letter written and away. I enclose some little poems recently written. One poem is distinctively Irish. I am getting on well now.

He was still in Cairo on 3 April according to the manuscript copy of a poem, *The Five Roads* (which meet at the Hill of Skreen). Shortly afterwards the doctor succeeded in getting him transferred to England. The ship conveying Ledwidge put in at Naples for several days. All the soldiers returning from the East looked forward to this stop-over because the Neapolitans were very friendly. The ladies used to show their sympathy for the Allied cause by going on board the hospital ships, followed by Boy Scouts carrying stretchers laden with flowers to distribute among the patients.

The next letter from Ledwidge to Dunsany reports his arrival in Manchester.

2nd Western General Hospital,
(A Ward), Lilly Lane, Moston,
Manchester. 20th April 1916

I arrived in England late last night. I cannot tell you how glad I was to return to western civilisation once again. Coming from Southampton in the train, looking on England's beautiful valleys all white with Spring, I thought indeed its freedom was worth all the blood I have seen flow. No wonder England has so many ardent patriots. I would be one of them myself did I not presume to be an Irish patriot. I am not yet very well, indeed I am far from it; nevertheless I am asking to be sent to Ireland soon. I remember you once said of Manchester that God only sends fogs to it. You are quite right, but even the English fog is dear to me now and prized by me above Turkish sunshine, or Serbia's beautiful autumn.

I expect to be home in the course of a week, if I succeed in pretending that my back is strong again. I am so accustomed to asking you to do me favours that I venture this one with no reluctance. I request you to find me clerical work in the Orderly Room for a while, as I am not fit for parades and can't carry anything on my back. The doctors call my disease 'cholecystitis', that is the insane name the medical profession give a bad liver.

('Cholecystitis' is in fact inflammation of the gall bladder.)

The campaign in Serbia proved even more inconclusive than the Gallipoli expedition. All the Allies ever accomplished there was to hold the Bulgar army and keep it from being a trouble elsewhere, a 'containment' that required immense forces. More men were drafted to Salonika than had perished in Gallipoli, three-quarters of a million as compared with half a million. The Bulgars were not finally defeated until the autumn of 1918 and then only by a combined Allied offensive.

As Ledwidge recuperated in the Manchester hospital he had reason to be thankful for his good fortune. A survivor of two battle-fronts before the war was half-way through, he had deeply experienced its crass futility: the criminal waste of human life in Gallipoli; the tragicomedy of Serbia. Meanwhile he was slowly recovering physical strength and he had abounding hopes for his future.

IX

News reached Ledwidge of the insurrection in Dublin while he was in the Manchester hospital. Always in his heart an Irish Volunteer, he was shaken to the depths of his being. First a wild exultation leaped up in him that, despite everything, the Volunteers had managed to close the ranks again. They had acted on the old adage 'England's difficulty is Ireland's opportunity,' which he had quoted in his final public statement to the Rural Council. His first heady excitement was quickly succeeded by frantic grief over the executions. All the first reports of the rising slighted it as a total failure. Nevertheless Ledwidge's world was now utterly changed. He would have to get out of the army. Under the silence clamped down on Ireland he knew that a mighty spirit was stirring; it would speak again.

Padraic Pearse, Thomas MacDonagh and James Connolly had long been heroes to the poet. Ledwidge had always been a devoted champion of the workers' movement. Connolly and the Citizen Army, the trade union group, had thrown in their lot with the insurgents.

The Easter Week insurrection is now so well known, it need not be retold here. But to the majority of people outside the capital, the rising at first appeared sheer lunacy: a handful of badly armed men setting themselves up against the might of the British Empire. The number of Volunteers to go into action has been variously estimated; some calculations place it at 600; there were 1,200 British troops in Dublin on Easter Monday morning, but by Tuesday, reinforcements increased their strength to 5,000. Pearse had clearly foreseen this probability. These lines in his play *The Singer* are held to be prophetic:

> *Diarmid:* We thought it a foolish thing for fourscore to go into battle against four thousand, or maybe forty thousand.
> *MacDara:* And so it is a foolish thing. Do you want us to be wise?

Dublin had become so accustomed to the parading of the Volunteers that they attracted little attention when they marched through the streets that Easter Monday morning. They walked into the General

Post Office, chosen as headquarters of the Provisional Government, and ordered the staff to evacuate. The clerks had hurriedly complied. The Tricolour was run up over the building and Pearse returned to the steps to read the Proclamation of Freedom. It had been signed by seven men: Thomas Clarke, Sean MacDiarmada, P. H. Pearse, James Connolly, Thomas MacDonagh, Eamonn Ceannt and Joseph Plunkett. As it was a bank holiday, most people's thoughts were fixed on relaxation. Only a handful of people on their morning rounds even paused to listen to Pearse. It was not a spectacular *coup d'état*, yet it changed the whole course of Ireland's history.

Other strategic points in the city had been simultaneously occupied. As the week went by, the Republican posts were recaptured one after the other, but the General Post Office held out. On Wednesday, field-guns set up in Trinity College and on a gunboat in the Liffey demolished half O'Connell Street, including the upper storey of the Post Office. On Friday afternoon the ruined building went on fire and the garrison evacuated across Henry Street with seventeen casualties. By midday on Saturday their position had become untenable and Pearse surrendered, sending a written order to the other commands around the city to do likewise.

The seven men who signed the Proclamation were secretly court-martialled. Nothing was known of them until the evening of 3 May, when an official notice posted on the gate of Arbour Hill prison announced that Pearse, MacDonagh and Clarke had been executed. Other executions to the number of fifteen quickly followed. It was a period of public mourning long remembered in Ireland.

Ledwidge had planned to go straight home the day he was released from hospital. But in the event he could not travel to Ireland because all passenger services were suspended on account of the rising. He was obliged to wait at the home of his married sister, Mary, until he could get on a boat. On his first morning of civilian life, he was cheered by a letter from Bob Christie, which he answered at once:

> 68H Cambridge Street,
> C. on M.
> Manchester
> 4th May '16

My dear Bob,

How glad I was to receive your letter this morning, forwarded to me from the hospital. I had a letter from you in Serbia, which I answered, but about that time several mail-boats were waylaid on the sea and my replies are probably safe in Davy Jones's locker.

We had a terrific time since you left us. It was hell! hell!! hell!!! We lost two-thirds of our men on the day you were wounded, several more the next day, and an occasional man in the trenches which we held until we left Suvla for other arenas. I cannot write you of our hardships in Serbia, as no words could describe the cold, the blizzards, the frost and the hunger. We did not fear the Bulgars even though we were outnumbered; we only thought it unfair of England to send us, a broken division, up there where so many had failed. When we were finally beaten on the Vardar, the retreat to Salonika was more than our strength was equal to, especially as the weather was so severe and the journey so rugged. Many of us were sent to hospital when we got there, and a good few are now home. My liver started troubling me, and does still. I can't sleep at night. Though I am discharged from hospital I am far from being well, but I hope, nevertheless, to recuperate fully in the green fields of Ireland. I am only waiting for the boats to resume their wonted trips to hasten home once again.

I know all about Lynch's D.C.M. I tried to get *you* that, as Lynch, or Captain Adams can tell you, for I believe you deserved it, so did Mason. I wrote about you to the General from the trenches, and afterwards was summoned before Adams. I will tell you all later. Bob, I had hard graft in Suvla and Serbia. I was on 'listening post' every alternate night. The first night I shot a Turk who came spying and got a certain amount of fame and—more dangerous work—and a stripe. I will hardly fight any more.

But to talk of things that matter. I often talk with Corney and cry for you. Corney always told me you were safe. We will write that play this summer (D.V.). Your verse is excellent. Keep on. We must take out a book of your verse in Autumn. I have one more ready. 'Songs of the Fields' is a great success. It is in the third edition now.

Yes, poor Ireland is always in trouble. Tho' I am not a Sinn Feiner and you are a Carsonite, do our sympathies not go to *Cathleen ni Houlihan*? Poor MacDonagh and Pearse were two of my best friends, and now they are dead, shot by England. MacDonagh had a beautiful mind. Don't you know his poetry:

Sweeter than violin and lute
Is my love—and she left me behind.
I wish that all music were mute
And I to all beauty were blind.

That is a verse from one of his Irish love songs. My recollections of
poor MacDonagh are for evermore full of sorrow.

Have no fears. The 'Saturday' will pay you. They are always slow.
You may write if you like. I often wrote when hard up. I have no
rest because of Ellie, even yet. I wrote many keens for her. The poem
in 'The Saturday Review', if it was *Nocturne* is of her. The 'Saturday'
has another of mine, one written in Greece. I hope to get home
in a few days, but you must write again. I will run to see you when
I go to Derry. I hear often from Lord Dunsany. He wrote to welcome
me home. I didn't know his mother was dead. I must write condoling
with him.

P.S. But how are you? Have you a leg at all? I have many humorous
stories of Cassidy to tell you. He is still alive. Poor Moyers was never
heard of after the 15th August. He must have got killed. Patterson
told me he saw him and that he was hit in the lungs and dying.
Others say this may not be true. He is dead anyhow. Upson also
disappeared in the same way.

'I have no rest because of Ellie, even yet,' was a confidence torn from
his innermost heart in the relief of being in touch again with his closest
friend. It was almost a year since Ellie's death: he was still mourning
her loss, still torturing himself with useless regrets; they had been
bound together in a mysterious affinity and it was *he* who had allowed
it to be broken, a love affair that he would never again experience.
What a different course their lives might have taken *if* . . . They
might have been happy together at that moment in Slane *if* . . .

The late Con O'Leary, a popular journalist, described a visit Ledwidge paid him about this time, an account that has been much quoted:

During Easter Week 1916, he was on leave in Manchester and came
to see me. He was very excited and said he was going to Ireland that
night with some wild aspiration of making cause with the rebels.
He was a great friend of one of the leaders, his fellow-poet, Thomas
MacDonagh. On his arrival in Dublin he found contact with the
rebels was impossible. They were hemmed in, swept by a purgatorial

fire. A week later he was in Manchester again, returning to the front. It was the evening of the day on which the executions of Pearse, Clarke and MacDonagh were announced in the House of Commons, when that fierce little campaigner, the late Larry Ginnell, from his place below the gangway, startled Ministers with the taunt 'Huns'. I never saw a man more distressed than Ledwidge was. He had a capacity for deep feeling and that night he wore his heart on his sleeve. He repeated several times the lines from *Cathleen ni Houlihan* which began:

> I will cry with the women
> For yellow-haired Donagh is dead;
> With a hempen rope for a neck-cloth
> And a white clout on his head.

He stayed in my rooms till two o'clock in the morning, talking of many things, but ever reverting to the one sad theme. I saw the pathos of this man wearing the uniform which his friend had taken the field against, and I foresaw the possibility that he, too, might be cut off in his bloom and join his friend in the impartial bivouac of death. Finally, I went some way towards his sister's home with him, and, as we passed the illuminated public clock at the junction of Great Jackson Street, he quoted lines from Padraic Colum:

> The city clocks point out the hours
> They look like moons on darkened towers.

Joe (Frank's brother), however, told me positively that O'Leary's account is inaccurate:

Frank spent Easter Week in a Manchester hospital and was then detained over there because the passenger boat service was not running. As he couldn't get home, he went to stay with my married sister, Mary. He told us later on how much he fretted at the delay because he wanted to spend all his short leave at home.

Paddy Mullen, Matty McGoona's uncle, corroborated. He told me that during Holy Week Matty had received a letter from Ledwidge, written in the Manchester hospital, saying that he hoped to be home soon. Uncle and nephew, who were close enough in age to be companionable, went into Slane together on Easter Monday morning to call at Janeville and find out when Frank was coming. But the family there had no news of him except that he was to come 'any day'. None of them knew that an insurrection had broken out in Dublin that morning. Of course the telephone wires had been cut and no news could come from the city except through people in cars and there were few cars in those days. The only unusual activity Matty and Paddy noticed in Slane was a few sidecars drawn up outside the police barracks. They accompanied Joe to a dance in the village that night, still unaware of the rising.

Dunsany has described in his book *Patches of Sunlight* how he became involved in the Easter Week events in Dublin. The army having given him forty-eight hours' leave for Easter, he and his wife left Derry on Good Friday to spend the holiday at home. Their guests for the weekend were Captain Lindsay and Brigadier-General Hammond. Easter Monday went by in the usual country tranquillity. But on Tuesday morning, when Dunsany came down to breakfast, he found that one of his guests had left. An armoured car had arrived early for Hammond and taken him off to the Curragh. No one had any idea of what was happening in Dublin, but as the rumours were growing hourly more serious, he and Captain Lindsay decided to drive up and find out. When they reached the city, they reported at G.H.Q. and Dunsany was sent to help Major Carter at Amiens Street. He was advised by the military post in the Park not to attempt to cross the city, but he insisted on going by the north quays. The street was barricaded at the Four Courts and he was stopped by the insurgents, who needed his car.

They stood up from behind the barrels with their rifles already at their shoulders, with the bayonets fixed and the scabbards still on the bayonets, and as soon as they were standing they began to fire. I got out and lay down in the road and many bullets went by me before I was hit. The chauffeur was shot at the wheel, but not fatally.

A bullet hit Dunsany in the nose, lodging in the wall of the antrum. He was then disarmed by the insurrectionists and taken to Jervis Street hospital. Later he was transferred to the King George V Hospital, where the bullet was extracted. He was discharged from hospital during the second week of May and went home on a month's sick leave.

In the meantime, people in Meath had been reading an extraordinary deflation of the rising. The *Drogheda Independent* of 29 April did not disguise its contempt:

Since Monday last the people of Ireland have been hearing of strange doings in Dublin—a 'rising' of the Sinn Fein Volunteers, street disturbances, and such like. It would appear that an armed conjunction of the Liberty Hall heroes, with some of the Sinn Fein Volunteers, has made an attempt at some kind of miserable rising. The King's troops and the police force have now got the Larkinites and the Sinn Feiners well in hand, and the ridiculous 'rising' has been crushed and broken.

Elsewhere in the same number, the happenings of Easter Monday are described as 'a madcap escapade, lunatic folly, a gallows-trap, a Dublin street brawl'. The Sinn Feiners are dismissed as the merest handful and a miserable minority. To readers of today, this will sound like a classic of journalistic obtuseness, but one must always remember that it expressed the majority reaction at the time.

The *Meath Chronicle*, however, was more percipient. It devoted an editorial to the events of Easter Week, calling them 'A Tragic Blunder' and conceding: 'No one, we feel sure, can refuse a tribute to these gallant young fellows who harkened to the call of duty to fight against desperate odds for the liberation of their country.'

Ledwidge would not have been unduly influenced by such accounts. He knew that the *Drogheda Independent* was behind Redmond and that to belittle the rising would be its consistent policy. He had not to be told by the *Chronicle* that the rebels were gallant. He had been a Volunteer himself and he knew the fierce honesty of their patriotism better than any journalist.

The public transport services were not back to normal schedule until 10 May and that is about the date when Ledwidge arrived home. His appearance in Slane was a local sensation. Mrs Joseph Ledwidge, then a little girl, told me she remembers seeing a large group in the middle of the Square one morning, all laughing and talking. Curious to find out what was up, she ran to the outskirts of the crowd and saw Frank in the middle of it giving a humorous account of his experiences.

The *Meath Chronicle* of 13 May, under the heading 'Meath Poet-Soldier Among the Serbians', announced his return:

Mr Francis Ledwidge, the gifted Meath poet, who joined the Inniskilling Fusiliers, and who has been on active service for the past year, and at present home on leave, speaking to our representative, remarked: 'The Serbians impressed me very much. I consider Serbia, poetically, like Ireland—a poor old woman wandering the roads of the world.' In the course of further conversation he stated that they found strips of cloth in some of the Serbian houses bearing in faded letters the word *Welcome* .Those cloths had been hung across the streets. 'While in the Dardanelles', he said, with a smile, 'we were not short of cigs. The Turks exchanged cigs with us for beef and biscuits. If I give you more information I'll have nothing left for the book I am going to write on my experiences out there.'

The outstanding aspect of his brother's homecoming in Joe's memory was the newly minted poem on Thomas MacDonagh that he read out to them the first evening. He could talk of nothing else. The family wanted to hear about his war experience, but he brushed aside their queries. The poem was 'the thing that mattered'. He told them he would have to see Dunsany at once to find out whether he passed it for publication. Later he was elated when Dunsany liked the poem and agreed to include it in his next book.

THOMAS MACDONAGH

He shall not hear the bittern cry
In the wild sky, where he is lain,
Nor voices of the sweeter birds
Above the wailing of the rain.

Nor shall he know when loud March blows
Thro' slanting snows her fanfare shrill,
Blowing to flame the golden cup
Of many an upset daffodil.

But when the Dark Cow leaves the moor,
And pastures poor with greedy weeds,
Perhaps he'll hear her low at morn
Lifting her horn in pleasant meads.

Ledwidge had begun to model his verse on Irish poetry, using the metre with the *aicill*-rhyme, from the end of one line to the middle of the next. He probably learnt this from Douglas Hyde's *Love Songs of Connacht*, and *The Literary History of Ireland*. The poem is also a moving recall to the executed leader's translation from the Irish of the poem *The Yellow Bittern*. John Drinkwater described it as 'Ledwidge's first encompassing of profound lyric mastery', 'a poem of that limpid austerity that comes only from minds slowly but irresistibly disciplined to truth'. As in the case of all artists, Ledwidge's craft is seen here in the process of being perfected by suffering.

In a letter to me from Mrs Thomas Dillon, formerly Geraldine Plunkett, sister of the executed Joseph Plunkett, she says she 'remembers Thomas MacDonagh talking about him to my brother Joe and praising his work very highly. He was anxious to bring Ledwidge into his own circle. He thought Ledwidge had been far too isolated and without criticism from other poets'.

In Dublin he mingled with the crowds who gathered in O'Connell Street every day to stare at the still-smoking ruins. The newspaper reports of the devastation said that from the Pillar to the quays on both sides, all the buildings were gone, leaving only a mass of rubble. The walls and portico were all that was left of the Post Office, but from the gutted interior smoke was still rising into the air. The Imperial Hotel opposite had also been demolished, but the name in gilt letters still remained on the front wall. The Metropole Hotel and the whole block of which it formed part had disappeared, leaving a debris of bricks and stones. The statues of Nelson and O'Connell remained intact. Ledwidge wrote eight lines of verse on his brooding:

O'CONNELL STREET

A noble failure is not vain
But hath a victory its own
A bright delectance from the slain
Is down the generations thrown.

And, more than Beauty understands
Has made her lovelier here, it seems;
I see white ships that crowd her strands,
For mine are all the dead men's dreams.*

Yes, indeed, he could claim that their dreams had been his, too.

At home he tried to resume the life he had so greatly longed for in foreign countries. He dropped into the Conyngham Arms at night and picked up the threads of old friendships. This is where he used to enjoy relaxing in congenial company, a couple of drinks putting him into sparkling conversational form. But his friends found him changed. He had become morose; it was difficult to get him to talk about his army experiences. He had been completely disillusioned. He told Joe: 'If I heard the Germans were coming in over our back wall, I wouldn't go out now to stop them. They could come!'

* Unpublished poem in the Dunsany papers.

157

He made no attempt to see Lizzie. She had by this time left the Farrellys' home and had taken up what she considered more attractive employment in Dun Laoghaire, near enough for Ledwidge to have been able to arrange a meeting if he wanted it. Almost perversely, he seemed to prefer to live with his grief.

May was a warm, sunny month that year but to Ledwidge there was a shadow on the bright days. Slane in early summer was full of memories of Ellie; every turn of the road proclaimed his loss. He stood again in the trysting place commemorated in the poem *Evening in May*. She was the beloved of those other verses:

> The light of one fair face that fain would stay
> Upon the heart's broad canvas . . .

She had haunted him in the mountain camp of Serbia, but here there was no escape from memory. Ellie was so much part of summertime in Meath that the May scene was desolate without her.

He tried to work at his poetry, but the shadow was there too. The war showed no signs of ending and that meant he would probably have to return to active service. His poem *The Dream of Artemis* concludes with the lines:

> Oh, Artemis, what grief the silence brings!
> I hear the rolling chariot of Mars!

Elsewhere in the poem he refers to the 'grey future' and wistfully speaks of himself at home as 'an exile in Arcadia'.

The tide of public sympathy began to turn in favour of the insurrection even during his leave in Slane. The *Meath Chronicle* recovered from its first numbness and came out clearly on the side of the rebels. It proudly claimed that Pearse's poem of farewell to his mother was first published in its columns. It reported anecdotes of Easter Week and after. The insurgents had answered field-guns with rifles, cooled with oil from sardine tins. Father M'Cabe, the Carmelite Prior, going into Jacob's Factory to remonstrate with the men: 'Do you think a fly can fight an elephant?' he asked them. They listened to him gravely but ignored his appeal. MacDonagh's sister, a nun, summoned by soldiers to see her brother before his execution. 'She bore up bravely and said her brother was happy and "glad to die for Ireland" '. Joseph Plunkett's marriage to Grace Gifford just before he was led out to be executed, 'We want her to know that our deepest love and sympathy are with the poor, brave young thing.'

Ledwidge had been ordered to report in Derry on 18 May. But as he had lost days waiting in Manchester for a passenger boat to sail, he felt that an extension of leave was due to him. He went to Richmond Barracks to arrange for this extension. It was a changed barracks from the place he had known. Used by the British as one of their five main garrisons during the insurrection, here is where Pearse, MacDonagh, Ceannt and others had been sentenced. The smell of their untimely death seemed to assail the nostrils of the sensitive poet. The officer before whom he was brought curtly refused any extension and made some offensive reference to the rising. Ledwidge told him angrily that when he fought on two battlefronts, he had been fighting for Ireland's freedom. This led to some acrimonious exchanges. The officer said he would report Ledwidge to Derry where he would be dealt with in due course. On his journey north, although he was already late, Ledwidge stopped at Belfast to see Christie.

When the latter was discharged from the army, as soon as he was able to walk without crutches, he studied dentistry. He was at this period living with his family at Duncairn Gardens, Belfast. The two friends had a happy reunion. They had not met since the night the poet had picked up Christie on the Suvla Bay battlefield. The hours sped while they talked. Ledwidge confided to Christie an account of what had happened in Richmond Barracks. Christie's comment on Frank's plain speaking was:

All this only a few weeks after British soldiers had been shot down in Dublin! The trouble that Frank was now heading for was due to his talk. Need I say that there was no right or wrong in any opinion expressed unless it was one hundred per cent loyal.

Ledwidge found it hard to tear himself away from his Belfast friends. Mrs Christie invited him to stay with them for a few nights. He was just explaining to her that he was already two weeks overdue in Derry when another visitor arrived, Stanley Prosser, a friend of Christie's, who was a music teacher, well read and versatile, one of the Belfast literary and artistic circle. His brother-in-law was James Craig, the landscape painter, among his friends were Padraic Gregory, the poet, and Forrest Reid, the novelist. Prosser was glad to meet Ledwidge and soon he, too, was urging the poet to stay another night. Ledwidge gave in.

Christie, too, by this time had become completely disillusioned with the war and army life. He was very glad to be finished with it and urged Ledwidge to seek for a discharge on medical grounds. Ledwidge shook his head; he was all right again except for a weak back.

So I made him lie down on the couch and with my newly acquired medical knowledge, I told him where to show reaction when the doctor examined him. 'When he presses here, just where my hand is now, remember, you're to give an almighty yell. If you do that, no doctor on earth can send you back to active service.' But he only laughed at me; he said he would have to get an honourable discharge. His sympathies were with the men who had risen in Dublin, so I told him that if he wanted to join the hill-men, I would even get him the clothes, but he shook his head again. It was against his principles to desert.

They arranged a code to defeat the censor: 'good news for Mollie' would mean that he had been given his discharge. Promising Christie to send him this good news soon, Ledwidge left with him an old exercise, and a book he had been reading in the train, Patrick McGill's *Children of the Dead End*. He said he would be back soon to claim them. They would have happy times together yet writing that play about Corney Noggins.

He wrote to his friend the following day:

> 5 Co., Ebrington Barracks,
> Derry. 2nd June 1916

My dear Bob,

I have not much news for you yet awhile. I got back here all right, and hope to work the oracle. My back is still bad, but the doctor gave me light duty today and tomorrow. That means, as you know, an hour's standing and a backsheesh drink. Some day you will be writing to Mollie that all is well.

Remember me many times to your dear mother and father, nor forget to mention to your sisters and brothers-in-law that I wish to be remembered to them. I shall never forget your mother's kindness to me, while, a self-invited guest, I stopped at your house. I won't promise her a Turkish carpet as I did Mrs Carter, but I promise her a warm corner in my memory always.

Prosser and a lady of the Literary Society came to see me off at the Great Northern. I think more of that than Prosser can ever know. He is a splendid boy and I consider it a great honour to be recognized by him. I had several letters here already, but then I should be here fourteen days ago and yet expect to be called upon for an account of my absence. But my trust is in Dunsany when he comes on Monday. I will write to you often letting you know my progress.

Somebody from Derry who has been expecting me here is to call to see me tonight. I wonder who he be!!

Now dear Bob remember me all around my new friends and tell your mother I actually cried in the train.

But when Dunsany returned he could do little for him.

Ledwidge was not in my Company and I was glad of that, for his movements had a little of the unpredictable nature of will-o-the-wisps roaming bogs of the land that he loved; as you might expect of a poet in a lance-corporal's uniform. One day he had a bit of a night out, and I was too much annoyed to feel very sympathetic about the trouble in which it landed him, for it looked as if he was almost deliberately harming his own prospects. Being a lance-corporal, and not a private soldier, it landed him in a court-martial; and I said to Major Willock, who was president of the court-martial, 'You will go down to posterity as an afflicter of poets.' Major Willock was quite distressed but found no way of avoiding sentencing Ledwidge to lose his lance-corporal's stripe.

(*Patches of Sunlight*)

According to Christie, however, Ledwidge was court-martialled for overstaying his leave and for insubordinate talk and behaviour in the presence of the commanding officer in Dublin to whom he had applied for an extension. Irishmen—he said—received rough treatment in the British Army after Easter Week, especially those from the Twenty-six Counties.

Ledwidge's own comment on the episode is given in his poem *After Court Martial*:

> My mind is not my mind, therefore
> I take no heed of what men say,
> I lived ten thousand years before
> God cursed the town of Nineveh.

> The Present is a dream I see
> Of horror and loud sufferings,
> At dawn a bird will waken me
> Unto my place among the kings.

And though men called me a vile name,
And all my dream companions gone,
'Tis I the soldier bears the shame,
Not I the king of Babylon.

The name flung at him was probably *traitor* and the episode was no joke to the accused.

Ledwidge's visit had stimulated Christie to write poetry again. He began sending his verses to Derry for his friend's approval. Ledwidge was always generous in literary encouragement. He wanted all his friends to end up as immortals in the Hall of Fame. The following letter is characteristic:

21st June 1916

My dear Bob,

Very many thanks for your letter and copies of poems. The poem: 'Where be to be ups and downs, etc.' is charming. I wish I could tell you how much it delights me. It is much better than the *Drover* poem, beautiful as that is. 'All that I lost was a wee blue tin,' is a line which has written itself in my memory. Were the tin a *white* tin the line had no charm, but as it is it is fresh and pure—and I know how much old women like tins painted over. You have achieved the chief achievement.

A few lines of the Drover love song to my ear are slightly out of tune. A word here and there will add the missing pulses, may I do this and then send the two off to Hone for publication in the anthology of which I told you? From my heart I congratulate you, and you should know ere now I am always sincere in my appreciation, or criticism.

I am afraid the insurance people are right. You can't get treatment from their doctor, but are entitled to periodical visits from him and free certificates. Let me know all the correspondence which passes between you. I am going on with the good news for Mollie. I shall certainly go up to see you on a very near weekend and talk once more of things that matter.

Remember me to your dear mother and all the friends I found at your house. I am busy enough writing away, as ideas will keep coming on. Write now and let me know anything further. Tell me how your leg is. Joe and Annie were asking for you. Congratulations again on your recent poems.

Christie answered by return. He was in a tangle about insurance and his army pension. Ledwidge's past experience in the Meath Labour Insurance had made him knowledgeable in such matters. He immediately reassures his friend:

My dear Bob,

I must look up matters and see how far the Insurance Act applies to wounded soldiers. No doubt certain amendments have been made since the outbreak of the War. But you won't come off too badly. I am glad to know you are in such form for writing. Inspiration comes in spasms and it is worth months of inactivity to get an occasional week or two of what you are having now. I think I told you before that poets should always wait until the gods say 'Write!' and not try to do things when their souls are not *en rapport* with the divinities who dictate in their own good time.

I can't say what date Maunsell's anthology comes out. I have fallen out with them about my two poems and unless they concede to my wishes regarding their publication, I shall hardly hear from them again. They made me a mean offer which I promptly declined. You should send your two poems to 'New Ireland' for publication as they will best be understood there. I will send you back copies of them with slight revisions in the verses of the *Drover* on tomorrow. You have become a great man and shall still become greater. I have written a lot recently. I must send you copies of my late stuff tomorrow. I certainly expect to see you very soon. I haven't a minute to spare as I am busy finishing my autumn volume as well as writing 'pot boilers' for English weeklies.

Remember me to your dear mother and sisters and brothers-in-law, also to Orpheus Prosser.

When Dunsany was sent by the army authorities from Basingstoke camp to Ebrington barracks, Derry, he rented a house there for his wife. They gave Ledwidge a room where he had privacy to work whenever he could get away from the barracks. Here he sorted the poems written since his first volume went to the publishers and, with Dunsany's guidance, made a selection of thirty-nine, which he revised. Like his first collection the second group are strongly autobiographical. The headings gave his war itinerary to date: *At Home, In Richmond Barracks, In Basingstoke Camp, At Sea, In Serbia, In Greece, In Hospital in Egypt, In Ebrington Barracks.* But they only indirectly commemorate his military experience. This is conveyed in the title, *Songs of Peace.*

Since he contributed nothing to war poetry as such, he cannot be accurately described as a war poet.

His allegiance was to nature. He excelled in minute observation of the landscape of Meath and as it changed with the seasons, he brought it to life in his poetry with great descriptive power. But to acclaim him merely as a pastoral poet would be a disservice. When he devoted his lyrical gifts to the theme of love, he was successful, too. War proved to be a cruel assault on his gentle nature. As we have seen, during his first two months on active service, his mind was too stunned and bruised to rise above the horrors around him. Later, when he had recovered his poise and attuned himself to the tragedy of his involvement, he never saw anything in war but waste and futility. He tended to recoil from it even in his verse.

Preparing his second book was absorbing work and while Dunsany and he were engaged on it, they could shut out the menace shaping their lives. Ledwidge made selection difficult because he was always writing new verse and was usually excited about the latest he had written. Moreover, the events of Easter Week had shaken him. 'Things were touched in him,' said Robert Farren, 'that nothing had touched before, and his birthright began at last to serve his verse.' The year 1916 obsessed him in Derry. He wrote no less than twenty poems on the insurrection, of which four appear in his second volume.

Ledwidge thus at work under Dunsany's roof, however, was a different man from Ledwidge in the mess among his fellow soldiers. Sam Hughes of Londonderry sent me the following account:

I received this information from my brother George and from John McLaren, who survived the war and died in 1950. McLaren was possibly Ledwidge's closest friend in the company. Though a labouring man, he was widely read in his country's history and traditions. His gay, carefree disposition endeared him to Ledwidge as it did to all who knew him in later life. He did not join up until he was in his mid-thirties, so he was older than Ledwidge. My brother, George, was, like Ledwidge, a corporal. I do not think they were intimate, but George took pride in knowing the poet and their habits were in much the same mould. After their return from the Balkans in the spring of 1916, they were posted to Ebrington Barracks, Derry, to the 3rd (Reserve) Battalion of the 'Skins'. The 1916 Rising caused Ledwidge a great deal of mental suffering, as he knew many of its leading spirits. Possibly it was a sense of loyalty to his

C.O., Lord Dunsany, who, I understand, sponsored his poems, that prevented him deserting, like a few other bolder spirits, to the 'hill-men'—which was how the dug-out element among the N.C.O.s in the barracks referred to the rebels.

I think the atmosphere of the Mess would have been inimical to Ledwidge and discouraged any ideas of promotion for which he seemed fitted since, on McLaren's account, he was neat and soldier-like in his appearance and did not find the discipline unduly irk-some.

Ledwidge was moody and withdrawn at this period, but respected as an educated man and for his service at the Dardanelles. Every pay-night, as if to atone for his aloofness during the week, he spent his entire pay in treating his room mates. This was an unfailing ritual and the company 'hards' made a point of trailing him, he was then very talkative and usually ended up hilariously drunk. It is recalled how he once sought to explain the motives of the Sinn Feiners, then an unknown and suspected German force, to a hostile audience of Orange and Redmondite tipplers.

He lost his stripe several times but seemed indifferent. Promotion to a mess full of dug-out bullying, drill instructors was repellent to him. My brother, George, was also stripped for drunkenness and for an additional offence—striking a superior officer, that is, a military policeman. This landed him in Arbour Hill Detention Barracks. From Tom Jarvis, a fellow defaulter, I learn that hardly had they be-gun their sentences than they were bundled off to France for the coming offensive. George died of wounds on the 5th December 1917, and is buried at Ljssenthoek Military Cemetery, Poperinghe. Perhaps this is not relevant, but it shows the 'N.C.O. one day, private the next day' atmosphere of the Company.

I feel happy to pay tribute to the memory of those gallant men who, however divided their loyalties, or manifest their failings, showed their country's supreme virtue in dying for a cause.

Corporal John Dick, who knew Ledwidge in Serbia, met him again in Derry during the summer of 1916. He sent me his memories of their reunion in the barracks:

We were out together a few times, recalling our experiences in Salonika. I remember one day when we were walking together on Carlisle Road, he stopped at a bookshop window and pointed out to me a few of his books displayed there. Many a time in the barracks room, I would sit on my bed and watch him at his writing. He was a very fast writer and he could fill a foolscap sheet in no time. I remember he told me about the long walks he used to take when he was at home. He told me that his favourite walk when he wanted to think out poems was along by the river, which must have been near his home because he talked about it so much.

Henry Gallagher of Bunbeg, County Donegal, was in the same dormitory as Ledwidge for four months, July to October 1916, and also sent me his recollections. While working in England, Gallagher had been conscripted at the age of twenty-six into the Royal Inniskilling Fusiliers and drafted to Derry for training. He remembers Ledwidge as:

> dark-featured, of medium height, very athletic in appearance; a good soldier in dress, bearing and discipline; also a brave one because he had been invalided home from Gallipoli and Serbia before coming to Derry. There was a great deal of fuss made of him in the barracks because he was a poet. He was addicted to drink and lost his corporal's stripe for this reason. He often talked about the Easter Week Rising and said since it happened he regretted having joined the Army. He was really a great Irishman and his heart was with the men of 1916.

Ledwidge's health was restored. His back had improved to almost normal strength. He was able to shoulder a rifle again and attend parades. Unless the war came to a speedy end, he would probably have to fight again. As for 'good news for Mollie', hope of this receded week by week. He left unanswered Christie's eager inquiries.

Summer was over. The first winds of autumn began to whistle keenly around the corners of the hilly streets. The poet fell into a dark, fatalistic mood. He began a number of poems and threw them aside unfinished. Three excerpts from the verse he wrote during the autumn express his mind:

On *War*:

'I call
And shorten your way with speed to me.
I am love and hate and the terrible mind
Of vicious gods . . .'*

* There are many such fragments in the Dunsany papers.

These are his lines on *Fate*:

> These things I know in my dreams,
> The crying sword of Lugh,
> And Balor's ancient eye
> Searching me through,
> Withering my songs
> And my pipe yet new.

In *Song-time is Over*, he wrote:

> You will hear me no more awhile,
> The birds are dumb,
> And a voice in the distance calls
> 'Come,' and 'Come'.

The poems for his second volume were sent off. In the Introduction, Dunsany comments on his favourites and says that the keynote of the collection is devotion to the fields of Meath. He was touched by the poem on *Faughan* because Ledwidge told him no one had ever commemorated its hills, woods and streams that called for praise in verse.

In December General Nivelle had been appointed to the chief command of the French forces. He planned a great new offensive to break through the German lines. The British and French armies were to move into action together. Details were submitted to the British Commander-in-Chief, Sir Douglas Haig, who approved of them. This mighty joint offensive was to end the war. But *every* man was needed. Longer lists were daily posted of those assigned to the Western Front; Ledwidge's name appeared among them in mid-December.

Training and briefing were furiously intensified and then the company were packing up. Ledwidge did not tell Bob Christie that there was no 'good news for Mollie'. A few days' compassionate leave were conceded to the units for France and soon the poet found himself in the train speeding south to Slane.

Joe told me that on the final day of that short leave, all he knew was that his brother had to go that night. In the afternoon he went to the village on an errand and when he was returning from Gallows Hill, a car passed him and he thought he caught a glimpse of Frank sitting beside the driver. Astonished that they had not pulled up to speak to him, he stood staring after it. Dusk was falling, but as the car went up the hill on the Dublin road, he saw the passenger's back view clearly and recognized Frank, a scene etched for ever on the young brother's mind.

A few days later, Frank wrote to him apologizing for his summary departure. He gave the date when his troop-train would pass through Drogheda and said that if Joe could be there, they would have a few minutes' chat. Joe cycled to Drogheda and waited at the station for hours, but no train full of soldiers passed through. He haunted the station again the following day with the same result. No one there knew anything about the movements of troop-trains. They had a sad Christmas in Janeville.

Less than a week after his departure from Slane, Ledwidge was on the mail-boat for England among the throng of pack-laden soldiers. Then he was on a troop-train speeding south, one of the tens of thousands being assembled from all parts of the British Isles for Field-Marshal Haig's big push in the New Year. And now he is lost to our view for he has become a mere speck in the tide of khaki flowing out of Folkestone Harbour across the Channel. It was 26 December 1916.

X

Ledwidge's destination on the Western Front was Picquigny, a village north-east of Amiens. He was back in a nightmare world. The landscape differed in externals from Suvla Bay and Serbia, but it had the same atmosphere of doom. The p.b.i's (poor bloody infantry) as everyone in the army called them, were trapped in a similar plight.

The weather in France and Flanders, unprecedented in its severity, made news all that winter of 1916–17. The temperature remained below freezing point for nearly three months, intensifying the army's difficulties. Water carried up in petrol tins to the front line was frozen by the time it reached the men. The tins had to be stripped off and the solid blocks of ice broken up before they could be melted. Wounded men, waiting to be picked up, quickly died of exposure. The bodies of the dead were found frozen hard.

When Ledwidge reached Picquigny, he and his comrades were placed in reserve behind the lines. He had about a week in which to inure himself to the place before going into battle. He was no longer with the same unit. Having left the remnant of his old division in Salonika, he had now been drafted into B Company, 1st Battalion of the 29th Division, Royal Inniskilling Fusiliers. This division had been on active service at the Western Front for six months and had suffered heavy losses. The new arrivals from Derry had been sent to rebuild its strength.

Ledwidge wanted to survive the war in order to become the great poet of his ambition. It was essential for him to defend his spirit, too; to fortify it against despair was more important to him than saving his body. His single refuge was poetry, 'the thing that mattered'.

A helpful letter reached him at Picquigny from Katherine Tynan, enclosing a favourable review she had written of his *Songs of the Fields*. She, too, was a poet, as well as author and busy journalist. At this period her repute was considerable and her opinion carried weight. In her family home, a farm near Clondalkin, County Dublin, she used to keep open house for writers including Yeats, the Sigersons, Rose Kavanagh and patriots like Michael Davitt and John O'Leary. By 1917 she was married and had a son serving in the war. She had great sympathy for the men at the front. Her friendly gesture to Ledwidge initiated a correspondence between them, afterwards published in her book of reminiscences, *The Years of the Shadow*. His reply is dated 6 January 1917:

> If I survive the war, I have great hopes of writing something that will live. If not, I trust to be remembered in my own land for one or two things which its long sorrow inspired. My book has had a greater reception in England, Ireland and America than I had ever dreamt of, but I never feel that my name should be mentioned in the same breath with my contemporaries.

> You ask me what I am doing. I am a unit in the Great War, doing and suffering, admiring great endeavour and condemning great dishonour. I may be dead before this reaches you, but I will have done my part. Death is as interesting to me as life. I have seen so much of it from Suvla to Serbia and now in France. I am always homesick. I hear the roads calling, and the hills, and the rivers wondering where I am. It is terrible to be always homesick.

The more the horrors of war multiplied around him the more intensely his mind concentrated on remembered beatitude. On the same day that he wrote to Katherine Tynan, he finished a poem about rushes 'that nod so grave by the river', recalling the banks of the Boyne near his home.

His thoughts, too, continually dwelt on Easter Week. The following day, he finished another lament entitled *The Dead Kings*, a long poem of thirty-two lines in which he shows a confident mastery of the Irish internal rhyme technique. Here are three verses:

> All the dead kings came to me
> At Rosnaree, where I was dreaming.
> A few stars glimmered through the morn,
> And down the thorn the dews were streaming.

> And every dead king had a story
> Of ancient glory, sweetly told.
> It was too early for the lark,
> But the starry dark had tints of gold.

And one said: 'A loud tramp of men
We'll hear again at Rosnaree.'
A bomb burst near me where I lay.
I woke, 'twas day in Picardy.

Ledwidge remained in Picquigny only one week and was then
transferred to Carnoy camp, near Trones Wood, still in the Somme
region, where intensive preparations were in progress for another
British assault. This camp consisted of a small group of ugly round
huts known as elephant shelters, isolated at that date in a vast expanse
of snow. On the afternoon of 26 January, the Inniskillings paraded in
this depressing place for their march to the front line. All went well
as far as Ginchy where the road ended and the men had to take to the
duck-board track that wound away for miles over open country.
When trampled soft on the duck-boards, the snow quickly turned into
patches of ice. The infantry were heavily laden with Lewis-gun magazines, tins of water, bags of rations, shovels and other impedimenta.
Whenever the duck-board sloped, they found it impossible to keep
from slipping. Halts were frequently called while they tried tying sandbags over their boots, but the canvas wore out so quickly it was little
use. After a horribly wearisome journey, they reached their line, consisting of a series of shell-holes connected by a shallow trench.

In February the German Army began to withdraw from the Somme
battlefield where costly, indecisive fighting had gone on all through the
summer and autumn of 1916. This change in the disposition of the
forces was noted with hopeful interest by the Allies. It was not a retreat
but a strategic retirement to shorten the German line and conserve man-
power. Withdrawal, however, from the Allies' point of view, was
better than the long deadlock of inconclusive attack and counter-
attack. Reports from war correspondents became more optimistic.

The severe winter favoured the German tactics. The enemy fell back
on solid ground, while the troops following up found themselves bog-
ging down on soil that had been churned into an unspeakable condition. Passable while it remained frozen, even a slight drop in temperature turned the land into a sea of mud into which had been trampled
the horrible debris of innumerable battles.

Philip Gibbs, at that time war correspondent with the *Daily Chronicle*
and *Daily Telegraph*, described it:

Bodies, and bits of bodies, and clots of blood, and green, metallic-
looking slime, made by explosive gases, were floating on the surface

171

of that water below the crater banks. Our men lived there, crouched below the sandbags and burrowed in the sides of the craters. Lice crawled over them in legions. Human flesh, rotting and stinking, mere pulp, was pasted into the mudbanks. If they dug to get deeper cover, their shovels went into the softness of dead bodies who had been their comrades. Scraps of flesh, booted legs, blackened hands, eyeless heads, came falling over them when the enemy trench-mortared their position or blew up a new mine-shaft.

Katherine Tynan's heart had been touched by Ledwidge's mention of loneliness. She sent him a sympathetic letter, a box of sweets, and a copy of her latest book, *Lord Edward*. She says that in his letter of acknowledgement, he enclosed two poems: *In France* and *Had I a Golden Pound to Spend*, and that it was a happier letter than the first one. He told her she was not to think that he was always lonely. He had met a few people out there, too, who cared for 'the only thing that matters'. He had the consolation of letters from home: his mother, brothers, sisters and cousins, all wrote to him. A subsequent letter to her gives 'some indication of his odd ways of writing'.

When I read the proofs of *Songs of Peace* there were several poems I hardly recognised as my own, for I scribble them off in odd moments, and, if I do not give them to someone, they become part of the dust of the earth and little things stuck on the ends of hedges when the wind has done with them. My MSS are scattered about two hemispheres, some lost for ever, others wandering in the corners of newspapers like so many little Abrahams, changing their names as if they had given over an old faith and were set on new endeavours. I lament them in sober moments, and forget them again when some new tune breaks out in my mind.

I wish you would come to Louth. There are charming places about Dundalk and Drogheda, and the people are so beautiful. When I am in Louth I always imagine voices are calling me from one distance to another, and at every turn I half expect to see Cuchullain stride over the hills to meet some new champion of Maeve. You could only be happy in Louth or Meath.

What a pity the birds must suffer as we do! I had a special way of feeding them when I was at home in winter. I used to put potatoes on the garden wall for the crows and under a covering of sacks spread bread and meal for the smaller birds. It was taboo to open the kitchen door, for that would disturb them.

So AE has been telling you of my doings, but he did not know that the poems which I destroyed were very amateurish; and how sick I was of them, for I had repeated them until they became vapid. I try to keep my poems now by sending them to Lord Dunsany, or home, but out here one has not always the time or the convenience and, after all, when the pleasure of writing them has passed, what does it matter? I still have hundreds. My next book will be the best of mine. I may be in Ireland for May Day yet.

Father Devas was among the few congenial people Ledwidge met at this front. The Jesuit father was a poet, too. Ledwidge had already known him at Suvla Bay, where the chaplain had won the D.S.O. for bravery. Now in this new theatre of war, he continued to be a hero to the men. Preferring to stay in the front trenches with them, his steel-hatted figure was always a familiar sight after an engagement, when he went out with a few men to collect the identity discs of the dead, bury them, and if possible, mark their graves.

The German withdrawal went on steadily all through February and the reports from the front continued optimistic. As their army fell back, the German High Command ordered the destruction of the villages where they had been billeted. Wells were rendered useless by filling them with filth; churches were dynamited; bridges blown up; cross-roads mined. Booby-traps consisting of mines and bombs with slow-working fuses, were left in the most unexpected places. The saddest impression on the soldiers was made by the sight of humble little cottages gutted and the apple trees in orchards sawn off within a couple of feet from the ground—all done in the name of military necessity.

The momentum of the retreat slowed down at the end of February and the German Army began to consolidate its new line. The 1st Innis-killings were then transferred farther west to a camp at the village of La Neuville near Corbie. Ledwidge's tour of the trenches brought him back into camp again for the national feast day. In the morning there was an issue of shamrock to all the Irishmen. The Australians, who hap-pened to be going into action that day, also asked for shamrock and wore it in their caps. Most of the forenoon was taken up with a church parade. Then B Company had their photograph taken out of doors. Ledwidge, grim and unsmiling, his mouth set in a straight line, stands fourth from the left in the second row. In the afternoon, the Inniskilling fife and drum band played in the village to the great delight of the

French children, who crowded around them. The men got up a concert for themselves in the afternoon. The officers went into Corbie that night for dinner. The rations were greatly stepped up in honour of the feast and there was a good dinner, too, in the mess, after which most of the men also went into town to sample the *estaminets*. These kept open very late, as they did on Christmas Day. Despite the army concessions, however, commemorating their patron saint in such a setting inevitably made the Irishmen melancholy.

In the last week of March the 1st Battalion was sent northwards towards the city of Arras, then in British hands. They had to march continuously, sixteen to eighteen miles a day, for two weeks. When they were lucky, they spent the night in billets in some village, but they often had to bivouac in the open. The whole countryside was still locked in the grip of winter and it was bitterly cold. April set in with incessant rain.

The United States of America declared war on Germany on 3 April 1917. This guarantee of substantial help on its way gave new hope to the Allies of a speedy end to the war. The morale of the troops improved along the whole battle-front.

Arras was now in everyone's mouth as word filtered down the ranks that the next big battle they were preparing for would be launched from that city. Even the men on duty in the trenches had to help in the preparations for the big push. Enormous quantities of bombs had to be transported to the front line. As Ledwidge's unit approached Arras, they, too, had to help with the hauling of trench mortar bombs.

The region for which the opposing armies were now preparing to contend was the coal-mining district of the Artois, a tableland of pit-heads, slack-heaps and workmen's villages, diversified by little wooded hills and copses. Designed with military simplicity, the miners' settlements were readily turned into crown-works of fortification and as such the German Army had been quick to take advantage of them. They had seized this great system of forts, partly natural and partly built for peacetime industrial purposes, and strengthened them with all their military skill in their first big advance in 1914. Since that time they had successfully resisted every attempt by the British and French to dislodge them.

An Allied assault on this important position was planned for Easter Sunday, 9 April, to be launched from Arras. Underneath the almost ruined city was an ancient, complicated system of cellars, passages and large vaults used by the merchants for stores. This network of ready-made trenches was taken over by the British engineering corps, cleared, deepened and lengthened. The original passages were carried forward until they extended almost to the German front line.

Ledwidge's unit reached Arras in the first few days of April and joined the thousands of infantry already assembled underground. By this time the Germans were of course well aware that an attack was imminent. They shelled Arras continually, concentrating on the supply roads into the city, the station, barracks, streets and squares. Scarcely a house was left standing.

In addition to the huge concentration of soldiers, there were about seven hundred women and children living in the cellars. When the British took the city, these refugees would not leave as they had nowhere to go. The subterranean tunnels were better than the open road during that terrible winter.

Here Ledwidge became acquainted for the first time with massive artillery bombardment, always the prelude to a big infantry advance on the Western Front. Nothing exposed to that concentration of heavy gunfire could live overground. The unceasing, ear-splitting roar was harrowing to the nerves of the combatants on both sides.

The regimental history describes the bombardment before the battle of Arras:

> A fierce flame crackled and ran like chain-lightning for fifteen miles along our front. A thousand and more guns, from the giant 15-inch howitzers to the 18-pounders, began to discharge shells at the German positions. There were brought into action high-explosive shells of terrible power and instantaneous detonation, monster shells which would deliver their shattering message at the touch of a bird's wing, or of a single strand of wire; which did not wreck trenches, but obliterated them; which did not cut lanes through wire entanglements, but dissipated them into dust.

The soldiers waiting under the city felt their underground world vibrating in the bombardment, while loose chalk from the ceiling continually flaked down on their heads.

Ledwidge was not sent into action that Easter Sunday, the 29th Division being held back to consolidate the first advance. The weather could not have been worse. The infantry found their progress across the open ground impeded by driving wind and rain. Visibility was reduced to nil. Nevertheless the first wave of assault did well. The Germans were driven off the important Vimy Ridge and four miles of trenches north and south of the River Scarpe were captured; 11,000 prisoners were taken, including 235 officers.

Philip Gibbs walked through the underground cellars next day and described what he saw, giving us a glimpse of the soldiers among whom was Ledwidge, waiting to be called into action:

> I went through the tunnels when long columns of soldiers in single file moved slowly forward to another day's battle in the fields beyond, and when another column came back, wounded and bloody after their morning's fight. The wounded and the unwounded passed each other in these dimly lighted corridors. Their steel hats clinked together. Their bodies touched. Wafts of stale air laden with a sickly stench came out of the vaults. Faint whiffs of poison-gas filtered through the soil above and made men vomit. For the most time the men were silent as they passed each other, but now and then a wounded man would say, 'Oh, Christ!' In vaults dug into the sides of the passages were groups of tunnellers and other men half screened by blanket curtains. Their rifles were propped against the quarried rocks. They sat on ammunition boxes and played cards in the light of candles stuck in bottles, which made their shadows flicker fantastically on the walls. They took no interest in the procession beyond their blankets—the walking wounded and the troops going up. Some of them slept on the stone floors with their heads covered by their overcoats and made pillows of their gas-masks.

The weather became progressively worse. Snow fell on the afternoon of the 11th. There was a heavy snowstorm on the night of the 12th and wind swept the snow into drifts four feet high. On the 13th, a slight thaw melted the snow and flooded the tunnels. The ground above was like a marsh. Ledwidge's unit was summoned out of the cellars that day to support the line east of Monchy-le-Preux. This town had been knocked about here and there but most of it was still standing. The Inniskillings turned the cellars into dug-outs and in one of these Ledwidge cowered with his comrades under streets choked with unburied dead and the dead horses of a cavalry regiment.

The initial gains at the battle of Arras proved a costly victory. On sectors of the fifteen-mile line, the Germans counter-attacked seven and eight times. Rivers of blood were shed. Many of the wounded were suffocated in the mud where they fell. The stretcher-bearers sank to their knees in it, carrying their burdens shoulder-high.

Mutiny broke out in the French Army during the third week of

April. Eight French divisions refused to obey the orders of the High Command in protest against the reckless and futile expenditure of life. This news was kept from the British ranks. It meant for them longer spells of duty in the trenches and shorter periods of rest between orders to advance.

The seasons had become freakish. There was no transition between the wintry conditions of April and the excessive heat of summer. Temperatures rose suddenly at the end of April and May was unusually warm. The water dried out of the shell-craters and trenches; the mud turned to dust. Summer flowed over the land.

Back in reserve again, Ledwidge wrote to Katherine Tynan on 31 May:

> I would have written to thank you for the sweets, only that lately we were unsettled, wandering to and fro between the firing-line and resting billets immediately behind. This letter is ante-dated by two hours, but before midnight we may be wandering in single and slow file, with the reserve line two or three hundred yards behind the fire trench. We are under an hour's notice. Entering and leaving the line is most exciting, as we are usually but about thirty yards from the enemy, and you can scarcely understand how bright the nights are made by his rockets. These are in continual ascent and descent from dusk to dawn, making a beautiful crescent from Switzerland to the sea. There are white lights, green, and red, and whiter, bursting into red and changing again, and blue bursting into purple drops and reds fading into green. It is all like the end of a beautiful world. It is only horrible when you remember that every colour is a signal to waiting reinforcements of artillery and God help us if we are caught in the open, for then up go a thousand reds, and hundreds of rifles and machine-guns are emptied against us, and all amongst us shells of every calibre are thrown, shouting destruction and death. We can do nothing but fling ourselves into the first shell-hole and wonder as we wait where we will be hit.
>
> I am indeed glad to think you are preparing another book of verse. Will you really allow me to review it? I don't want money for doing it. The honour would be worth more than money. I reviewed Seumas O'Sullivan's poems a few years ago, and hope I helped him a little to a wider public, though he has not yet the fame he deserves. His very name is a picture to me of lakes and green places, rivers and willows, and wild things. *You* give me a picture of a long lane, with

many surprises of flowers, a house hidden in trees where there is rest, and beyond that mountains where the days are purple, and then the sea. AE sets me thinking of things long forgotten, and Lord Dunsany of gorgeous Eastern tapestry and carpets. Do you get such impressions from the books you love? I met a traveller in Naples who told me that he never reads Andrew Marvell but he remembers a dunce's cap and a fishing-rod he had when a boy, and never could trace the train of thought far enough back to discover where the connection lay.

I am writing odd things in a little book whenever I can. Just now I am engaged on a poem about the *Lanawn Shee*, who, you remember, is really the Irish Muse. One who sees her is doomed to sing. She is very close to you. I am writing it in the traditional style of 'The Silk of the Kine'. She tries many devices to woo a lover and to secure his pity, laments one who loved her for long but who left her for earth, 'fairer than Usna's youngest son'. If I do not tire you, I will read it all some day (D.V.). It is time I remembered you would be weary of this letter and will close with regret.

He enclosed the poem:

Ascension Thursday, 1917

Lord, Thou has left Thy footprints in the rocks,
That we may know the way to follow Thee,
But there are wide lands opened out between
Thy Olivet and my Gethsemane.

And oftentimes I make the night afraid,
Crying for lost hands when the dark is deep
And strive to reach the sheltering of Thy love
Where Thou art herd among Thy folded sheep.

Thou wilt not ever thus, O Lord, allow
My feet to wander when the sun is set,
But through the darkness, let me still behold
The stony bye-ways up to Olivet.

He also sent Katherine Tynan in the same letter seventeen lines of the *Lanawn Shee*.

Every time he got away from the firing-line in the following week, he continued to work at this, one of the longest of his poems, running to twenty-seven four-line verses. It describes the poet meeting the Gaelic Muse of Poetry in the form of a beautiful maiden, singing beside a stream in Meath. She tells him about *Tir na n'Og*, an earthly paradise, many of whose denizens mourn human loves. She then confides to the poet her own pathetic story. While concentrating on this poem, Ledwidge had such a vivid dream of Ellie that he believed it portended his death. He told Dunsany his premonition in a letter enclosing the poem. In the final verses, the subject moves from the legendary Muse to the real woman he is still mourning:

> From hill to hill, from land to land,
> Her lovely hand is beckoning for me,
> I follow on through dangerous zones,
> Cross dead men's bones and oceans stormy.
> Some day I know she'll wait at last
> And lock me fast in white embraces,
> And down mysterious ways of love
> We two shall move to fairy places.

There is hardly need to underline Ledwidge's marked psychic character, or mention that he believed in telepathy. He inflicted his dreams on all his friends, speculating on their meaning. His brother, Joe, told me a story in this connection. One day they were cycling together along an empty country road when Frank began to recount his strange dream of the night before. Joe lost patience and did not want to hear it; he was tired of dreams. 'Well, I'll tell you one thing,' said Frank. 'A boy will come over the brow of that hill in a moment.' He then repeated the conversation that would take place. Joe tossed his head in disbelief and they pedalled on in silence. A few minutes later, a boy appeared in the far distance. As he came abreast, Frank greeted him and asked him some questions to which he got the exact answers he had predicted. 'After that', concluded Joe, 'I had no more to say.'

Early in June, Ledwidge received an enquiry from an American admirer, Professor Lewis Nathaniel Chase of the University of Wisconsin, asking for biographical information and poems to use in a series of lectures he was giving on contemporary poets. Fortunately Ledwidge was free to reply on the day the enquiry reached him. A number of excerpts have already been taken from his lengthy answer and used in chronological order throughout this book.

> B.E.F.
> France, 6th June 1917

Your letter of May 15th reached me this afternoon. I have to thank you for introducing my books into your library and for the interest which you take in my poems and will endeavour to supply you with what details you require of myself and my work for the composition of your proposed lecture. You will, of course, understand that I am writing this under the most inept circumstances between my watches, for I am in the firing line and may be busy at any moment in the horrible work of war. I am on active service since the Spring of 1915, having served in the Dardanelles and the first British expeditionary force to Serbia and after a brief interval at home came to France in December 1916.

I am sorry that party politics should ever divide our own tents but am not without hope that a new Ireland will arise from her ashes in the ruins of Dublin, like the Phoenix, with one purpose, one aim, and one ambition. I tell you this in order that you may know what it is to me to be called a British soldier while my own country has no place amongst the nations but the place of Cinderella.

I set myself certain studies and these I pursued at night when I should have been resting from a laborious day. I read books on logic and astronomy and could point out the planets and discuss the nebulae of the Milky Way. I read and studied the poets of England from the age of Chaucer to Swinburne, turning especially to the Elizabethans and the ballads that came before the great renaissance. I thirsted for travel and adventure and longed to see the Italy of Shelley and the Greece of Byron. But the poems of Keats and his sad life appealed to me most. I began to pick faults with Longfellow and Tennyson, and the poems of the former which had erstwhile pleased me seemed too full of colour, too full of metaphor and often too disconnected, like a picture which an artist began at one window and finished at another. Tennyson was too conventional for my taste and nearly always spoiled his work with a prologue, or an epilogue, full of loud bombast or conceit. Shelley was innocent of such sins and poor Keats never heard of them. For a long time I did little but criticize and re-arrange my books, separating as it were the sheep from the goats. I put Longfellow and Tennyson at the back of the shelf and gave Keats, Swinburne, Shelley and the anthologies the foremost place in the light. I burned many copy-books which contained fugitive pieces of my own because I thought it were better for them to die young and be happy than live to be reviled.

My taste, I think, became extremely acute and I was more inclined to blow warm and cold over such works as Yeats' than sit to admire as I do now. I have never met Yeats but I hope to one day for I have much to say to him. I don't think he has quite ever reached the hearts of the people and if any of his works live it will be his early poems on Maeve and Cuchullain. If you remember his earlier works you will agree with me in saying that the revisions which he made in them in later years have robbed them of much enchantment. I agree that many of his far-fetched metaphors required elucidation, but, in attempting this, he has not always been successful. Take for instance two lines which appeared in the first version of *The Wanderings of Ossian*:

Empty of purple hours as a beggar's cloak in the rain
As a grass seed crushed by a pebble, or a wolf sucked under a weir.

I always pointed out these similes as the most ludicrous of Yeats. They do not illustrate his meaning, and were probably written in a rainstorm in a moment certainly happy for rhyme, not for reason. In the revised edition it reads:

As a haycock out on the flood, etc.

which is better because it gives you a picture of things adrift, of loneliness and the beauty of a cataclysm. This is the single exception in his work of where his second thoughts were better than his inspiration. I am afraid Masefield is getting this bad habit also. When his *Dauber* appeared first in *The English Review*, I was struck by a wonderful line in the kitchen scene of which Dauber spoke. His sister was dusting and

A wagging corner of the duster flicked

but when it appeared in book-form this line was replaced by another which had no thought. What a pity it is that these men won't remember that they do the Gods' work and not their own. I never revise. It is too dangerous. I can't dictate to the Gods.

Georgian Poetry (with my three excluded) contains, I think, the best poems of the century. What could be sweeter than the songs at the gates of Damascus, or Stephens' *Goat-paths*? It is not always Stephens plucks all flowers but I have not found a weed on the crooked paths that wind every way up the hill.

Of myself: I am a fast writer and very prolific. I have long silences, often for weeks, then the mood comes over me and I must write and write no matter where I be or what the circumstances are.

I do my best work in the Spring. I have had many disappointments in life and many sorrows but in my saddest moment song came to me and I sang. I get more pleasure from a good line than from a big cheque. Tho' I love music I cannot write within earshot of any instrument. I cannot carry a watch on account of the tick, real or imaginary, and might as well try to sleep under the bell of Bruges as in a room where a clock stands. I write a lot late at night in my room, though mostly my poems are written out of doors.

I have been to Naples, Egypt, Greece, Serbia, Spain and France, but in no country have I found a people as wonderful or as strange as my own. I have written many short stories and one play. *The Wife of Llew* was written in a meadow full of flowers and singing birds. *The Lost Ones* was written in a sad mood when I remembered all whom I knew and who were lost and away for ever. I wanted someone to console me by assuring me that beyond the dark they would meet me again.

My favourite amongst my own are always changing. Of my published works, I perhaps like *Thomas MacDonagh* best. Better work than any you have yet seen from me is being selected for my next book, but my best is not yet written. I mean to do something really great if I am spared, but out here one may at any moment be hurled beyond life.

He enclosed with the letter two poems: *With Flowers* and *Pan*.

Ledwidge wrote again to Katherine Tynan on the 19 June. The soldiers in reserve were now basking in radiant summer weather. Behind the lines, conditions were often idyllic. His letter is full of this contrast:

This is my birthday. I am spending it in a little red town in an orchard. There is a lovely valley just below me, and a river that goes gobbling down the fields, like turkeys coming home in Ireland. It is an idle little vagrant that does no work for miles and miles except to turn one mill-wheel for a dusty old man who has five sons fighting for France. I was down here earlier in the spring and was glad to return again in the sober moments of June. Although I have a conventional residence I sleep out in the orchard, and every morning a cuckoo comes to a tree quite close, and calls out his name with a clear voice above the rest of the morning's song, like a tender stop heard above the lower keys in a beautiful organ.

I am glad to hear the experience of your boy in Macedonia. I had

182

a rather narrow escape above Lake Doiran in the winter of 1915. Ten of us went out to rescue a few sheep which we had discovered on a mountain tip, and we were attacked by a Bulgar force. We sought the cover of rocks in a deep ravine, and we were able to keep the attackers off, although we could not return until help arrived. We secured three sheep, after which we named the battle. I wrote the song of it for *The Sunday Chronicle* in Manchester last year.

I hope he will be duly rewarded for his coolness and bravery, for, after all, is not every honour won by Irishmen on the battlefields of the world Ireland's honour, and does it not tend to the glory and delight of her posterity?

You are in Meath now, I suppose. If you go to Tara, go to Rath-na-Rí and look all round you from the hills of Drumcondrath in the north to the plains of Enfield in the south, where Allen Bog begins, and remember me to every hill and wood and ruin, for my heart is there. If it is a clear day you will see Slane Hill blue and distant. Say I will come back again surely, and maybe you will hear pipes in the grass, or a fairy horn and the hounds of Finn. I have heard them often from Tara. I am greatly afraid your *Lord Edward* will never reach me. My next book is due in October.

It is growing dusk now, it is the 'owls' light', and I must draw to a close.

He enclosed three poems: *The Find, Stanley Hill* and *The Old Gods*.

Ledwidge's birthday, however, was still two months away. He was born on 19 August, not 19 June. Birthdays at that time were—and still are—mostly ignored in rural Ireland and were never celebrated in the Ledwidge family. Anne Ledwidge was the only person who might know the dates when her children were born. But as she had never kept a record, her memory was confused by the time they were grown up. When Ledwidge enlisted, he was asked for the first time in his life to give the date and year of his birth. He referred to her and she scribbled it down on a slip of paper for him which he handed to the recruiting officer; afterwards it was found that she had given Joe's date instead of Frank's.

On 26 June, the first of the American contingents arrived at the Western Front. They were well equipped and accoutred, speaking with a lazy drawl, looking bronzed and fit. The news of their arrival sped along the line bringing new hope. Their presence was a promise of almost unlimited fresh reserves that would certainly turn the tide.

July 1st found Ledwidge writing to Edward Marsh, who was bringing out a third volume of *Georgian Poetry* and was considering for inclusion another selection of Ledwidge's poems. The poet says:

Just now a big strafe is worrying our dug-outs and putting out our candles, but my soul is by the Boyne cutting new meadows under a thousand wings and listening to the cuckoos at Crocknaharna. They say there will be peace soon.

If you visit the Front don't forget to come up the line at night to watch the German rockets. They have white crests which throw a pale flame across no-man's-land and white bursting into green and green changing into blue and blue bursting and dropping down in purple torrents. It is like the end of a beautiful world.

Marsh, however, did not visit the Western Front with Churchill until the following September.

Ledwidge's unit was ordered north at the beginning of July. They marched over the Franco-Belgian border into what they called 'the Ypres salient'. As they travelled, they found every road jammed with troops, trucks of ammunition and an endless procession of powerful guns. It was evident that preparations were being made on a vast scale for another major offensive. When General Nivelle's plan for a decisive break-through had failed, he was relieved of his command and replaced by Marshal Foch. Now the Allied Command had again decided that the French and British armies were to go into action together. The new attack was planned on a line running from Boesinghe, a village about three miles north of the ruined, ghost city of Ypres (where two major battles had already taken place), and continuing on as far as the River Lys, roughly fifteen miles.

Leave was now overdue for the men spending their seventh month on active service. Most of them were worn out. But the progress of the war made leave out of the question. Nevertheless, Ledwidge must have had reason to hope that he would escape the next battle. His thoughts ran in a more optimistic current. This nightmare would end. He had been mourning Ellie for two years. Surely, now, he should move out of the shadows and go forward towards life again? On 12 July he broke his long silence in a letter to Lizzie Healy:

You will be surprised to hear from me again after a silence nearly three years long. The reason I write is because I have been dreaming about you and it has made me rather anxious. I sincerely hope that nothing troubles you in body or soul.

184

It must be quite beautiful on the bog now. How happy you are to be living in peace and quietude where birds still sing and the country wears her confirmation dress. Out here the land is broken up by shells and the woods are like skeletons and when you come to a little town it is only to find poor homeless people lamenting over what was once a cheery home. As I write this a big battle is raging on my left hand and if it extends to this part of the line I will be pulling triggers like a man gone mad.

Please, dear Lizzie, send me a flower from the bog, plucked specially for me. I may be home again soon. In fact I am only waiting to be called home. God send it soon.

Three days after he had sent off that letter, the preliminary bombardment opened for the third battle of Ypres. Soon houses twelve miles behind the lines vibrated in the blasts, the most concentrated, continuous, and ear-splitting yet experienced. When the guns stopped for a brief spell, the silence assailed the ear with a kind of shock. The uproar of the guns was the prelude to a formidable assault, 'the battle which all the world had been expecting' according to Philip Gibbs.

One morning, during a lull in the bombardment, Ledwidge heard a robin singing. He stopped short and listened to the brave trilling until the noisy tumult of the guns roared again and drowned the little roundelay. This inspired the poem *Home*:

> A burst of sudden wings at dawn,
> Faint voices in a dreamy noon,
> Evenings of mist and murmurings,
> And nights with rainbows of the moon.
>
> And through these things a woodway dim,
> And waters dim, and slow sheep seen
> On uphill paths that wind away
> Through summer sounds and harvest green.
>
> This is a song a robin sang
> This morning on a broken tree,
> It was about the little fields
> That call across the world to me.

Back from the firing-line on 20 July, he found Katherine Tynan's book *Lord Edward* waiting in his billet and immediately acknowledged it:

We have just returned from the line after an unusually long time. It was very exciting this time, as we had to contend with gas, lachrymatory shells, and other devices new and horrible. It will be worse soon. The camp we are in at present might be in Tir-na-n'Óg, it is pitched amid such splendours. There is barley and rye just entering harvest days of gold, and meadow-sweet rippling, and where a little inn named *In Den Neerloop* holds its gable up to the swallows, bluebells and goldilocks swing their splendid censers. There is a wood hard by where hips glisten like little sparks, and just at the edge of it mealey leaves sway like green fire. I will hunt for a secret place in that wood to read *Lord Edward*. I anticipate beautiful moments.

I daresay you have left Meath and are back again in the brown wilds of Connaught. I would give £100 for two days in Ireland with nothing to do but ramble on from one delight to another. I am entitled to a leave now, but I'm afraid there are many before my name in the list. Special leaves are granted, and I have to finish a book for the autumn. But, more particularly, I want to see again my wonderful mother, and to walk by the Boyne to Crewbawn and up through the brown and grey rocks of Crocknaharna. You have no idea of how I suffer with this longing for the swish of the reeds at Slane and the voices I used to hear coming over the low hills of Currabwee. Say a prayer that I may get this leave, and give as a condition my punctual return and sojourn till the war is over. It is midnight now and the glow-worms are out. It is quiet in camp, but the far night is loud with our guns bombarding the positions we must soon fight for.

But special leave to a poet because he has a book coming out was only a day-dream. All furlough had now been cancelled until after the battle. The soldiers in their billets talked of nothing else. The air was full of brooding, nervous tension. News had filtered down the ranks that Pilckem Ridge west of Boesinghe was to be the objective. This height had to be carried from the low floats around Ypres. The Allied troops were at the bottom of a saucer and the Germans entrenched on its rim, a disposition of forces not unlike Suvla Bay. But here at Ypres, as his comrades probably reasoned, they at least had the guns, the sheer pressure of which would carry the day.

On 22 July, Ledwidge's thoughts dwelt affectionately on his old friend, Matty McGoona and he wrote the poem, *To One Who Comes Now and Then*, recalling Matty's fiddle-playing in the twilight.

The weather broke during the last week of July. Day after day, the horizon was veiled in a dense mist and cold rain fell incessantly from a dark sky. The contending armies were swallowed up in the gloom of what looked like a Flemish winter. 'By universal consent the Third Battle of Ypres represents the utmost that the war has so far achieved in the way of horrors,' says Gillon:

> The cramped theatre with its slimy canals, becks, sloughs, bogs, and inundations; its shelled duck-board tracks, its isolated outposts, its incessant shelling and incessant rain, its mists and fogs, its corpses and its pestilential, miasmic odours, outdid anything that even the Somme or Arras could boast. The craters were more numerous and the mud deeper. There was also the added horror of mustard gas, which could cling about a dug-out for days in spite of fires. It was lethal but was still more effective as an incapacitator. It was first felt on July 12, 1917, and in ten days had inflicted 3,500 casualties. On the night of 23rd–24th July, in consequence of a steady rain of gas shells, gas masks had to be worn at the batteries for six hours.

July 31 was the date fixed for the attack. On the night of 30 July, hundreds of thousands of men slept out in puddles and mud-holes. Ledwidge was not among them, being still in reserve. It was 3.50 a.m. when they received the signal to go forward in one huge wave of assault—the battle that would end the war.

The results disappointed expectation. The German defences were only dented, not broken; the haul of prisoners was less than had been hoped. Some of the commanders blamed the rain; others the hasty training of the troops. One of the districts seized by the British was called the Boesinghe sector from the village of that name just west of the Ypres Canal.

In his book *The Fading Vision*, John North said:

> Never before have Englishmen been slain at such a rate on such a scale. No High Command in the whole history of war—where success is 'almost in mathematical ratio' to the degree of surprise—can have contributed less in manœuvre, or demanded more in slaughter; its appetite for men to fling into the cauldron of its offensives knew no appeasement: 'I want *Men*,' wrote the Commander-in-Chief at Passchendaele.

It was afterwards calculated that 135,000 men had been killed in one day at this sector for a gain of one hundred yards.

All during the morning of 31 July the tide of wounded flowed back from the front line. Once again the stretcher-bearers had to raise their burdens shoulder-high as they sloshed along. Questioned how the day went, there was not much they could tell. Soldiers in the ranks usually know little about the progress of a battle. All they could say was that the German front line of shell-craters was quickly taken, as it was manned by only scattered outposts. But immediately they found themselves in an inferno of gunfire as wave after wave of Germans came out against them, fighting like tigers.

Ledwidge and his comrades in reserve had been toiling since early morning at road-making. The army's first need was men; their second, guns; their third, roads. These latter consisted mainly of heavy beech planks bolted together, which could be rapidly laid down. No advance could be supported in that sodden land without a sufficiency of these communication tracks, six or seven feet wide. Supplies were conveyed by pack-mules over the wooden paths. Survivors concur in placing the road-work done by B Company that day one mile north-east of Hell Fire Corner, so called because it was very exposed to German shelling.

There was a violent rainstorm in the afternoon, shrouding the region in a grey monochrome. Sullenly, the enemy's long-range guns continued to fling their shells far behind the lines. Road-work could not be suspended, however, as the tracks were in use as fast as they were laid down. Tea was issued to the men and, drenched to the skin, they stopped to swallow it. A shell exploded beside Ledwidge and he was instantly killed.

Father Devas was among the first to arrive on the scene. He rubbed the mud off the identification disc and stood stricken at the message it conveyed. That night he wrote in his diary:

July 31st 1917
Forest Area. Mass in Forest.

Crowds at Holy Communion. Arrange for service but washed out by rain and fatigues. Walk in rain with dogs. Ledwidge killed, blown to bits; at Confession yesterday and Mass and Holy Communion this morning. R.I.P.

XI

Father Devas wrote to the poet's mother:

4th August 1917

Dear Mrs Ledwidge,

I do not know how to write to you about the death of your dear son, Francis. Quite apart from his wonderful gifts, he was such a lovable boy and I was so fond of him. We had many talks together and he used to read me his poems. He died on the Feast of St. Ignatius Loyola. The evening before he died he had been to Confession. On the morning of the 31st he was present at Mass and received Holy Communion. That evening while out with a working party a shell exploded quite near to them killing seven and wounding twelve. Francis was killed at once so that he suffered no pain. I like to think that God took him before the world had been able to spoil him with its praise and he has found far greater joy and beauty than ever he would have found on earth. May God comfort you and may His Holy Mother pray for you. I shall say a Mass for Francis as soon as I can.

Entries in Father Devas's diary show that he said the promised Mass the following Sunday. A year later, another entry records that he remembered Ledwidge and again offered Mass for him on the anniversary of his death.

Thirty-five years later, a further and unexpected glimpse of Ledwidge on the eve of his death was given to Mr Tony Lane of Slane, who had been making inquiries from another priest who served as wartime chaplain, Father J. J. Fitzpatrick:

Bordean House,
Petersfield, Hants.
11th October 1952

Dear Mr Lane,

I am sorry I was not able to answer your letter sooner. I am afraid

I can add nothing to what I told Mr Smyth. On the eve of the battle we were very busy, and I was hearing Confessions at a C.C.S. Centre on the Poperinghe–Ypres road. One of those who came to me said he was the Irish poet, Francis Ledwidge. That meant nothing to me at the time. He didn't belong to our Brigade. I never saw him again. It was only months afterwards that I heard he was killed. Father Devas was Chaplain to the Irish Division. He died about four or five years ago.

During the Battle we buried the dead where they fell. They were later gathered into cemeteries, but many were blown to pieces by shell fire. If he is in a cemetery it must be in one of those along the road to Ypres, which in those days we called the 'Salient'.

As Ledwidge was not killed in battle he was probably buried at once in a graveyard. At any rate, his grave has since been traced: number 5 in Row B of the second plot in Artillery Wood cemetery, situated three-quarters of a mile east of the village of Boesinghe in Belgium, about three miles north of Ypres.

Christie did not know that Ledwidge had been sent to the Western Front until he read of his death in a newspaper. As was clear from the way the poet parted from his family in Slane, there were farewells he could not make. So many letters were lost at that period, it is possible that Ledwidge later communicated and that his letter never reached Christie.

Dunsany wrote Ledwidge's elegy in an imaginative story called *The Road*, a characteristic medley of fact and fantasy. The road the soldiers were making is carried forward until it becomes a splendid thorough-fare on which crowds of people are walking and laughing as if on their way to a fair. Palaces line the thoroughfare as it enters a mighty city where peace and victory are being celebrated. Mingling with the flag-bearers and the generals are the ghosts of the working-party killed at Boesinghe. One of them turns round to the lance-corporal in charge to say: 'That was a fine road we made, Frank!'

Three months after Ledwidge's death, his *Songs of Peace* appeared under the imprint of Herbert Jenkins. Dunsany had written the Intro-duction in Ebrington barracks during September 1916 and it was printed without an addendum so that it reads as though the poet were still alive. Again the critics gave it a flattering reception. Its sales were enhanced by the sentimental appeal of a 'Soldier Poet Fallen in the War'.

A contemporary poet, John Drinkwater, reacted sharply against this cant:

> The continual insistence, not that his devotion is splendid, but that it is upon us that his devotion may splendidly bestow itself, is contemptible. Ledwidge died heroically: that I can reflect with deep reverence; that he died for me I can remember only in forlorn desolation and silence. But his poetry exults me, while not so his death. And it is well for us to keep our minds fixed on this plain fact, that when he died, a poet was not transfigured, but killed, and his poetry was not magnified, but blasted in its first flowering . . . To those who know what poetry is, the untimely death of a man like Ledwidge is nothing but calamity.

The war is present in the second book of poems in a subtle and accusing way. Its baneful effect is on the meagre output, the promise unfulfilled, the bitter struggle for expression that the poet seems always on the point of losing. Dunsany, in his Introduction, describes *A Dream of Artemis* as incomplete and hurriedly finished. But throughout the whole of this first posthumous volume there is a sense of haste and displacement eloquent of the poet's ordeal. He had been silent for eight weeks in Gallipoli; he lost his manuscripts in the Serbian retreat and the few rain-soaked pieces of paper he had managed to keep in his haversack could hardly be deciphered afterwards. There was another period of enforced silence in his hospital bed when, as he complained, 'there are Navvy imps in my head' and the Muse had withdrawn. But far more than the physical strain was the shadow of a deeper tragedy. After the 1916 insurrection, his heart was broken by the fate of his former comrades in the Volunteers. He identified himself with them in a series of poignant laments, conscious of the painful irony of his predicament.

Of the seven signatories to the Proclamation of Freedom, executed after Easter Week, three were poets: Pearse, Plunkett and MacDonagh. In addition to the communion of mind between all poets, Ledwidge was particularly drawn to MacDonagh for his panache and gaiety. The latter's verse translations from the Irish were very popular, especially *The Yellow Bittern* by the Gaelic poet Cathal Buidhe Mac Giolla Ghunna, in which the translator proved his own mastery of the internal rhyme and assonance:

> The yellow bittern that never broke out
> In a drinking bout, might as well have drunk;

His bones are thrown on a naked stone
Where he lived alone like a hermit monk.

The translator revived great interest in the original poet, Mac Giolla Ghunna, in the old Irish verse-forms, and even in the bittern.

After Ledwidge's death, Dunsany continued to collect his poems with a view to publication. The Ledwidge family sent him all the writings left at Janeville and everything sent home from the Western Front. But a great deal of Ledwidge's work is irretrievably lost. He had truly described the position in one of his letters to Katherine Tynan.

A few months after the appearance of *Songs of Peace*, another thirty-three poems were put together by Dunsany and sent to Jenkins, who published them in 1918 under the title *Last Songs*. These had been written in Derry barracks and at the Western Front. Brief though it is, the little book continues the poet's personal history and records his changed attitude to army life. Three in this final collection are again Laments for 1916, but most of the verse dwells on the landscape around his home in Meath. The notable point about these songs is that they are not visual but remembered descriptions, drawn with the same fidelity of detail as if he wrote within sight of the hills and the river: *Autumn, Dawn, Ceol Sidhe, Soliloquy, The Rushes, The Dead Kings* and many other poems contain vivid pictures of home as he saw them in his mind's eye. His *Complete Poems*, numbering 122, were published a year later, in 1919.

Ledwidge's reading may be clearly traced in his poems and is confirmed by allusions in his letters: the Bible, Dante's *Divine Comedy*, Homer's *Odyssey*, the *Mabinogion* (Welsh medieval romances) and the Celtic Sagas. All these books were the common font of his fellow poets of the Anglo-Irish Renaissance. The vast canvas of the Old Testament particularly appealed to Ledwidge and his verses contain many allusions to Biblical personages. He was in the current fashion, too, in his continuous flow of classical references. He shared the contemporary enthusiasm for the Celtic Sagas, popularized through the verse translations of Samuel Ferguson and the later work of Standish O'Grady and Lady Gregory. Thus Ledwidge uses place names like Dun Dealgan and Emain Macha. Also Ailill, Maeve, Findebar, Cuchullain, Sualtem, Ferdia, King Connor, Deirdre, Cathbad, Leag, Emer, Conall, Caoilte, Oscar, Finn, Conan, Fand and many others come thronging from the native pantheon into his verse.

Ledwidge's poetry is of the Romantic School, which enjoyed great prestige in the Victorian era, but was rapidly losing favour in the second decade of the twentieth century. It was revived through the active, practical patronage of Edward Marsh whose volumes of *Georgian Poetry* and the interest aroused by the Poetry Bookshop infused new life into it. The influence of the Celtic Twilight, too, is on Ledwidge's poetry in its dreamy moods and dim landscapes.

Among the poets of the past on whom Ledwidge modelled his early work, Keats came first as is well known and has been too often said. The conformities in their lives attracted too the sympathy of the Irish poet: both had to fight against poverty and mockery in their youth; the shadow of tuberculosis (Keats died of this disease and also his mother and brother) lay on both families.

The influence of Yeats's early poetry is also evident on Ledwidge's work: dwelling on unrequited love, repining for a lost Arcadia, recalling the heroic personages of the Celtic Sagas, being comforted by fairy visitants. But Ledwidge very soon learned to dominate the echoes of his contemporary and develop his own mature and distinctive mode of expression.

The best feature of his style is simplicity, not achieved without immense effort and for that reason deceptive to the uninitiated. People like Lady Dunsany and Joseph Ledwidge, who had the opportunity of observing him at work, told me that he slaved at perfecting his verse. 'You know how I love short words,' he wrote in a letter to Dunsany. He preferred not only short words, but short lines, too, and short poems. This passion for terseness and economy sometimes led him into awkward constructions and flawed lines, but on the other hand its effect when completely successful was a dewy freshness, a delicate airy lightness as in that near perfect lyric *A Little Boy in the Morning*.

He pursued intensity of expression not only in his choice of words and in the calculated length of lines and poems, but in his metre. Most of his first fifty poems are in lines of two-syllable feet, usually four or five iambs, varied with the trochee. But if the ground beat of his verse is simple, his rhyme patterns are attractively original. In his later period, Ledwidge becomes more adventurous, embarking on two long poems, *A Dream of Artemis* and *The Lanawn Shee*, and using a greater variety of two-syllable metre. But he never resorts to novel experimental verse merely to convey effect.

The notable development of his personal poetic genius was when he made his own of the Gaelic verse form of internal rhyme and assonance. The deep satisfaction of communicating with the past then thrilled through his poems. Notice the new assurance in the metre of his laments for Easter Week: *The Blackbirds, Thro' Bogac Ban, The Dead Kings*. If the poet was snuffed out of life in his springtime, his genius had reached maturity in more than one enchanting lyric, such as:

> Had I a golden pound to spend,
> My love should mend and sew no more.
> And I would buy her a little quern,
> Easy to turn on the kitchen floor.
>
> And for her windows curtains white,
> With birds in flight and flowers in bloom,
> To face with pride the road to town,
> And mellow down her sunlit room.
>
> And with the silver change we'd prove
> The truth of love to life's own end,
> With hearts the years could but embolden,
> Had I a golden pound to spend.

'Let us not call him the Burns of Ireland, you who may like this book, nor even the Irish John Clare, though he is more like him, for poets are all incomparable,' wrote Dunsany in his Introduction to *Songs of the Fields*. Since that time, however, Ledwidge has been likened with monotonous repetition to the Scottish national poet and to the English rural one. Burns, too, was born in poverty, lived in the country, made nature his inspiration, had to earn his living before he was fifteen, struggled for expression without benefit of formal education. But there the resemblance ends. Burns was a tedious moralist, Ledwidge was never didactic.

The nineteenth-century John Clare was also the son of a farm labourer, poor, uneducated, and would probably never have been heard of without the energetic help of a patron. Clare, too, had a deep appreciation of nature and of his homeland. He could conjure up rural scenes in vivid detail. But in a sense the comparison between Ledwidge and Clare is futile because the latter left a huge output, about 860 published poems.

Since the death of Patrick Kavanagh, Ledwidge's name has been evoked in his connection, too, because of the resemblance in their circumstances. Both were isolated phenomena in their native counties.

Ledwidge's first book went through three editions; his second two;

and his *Complete Poems* followed his third book so quickly that it superseded the separate volumes. This final collection was reprinted three times, the last date being 1955. The book is still selling and the original publishers still hold the copyright. These hard facts prove that the poems acquired a vitality of their own. In 1925, Lennox Robinson with the help of W. B. Yeats and AE, edited *A Golden Treasury of Irish Verse* and included in it five of Ledwidge's poems. More than thirty years later, Robinson was called on to edit *The Oxford Book of Irish Verse* (1958). This time he was aided by Donagh MacDonagh and they again included five of Ledwidge's poems. When Padraic Colum edited an *Anthology of Irish Verse* for an American publisher in 1948, he included four of Ledwidge's. Hundreds of poets have gone down into the Limbo of the forgotten during the past fifty years, but Ledwidge's poetry lives on. It is no small triumph that it has survived the death of the Romantic School and the final fading of the Celtic Twilight. His permanent place among the poets of the Irish Renaissance is secure.

Robert Farren, one of our leading contemporary poets who has made a distinguished contribution to Irish letters, wrote a book in 1948 called *The Course of Irish Verse*, in which he movingly recalled Ledwidge: 'His verse has always fluidity, euphony and a soft, white light which distinguishes it.'

A more complete volume of Ledwidge's *Complete Poems* is long overdue for publication. Another selection could be made from the Dunsany papers; a contemporary editor's judgment would be probably different. Moreover every poem did not pass through the Dunsany sieve, especially after the poet began to travel. A large amount of his work could still be retrieved from periodicals and newspapers.

A play *The Bird in the Net*, by Sean Dowling, was produced b y the Abbey in 1960, had a successful run and was acclaimed a success. It tells the story of a young Irish officer in the British Army who was a poet, too, and whom Dublin audiences immediately recognized as Ledwidge, thinly disguised. The action of the play is set in the week following the 1916 insurrection. The young officer, Michael Tyrrell (or Ledwidge) has just arrived back from the Western Front and is paying a call on Sir William D'Arcy, who had sponsored the publication of his poems, when the house is surrounded by the local Volunteers and taken as headquarters. Tyrrell's sympathies are with the insurrectionists. He tries to join them but when news reaches them that the rising has failed in Dublin, they refuse to accept him because they are disbanding. This play by its many implications and especially by the misleading final scene cast a false light on the friendship between Dunsany and Ledwidge and provoked an unfortunate spate of newspaper comment, most of it uninformed.

Dunsany survived Ledwidge by more than forty years, and his admiring and affectionate memories of the poet lasted to the end of his days. In his book *My Ireland*, he included a long chapter on Ledwidge and said that the woods and hills around Slane were to him for ever haunted by the memory of the apprentice poet.

The association between Dunsany and Ledwidge began with friendly patronage on the one hand and a timid acceptance of help on the other; but it developed into one of the most unusual friendships in the history of letters. They had the same aspiration of self-fulfilment, although they approached it from opposite poles. Dunsany was hampered by an abundance of material good fortune; Ledwidge by the lack of it. They found in the meeting of extremes, they had an identical problem: how to have their work valued objectively without reference to background. Dunsany found his title coming between him and his goal; Ledwidge's poems were popularized under false labels: 'the scavenger poet', or 'our soldier poet'.

I discussed the unusual friendship at some length with three people intimately acquainted with it though from totally different angles: the late Dowager Lady Dunsany, Joseph Ledwidge and Robert Christie; they had not all met and they had lived far apart. All three, however, had the same anxiety to give that friendship its final and truthful definition. They chose their words carefully and it was an extraordinary experience to hear them arrive at almost the same phrases.

It is a friendship that has been assailed—and is still being assailed—from every side; Dunsany's friends believed he made too much of a working man; Ledwidge's neighbours and patriotic friends were anxious to detach him from an influence they considered embarrassing, if not baneful. The Irish genius for denigration has been fully expended on the bond between the two writers. But is it so impossible to understand? Dunsany honoured the young poet's genius and did all in his power to help him to express it; this belief in him was to Ledwidge a matter of life or death. The established writer gave the beginner the encouragement and stimulus without which even genius could flicker out. A magnanimous streak in Dunsany sounded depths of loyalty in Ledwidge. The bond between them leaped over religious and social barriers; survived even the sundering effect of 1916 with its fierce passions, and the squalor of a world war, on which they had opposing ideological views. The history of ascendancy versus native Irish is a black, bitter story and this friendship flowered on wintry soil, but there it shines. Dunsany should be for ever honoured for his befriending of the poet. According to the creed of writers, it is among the greatest works of mercy, if not the greatest.

A bronze plaque to the memory of Ledwidge was unveiled on the Boyne Bridge in Slane in September 1962. Designed by the Cork sculptor, Seamus Murphy, the memorial is of modest dimensions and timidly sited; it carries the first four lines of the poem to Thomas Mac-Donagh, so applicable to Ledwidge himself. The Slane Guild of *Muintir na Tire* (the Irish Community movement), through whose efforts the plaque was erected, regard it as only a token gesture towards a more worthy monument at a later date.

The hosting of people in Slane that day reminded village elders of the crowds that congregated on the historic Lady Day of 1914. The town was so thronged with visitors that for some hours wheeled vehicles could not pass through the streets. There was an *Aeriocht*, a parade of bands, and the Boyne Valley Festival, which has since become an annual event, was formally inaugurated.

It was a long deferred honouring of the poet in his native place, in a sense his homecoming. Autumn had as yet barely touched the nearby woods, but it had coloured the great cornfields on the surrounding hills. Bands paraded on the bridge, looking down on the sparkling river. Did anyone remember Ledwidge's lines in *Music on Water*?

Today
Let me be part of all this joy.
Methinks I see the music like a light
Low on the bobbing water, and the fields
Yellow and brown alternate on the height,
Hanging in silence there like battered shields,
Lean forward heavy with their coloured yields.

At the unveiling of the Ledwidge monument at Ieper on 31st July 1998, (from left) Dermot Bolger, Luc Dehaene, Mayor of Ieper, and Joe Ledwidge.

Afterword

A Tricolour Flies in Flanders

Dermot Bolger

Alice Curtayne's labour-of-love biography ends with a monument to Francis Ledwidge finally being unveiled in the place where he was born, as she was finishing the proofs for the first edition of this book.

It is appropriate therefore that as this, the first ever softback edition of her book, was going to press, a second monument to him was being unveiled, far from Slane, in the exact spot where he had died.

There were potato fields ready for harvesting, black and white cows lazily swishing their tails in a quiet field. The evening was warm, the country road thronged with country people and an Irish tricolour finally flew over Flanders.

Eighty-one years before, on July 31st 1917, the nightmare that was the Third battle of Ypres had commenced, with 30,000 young men killed for the gain of several hundred yards of no-man's land during that single first day.

One of them (working at a job he knew only too well — that of road building) was Francis Ledwidge. Not surprisingly, he was buried in the hole the shell had made, and it was not until 1919, when an eerie calm had settled around the flattened, featureless and rat-infested land where the beautiful town of Ypres had once stood, that those of Ledwidge's limbs they could salvage were re-buried nearby.

Now in 1998, on that 81st anniversary, two hundred local Flemish people had gathered at his rarely visited grave in Artillery Wood Cemetery to see wreaths laid by Luc Dehaene, the Mayor of Ieper, and by the poet's nephew, Joe Ledwidge (the only son of Francis' brother Joseph) from Slane. Flemish musicians sounded The Last Post before the sound of Irish piping filled the air.

199

Those locals who came knew little about Francis Ledwidge, but each year now they try to understand the fields of seemingly endless white crosses around them by focusing on the life of one individual buried there.

After the Last Post they walked slowly down the lane to where one Irish tricolour flew in the evening sky and another covered a monument to Ledwidge, marking the exact spot where he fell. Walking among them I thought of his lines in 'At Currabwee': *For am I not of those who reared / The banner of old Ireland high, / From Dublin town to Turkey's shores...*

Here, at last the banner of Ireland was raised high over the spot where he died, and even if it was the Belgium authorities and not his own government who had the decency to honour him, it mattered little as Joe Ledwidge (as a family member) and myself (representing his fellow Irish poets) were invited to remove the tricolour and unveil the simple, yet highly evocative monument.

Poetry lives on in a thousand ways, with poems undergoing strange journeys to rival even the spawning salmon. So it has been with Ledwidge's work — cast into the limbo of being out of print for various decades, but always surviving in the minds of poetry lovers — from fellow writers to the children of neighbours in Slane or comrades who fought with him abroad.

And indeed this new interest in Ledwidge in Boezinge (now part of Ieper, as Ypres has been renamed) was ignited by a former comrade's son writing by hand the entire text of Ledwidge's poem 'Crocknaharna' in the visitors' book in the tiny cemetery where he is laid.

Its discovery led to the superb 'In Flanders Fields Museum' in Ieper (under the direction of Piet Chielens) researching just who this soldier-poet had been, painstakingly locating the exact spot of his death, constructing the monument (combining glass and yellow Ieper brick to give a ghostly effect) and commissioning the noted Dutch poet Benno Barnard to translate Ledwidge's poem, 'Soliloquy' (both texts are on the monument).

After the unveiling local people crammed into a school hall in Boezinge to hear Flemish musicians set his poems to music, followed by a talk about his life and readings from his work. Then finally a Ledwidge voice was heard again in Flanders as the elderly Joe Ledwidge was coaxed onto the stage. For several electrifying minutes, Joe Ledwidge bridged any language barriers with a piece of mesmerising singing that seemed to bring the very ghost of the poet into the hall.

If Ledwidge had known a life of hardship, followed by decades of bigoted whispers, then, in that moment, his memory was truly and finally honoured.

Today, a quarter of a century after it was first published, Alice Curtayne's biography can occasionally be seen to show signs of the age and the Ireland in which it was written. Curtayne was a writer of her time and contemporary readers may argue about this conclusion or that. Yet what there can be no doubt about is that without her pioneering and selfless work (both in this biography and in compiling his *Complete Poems*) much of Ledwidge's work and many facts about his life would have been as lost and forgotten as the lives and memories of so many of his comrades in that Flanders graveyard.

Seamus Heaney (in his introduction to Ledwidge's *Selected Poems*) is only one of the many writers who have expressed their indebtedness to her labour and research. Without this book, I very much doubt if a small band of Slane people (including Pearl Baxter, the niece of Ellie Vaughey) would have banded together to restore his cottage and open it as a fascinating museum, and to organise an annual day of celebration, poetry and music in his native village in his honour. I wonder if there would be a society in Dublin dedicated to his memory, or if the work of Francis Ledwidge would still be so well known in Ireland today.

On a personal note I still recall the excitement of walking home from Dublin, having spent all my savings, plus the bus fare, on buying a copy of Alice Curtayne's biography as a young schoolboy in 1973. It was the first hardback book I ever owned and the most precious. I literally devoured every detail. What stirred me most vividly was Curtayne's story of him being sent to work as a grocer's apprentice in Rathfarnham. Consumed with homesickness, he had composed 'Behind the Closed Eye' and been so moved that he had abandoned his job to walk the thirty miles home to Slane through the dark, pausing to rest at each milestone along the way.

Anyone writing at sixteen is yearning for some link or affinity to make one feel less alone. For me at that age Ledwidge's story had a special resonance because, on the edge of the Slane Road close to where I lived in Finglas, one such milestone still existed. At night I would sit there, feeling as uncertain of the future as most people that age are, and taking a curious solace from the fact that Ledwidge, at the same age and perhaps even more uncertain of his future, had rested upon the very same milestone under a similar dark sky.

Many readers I have met over the years have similar memories of coming across Alice Curtayne's book, which — due to the virtual collapse of the company which first published it (although tribute should be payed to Timothy O'Keeffe for doing so) — was nearly impossible to get for almost two decades.

Its republication now will no doubt resurrect the old debate as to why Francis Ledwidge, as a committed Irish Nationalist, joined the British Army. I don't propose to join that argument, as it seems to me that to do so suggests that excuses need to be made for the actions of Francis Ledwidge and – by extension – for the actions of countless thousands of other brave young Irishmen who died along with men from sixty other nations in that international conflict. Men who marched away from home to the cheers, thanks and gratitude of neighbours and clergy (Cardinal Mercier's famous pastoral letter deemed it a Catholic duty to fight for Belgium) and returned home to hostility and abuse.

For many Irishmen who survived the killing fields of Passiondale, their lives were like those of the recent Soviet cosmonauts who were launched into space as heroes and returned to earth to find that the country that had sent them into orbit had ceased to exist in the meantime.

I have no doubt that if he had died with his friends in the Easter Rising he would have quickly become an icon, instead of enduring suspicion before Alice Curtayne began the process of bringing his work back into the light.

The work continues today. In 1992 I fulfilled a lifelong ambition in editing his *Selected Poems* (which Seamus Heaney introduced) and more recently a more comprehensive edition of his poems has been edited by Liam O'Meara.

His cottage museum in Slane is now open seven days a week and the hungry child who passed through its doors to work in the fields with his mother could never have dreamt that his native village — dominated by the castle and rule of an aristocratic and at times autocratic family — would today be known as Ledwidge Country, and that the youth of Slane now gather in the evenings on benches which commemorate him.

Francis Ledwidge lived for poetry. He lived for his fellow men as a union organiser and strike leader. He lived for sport and for music played on an old gramophone in the Cunningham Arms. He lived for his friends like Matty McGoona who saw his ghost in Navan on the night of his death.

He lived for his family, his mother who slaved through his childhood and for his young brother Joe. He lived by his labouring hands and by the promise of the future.

He died trying to mend the tiny patch of earth where he was buried. He died for an Ireland who has slowly come to recognise and acknowledge that fact. And he died also for Belgium, that small occupied nation whose freedom from oppression so many Irishmen believed would in turn bring about their own.

Thanks to people like Alice Curtayne his memory has lived on since the terrible day when he was killed until, eighty-one years later, his nephew, along with lovers of his work from Dublin and Slane, would gather with locals in the quiet Flanders evening.

I have rarely been so moved as to stand by that monument marking the spot where so much talent and hope and gaiety was blown to pieces by a random shell on a terrible day, when men paused at their work to drink scalding tea and turned their thoughts to home, to the secret places in their hearts to which they would never return.

Dermot Bolger
Flanders, 31ˢᵗ Aug, 1998

Bibliography

LEDWIDGE, Francis: *Complete Poems with Introduction by Lord Dunsany*, London, 1955
The Crock of Gold, unpublished play
Dunsany Papers, containing letters, poems and memoranda
Autobiographical Letter to Professor Lewis N. Chase. Ledwidge Folder, Lewis Chase Papers, Ac. 9468, Box 7, Library of Congress, Washington, D.C., 20540
'The Wallflower', a poem with a covering letter from Ledwidge to Miss O'Malley, 14 April 1914. The National Library, Dublin, Ms. 15,455
Original manuscript of poem 'Thomas MacDonagh' with a letter from Lord Dunsany to Donagh MacDonagh, 30 June 1940. The National Library, Dublin, MS. 15,542

ADCOCK, A. St. John: *For Remembrance: Soldier Poets who have fallen in the War*, London, 1918
ASHMEAD-BARTLETT, E.: *The Uncensored Dardanelles*, London
BERGIN, Maureen: *The Blackbird of Slane*. A Presentation of his Life and Verse
BRADY, Rev. John: *Short History of the Diocese of Meath*, 1867–1937
CAULFIELD, Max: *The Easter Rebellion*, London
COFFEY, Thomas M.: *Agony at Easter*, London, 1969
COGAN, Rev. A.: *The Diocese of Meath Ancient and Modern*, Dublin, 1862
COLE, Grenville A. J.: *Memoirs of the Geological Survey of Ireland*, Stationery Office, Dublin, 1922
COLUM, Padraic: *The Road Round Ireland*, New York, 1926
The Island of the Mighty, retold from the Mabinogion, New York, 1924
Anthology of Irish Verse, New York, 1948
COOPER, Major Brian: *The Tenth (Irish) Division in Gallipoli*, London, 1918

CURTAYNE, Alice: *Francis Ledwidge*. Radio Eireann Thomas Davis Lecture, 1967

The Poet of the Blackbird. Documentary for Radio 4, Home Service, Northern Ireland, produced by Sam Hanna Bell, 22 December 1967

DENSON, Alan (Editor): *Letters from AE*, Abelard-Schuman, London, 1961

DEVAS, Charles H.: Unpublished Wartime Notebooks

Devoy's Post Bag, 1871–1928. 2 vols., Dublin, 1948, 1953

DOWLING, Sean: *The Bird in the Net*, Duffy Ltd., Dublin, 1961

DRINKWATER, John: *The Lyric*, Martin Secker, London

The Muse in Council, Houghton Mifflin Co., 1925

DUFFY, T. E.: *Francis Ledwidge*. Souvenir brochure of Slane Muintir na Tire Guild's Memorial Plaque to Francis Ledwidge, 9 September 1962

DUNSANY, Lord: *Tales of War*, Talbot Press, Dublin, 1918

Unhappy Far-off Things, Elkin Mathews, London, 1919

Patches of Sunlight, Heinemann, London, 1938

My Ireland, Jarrolds, London, 1957

While the Sirens Slept, Jarrolds, London

FORESTER, C. S.: *The General*, Michael Joseph, London, 1958

FOX, Sir Frank, O.B.E.: *The Royal Inniskilling Fusiliers in the World War* Constable, London, 1928

Regimental History, Vol. II

GIBBON, Monk: *The Living Torch*, Macmillan, London

GIBBS, Philip: *From Bapaume to Passchendaele*, Heinemann, London, 1918

GILLON, Capt. Stair: *The Story of the 29th Division*, Nelson, London, 1925

GOGARTY, Oliver St J.: *As I was going down Sackville Street*, Rich and Cowan, London, 1937

It isn't This Time of Year at all, Doubleday, New York, 1954

GUEST, Lady Charlotte: *The Mabinogion* (translated by). Mediaeval Welsh Romances, Sign of the Phoenix, London, 1904

HARGRAVE, John; *At Suvla Bay*, Constable, London, 1916

The Suvla Bay Landing, Macdonald, London, 1964

HERBERT, A. P.: *The Secret Battle*, Methuen, London, 1949

HIGGINS, F. R.: *Island Blood*, John Lane The Bodley Head, London, 1925

HINKSON, Pamela: *Seventy Years Young*, Collins, London, 1937

205

HOBSON, Bulmer: *Short History of the Irish Volunteers*, Dublin, 1918
HOUSMAN, A. E.: *The Name and Nature of Poetry*, Cambridge University Press
JENKINS, Herbert: *Bindle*, Herbert Jenkins, London, 1917
JUVENIS (Capt. O .G. E. MacWilliam): *Suvla Bay and After*, Hodder & Stoughton, London, 1916
KENNEDY, Capt. J. J.: *With the 5th (Service) Battalion during the Great War*
MACGIVNEY, Rev. Joseph: *Place Names of the Co. Longford*
MACKENZIE, Compton: *Gallipoli Memories*, Cassell, London, 1929
MACLYSAGHT, Edward: *Irish Families*, Dublin, 1957
More Irish Families, Dublin & Galway, 1960
Supplement to Irish Families, Dublin, 1964
Guide to Irish Families, Dublin, 1964
McCUSTRA, Trooper L.: *Gallipoli Days and Nights*, Hodder & Stoughton, London, 1916
MACNEILL, Eoin (Editor): *The Irish Volunteer*
MARTIN, F. X., O.S.A.: *The Irish Volunteers 1913–1915*, Duffy, Dublin, 1963
Leaders and Men of the Easter Rising, Methuen, London, 1967
MASEFIELD, John: *Gallipoli*, Heinemann, London, 1916
MOORE, Thomas Sturge: *Some Soldier Poets*, Harcourt Brace & Howe, New York, 1920
MOOREHEAD, Alan: *Gallipoli*, Hamish Hamilton, London, 1956
MORTON, David: *The Renaissance of Irish Poetry*, Ives Washburn, 1929
NORTH, John: *The Fading Vision*, Faber and Faber, London, 1936
O'FARACHAIN, Roibeard: *The Course of Irish Verse*, Sheed & Ward, London, 1947
O'HIGGINS, Brian: *My Songs and Myself* (Wolfe Tone Annual, 1949)
O'LEARY, Con: *An Exile's Burden*, 1923
A Wayfarer in Ireland, Methuen, London, 1935
Oxford Book of Irish Verse, The, Clarendon Press, Oxford, 1958
PLUNKETT, Joseph Mary: *The Circle and the Sword*, Maunsell, Dublin, 1911
Poets of 1916 (Undated pamphlet). Educational Co. Ltd., Dublin
Poets of the Insurrection. Maunsell, Dublin, 1918
RAYMOND, Ernest: *Tell England*, Cassell, London, 1922
ROBINSON, Lennox (Editor): *A Golden Treasury of Irish Verse*, Macmillan, London, 1925
The Oxford Book of Irish Verse, Oxford, 1958

206

ROONEY, Philip: *Blackbird of the Boyne*, Radio Eireann Documentary
RYAN, Desmond: *Remembering Sion*, Arthur Barker, London, 1934
  The Rising, Standard House, Dublin, 1949
SASSOON, Siegfried: *Memoirs of a Fox-Hunting Man*, Tauchnitz Edition, Vol. 4975, Paris, Gaulon, 1931
  The Complete Memoirs of George Sherston, Faber, London, 1949
STANNARD, Russell: *With the Dictators of Fleet Street*, Hutchinson, London, 1934
TIBBLE, T. W. (Editor): *The Poems of John Clare*, Dent, London, 1935
TYNAN, Katherine: *Lord Edward*, A Study in Romance. Smith Elder, London, 1916
  The Years of the Shadow, Constable, London, 1919
WALSH, Rev. Paul: *The Placenames of Westmeath*
  Some Place Names in Ancient Meath
WARD, Aileen: *John Keats*, The Making of a Poet. Secker & Warburg, London, 1963
Walton's Treasury of Songs and Ballads, Walton, Dublin, 1947
WOULFE, Rev. Patrick: *Irish Names and Surnames*
The Young Gael, April and May, 1911

PERIODICALS AND NEWSPAPERS

Drogheda Independent. Issues from 1903 to 1918; also 18 December 1937
Edinburgh Review, July, 1918
Irish Press. Five articles by Philip Rooney, January 1962
The Lanthorn (Yearbook of the Dominican College, Eccles Street, Dublin), Christmas, 1919
Living Age, September 1918
Meath Chronicle. Issues from 1903 to 1918; also 11 June 1955
Reminiscences. F.E.L. by Katherine Ryan (pseudonym of Margaret Shaw)
Sprig of Shillelagh, Journal of the Royal Inniskilling Fusiliers, September 1917 et al.
Sunday Graphic and Sunday News, 16 September, 1934
The Weekly Dispatch, 19 August 1917 ('The Tragedy of a Great Poet' by H. Russell Stannard)

Index

210

IT SERVICE MANAGEMENT
A Guide for ITIL® V3 Fou
Exam Candidates

C000299543

BCS THE CHARTERED INSTITUTE FOR IT

BCS The Chartered Institute for IT promotes wider social and economic progress through the advancement of information technology, science and practice. We bring together industry, academics, practitioners and government to share knowledge, promote new thinking, inform the design of new curricula, shape public policy and inform the public. As the professional membership and accreditation body for IT, we serve over 70,000 members including practitioners, academics and students, in the UK and internationally. A leading IT qualification body, we offer a range of widely recognised professional and end-user qualifications.

Joining BCS
BCS qualifications, products and services are designed with your career plans in mind. We not only provide essential recognition through professional qualifications but also offer many other useful benefits to our members at every level.

BCS Membership demonstrates your commitment to professional development. It helps to set you apart from other IT practitioners and provides industry recognition of your skills and experience. Employers and customers increasingly require proof of professional qualifications and competence. Professional membership confirms your competence and integrity and sets an independent standard that people can trust. Professional Membership (MBCS) is the pathway to Chartered IT Professional (CITP) Status.
www.bcs.org/membership

Further Information
BCS The Chartered Institute for IT, First Floor, Block D, North Star House, North Star Avenue, Swindon, SN2 1FA, United Kingdom.
T +44 (0) 1793 417 424
F +44 (0) 1793 417 444
www.bcs.org/contact

IT SERVICE MANAGEMENT
A Guide for ITIL® V3 Foundation Exam Candidates

Ernest Brewster, Richard Griffiths, Aidan Lawes, John Sansbury

bcs

The
Chartered
Institute
for IT

Published by British Informatics Society Limited (BISL), a wholly owned subsidiary of BCS
The Chartered Institute for IT, First Floor, Block D, North Star House, North Star Avenue, Swindon, SN2 1FA, United Kingdom.
www.bcs.org

ISBN 978-1-906124-19-9

British Cataloguing in Publication Data.
A CIP catalogue record for this book is available at the British Library.

Typeset by Lapiz Digital Services, Chennai, India.
Printed at CPI Antony Rowe, Chippenham, UK.

CONTENTS

LIST OF FIGURES AND TABLES

Figures 1.1, 1.2, 1.4, 1.5, 1.6, 4.1, 6.1, 9.1, 9.2, 11.1, 11.2, 13.1, 15.1, 16.1, 17.1, 17.2, 18.1, 18.2, 18.3, 19.1, 20.1, 20.2, 23.1, 24.1, 29.1, 31.1, 31.2 are based on OGC ITIL material. Reproduced under licence from OGC.

AUTHORS

Ernest Brewster has over 30 years' experience in IT, including 20 years as a senior manager in various public sector organisations, latterly as Head of IT at Fife Council, one of Scotland's largest local authorities with over 15,000 personal computers and a network linking several hundred separate sites. He is a long-time champion of ITIL® Service Management, with a record of implementing ITIL-based good practice in complex organisations, and an expert in strategy development, programme and project management, business process re-engineering and public procurement. Ernest is an ex-member of SOCITM's National Executive Committee and a contributor to several of SOCITM's MAPIT (now Insight) publications.

Richard Griffiths is an experienced and respected Service Management expert, and has worked as practitioner, trainer and consultant in all aspects of ITIL for a number of organisations worldwide. He has been a question compiler and examiner at all levels for ten years and uses the knowledge gained from running many Foundation courses to tailor his writing to the audience of potential candidates.

Aidan Lawes is one the world's leading independent authorities on, and a passionate champion of, IT Service Management (SM). Educated in New Zealand, he started his working life there in the insurance industry, before leaving to travel. On settling in the UK, he joined the Civil Service and entered the world of IT. There followed 20 years working for ICL in a variety of training and consultancy roles around the globe, including working on major service management projects in the financial and public sectors in Europe. From 1999 to 2007, he was CEO of *it*SMF UK and International, overseeing phenomenal membership and revenue growth, and spreading the SM gospel globally. Aidan is a Fellow of both the ISM and BCS, and has contributed to many ITSM publications (including ITIL), co-authored the BSI standard and its International successor (ISO/IEC 20000), chaired the ITIL V3 refresh programme board and participates in many initiatives to raise professional standards. In his spare time, Aidan is a passionate rugby fan, supporting the All Blacks and anyone playing against Australia.

John Sansbury has completed the ITIL-experience jigsaw with the publication of this, his first book, having been a service management practitioner for 25 years, a consultant for 14 years, an ITIL examiner since 1996 and a trainer for three years. Since his career started in IT Operations in the 1970s, John has shunned the technical aspects of IT, partly because it's boring and partly because he's rubbish at it! Instead, he has excelled at helping organisations deliver real business value from IT. As a practitioner, John learnt his trade with Philips and London Electricity (now EDF) where he helped implement Capacity Management (the interesting bit where you meet business representatives to understand their plans, not the techie, modelling stuff), negotiated the SLAs with the business and developed one of the world's first business-unit based chargeback systems. As a consultant, he has worked with organisations across the world to analyse and improve their IT processes and deliver increased stakeholder value. John is a Chartered Fellow of BCS, the Founder of the Classic Corvette Club UK, a husband of 26 years and the proud father of two successful sons. He's also a masochist, having accepted a commission to write his second book, on the OSA Capability exam.

"ITIL® is a Registered Trademark of the Office of Government Commerce in the United Kingdom and other countries."

ABBREVIATIONS

BCM	Business Continuity Management
BIA	Business Impact Analysis
BRM	Business Relationship Management
CAB	Change Advisory Board
CI	Configuration Item
CMDB	Configuration Management Database
CMIS	Capacity Management Information System
CMMI	Capability Maturity Model Integration
CMS	Configuration Management System
COBIT	Control Objectives for Information and related Technology
CRM	Customer Relationship Management
CSI	Continual Service Improvement
DIKW	Data → Information → Knowledge → Wisdom
DML	Definitive Media Library
ECAB	Emergency Change Advisory Board
EFQM	The European Foundation for Quality Management
eSCM–SP	eSourcing Capability Model for Service Providers
ISM	Information Security Management
ISMS	Information Security Management System
ISO	International Organization for Standardization
ITSCM	IT Service Continuity Management
ITSM	IT Service Management
itSMF	IT Service Management Forum
KPI	Key Performance Indicator
MTBF	Mean Time Between Failures

MTBSI	Mean Time Between System Incidents
MTRS	Mean Time to Restore Service
OGC	Office of Government Commerce
OLA	Operational Level Agreement
PBA	Pattern of Business Activity
RACI	An example of an authority matrix: Responsible, Accountable, Consulted, Informed
RFC	Request For Change
ROI	Return On Investment
SACM	Service Asset and Configuration Management
SCD	Supplier and Contracts Database
SD	Service Design
SDP	Service Design Package
SIP	Service Improvement Plan
SKMS	Service Knowledge Management System
SLA	Service Level Agreement
SLAM	SLA Monitoring
SLM	Service Level Management
SLP	Service Level Package
SLR	Service Level Requirements
SM	Service Management
SO	Service Operation
SOX	Sarbannes–Oxley
SPM	Service Portfolio Management
SS	Service Strategy
ST	Service Transition
TCO	Total Cost of Ownership
TSO	The Stationery Office
UC	Underpinning Contract
VBF	Vital Business Function
VOI	Value Of Investment

GLOSSARY†

Alert   A warning that a threshold has been reached, something has changed or
a failure has occurred.

Capabilities   The ability of an organisation, person, process, application,
configuration item or IT service to carry out an activity. Capabilities are
intangible assets of an organisation.

Configuration Item   A Configuration Item (CI) is any component that needs to
be managed in order to deliver an IT service. Information about each CI is
recorded in a configuration record within the Configuration Management System
and is maintained throughout its lifecycle by Configuration Management. CIs are
under the control of Change Management. CIs typically include IT services,
hardware, software, buildings, people and formal documentation such as process
documentation and SLAs.

Configuration Management Database   A Configuration Management
Database (CMDB) stores configuration records containing Attributes of CIs and
their relationships. A CMS may include one or more CMDBs.

Configuration Management System   A Configuration Management System
(CMS) is a set of tools and databases used to manage an IT service provider's
configuration data. The CMS also includes information about Incidents, Problems,
known errors, changes and releases, and may contain data about employees,
suppliers, locations, business units, customers and users. The CMS includes tools
for collecting, storing, managing, updating and presenting data about all CIs and
their relationships. The CMS is maintained by Configuration Management and is
used by all IT Service Management processes.

Configuration Model   A Configuration Model is a model of the services, assets
and the infrastructure that includes relationships between CIs, enabling other
processes to access valuable information (e.g. assessing the impact of Incidents,
Problems and proposed changes; planning and designing new or changed services
and their release and deployment; optimising asset utilisation and costs).

Definitive Media Library   A Definitive Media Library (DML) is one or more
locations in which the definitive and approved versions of all software CIs are
securely stored. The DML may also contain associated CIs such as licences
and documentation. The DML is a single logical storage area even if there are
multiple locations. All software in the DML is under the control of Change and

Release Management and is recorded in the Configuration Management System. Only software from the DML is acceptable for use in a release. See Figure 18.2.

Deployment   Deployment is the activity responsible for the movement of new or changed hardware, software, documentation, process etc. to the Live Environment.

Event   An Event can be defined as any detectable or discernable occurrence that has significance for the management of the IT infrastructure or the delivery of IT service and evaluation of the impact a deviation may cause to the services. Events are typically notifications created by an IT service, Configuration Item or monitoring tool.

Event Management   The Process responsible for managing Events throughout their lifecycle. Event Management is one of the main Activities of IT Operations.

Function   A team or group of people and the tools they use to carry out one or more Processes or activities (e.g. the Service Desk or IT Operations).

Incident   An Incident is an unplanned interruption to an IT service or reduction in the quality of an IT service. Failure of a Configuration Item that has not yet impacted service is also an Incident.

Key Performance Indicator   Only the most important metrics are defined as KPIs. KPIs should be selected to ensure that Efficiency, Effectiveness and Cost-Effectiveness are all managed.

Known Error   A Problem that has a documented root cause and a workaround. Known Errors are created and managed throughout their lifecycle by Problem Management. Known Errors may also be identified by Development or Suppliers.

Metric   Something that is measured and reported to help manage a Process, IT Service or Activity.

Operational Level Agreement   An Operational Level Agreement (OLA) is an agreement between an IT service provider and another part of the same organisation. An OLA supports the IT service provider's delivery of IT services to the customers. The OLA defines the goods or services to be provided and the responsibilities of both parties.

Problem   A Problem is the cause of one or more Incidents.

Process   A Process is a structured set of activities designed to accomplish a specific objective. A Process takes one or more defined inputs and turns them into defined outputs. A Process may include any of the Roles, responsibilities, tools and management controls required to reliably deliver the outputs. A Process may define policies, standards, guidelines, activities and work instructions if they are needed.

Release   A Release is a collection of hardware, software, documents, processes or other components required to implement one or more approved Changes to

IT services. The contents of each Release are managed, tested and deployed as a single entity.

Resource   A generic term that includes IT infrastructure, people, money or anything else that might help to deliver an IT service. Resources are considered to be assets of an organisation.

Risk   Risk is defined as uncertainty of outcome, whether positive opportunity or negative threat. A possible event that could cause harm or loss, or affect the ability to achieve Objectives. A Risk is measured by the probability of a Threat, the Vulnerability of the Asset to that Threat, and the Impact it would have if it occurred.

Role   A set of responsibilities, activities and authorities granted to a person or team. A Role is defined in a Process. One person or team may have multiple roles (e.g. the roles of Configuration Manager and Change Manager may be carried out by a single person).

Service   A service is a means of delivering value to customers by facilitating outcomes that customers want to achieve without the ownership of specific costs and risks.

Service Change   Service Change is the addition, modification or removal of anything that could affect IT services. The scope should include all IT services, CIs, processes, documentation etc.

Service Design Package   (Service Design) Document(s) defining all aspects of an IT Service and their Requirements through each stage of its Lifecycle. A Service Design Package is produced for each new IT Service, major Change or IT Service Retirement.

Service Improvement Plan (SIP)   A formal Plan to implement improvements to a Process or IT Service.

Service Level Agreement   ITIL defines a Service Level Agreement (SLA) as an agreement between an IT service provider and a customer. The SLA describes the IT service, records service level targets, and specifies the responsibilities for the IT service provider and the customer. A single SLA may cover multiple IT services or multiple customers.

Service Level Package   A Service Level Package is a defined level of Utility and Warranty for a particular Service Package. Each SLP is designed to meet the needs of a particular Pattern of Business Activity.

Service Management   Service Management is a set of specialised organisational capabilities for providing value to customers in the form of services.

Service Package   ITIL defines a Service Package as a detailed description of an IT service that is available to be delivered to customers. A Service Package includes a Service Level Package (SLP) and one or more Core Services and Supporting Services.

Service Request   A Service Request is a request from a user for information, for advice, for a Standard Change or for access to an IT Service.

Standard Change   A Standard Change is a pre-approved Change that is low risk, relatively common and follows a Procedure or Work Instruction.

Strategic asset   Strategic assets are assets that provide the basis for core competence, distinctive performance, durable advantage, and qualifications to participate in business opportunities. IT organisations can use the guidance provided by ITIL to transform their Service Management capabilities into strategic assets.

Supplier   A third party responsible for supplying goods or services that are required to deliver IT services.

Utility   Functionality offered by a product or service to meet a particular need. Utility is often summarised as 'what it does'.

Warranty   A promise or guarantee that a product or service will meet its agreed requirements.

USEFUL WEBSITES

www.efgm.org
European Foundation for Quality Management

www.isaca.org
Information Systems Audit and Control Association

www.iso.org
International Organization for Standardization

www.isoiec20000certification.com
ISO/IEC 20000 certification and qualification schemes

www.itil-officialsite.com
The official ITIL® website

www.itsmf.co.uk
The IT Service Management Forum

www.itsmf.org
*it*SMF International

www.sarbanes-oxley.com
Sarbanes-Oxley

www.sei.cmu.edu/cmmi/
Carnegie Mellon University Capability and Maturity Model

PREFACE

This ITIL Foundation book represents a very different approach to ITIL than any other and in so doing, we believe it will help you understand ITIL at a Foundation level better than any other publication. As a result, you are more likely to score higher in your Foundation exam, more likely to pass the exam and more likely to retain your knowledge of ITIL and use it to benefit you and your organisation. Why? Because we have used our collective experiences to help you understand ITIL, not just memorise it. This gives you an edge in your exam because you will have the potential to work out the right answer, not just rely on your memory from the training course. Furthermore, when you take this back to your organisation, you will have an appreciation of the subject on which you can start to build your expertise, instead of a head full of facts and figures that will rapidly vanish.

The authors have actively helped organisations, ranging from a handful of people to multinational corporations in all industry sectors, adopt ITIL and reap the benefits of better performance, greater consistency and lower cost. We have worked for these organisations, advised them in a consultative capacity, trained their staff and run international forums for their people – yourselves – to benefit from shared experiences.

That is why this ITIL Foundation book will help you make sense of ITIL and we believe it will help you make a difference in your organisation. We know it will help you with your Foundation examination.

Ernest Brewster
Richard Griffiths
Aidan Lawes
John Sansbury

INTRODUCTION

HOW TO USE THIS BOOK

This book covers everything you need to know in order to pass the ITIL Foundation exam. However, we also recognise that many people simply want to understand the ITIL concepts without necessarily taking the exam itself. This book caters for both needs through its simple four-section structure.

- **Section 1:** An overview that introduces the basic concepts of Service Management and good practice, the ITIL framework, the Service Lifecycle and some of the key ITIL concepts such as processes and functions.

- **Section 2:** A view of each of the five stages of the lifecycle from Service Strategy to Continual Service Improvement. Each chapter contains an easy-to-read summary of the core elements of that part of the lifecycle.

- **Section 3:** The core of the book with a chapter describing each of the ITIL processes and functions.

- **Section 4:** Guidance on measurement and metrics, and the Deming improvement cycle.

In addition, the Appendix contains some useful exam techniques.

Naturally we suggest you start by reading Section 1, but, after that, we have designed each chapter to be self-contained and capable of being read in any sequence and without reference to other chapters. Each chapter can be read in 5–10 minutes.

For convenience, we have cross-referenced the chapters in Section 3 (and where applicable in Section 4) with the relevant chapters in the core books for further, more detailed content if the reader wishes to refer to it.

The structure of this book is also aligned with its companion book, *IT Service Management Foundation Practice Questions*. This helps in two ways:

- Questions in *IT Service Management Foundation Practice Questions* related to a particular learning element are listed at the end of the relevant chapters in this book so you can test your knowledge.

- When using *IT Service Management Foundation Practice Questions*, if you find your knowledge of a particular topic needs strengthening, it is easy to find and revise the relevant section in this book.

Within the core ITIL lifecycle volumes, the use of 'Goals', 'Purpose' and 'Objectives' is not always consistent and they are sometimes interchanged. For the benefit of clarity, the authors have standardised on the same heading for each process. The sharp-eyed reader will also notice that not all processes contain the same subheadings. Again, the core volumes are inconsistent in this respect, so the authors have included appropriate headings based on a combination of the Foundation syllabus and reader assistance.

Throughout the book, portions of text have been taken directly from ITIL manuals. This text is indicated by the use of quotation marks and the † symbol. All definitions, which are given in the Glossary and appear in boxes in the text, are taken directly from the OGC source material.

SECTION 1: OVERVIEW

1 WHAT IS SERVICE MANAGEMENT?

INTRODUCTION

In order to understand what Service Management is, and why it is so important to enterprises, we need to understand what services are, and how Service Management can help service providers to deliver and manage these services.

ITIL defines a service as follows:

SERVICE

A service is a means of delivering value to customers by facilitating outcomes that customers want to achieve without the ownership of specific costs and risks.

The outcomes that customers want to achieve are the reason why they purchase or use a service. Typically this will be expressed as a specific business objective (e.g. to enable customers of a bank to perform all transactions and account management activities online or to deliver state services to citizens in a cost-effective manner). The value of the service to the customer is directly dependent on how well a service facilitates these outcomes.

Although the enterprise retains responsibility for managing the overall costs of the business, they often wish to devolve responsibility for owning and managing defined aspects to an internal or external entity that has acknowledged expertise in the area.

This is a generic concept that applies to the purchase of any service. Consider financial planning. As a customer, we recognise that we don't have the expertise, or the time, or the inclination to handle all the day-to-day decision-making and management of individual investments that are required. Therefore, we engage the services of a professional manager to provide us a service. As long as their performance delivers a value (increasing wealth) at a price that we believe is reasonable, we are happy to let them invest in all the necessary systems and processes that are needed for the wealth creation activities.

In the past, service providers often focused on the technical (supply side) view of what constituted a service, rather than on the consumption side. Hence it was not unusual for the service provider and the consumer to have different definitions and perceptions of what services were provided, or for the provider to know all about the cost of individual components, but not the total cost of a service that the consumer understood.

Service Management is what enables a service provider to:

- understand the services that they are providing from both a consumer and provider perspective;
- ensure that the services really do facilitate the outcomes that their customers want to achieve;
- understand the value of those services to their customers and hence their relative importance;
- understand and manage all of the costs and risks associated with providing those services.

SERVICE MANAGEMENT

Service Management is a set of specialised organisational capabilities for providing value to customers in the form of services.

These 'specialised organisational capabilities' include the processes, activities, functions and roles that a service provider uses to let them to deliver services to their customers, as well as the ability to establish suitable organisation structures, manage knowledge, and understand how to facilitate outcomes that create value.

Although there is no single definition of a profession practice, it is widely accepted that the word profession applies where a group of people share common standards and disciplines based on a high level of knowledge and skills, which are gained from organised education schemes supported by training through experience and are measured and recognised through formal qualifications. Moreover, a profession seeks to use its influence through the development of good practice guidance and advice in order to improve the standard of performance in its given field. Service Management has a clear right to regard itself as a profession and the exercise of Service Management disciplines as professional practice.

Service Management is also a professional practice performed and supported by a global community drawn from all market sectors. There is a rich body of knowledge and experience including formal schemes for the education of individuals.

'BEST PRACTICE' VERSUS 'GOOD PRACTICE'

Enterprises operating in dynamic environments need to improve their performance and maintain competitive advantage. Adopting practices in industry-wide use can help to improve capability.

The term 'best practice' generally refers to the 'best possible way of doing something'. As a concept, it was first raised as long ago as 1919, but it was popularised in the 1980s through Tom Peters' books on business management.

The idea behind best practice is that one creates a specification for what is accepted by a wide community as being the best approach for any given situation. Then, one can compare actual job performance against these best practices and determine whether the job performance was lacking in quality somehow. Alternatively, the specification for best practices may need updating to include lessons learned from the job performance being graded.

Enterprises should not be trying to 'implement' any specific best practice, but adapting and adopting it to suit their specific requirements. In doing this, they may also draw upon other sources of good practice, such as public standards and frameworks, or the proprietary knowledge of individuals and other enterprises as illustrated in Figure 1.1.

Figure 1.1 Sources of good practice (Source: OGC ITIL Service Strategy ISBN 978-0-113310-45-6)

These sources have different characteristics:

- Public frameworks and standards have been validated across diverse environments.

- Knowledge of them is widely distributed among industry professionals.

- Training and certification programmes are publicly available.

- The acquisition of knowledge through the labour market is more readily achievable.

The proprietary knowledge of enterprises and individuals is usually customised for the local context and specific business needs of an organisation. It may only be available to a wider market under commercial terms and may be poorly documented and hard to extract. If embedded within individuals it may not be documented at all.

Enterprises deploying solutions based on good and best practice should, in theory, have an optimal and unique solution. Their solution may include ideas that are gradually adopted by other enterprises and, having been widely accepted, eventually become recognised inputs to good and best practice.

THE ITIL FRAMEWORK

ITIL is not a standard in the formal sense but a framework which is a source of good practice in Service Management. The standard for IT Service Management (ITSM) is ISO/IEC 20000, which is aligned with, but not dependent on, ITIL.

As a formal standard, ISO/IEC 20000 defines a set of requirements against which an organisation can be independently audited and, if they satisfy those requirements, can be certificated to that effect. The requirements focus on what must be achieved rather than how that is done. ITIL provides guidance about how different aspects of the solution can be developed.

The International Organization for Standardization (ISO) and the Office of Government Commerce (OGC), with the cooperation of the independent user group *it*SMF (the IT Service Management Forum), have publicly committed to keeping the standard and the framework as aligned as possible. However, it has to be accepted that they serve different purposes and have their own development lifecycles so it is unlikely that they will ever be completely synchronised.

The ITIL Library has the following components:

- **ITIL Core:** Publications describing generic best practice that is applicable to all types of organisation that provide services to a business.
- **ITIL Complementary Guidance:** A set of publications with guidance specific to industry sectors, organisation types, operating models and technology architectures.

The objective of the ITIL Service Management framework is to provide guidance applicable to all types of organisations that provide IT services to businesses, irrespective of their size, complexity, or whether they are commercial service providers or internal divisions of a business. The framework shouldn't be bureaucratic or unwieldy provided it is used sensibly and in full recognition of the business needs of the specific enterprise.

ITIL-based solutions have been deployed successfully around the world for over 20 years. Over this time, the framework has evolved considerably. The original publications, of which there were over 40, tended to be single topic and function-based. The next iteration reduced the number of books considerably, taking a process-based view and concatenating topics together to reinforce the integrated nature of service management solutions. The latest iteration (commonly referred to as v3) now provides a broader, holistic Service Lifecycle approach.

The generic nature of ITIL is both a strength and a weakness. Since it is generic, it truly can be applied to any organisation of any size in any market sector and regardless of whether the service provider is internal to the business or a commercial enterprise. However, organisations have to adopt and adapt the guidance that it contains to their specific requirements, which in some cases requires considerable effort and commitment.

Unfortunately, much of the focus in learning programmes is on the specifics of terminology and process definitions included within the ITIL volumes, which means that individuals aren't always equipped to make the necessary decisions about how to implement key processes and functions. Organisations should not be seeking to 'implement ITIL', but to implement a service management solution based on ITIL that meets the needs of the organisation.

THE ITIL CORE

The Service Lifecycle is an approach to IT Service Management that emphasises the importance of coordination and control across the various functions, processes and systems necessary to manage the full lifecycle of IT services. The Service Management Lifecycle approach considers the strategy, design, transition, operation and continual improvement of IT services. The Service Lifecycle is described in a set of five publications within the ITIL Core set. Each of these publications covers a stage of the Service Lifecycle (see Figure 1.2) from the initial definition and analysis of business requirements in Service Strategy (SS) and Service Design (SD), through migration into the live environment within Service Transition (ST), to live operation and improvement in Service Operation (SO) and Continual Service Improvement (CSI). The term 'continual' is used in preference to 'continuous' to emphasise that this activity is not performed on a constant basis, but as a series of planned and controlled actions.

Figure 1.2 The Service Lifecycle (Source: OGC ITIL Service Strategy ISBN 978-0-113310-45-6)

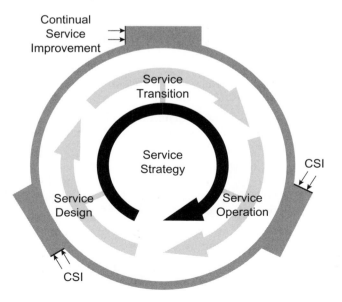

Service Strategy is the hub around which everything revolves. Strategy drives all the decisions that are subsequently taken. Design, Transition and Operation are the more iterative cyclic activities. At all stages throughout the lifecycle, opportunities arise for improvement.

COMPLEMENTARY MATERIAL

Although the material in the Core is likely to remain fairly constant, Complementary material is likely to be more dynamic. Complementary material may take the form of books or web-based material and may be sourced from the wider industry, rather than from the Office of Government Commerce (OGC)/The Stationery Office (TSO).

Examples of such material are glossary of terms, process models, process templates, role descriptions, case studies, targeted overviews and study aids for passing examinations. These will typically be officially commissioned and published by TSO.

Other publications that focus on specific market sectors, techniques or technologies are more likely to be produced by organisations such as *it*SMF or by the vendor community.

RELATED MATERIAL

Apart from the ISO/IEC 20000 standard, ITIL is also complementary to many other standards, frameworks and approaches. No one of these items will provide everything that an enterprise will wish to use in developing and managing their business. The secret is to draw on them for their insight and guidance as appropriate. Among the many such complementary approaches are:

- **Balanced Scorecard:** A management tool developed by Dr Robert Kaplan and Dr David Norton. A balanced scorecard enables a Strategy to be broken down into Key Performance Indicators (KPIs). Performance against the KPIs is used to demonstrate how well the Strategy is being achieved. A balanced scorecard has four major areas, each of which are considered at different levels of detail throughout the organisation.

- **COBIT:** Control Objectives for Information and related Technology provides guidance and best practice for the management of IT Processes. COBIT is published by the IT Governance Institute.

- **CMMI-SVC:** Capability Maturity Model Integration is a process improvement approach that gives organisations the essential elements for effective process improvement. CMMI-SVC is a variant aimed at service establishment, management, and delivery.

- **EFQM:** The European Foundation for Quality Management is a framework for organisational management systems.

- **eSCM–SP:** eSourcing Capability Model for Service Providers is a framework to help IT service providers develop their IT Service Management Capabilities from a Service Sourcing perspective.

- **ISO 9000:** A generic quality management standard, with which ISO/IEC 20000 is aligned.

- **ISO/IEC 19770:** Software Asset Management standard, which is aligned with ISO/IEC 20000.

- **ISO/IEC 27001:** ISO Specification for Information Security Management. The corresponding Code of Practice is ISO/IEC 17799.

- **Lean:** a production practice centred around creating more value with less work.

- **PRINCE2:** The standard UK government methodology for project management.

- **SOX:** the Sarbannes–Oxley framework for corporate governance.

- **Six Sigma:** a business management strategy, initially implemented by Motorola, which today enjoys widespread application in many sectors of industry.

Each of these contributes something different, as can be surmised from the brief descriptions, whether it be as legislation to comply with, as a standard to aspire to or as a method of measuring success. Enterprises globally have developed total corporate solutions embracing many permutations of these approaches.

THE ITIL SERVICE MANAGEMENT MODEL

Whether services are being provided by an internal unit of the organisation or contracted to an external agency, all services should be driven solely by business needs and judged by the value that they provide to the organisation. Decision-making therefore rests with the business. Within this context, services must also reflect the defined strategies and policies of the service provider organisation, which is particularly significant for external providers.

Figure 1.3 illustrates how the Service Lifecycle is initiated from a change in requirements at the business level. These new or changed requirements are identified and agreed at the Service Strategy stage and documented. Each of these 'packages' will have an associated defined set of business outcomes.

The package is passed to the Service Design stage where a service solution is produced, defining everything necessary to take this service through the remaining stages of the lifecycle. Solutions may be developed internally or consist of bought in components that are integrated internally.

The design definition is passed to the Service Transition stage, where the service is built, evaluated, tested and validated, and transitioned into the live environment, where it enters the live Service Operation stage. The transition phase is also responsible for supporting the service in its early life and the phasing out of any services that are no longer required.

Service Operation focuses on providing effective and efficient operational services to deliver the required business outcomes and value to the customer. This is where any value is actually delivered and measured.

Figure 1.3 Key activities of the Service Lifecycle stages

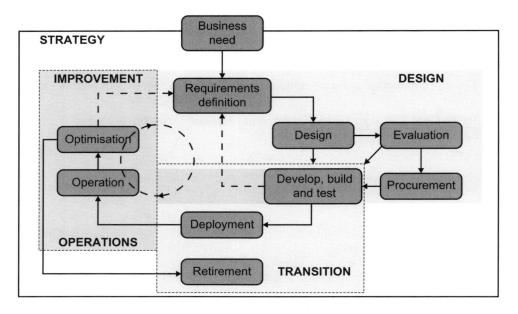

Continual Service Improvement identifies opportunities for improvement (which may arise anywhere within any of the lifecycle stages) based on measurement and reporting of the efficiency, effectiveness, cost-effectiveness and compliance of the services themselves, the technology that is in use and the Service Management processes used to manage these components. Although the measurements are taken during the operational phase, improvements may be identified for any phase of the lifecycle.

KEY CONCEPTS

Value
From the earlier definition of a service, it is clear that the primary focus is on delivering value to the service consumer. Value is created through providing the right service under the right conditions.

Customers value an IT service when they see a clear relationship between that IT service and the business value that they need to generate. In the past, both IT and business management have been very poor at understanding this link: IT has often known all about the costs of components, but not the cost of providing a service that the business understands, and the business has been unable to make value-based decisions about the worth of such solutions.

Value is created through two components:

- **Utility:** Value in the form of what the customer gets from the service. This will either be from providing new business lines or from the relaxation of existing constraints on the customer's ability to achieve their desired outcomes. Utility is about what the product or service does, determining whether it is 'Fit for purpose'.

- **Warranty:** Value in the form of how this 'utility' is delivered to the customer. This is seen as the positive effect of the service being available when and where it is required, in sufficient capacity to meet the business needs, and being sufficiently reliable in terms of continuity and security for it to be depended on (i.e. it is 'Fit for use').

UTILITY

Functionality offered by a product or service to meet a particular need. Utility is often summarised as 'what it does'.

WARRANTY

A promise or guarantee that a product or service will meet its agreed requirements.

Neither Utility nor Warranty can deliver full value on its own. A product or service may do exactly what the customer requires, but if it performs poorly, or is unavailable, insecure or unreliable, it cannot deliver maximum value. Conversely, a service will not deliver value if it does not provide the functionality needed, even though it may be highly available, reliable and secure and offer high levels of performance.

Figure 1.4 shows that value is only created when both Utility and Warranty are satisfied. A service that seems potentially attractive on paper to a customer in terms of the Utility that it offers won't be perceived as providing real value if the way it is delivered is highly unreliable or it is delivered in an insecure manner. A customer's ability to realise value from an IT service is dependent on both the Utility associated with the service and the degree to which they can rely on the consistent delivery of that service (the service Warranty).

Figure 1.4 Utility and Warranty (Source: OGC ITIL Service Strategy ISBN 978-0-113310-45-6)

EXAMPLE

When ATMs were introduced, they removed the time constraint of customers being able to withdraw cash from their account only when the bank branch was open. Since their introduction, further functionality has been added (account balances, mini statements, bill payment etc.). These are all aspects of utility, but they are of course useless unless ATMs are sited in convenient locations, are kept topped up with cash and printer paper, have secure access controls and are reliable.

Internet banking offered new utility through additional functions (e.g. transfers and online account creation) as well as allowing the customer to do all these anytime, anywhere. Different security, capacity and availability aspects are required in order to ensure the functionality is provided.

Service assets

Service providers create value through using their assets in the form of resources and capabilities.

RESOURCES

A generic term that includes IT infrastructure, people, money or anything else that might help to deliver an IT service. Resources are considered to be assets of an organisation.

CAPABILITIES

The ability of an organisation, person, process, application, configuration item or IT service to carry out an activity. Capabilities are intangible assets of an organisation.

Figure 1.5 shows how an IT service provider uses its service assets in the form of resources and capabilities to create each service that it provides.

The key difference between resource assets and capability assets is that, typically, resources can be purchased in the marketplace while distinctive capabilities can only be developed over time. Capabilities reflect the knowledge and experience of the organisation and are used to transform physical resources into services. The distinctive capabilities of a service provider, often quite intangible, set it apart from its competitors, and enable it to attract and retain customers by offering unique value propositions.

Figure 1.5 Service delivery through service assets (Source: OGC ITIL Service Strategy ISBN 978-0-113310-45-6)

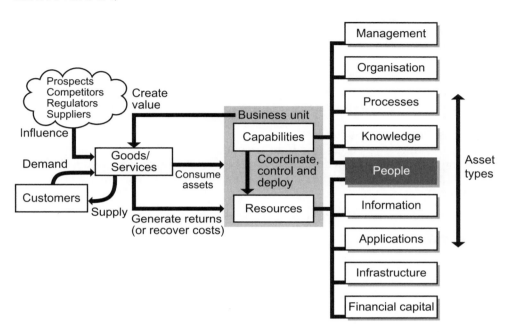

The business unit to which the service is provided will also have resources and capabilities that are harnessed to provide the end service to the customer. The integration between the service and the business unit's own assets may be very tight, making it hard to distinguish between the two, or it may be much more clearly separated.

Service Model

A Service Model describes how a service provider creates value for a given portfolio of customer contracts by connecting the demand for service from the assets of its customers with the service provider's service assets. It describes both the structure and the dynamics of the service:

- **Structure:** The particular service assets needed to deliver the service and the patterns in which they are configured.

- **Dynamics:** The activities, flow of resources, coordination, and interactions between customer and service provider assets (e.g. interaction between service users and service agents). Service dynamics include Patterns of Business Activity (PBAs), demand patterns, exceptions and variations.

A Service Model may include:

- process maps;
- workflow diagrams;
- queuing models;
- activity patterns.

Once defined, variants of a service model can be generated in order to tailor a service to a customer's specific needs.

Functions, Processes and Roles

The terms Function, Process and Role are often confused. This is not surprising since they are so intertwined. In addition, the way the words are used in ITIL is precise, and may be confused with the way these words are used in a more general context.

FUNCTION

A team or group of people and the tools they use to carry out one or more Processes or activities (e.g. the Service Desk or IT Operations).

In this context a Function is a structural part of an organisation (e.g. a division or a business unit) established to do specific things. For example, the Service Desk is a Function that is created to perform defined activities and produce specified outcomes. People within a function have defined roles that they perform to deliver the outcomes required. By their nature, functions are specialised and have their own disciplines, skills, performance measures and knowledge base. Functions perform activities that are elements of Processes. Individual Functions may perform an entire Process or, quite commonly, share Processes with other Functions.

PROCESS

A Process is a structured set of activities designed to accomplish a specific objective. A Process takes one or more defined inputs and turns them into defined outputs. A Process may include any of the Roles, responsibilities, tools and management controls required to reliably deliver the outputs. A Process may define policies, standards, guidelines, activities and work instructions if they are needed.

A process consists of a set of coordinated activities using resources and capabilities to produce an outcome, which, directly or indirectly, creates value for an external customer or stakeholder.

Every process consists of a number of elements, as shown in Figure 1.6. A process takes inputs and transforms them, using the appropriate enablers, to produce the required outputs in a closed-loop system that allows for feedback and improvement. Process control ensures that consistent repeatable processes are established, regulated and managed so that their performance is effective and efficient.

Process characteristics

A process transforms a prescribed set of data, information and knowledge into a desired outcome, using feedback as a learning mechanism for process improvement. Every process consists of a number of elements, as shown in Figure 1.6.

Figure 1.6 Process structure (Source: OGC ITIL Service Design ISBN 978-0-113310-47-0)

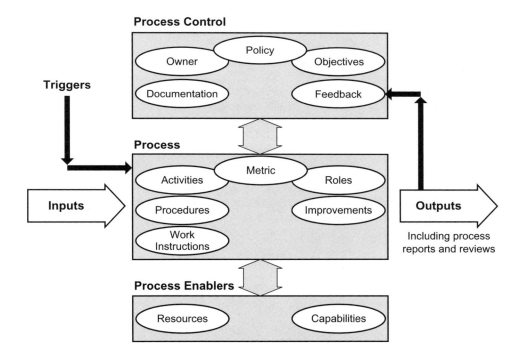

Figure 1.6 illustrates some of the basic features of a Process. First, a Process, initiated by an event or trigger, transforms inputs into outputs through a series of activities carried out by people or systems with specific roles with procedures or work instructions. It makes use of organisation resources and capabilities as process enablers. It is has an owner responsible for it. It has documented policy, terms of reference and objectives, and it is controlled to ensure it meets its specified purpose. The process is measured against defined metrics to determine how effectively it is operating and the results are fed back to drive continual improvement (this is what is known as a closed-loop feedback system).

In line with this, all processes will have certain characteristics:

- **Measurable:** We must be able to measure the Process. The performance of the Process is incredibly important. Managers will want to measure the cost and quality. People involved operationally with the Process are concerned with how long it takes and how easy it is to use.

- **Specific results:** A Process exists in order to deliver a specific result, which must be identifiable and countable.

- **Customers:** Each Process delivers its main results to a customer or stakeholder, who may be internal or external, and the results must meet their expectations.

- **Responds to a specific event:** Each Process, whether it is ongoing or iterative, will have a specific trigger.

EXAMPLE

Let's use a Process for booking theatre tickets by telephone as an example:

- **Measurement:** Management will want to ensure quality (e.g. bookings are correctly recorded, seats aren't 'double booked' etc.). The staff taking the bookings by phone may want a system that remembers details of customers from previous transactions, thus making it easier to use.

- **Results:** Each correct set of theatre tickets despatched on time or made available for collection might be the result.

- **Customer:** Customer expectations may be that the Process makes it easy to book tickets and that they are either received before they go to see the show or are available at the box office on arrival.

- **Trigger:** The customer telephone call.

Roles

ROLE

A set of responsibilities, activities and authorities granted to a person or team. A Role is defined in a Process. One person or team may have multiple roles (e.g. the roles of Configuration Manager and Change Manager may be carried out by a single person).

Therefore, a role describes what an individual actually does. Every organisation will define those Roles that it requires in order to perform the necessary tasks and will allocate individuals to perform those roles. The relationship between Roles and persons is a many-to-many one (i.e. an individual may perform more than one role and a role may be performed by more than one person). Roles may or may not be related to job titles.

As stated earlier, there should be one role that is accountable for any specific task or process. ITIL advocates that two generic roles should be defined:

Process Owner – accountable for ensuring that all activities within a Process are undertaken with responsibility for:

- defining the process strategy;
- assisting with the design of the process;
- ensuring that process documentation is available and current, and that all staff are trained correctly;
- defining policies and standards to be followed;
- defining KPIs and auditing to ensure that the Process is being followed correctly and is effective and efficient;
- reviewing proposed enhancements and providing input to the Service Improvement Plan.

Service Owner – accountable to the customer for a particular service with responsibility for:

- acting as the prime customer contact for all service-related enquiries and issues, and as an escalation point for major incidents;
- representing the Service in CAB and customer meetings;
- participating in negotiating SLAs and OLAs, and ensuring the Service is correctly defined in the Service Catelogue;
- ensuring that the service is delivered as agreed (i.e. service levels are met);
- identifying opportunities for improving the service provided;
- ensuring that effective service monitoring is implemented.

One reason why people get confused about Processes and Functions is that it is common to give names to organisation units that are the same as the names of Processes. For example, Configuration Management is an SM Process, but many organisations will have a unit called Configuration Management with responsibility for the Configuration Management Process. It is important to recognise that organisation structures are a matter of choice, but irrespective of how the organisation is structured and what the elements are called, the Service Management Processes are not a matter of choice.

The interrelationship between Functions, Process and Roles
Figure 1.7 illustrates the typical interrelationship between the three entities. Processes can span one or more Functions and require activities to be performed by one or more Roles within any function. In fact, it is usually even more complex than this, since each Role may have a different type of engagement in any individual process.

Figure 1.7 Functions, Roles and Processes

Authority matrix

An authority matrix is often used within organisations to indicate specific roles and responsibilities in relation to Processes and activities.

The RACI model is an example of an authority matrix. It is used to map the Process activities to the Roles involved in their execution. The acronym RACI is derived from the distinct ways a Role can be involved in a Process.

Responsible executes the process or activity   (does the work)
Accountable has ownership of quality and the end result   (ultimate owner)
Consulted   provides input of knowledge and information (provides assistance)
Informed   receives information about execution   (needs to know)

Within the RACI model, each activity must have a role identified as Accountable and Responsible, whereas Consulted and Informed are optional. There must be exactly one Accountable role for each activity.

Generic roles are normally used in the RACI model, but it is vitally important that the Role–Activity links it describes are mapped back to specific individuals within the organisation.

Separating the role involvement from the organisation allows flexibility in the application of Role–Activity relationships to the realities and constraints of organisational design:

- It recognises that the same Process (or activity) may be carried out by more than one organisational role or unit.

- It allows organisation design to change without impacting the underlying process model.

- It recognises constraints of geographically diverse organisations which may have to combine many responsibilities in fewer roles in smaller sites.

- It allows for complex organisations covering diverse businesses to adopt the same underlying process model without extensive adaptation.

ITIL Processes and Functions

Table 1.1 lists the ITIL Service Management Processes and Functions in alphabetical order, identifying the publication in which they are primarily defined, where significant further expansion is provided and the chapter in Section 3 that contains greater detail. Most Processes play a Role during each lifecycle stage, but only significant expansion references are included. The shaded Processes are not part of the Foundation syllabus and are not covered in detail in this book.

Table 1.1 ITIL v3 Service Management Processes and Functions

Service Management Process/Function	Core book	Further	Section 3
Seven-step Improvement Process	CSI		29
Access Management	SO		16
Application Management	SO		27
Availability Management	SD	CSI	14
Capacity Management	SD	SO, CSI	13
Change Management	ST		19
Demand Management	SS	SD	8
Evaluation	ST		
Event Management	SO		26
Financial Management	SS		7
Incident Management	SO	CSI	23
Information Security Management	SD	SO	16
IT Operations	SO		25
IT Service Continuity Management	SD	CSI	15
Knowledge Management	ST	CSI	17
Problem Management	SO	CSI	24

(Continued)

Table 1.1 *(Continued)*

Service Management Process/Function	Core book	Further	Section 3
Management of Organisational and Stakeholder Change	ST		
Release and Deployment Management	ST	SO	20
Request Fulfilment	SO		22
Service Asset and Configuration	ST	SO	18
Service Catalogue Management	SD	SS	10
Service Desk	SO		21
Service Level Management	SD	CSI	11
Service Measurement	CSI		30
Service Portfolio Management	SS	SD	9
Service Reporting	CSI		30
Service Validation and Testing	ST		
Strategy Generation	SS		
Supplier Management	SD		12
Technical Management	SO		28
Transition Planning and Support	ST		

TEST QUESTIONS FOR CHAPTER 1

CSI 09
SM 01, SM 02, SM 03, SM 04, SM 05
SL 08
PR 01, PR 03, PR 04, PR 05
A 9

SECTION 2:
THE SERVICE LIFECYCLE

2 SERVICE STRATEGY

INTRODUCTION

The objective of Service Strategy is to offer better services than the competition. You need to beat the opposition to survive. Of course, to be successful in the longer term, as the industrial landscape adjusts to the inevitable economic, social, technological and political changes, organisations have to think long term. So Service Strategy is not just about the strategy for individual services today, but also about positioning the IT service provider for the long haul. It also includes the design, development and implementation of Service Management as a foundation for sound governance and as part of the organisation's strategic asset base.

GOVERNANCE

The concept of governance is central to the sound operation and management of all healthy organisations. It covers the various policies, processes and structures established by senior management to ensure the smooth running and effective control of the organisation. The guidance provided through the ITIL disciplines offers a sound foundation for the development of effective governance, which is as important to the IT provider as to any other organisation.

The international standard for IT governance, ISO/IEC 38500:2008, 'provides a framework for effective governance of IT to assist those at the highest level of organisations to understand and fulfil their legal, regulatory, and ethical obligations in respect of their organisations' use of IT'. This framework sets out six principles for good corporate governance of IT, covering responsibility, strategy, acquisition, performance, conformance and human behaviour, making it clear that IT Governance is about much more than IT processes and controls. It is a management system used by directors of an organisation to ensure the proper and effective stewardship of the IT resource.

Nevertheless, effective IT procedures and controls are a vital component of good governance. The ITIL framework can be a key part of the foundations for excellent IT governance.

IT is a service business, and the adoption of ITIL Service Management practices is an effective way to address IT governance. Every part of the Service Lifecycle has a role to play. For example, Service Strategy ensures that IT investments not only address issues that are important to the business, but also that they are sound investments that take proper account of costs, benefits and risks. Continual Service Improvement helps the business achieve greater value and higher levels of efficiency while conforming to standards such as ISO/IEC 20000 and external constraints such as Sarbanes–Oxley (SOX). Further specific references to IT governance can be found in Chapter 7 IT Financial Management (a Service Strategy process) and Chapter 16 Information Security Management and Access Management (Service Design and Service Operation processes).

RISK

The effective management of risk, an important issue for all successful organisations, is a key component of governance.

RISK

Risk is defined as uncertainty of outcome, whether positive opportunity or negative threat.

Effective risk management requires a consistent framework in which risks are identified and analysed and appropriate measures put in place to deal with them.

KEY PROCESSES

The key processes in Service Strategy are:

- Service Strategy Development;
- Demand Management (see Chapter 8);
- Service Portfolio Management (see Chapter 9);
- Financial Management (see Chapter 7).

The final three are covered in the chapters indicated and are not described in any detail here.

SERVICE STRATEGY DEVELOPMENT

The building blocks
The long-term success of a business can be analysed in terms of three strategic factors or building blocks:

- The market focus and position of the organisation, which define where and how to compete in the marketplace.

- Performance anatomy, which is about the cultural and organisational attributes of the service provider; it is about values and mindsets that colour key decisions taken by the organisation and the individuals within it.

- Distinctive capabilities, which are capabilities the organisation has that the competition would find difficult to equal or copy. These differentiate the service provider at the delivery level.

IT SERVICE PROVIDER TYPES

In considering these factors it is important to recognise that there are different types of IT service provider, and that although all will have things in common in relation to Service Management, there will be unique aspects, for example those concerning the commercial relationship with customers and the business served by the provider.

In practice, there is a tremendous variation in the types of IT service provider. Different providers are characterised by their relationship with customers and their positioning in relation to the business or businesses they service. It is helpful to simplify this complexity and identify a small number of provider types that represent the wider variety in the marketplace. This simplification leads to the following three types:

- **Type I – Internal service provider:** This is the in-house IT unit typically positioned within the business units they serve, although it is common for these smaller scale IT units to be consolidated into a corporate IT department that has to balance the interests, demands and priorities of the corporate organisation against those of individual business units.

- **Type II – Shared services unit:** This is where a range of functions, regarded as non-core to the business, are grouped together into a corporate shared service unit. The functions involved are typically IT, finance and HR, sometimes with legal service, logistics and facilities management.

- **Type III – External service provider:** This is a separate commercial entity from the businesses it services, and operates as a competitive business in the marketplace.

THE FOUR Ps OF STRATEGY

Having considered the IT service provider's strategic approach to the marketplace, the next part of the strategic equation is the IT service provider's approach to Service Strategy. This may be analysed in terms of the four Ps:

- Strategy as a **Perspective:** This relates to vision, direction and the IT service provider's philosophy for doing business with its customers.

- Strategy as a **Position:** This describes strategy in terms of the IT service provider's general approach to its service offerings (e.g. high value or low cost, emphasis on utility or warranty).

- Strategy as a **Plan:** This describes strategy as a plan showing how the IT service provider will move from where it is today to where it wants to be.

- Strategy as a **Pattern:** This describes strategy as a consistent way of making decisions.

SERVICE MANAGEMENT AS A STRATEGIC ASSET

There are two components of Service Strategy. Service strategy is clearly about developing strategies for the delivery of specific services, but there is also the development of Service Management as a competence for providing services as part of the business strategy and as a basis for good governance.

The development of Service Management as a strategic asset is central to Service Strategy.

STRATEGIC ASSET

Strategic assets are assets that provide the basis for core competence, distinctive performance, durable advantage, and qualifications to participate in business opportunities. IT organisations can use the guidance provided by ITIL to transform their Service Management capabilities into strategic assets.

Service Management provides the framework within which value is delivered to the customer in the shape of specific services represented collectively in the Service Catalogue. The customer's confidence in commissioning new service offerings depends on the Service Management capabilities of the IT service provider.

DEVELOPING STRATEGY FOR SPECIFIC SERVICES

In terms of the development of a strategy for a specific service offering, the key elements are concerned with a series of activities that involve:

- understanding the customer and the ways IT can deliver value to them;

- understanding the outcomes the customer wants from the service and how the service will deliver benefit;

- defining critical success factors for the service;

- developing a specification based on the outcomes required by the customer, including the utility and warranty required;

- developing through Demand Management an understanding of the customer's priorities in relation to Patterns of Business Activity (PBAs).

It is important to remember that individual services have to operate in a broader context. New services must fit into the framework of existing services and any other new services with which they will likely share common services and compete for resources. The development of a Service Strategy has to take this fully into account.

At an early stage in the development of the Service Strategy, the initial, conceptual details of the new service will be captured in the Service Portfolio and the new service will begin its journey through its lifecycle. Through Service Portfolio Management, the new service offering will be put into the broader context of other services, business trends, regulation, the developing marketplace, emerging technologies, competition, risks and so on. The business case, developed in conjunction with Financial Management, will reflect these factors and explain why the Service Strategy developed represents the best way forward as well as describing how and to what extent it will deliver value.

The outcome of the Service Strategy process is a decision to continue with the service or not. Approved services are 'chartered' at which point they are ready to move forward to Service Design. The transfer into Service Design requires the production of a Service Package, which describes in detail the IT service to be delivered to the customer, including the service levels to be achieved and the supporting services that will underpin its delivery.

SERVICE PACKAGE

ITIL defines a Service Package as a detailed description of an IT service that is available to be delivered to customers. A Service Package includes a Service Level Package (SLP) and one or more Core Services and Supporting Services.

SERVICE LEVEL PACKAGE

A Service Level Package is a defined level of Utility and Warranty for a particular Service Package. Each SLP is designed to meet the needs of a particular Pattern of Business Activity.

SERVICE ASSETS

In delivering a service, the IT service provider exploits its own assets to add value to the customer's assets and generate value for the organisation.

The assets used by the IT service provider can be described in terms of its capabilities and resources, which were first introduced in Chapter 1 on page 12. The development of a successful Service Strategy needs to be built on an understanding of the service assets that can be brought into play in service delivery. There is no point in formulating a Service Strategy that requires service assets that will not be available. Making assumptions about the organisation's ability to improve its service asset base, especially its capabilities, introduces an element of risk that needs to be acknowledged, understood and managed.

Figure 2.1 Generation of value from service and customer assets

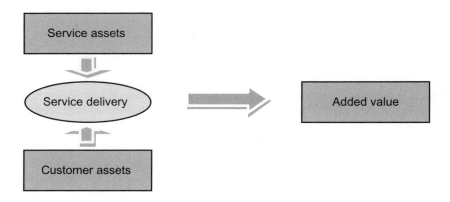

In developing a Service Strategy it is essential to recognise that generation of value to the business requires a combination of the IT service provider's assets and the customer's assets. This means that the development of Service Strategy must be informed by knowledge of the customer's resources and capabilities, and the opportunities, threats, vulnerabilities and risks associated with them. The IT service provider must look outwards as well as inwards.

VALUE

The idea that services add value is fundamental to IT service delivery and is a key input to the development of Service Strategy. There is little point in developing services that have no recognised value. In Chapter 1 on Page 11, we discussed how value is created through Utility or fitness for purpose, and Warranty or fitness for use. We can measure value not only in terms of quantifiable benefits such as financial savings or increased income, but also in terms of benefits such as service quality, which are less easily quantified and often depend on the perception of the customer or service user. The principle that value depends on customer perception leads us to conclude that effective service strategy requires a way of thinking, a 'marketing mindset', which captures the customer's perspective, through which we can understand both the customer and the outcomes that the customer really values and why, and to what extent they are valued.

AUTOMATING SERVICE MANAGEMENT PROCESSES

Automating business processes delivers higher Utility and Warranty thereby generating better performance and value from service and customer assets.

The same applies to IT Service Management. Earlier in this chapter, we identified IT Service Management capability as a strategic asset. Building this capability through automation is fundamental to providing value to the business by remaining competitive.

Of course, effective Service Management in all but the smallest organisations is inconceivable without a level of automation. For example, Configuration Management based on paper records could hardly deliver in an organisation of any significant scale. Beyond this basic level, we can identify a number of areas where automation can improve capability. For example:

- Monitoring and measuring to an extent not possible by other means, handling high levels of complexity and volume irrespective of time or location.
- Generating automated alerts helps us respond more rapidly to events, helping us maintain service availability.
- Discovery tools enable us to maintain an up-to-date Configuration Management System and identify and deal with a range of control related problems.
- Sophisticated modelling and simulation helps us design infrastructure and applications, and model complex options for service delivery.
- Artificial intelligence is able to offer a range of capabilities from root cause analysis, through sophisticated alarm and control systems, to complex scheduling and resource management.
- Workflow management systems improve customer service and efficiency across a range of processes.

At a more basic level, automation increases productivity, enables us to handle fluctuating demand and generally do more for less. Critically for IT Service Management, it also enables us to integrate across different Service Management Processes and Functions, for example through improved coherence, shared workflow and escalation processes, shared alarms and alerts, better inter-process communication, information sharing and organisational learning. This improves efficiency, helps reduce errors and duplication of effort, and delivers better value and better service to the customer.

TEST QUESTIONS FOR CHAPTER 2

SL 04, SL 05, SL 11
SS 01, SS 02, SS 04, SS 07, SS 08, SS 09, SS 10, SS 13, SS 15

3 SERVICE DESIGN

INTRODUCTION

Once an organisation has determined the IT strategy it wishes to pursue, it uses the Service Design phase of the lifecycle to create new services which Service Transition then introduces into the live environment. In so doing, Service Design aims to take the necessary steps to ensure that the new service will perform as planned and deliver the functionality and benefits intended by the business. This principle is at the heart of the ITIL approach and is why the majority of the Service Design processes are focused on operational control:

- Service Catalogue Management;
- Service Level Management;
- Capacity Management;
- Availability Management;
- IT Service Continuity Management;
- Information Security Management;
- Supplier Management.

The contribution that the Service Design phase of the lifecycle makes can therefore be summarised as ensuring the creation of cost-effective services that provide the level of quality required to satisfy customers and stakeholders throughout the life of the service.

However, the fact that business requirements change over time and generate the need or opportunity for further improvement, means that even an organisation with mature Service Design processes will need to make changes to services throughout their life. Service Design therefore has an important role to play in supporting Continual Service Improvement and is as important for managing changes to existing services as it is in designing new services. In this respect, Service Design must also consider the impact of its activities on the overall services, systems, architecture, tools and measurements in order to minimise the potential for disruption when a new or changed service is introduced into the live environment.

WHY SERVICE DESIGN?

Without well-established Service Design, services will become less stable and more expensive to maintain and become increasingly less supportive of business and customer needs. Furthermore, the cost of correcting these deficiencies is almost always higher than the costs that would have been incurred to prevent them at the design stage.

Not every change will require Service Design activities. Rather these are reserved for 'Significant' changes. Each organisation must decide its own definition of 'Significant' and use the Change Management process to assess the significance of each change and therefore whether or not Service Design activities need to be used.

Good Service Design will deliver a range of business benefits that help to underline its importance in the design of new and changed services. These are summarised below:

- Lower cost services because of the lower support and enhancement costs, leading to lower Total Cost of Ownership (TCO).
- Services that consistently provide the required level of quality and alignment to business and customer needs.
- Faster and easier introduction of new services and service changes.
- Better governance to ensure compliance to legal and corporate rules and guidelines.
- Better measurement capability to support decision-making and continual improvement.

Poor planning, preparation and management are common reasons for the failure of plans and projects in general and the design and deployment of new and changed services in particular. ITIL helps prevent this by offering guidance on preparing and planning the use of people, processes, products and partners: the Four Ps of Service Design. (N.b. It is important not to confuse these with the Four Ps of Service Strategy discussed on page 25.)

THE FIVE MAJOR ASPECTS OF SERVICE DESIGN

ITIL formally recognises five separate aspects of Service Design that together describe the scope of this part of the Service Lifecycle:

- The introduction of new or changed services through the accurate identification of business requirements and the agreed definition of service requirements.
- The Service Management systems and tools such as the Service Portfolio, ensuring mutual consistency with other services and appropriate tools support.

- The capability of technology architectures and management systems to operate and maintain new services.

- The capability of all processes, not just those in Service Design, to operate and maintain new and changed services.

- Designing in the appropriate measurement methods and metrics necessary for performance analysis of services, improved decision-making and continual improvement.

GOALS OF SERVICE DESIGN

From the considerations above, we can appreciate that the main goals of Service Design are:

- to design services that not only satisfy business and stakeholder objectives in terms of quality, ease-of-use, compliance and security, but also minimise the Total Cost of Ownership;

- to design efficient and effective policies, plans, processes, architectures and frameworks to manage services throughout their lifecycle;

- to support Service Transition in identifying and managing the risks associated with introducing new or changed services;

- to design measurement systems for assessing the efficiency and effectiveness of Service Design and its deliverables;

- to contribute to Continual Service Improvement (CSI), particularly by designing in features and benefits and then responding to improvement opportunities identified from the operational environment.

THE SERVICE DESIGN PACKAGE

The Design Stage takes a set of new or changed business requirements and develops a solution to meet them. The developed solution is passed to Service Transition to be built, tested and deployed into the live environment.

However, it is not enough simply to pass the technical or architectural design to Service Transition. The Service Transition teams will need more than this to deliver a fully functioning service that provides the Utility and Warranty expected. They need a blueprint that covers all aspects of the new service. This blueprint is known as the Service Design Package.

SERVICE DESIGN PACKAGE

(Service Design) Document(s) defining all aspects of an IT Service and their Requirements through each stage of its Lifecycle. A Service Design Package is produced for each new IT Service, major Change or IT Service Retirement.

The key contents of the Service Design Package include:

- the Service definition, agreed business requirements and how and where the Service will be used;
- the Service Design including the architectural design, functional requirements, SLRs/ SLAs (if available), service and operational management requirements including metrics and key performance indicators, supporting services and agreements;
- a service model showing the overall structure and dynamics of the Service, showing how customer and service assets, Service Management Functions and Processes come together to deliver value;
- an assessment of organisational readiness and its implications;
- a plan covering all stages of the Service Lifecycle;
- plans for Service Transition (covering build and assembly, test, release and deployment) and for operational service acceptance;
- acceptance criteria and the strategy and plan for User Acceptance Testing.

TEST QUESTIONS FOR CHAPTER 3

SL 07, SL 12
SD 03, SD 04, SD 07, SD 17

4 SERVICE TRANSITION

INTRODUCTION

There has frequently been a disconnection between the Development and Operations departments within IT, which has consequently led to many failed implementations of new or changed services. Service Transition is concerned with bridging that gap smoothly, ensuring that operational requirements are fully considered and catered for before anything is moved into the live environment, including documentation and training for users and support staff. Service Transition is also responsible for the decommissioning and removal of services that are no longer required.

Smooth transition is achieved by taking a new or changed Service Design Package (SDP) from the Service Design stage, testing it to ensure that it correctly meets the needs of the business, and deploying it within the production environment.

Some of the processes that are described within this phase are also used within other phases, in particular Service Knowledge, Change and Configuration Management.

Figure 4.1 shows the seven processes covered by Service Transition, along with Managing organisational and Stakeholder Change, which is a key Service Transition activity.

The Foundation syllabus only requires detailed knowledge of the four shaded areas in the diagram (i.e. Change Management, SACM, Release and Deployment Management and Knowledge Management), each of which has a separate chapter in Section 3. The remainder are covered later in this chapter.

GOALS, PURPOSE AND OBJECTIVES

The goals of Service Transition are to:

- set customer expectations on how the new or changed service will enable business change;
- enable the customer to integrate a release seamlessly into their business processes and services;

- reduce variations in the predicted and actual performance of the services once they are introduced;

- reduce known errors and minimise the risks from change;

- ensure that the service can be used in the manner in which it is required.

Figure 4.1 Service Transition processes (Source: OGC ITIL Service Transition ISBN 978-0-113310-48-7)

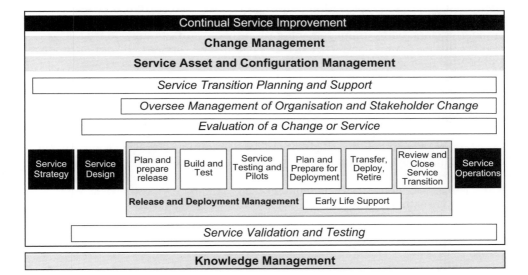

The objectives are to:

- plan and manage the resources to introduce and activate a new or changed service to the live environment within the predicted cost, quality and time estimates;

- minimise any unpredicted impact on the production services, operations and support organisation;

- increase customer, user and service management staff satisfaction with the deployment of new or changed services, including communications, release documentation, training and knowledge transfer;

- increase correct use of the services and any underlying applications and technology solutions;

- provide clear and comprehensive plans that enable alignment between the business and Service Transition.

Service Transition includes the management and coordination of the resources that are needed to package, build, test and deploy a release into production and to establish new or changed services as specified by the customer and stakeholder requirements. Service Transition also manages the transfer of services to or from external service providers.

When it is done well, Service Transition helps organisations to be more agile, with the capability and capacity to respond more rapidly and with greater certainty of success to change. This ability to adapt makes organisations more competitive as market places adjust to economic, social, environmental and political change.

Mergers, acquisitions and other major organisational changes are better managed, productivity losses through change are minimised, and risks are identified and dealt with. It also underpins sound financial management, as effective planning and budgeting for transition means fewer surprises, less disruption, higher productivity and better management of resources. As an example, in transitions that involve decommissioning of existing systems and services, the organisation will be able to identify opportunities for cost reduction through the timely termination of support contracts, maintenance agreements and licences. Services are better aligned with the needs of the business and, because training needs are identified in transition planning, people know what to expect from new or changed services and are ready to make best use of them.

In summary, effective Service Transition is an essential part of good governance. Change can be embraced more rapidly and more effectively without damaging the business, and the business, its customers and its employees can all face change with greater confidence in the outcome. Everyone knows what to expect and, if Service Transition is effective, those expectations will be borne out in reality.

PROCESS OBJECTIVES AND VALUE

Section 3 contains details on four of the processes in this phase. The remaining three processes and the activity 'Managing Organisational and Stakeholder Change' are described briefly below.

Transition Planning and Support
An integrated approach to planning improves the alignment of Service Transition plans with the plans of the customers, suppliers and the business, and can significantly improve a service provider's ability to handle high volumes of change and releases.

Service Validation and Testing
The objective of Service Validation and Testing is to ensure that a new or changed service and its associated release process will meet the needs of the business at the agreed cost.

Service Validation and Testing activities can be applied throughout the Service Lifecycle to provide quality assurance of any aspect of a service. The complete end-to-end service needs to be considered and both internally and externally developed service components included.

Service Validation provides value by preventing service failures that can harm the service provider's and the customer's assets, which can result in outcomes such as loss of reputation, financial loss, time delays, injury or even death.

Service Evaluation

Evaluation is a generic process that considers whether the performance of something is acceptable, value for money, fit for purpose and whether implementation can proceed based on defined and agreed criteria. The objectives of Service Evaluation are:

- to evaluate the intended effects of a service change and as much of the unintended effects as reasonably practical given capacity, resource and organisational constraints;

- to provide good quality outputs from the evaluation process so that change management can expedite an effective decision about whether a service change is to be approved or not.

The scope includes the evaluation of any new or changed service defined by Service Design, during deployment and before final transition to the production environment.

Managing organisational and stakeholder change

While Service Transition's basic role is to implement a new or changed service, a change of any significance may involve an organisational change, ranging from moving a few staff to work from new premises through to major alterations in the nature of business working (e.g. from face-to-face retail to web-based trading).

Organisational change efforts fail or fall short of their goals because changes and transitions are not led, managed and monitored efficiently across the organisation and throughout the change process. Service Transition therefore needs to ensure that any such implications are considered and brought to the attention of relevant stakeholders to ensure that the organisation is ready to receive and use the new service when it is introduced.

CHALLENGES

Establishing effective Service Transition can be challenging. The following are some of the issues that can arise and need to be managed:

- Ensuring that all change activity is driven through Service Transition.

- Balancing the evolving needs of the business against the need to protect live services (i.e. being responsive while maintaining suitable protection).

- Integrating with development and project lifecycles which traditionally are independent.

- Having the appropriate authority and empowerment to execute the processes as defined.

- Managing people's perceptions so that the processes are not seen as a barrier to change or as being over bureaucratic.

ROLES

The Service Transition Manager is responsible for planning and coordinating the resources to deploy a major release within the predicted cost, time and quality estimates.

TEST QUESTIONS FOR CHAPTER 4

SD 06
ST 03, ST 17

5   SERVICE OPERATION

INTRODUCTION

Service Operation is the phase of the IT Service Management Lifecycle that is responsible for 'business as usual' activities. If services are not utilised or are not delivered efficiently and effectively, they will not deliver their full value, irrespective of how well designed they may be. It is Service Operation that is responsible for utilising the processes to deliver services to users and customers.

Service Operation is where the value that has been modelled in Service Strategy and confirmed through Service Design and Service Transition is actually delivered. Without Service Operation running the services as designed and utilising the processes as designed, there would be no control and management of the services. Production of meaningful metrics by Service Operation will form the basis and starting point for Service Improvement activity.

GOALS, PURPOSE AND OBJECTIVES

The purpose of Service Operation is to organise and conduct the activities and processes needed to deliver services to business users at agreed levels of service. Additionally, Service Operation is responsible for the ongoing management of the technology (infrastructure and applications) that is utilised to deliver and support the services.

Service Operation is a balancing act. It is not just a matter of carrying out the processes on a day-to-day basis. There is a dynamic 'debate' that is taking place on four levels. These are known as the Four Balances of Service Operation:

- **Internal IT view versus external business view:** The external business view of IT will relate to the services delivered to users and customers while, internally within IT, those services will be viewed as a number of components. Individuals or teams responsible for the running of particular components may not understand how their components fit into the overall delivery of a particular service. If an organisation is too externally focused, there is the risk that agreements will be made with the business that cannot be actually delivered due to a lack of understanding of how the internal constituent parts need to operate. Conversely, an organisation that is too internally focused is likely to struggle to understand and deliver business requirements.

- **Stability versus responsiveness:** Changes are frequently the causes of Incidents and loss of availability, so it may be tempting to limit the number of changes in order to boost the stability of services. However, changes will always be needed in order to keep service up to date and to adopt to evolving business needs. The balance is between being able to speedily respond to changes and focusing on the stability of the infrastructure.

- **Quality of service versus cost of service:** There will always be pressures to boost the quality of IT services while controlling costs. Intense budgetary pressures may lead to reduced levels of service with more failures and less support. On the other hand, organisations out of balance on the 'other side' may be paying too much for their services with resilience built in that cannot be justified. The key is to have a meaningful dialogue over costs ensuring that the business fully understands what it gets and does not get for a certain amount of money and what it would get if it spent a bit less or a bit more.

- **Reactive versus proactive:** An extremely proactive organisation will always be predicting where things could go wrong and taking action to mitigate or prevent the situation. Taken to the extreme, such organisations may over monitor and apply unnecessary changes. Conversely, organisations that are purely reactive spend most of their time 'fire fighting' and dealing with situations as they arise, and they need to move more to the 'fire prevention' approach of predicting and avoiding Incidents and Problems.

THE VALUE OF SERVICE OPERATION

Each of the stages of the ITIL Service Lifecycle adds and provides value to the business. Service Operation does this by carrying out the processes and running the services as intended by the Service Strategy, Service Design and Service Transition stages of the Lifecycle. Service Operation is the visible face of the IT organisation and is the 'nearest' to the users and customers. Effective and efficient delivery of service is what is expected of Service Operation.

KEY ACTIVITIES AND FUNCTIONS

The processes performed by Service Operations are:

- **Event Management:** This is the process responsible for the monitoring of all events throughout the IT infrastructure and applications to ensure normal operation. Event Management is there to detect, escalate and react to exceptions.

- **Incident Management:** This is the process for dealing with all Incidents. These may be Incidents where service is being disrupted or where service has not yet been disrupted.

- **Request Fulfilment:** This is the process that carries out Service Requests from users. Request Fulfilment covers Standard Change requests, requests for information and complaints. From a Service Desk perspective, the process of Request Fulfilment tends to cover all the calls that are neither Incidents nor relate to Problems.

- **Problem Management:** This process is responsible for the management of all Problems in the IT infrastructure. The process includes root cause analysis and arriving at the resolution of Problems. Problem Management remains responsible until resolutions are implemented via the processes of Change Management and Release Management.

- **Access Management:** This process enables users with the correct level of authorisation to access an application or service. It is also ensures that those without the required level of authorisation are not able to access applications and services. Access Management allows an organisation to control access to applications and services.

The functions of Service Operation are:

- **The Service Desk:** This conducts a number of processes, in particular Incident Management and Request Fulfilment. The Service Desk is made up of a group of staff trained to deal with service events. Service Desk staff will have access to the necessary tools to manage these events. The Service Desk ought to be the single point of contact for IT users within an organisation.

- **Technical Management:** This is the function that provides the resources and ensures that knowledge of relevant technologies is kept up to date. Technical Management covers all the teams or areas that support the delivery of technical knowledge and expertise. This includes teams such as Networks, Mainframe, Middleware, Desktop, Server and Database.

- **Application Management:** This will manage applications through the totality of their lifecycle. This starts with the first business 'idea' and completes when the application is taken out of service. Application Management is involved in the design, testing and continual improvement of applications and the services that the applications support.

- **IT Operations Management:** This is responsible for operating the organisation's IT infrastructure and applications on a day-to-day basis.

The area which delivers the value has been modelled and designed elsewhere, so Service Operation will have many interfaces to processes that are part of the other Lifestyle phases, in particular Service Asset and Configuration Management, Release and Deployment Management, Knowledge Management, IT Service Continuity Management and Service Level Management.

SELF HELP

Organisations are increasingly utilising Self Help offerings to enable users to resolve issues as they arise. The technology needs to be put in place to allow users to access information that will be helpful to them via a web-based front-end. Incident reporting and Service Requests can be handled in a similar fashion.

Self Help is cost-effective and aims to keep users active in their roles. Statistics can be gathered on the most frequently asked questions or most visited pages. This reduces the risk that training needs or technology gaps are not identified even though there has not been a logged Service Desk call.

Good communication is crucial for Service Operation. There needs to be active communication between IT teams and departments and with business areas and users. Members of staff undertaking Service Operation processes should be aware of the requirement to communicate on a regular basis with members of staff conducting other processes.

One should remember, however, that effective communication must have an understood purpose and, ideally, a specified audience. Too much communication without specific purpose or desired outcome can and usually will be counterproductive. Information overload tends to dull people's attention to new information, and this can be just as bad as not communicating.

TEST QUESTIONS FOR CHAPTER 5

SO 07, SO 21, SO 23, SO 24
A 12

6   CONTINUAL SERVICE IMPROVEMENT

INTRODUCTION

Once a Service Management solution has been implemented, it is essential not to sit back and think that the job has been done. All aspects of the environment will be continually changing, and the service provider must always continue to seek improvements. Continual Service Improvement is responsible for ensuring that these improvements are identified and implemented. The performance of the IT service provider is continually measured and improvements are made to processes, IT services and the IT infrastructure in order to increase efficiency, effectiveness and cost-effectiveness.

GOALS, PURPOSE AND OBJECTIVES

Goals
Continual Service Improvement (CSI) aims to deliver business value by ensuring that the Service Management implementation continues to deliver the desired business benefits.

Objectives
CSI has the following objectives:

- To review, analyse and make recommendations on where improvements could be made at any point throughout the lifecycle.
- To review and analyse service level achievements against targets.
- To identify and implement individual activities to improve service quality and the efficiency and effectiveness of service management processes.
- To improve the cost-effectiveness of delivering IT services without impacting customer satisfaction.
- To apply quality management methods to support continual improvement activities.

CSI must be an objective for everyone in the organisation, but improvement activities will only happen if they are properly managed. A senior responsible owner must be appointed and they must possess the appropriate authority to make things happen. This is not a trivial role, since improvements may mean significant disruption of current work patterns.

Improvement activities need to be planned and scheduled on an ongoing basis and their effects monitored to ensure that the desired improvement is achieved. Ideally, the culture of 'improvement' will become embedded within the organisation.

Scope

CSI is applicable across all stages of the Service Lifecycle and addresses three main areas:

- The overall health of Service Management as a discipline.
- Continual alignment of the Service Portfolio with current and future business needs.
- The maturity of the enabling IT processes.

Value to business

CSI recognises that the value IT provides to the business can be realised and measured in different ways:

- **Improvements:** Outcomes that are better when compared with the previous state.
- **Benefits:** The gains achieved through the implemented improvements.
- **Return on investment (ROI):** The difference between the realised benefit and the cost of achieving it.
- **Value of investment (VOI):** The extra value created by the improvement including non-monetary benefits and outcomes.

Implementing CSI means committing to continued investment in order to create and maintain Service Improvement Plans (SIPs).

The expected value from an investment is a critical component of any business case, and CSI stresses the need for periodic re-evaluation following the implementation of improvements by:

- checking that benefits/ROI/VOI are realised by specific improvements;
- identifying the best investments by estimating benefits from different initiatives;
- assessing the impact on current benefit of any proposed change of organisation structure or business strategy, or of regulatory or legislative change.

Many organisations have been traditionally very poor at checking that planned benefits have actually been delivered in the manner intended and hence often compound the situation by making future decisions on the assumption that some significant change in value has occurred.

KEY PRINCIPLES

Continual Service Improvement model

The Continual Service Improvement model (see Figure 6.1) can be applied to any improvement plan. The model consists of six steps:

Figure 6.1 Continual Service Improvement model (Source: OGC ITIL Continual Service Improvement ISBN 978-0-113310-49-4)

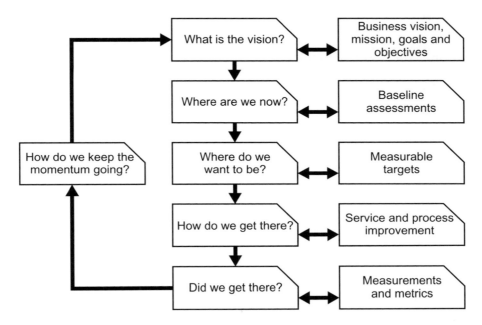

(1) Clarify the vision, taking into account both the business and IT vision, mission, goal and objectives, and ensuring that everyone has a common understanding. Visions are aspirational and represent a desired state.

(2) Assess the current situation and establish a baseline of exactly where the organisation is currently. This can be challenging and there is a need to be honest, which is why external input can be useful.

(3) Define steps towards the vision based on priorities for improvement and setting measurable targets. It is usually impossible to leap from wherever you currently are direct to the state represented by the vision.

(4) Document an improvement plan, using service and process improvement techniques.

(5) Monitor achievements, making use of appropriate measures and metrics as defined earlier.

(6) Maintain the momentum by ensuring that improvements are embedded and looking for further improvement opportunities.

Delivering improvements

A key to successful improvement is measurement. CSI advocates the use of industry approaches such as the Deming 'Plan–Do–Check–Act' model (see Chapter 31 on page 178) and a process known as the 'Seven-step Improvement Process' (see Chapter 29 on page 168).

TEST QUESTIONS FOR CHAPTER 6

CSI 01, CSI 02, CSI 04
A 11, A 13

TEST QUESTIONS FOR SECTION 2

SL 01, SL 02, SL 03, SL 06, SL 09
A 4, A 8

SECTION 3:
THE PROCESSES AND FUNCTIONS

7 IT FINANCIAL MANAGEMENT (SS 5.1)

INTRODUCTION

No business can survive for long, let alone flourish, if it fails to manage its money effectively. Like any other business, the IT service provider, whether run as a commercial business or not, needs sound financial management. It must ensure it has the right amount of money available to put its plans into action, to make sure that it understands how its money has been used, to determine if the money has been used effectively or whether a proposed new investment is sound. It needs to understand what individual services cost to deliver and how these costs should be divided among the service users, so that, among other things, it can assess the impact of changes in demand and levy charges for service use if appropriate.

Financial Management is about looking after the organisation's financial resources, making sure that they are prudently employed and that their use is properly accounted for. Financial Management makes sure the organisation has an understanding of the costs of its operations, the structure of these costs and the things that influence them. It helps the organisation make the best decisions about the services it should provide, the way services should be provisioned, the investments required for their delivery and the effect of changing patterns of demand. It evaluates the value of services to the business and, if relevant, a basis for setting prices for them. Working with Service Portfolio Management, it helps the organisation determine the services it should provide and those it should discontinue or change in some way.

Financial Management helps with financial planning, making sure that the organisation's plans align with its ability to support the financial costs and manage the risks. It keeps track of expenditure so that it is clear how the money has been used. By routinely comparing expenditure and income with financial plans and budgets, Financial Management will identify potential problems and take appropriate action to keep the organisation on track. Where the IT service provider charges for service, Financial Management will advise on how this should be done and what charges should be levied.

IT service providers must work in a rapidly changing world. Businesses, and the context in which they operate, are constantly changing, and the IT service provider must respond rapidly and effectively to these changes. Strong Financial Management enables the IT service provider to make better decisions and respond more rapidly to change. It enables better control over spending, ensures sound investment decisions and promotes value capture.

GOALS, PURPOSE AND OBJECTIVES

The goal of IT Financial Management is to ensure that optimal use is made of the organisation's financial resources and that this is achieved in compliance with the regulatory framework within which the IT service provider operates.

The purpose of Financial Management is to ensure that:

- money is managed and spent wisely;
- the financial resources available align fully with the organisation's plans and requirements for IT service delivery;
- investment decisions are sound and relevant to the organisations objectives;
- financial risks are identified and managed effectively;
- governance arrangements are in place to ensure the effective stewardship of financial resources and to define clear accountabilities;
- the organisation complies with all relevant financial regulatory obligations and the overall financial policy and strategy of the business.

The key objectives are to ensure that:

- there is an effective system for financial planning and budgeting;
- financial plans and budget allocations are aligned with the Service Portfolio;
- all proposed investments have a business case that meets the standards of the organisation;
- all significant financial risks are identified and fully managed;
- there is an appropriate governance framework in place with clear account- abilities and all those who need to be are properly trained in relation to it;
- all financial expenditure is properly accounted for and there is an audit process to ensure proper stewardship of financial resources;
- the costs and value of all IT services, processes and activities are monitored, measured and understood and appropriate actions are taken on the basis of their financial performance.

ACTIVITIES AND CONCEPTS

Service Valuation
Services are what the business sees and understands and if IT Financial Management adopts a service perspective, it will be using a language familiar to the business. Financial Management is concerned with quantifying the value of services and of the assets underlying their provision (Service Valuation). Service Value has two components: the Service Provisioning Value and the Service Value Potential. The first is the actual cost of provisioning the service. This 'Provisioning Value' is the sum of the actual costs of delivering the service. This has many similarities to the traditional cost model, where cost elements covering hardware,

software, personnel, accommodation etc. are allocated to specific services. Generally, the Provisioning Value represents the minimum value of a service since providers will rarely wish to provide service where the full provisioning cost cannot be recovered. The Service Value Potential is the added value of the service based on what the customer perceives as the financial benefit. The total value of the service is the sum of these two parts. This provides IT and the business with a common language for understanding what IT delivers, what it is worth to the business and, if charging is in place, what a fair price would be.

Demand Modelling, Service Portfolio Management and Service Provisioning Optimisation

Service Valuation information is used to forecast the cost of delivery against a pattern of changing demand (Demand Modelling). Financial Management provides financial information that enables the organisation to understand the costs and efficiencies of services included in the Service Catalogue and to make decisions about the best way of provisioning these services (Service Portfolio Management and Service Provisioning Optimisation).

Financial Management analyses data that enables the organisation to translate service costs and patterns of demand into financial resourcing requirements. The total operating costs for the IT service provider will cover all delivered services included in the Service Catalogue, the costs associated with new and changing services in the Service Pipeline and any other costs not otherwise included in service costs. For organisations where financial planning is based on a fixed budget cycle, this information, along with information on expected income, will be translated into budgets.

Governance and compliance

Financial Management will also establish rules for sound financial governance. For example, many organisations will have rules controlling expenditure that will create longer-term financial liabilities. There may be controls over the recruitment of permanent staff because this creates a continuing liability for salaries or redundancy payments. The procurement of fixed assets may mean a continuing commitment for maintenance. Without these controls, an organisation can easily build up problems for the future in the form of financial liabilities it cannot meet.

One responsibility of Financial Management is to ensure that the organisation complies with all elements of the regulatory framework, including any requirements for statutory returns and reports. Financial Management establishes internal structures and processes, including internal audits, to ensure compliance. Part of this responsibility will concern monitoring expenditure and income against financial plans and budgets to make sure that things are going as planned. Any significant variations from what was planned and expected must be identified and dealt with before they put the organisation at risk.

Budgeting

It is important to plan ahead to make sure that business plans match the money available. The product of this planning is a financial plan or budget covering expected expenditure and income for a specified period, usually a (financial) year. Expenditure and income will be divided into categories to facilitate financial planning, management and control.

The budget must reflect the services to be delivered, new projects, investments and other planned changes. It is not an articulation of what the business hopes to do: it is about what can be realistically achieved. Even so, a budget is a plan and plans do not always work out. Budgets should be the best prediction the organisation can make, but should include some contingency for the unexpected.

Budgets should show how expenditure and income is likely to change during the budget period (e.g. higher labour and transport costs at seasonally busy times).

Sound financial management requires regular monitoring against budgets. It tells the organisation when action is needed to maintain financial control, giving early warning that expenditure is too high or income too low; that planned projects cannot be funded or that others may be brought forward. Financial Management may require managers to reduce expenditure or increase income to get back on track. Sometimes, variations in one part of the budget will be offset elsewhere and the budget can be revised accordingly. For example, lower expenditure on in-house employees offset by higher expenditure on contractors.

However, budgets must never be changed simply to bring them into line with the real world. Significant variations are a warning that things are not as expected. Good governance requires managers to take considered action in response.

Accounting

The processes in IT accounting allow the IT service provider to account for expenditure and income, providing a breakdown of how costs and income are divided between customers, services and activities. This analysis helps determine the cost-effectiveness of services to make sound decisions about them. It provides details of how costs can be attributed to customers and customer groups, allowing the organisation to identify key customers and the impact of their service consumption. The information gathered through the Accounting Process provides budget monitoring with expenditure and income data, which will be used to evaluate the effectiveness of financial controls and to determine if action is required to rectify any significant variations from budget.

Charging

The decision whether to charge is a strategic decision to be taken with due care. Charging not only increases the operating costs of the IT service provider, but also increases accountability, exposure and transparency. Customers can compare what they get from IT with what they have to pay, and they can more easily compare their in-house IT provider with alternatives. Charging provides a means to influence customer behaviour, shaping demand and usage to match capacity, thereby reducing costs and risk. Without charging, many customers and users will see IT services as free and will make demands on these services with little interest in the financial or operational implications. The introduction of charging helps change attitudes.

Service Investment Analysis

All organisations need to invest wisely and a key role of Financial Management is to evaluate proposals for investment to determine whether they are worthwhile.

Sound Financial Management will require all proposals for investment to include a clear case for making the investment. This case normally takes the form of a Business Case.

A Business Case is a decision support and planning tool that projects the likely consequences of a business action. The core of the Business Case is usually a financial analysis, but the justification of investments frequently depends on more than financial considerations.

EXAMPLE

A local authority wished to establish a service for quickly identifying whether a child had been previously identified as being at risk. If a child appeared at the local hospital accident and emergency department, the duty doctor would be able to check the child's details against the At Risk Register and notify Social Services if there was a positive result. This involved a considerable investment in IT systems and support services but there was no direct financial benefit. Nevertheless, the potential benefits (e.g. in avoiding the unnecessary death or injury of a child at risk) overrode the financial cost.

Financial Management, in conjunction with business managers and other key stakeholders, will assess the business case in relation to the scale of the investment and the anticipated return, the impact on the business, the timescale for the realisation of benefits, the risks and contingencies involved, the robustness of the figures and their sensitivity to change. All of these should be covered in a sound Business Case.

It is essential that the Business Case makes it clear how the benefits and costs have been assessed, the assumptions on which it relies and the level of confidence in the figures. Business Cases sometimes depend on highly optimistic or even dubious views of the future, and it is crucial that this is made clear to the decision-makers. For example, it is common for Business Cases to predict staff savings based on individuals saving a few minutes of their time each day through a new investment. All these free minutes are aggregated, costed and presented as a benefit, even though there may be no practical way of realising a financial saving. It will also evaluate the resource requirements and take a view on whether the organisation has the resources and capabilities to deliver. An important concept is that of affordability. An investment may offer outstanding prospects, but the organisation should not give approval unless it can afford it.

RELATIONSHIPS WITH OTHER SERVICE MANAGEMENT PROCESSES

IT Financial Management is central to IT Service Management, and it has links with many of the other Service Management disciplines. The key interactions are with Service Level Management, Service Portfolio Management, Capacity Management and Configuration Management.

Service Level Management

Service Level Management (SLM) needs to work with Financial Management in relation to the costs of proposed levels of service required to meet the organisation's current and planned business needs. These costs will feed into the debate about what is affordable and deliverable and, therefore, what can be agreed in Service Level Agreements (SLAs). If charging is in place, Financial Management will be involved in determining charges, including the use of differential charging as part of Demand Management. Financial Management will assist in costing changes and evaluating new investments required to meet business needs.

Service Portfolio Management

Financial Management is concerned with business case development, assessment of investment opportunities, evaluation of different service options, the evaluation of financial risks and the determination of service value. All these are central to decisions about what should be included in the Service Portfolio or removed from it. Financial Management is able to contribute to decisions on how best to provision a given service, whether this should be through the in-house IT service provider or a third-party provider. Financial Management is also responsible for ensuring that funding is available to support the delivery of the Service Portfolio and for ensuring budget allocations align with it.

Capacity Management

Both Availability and Capacity Management are concerned with cost-effective delivery of services, and Financial Management can assist by providing costing information to enable assessment of the financial impact of desired levels of Capacity and Availability. Proposals to invest in new capacity or in increased resilience can be assessed by Financial Management before action is taken to purchase. Where charging is in place, Capacity Management will be able to provide information on resource usage that will help Financial Management determine charges.

Configuration Management

Configuration Management manages and maintains the Configuration Management Database (CMDB), which holds financial and other information on assets that are required by Financial Managements for a variety of uses. For example, from the CMDB, it should be possible to identify all the components required to deliver a given Service and this information is used by Financial Management to determine the overall cost of the Service. The CMDB also holds information on assets, such as equipment replacement dates and licence termination/renewal dates, which can be used in budget development and longer-term financial planning.

TEST QUESTIONS FOR CHAPTER 7

SS 05, SS 13, SS 14
A 6

8   DEMAND MANAGEMENT   (SS 5.5)

INTRODUCTION

Effective Demand Management avoids unnecessary spend on capacity and reductions in service levels caused by fluctuations in workload or demand.

As a service provider, IT is responsible for providing just enough capacity for services to meet their agreed service levels. Too much capacity is a wasted cost and too little puts service levels at risk. This is described in detail in the Capacity Management process (see Chapter 13 on page 89).

The process of Demand Management is necessary for two main reasons:

- The arrival rate of work, such as transactions sent to a server, print jobs sent to a printer or calls to a Service Desk, is not steady. In other words, there are peaks and troughs over the hour and day, as well as seasonal increases or decreases in demand. There is rarely sufficient flexibility in IT resources to provide just enough capacity to meet the demand at each and every point in time.
- Fluctuations in demand and the challenge of providing just the right amount of capacity are sources of risk that the service provider should minimise. The decision on how much risk is acceptable is taken by the business, which may accept a level of spare capacity (and therefore extra cost) to reduce the risk.

In ITIL terms, 'Demand' refers to the source of the work, such as the submission by the business/customers of batch jobs or a web search. It also refers to the activity that is subsequently generated on IT resources, such as network traffic and read/write calls to storage devices.

GOALS, PURPOSE AND OBJECTIVES

The goal of Demand Management is to optimise the use of capacity by moving workload to less utilised times and resources. In so doing, more efficient use is made of the resources because their utilisation can be evened out over time instead of having to cater for peaks or troughs in load.

The purpose of Demand Management is therefore to understand and influence customer demand for services in order to support the provision and management of minimum capacity to meet these demands.

The objectives include:

- characterising and codifying business activities into specific and recognisable patterns that have a common service consumption profile;
- characterising the usage of services by users into user profiles;
- encouraging the use of services at less busy times, for example by offering discounts at these times.

The first two objectives help to understand and predict the demand for resources better. This makes it easier for the service provider to match the services and resources to the identified needs of each user profile. Ultimately, this leads to improved value for both customers and suppliers by minimising costs and poor performance.

UNDERSTANDING DEMAND FLUCTUATIONS

Since the work that creates the demand comes from the business, ITIL recommends that to understand how demand fluctuates we identify Patterns of Business Activity. There is clearly a relationship between business activities and the consumption of IT resources. Our challenge is to understand that relationship well enough so that when the business shares its plans and forecasts with us, we can predict the impact on our resources. This in turn will tell us which resources need to be replaced or upgraded, and when, so that we can cost-effectively plan and budget our IT spend.

ATTEMPTING TO REDUCE PEAK DEMANDS

Provided the business agrees, IT can look to influence demand to reduce peak workloads and protect service levels without spending money on capacity that would otherwise be unused most of the time. Consider Figure 8.1 that shows a workload profile of demand over a twelve-month period.

In this scenario, IT has to provide capacity for 165 units of work in July and 172 in August. However, without this two-month peak, a capacity to handle only 130 units of work is necessary. Therefore, if IT can smooth out this peak demand and spread the workload in July and August across other months, it could potentially save the cost of providing capacity for up to 42 extra units of work.

One way of limiting demand is to increase the price for work units at peak times and/or reduce the price at off-peak times. Another way is to restrict the workload, for example in an online application by limiting the number of concurrent users, or in a Service Desk by reducing the number of lines available to callers.

PATTERNS OF BUSINESS ACTIVITY

Patterns of Business Activity (PBAs) can often be conveniently associatd with a small number of defined user profiles. In this way we can relate any new

Figure 8.1 Workload profile

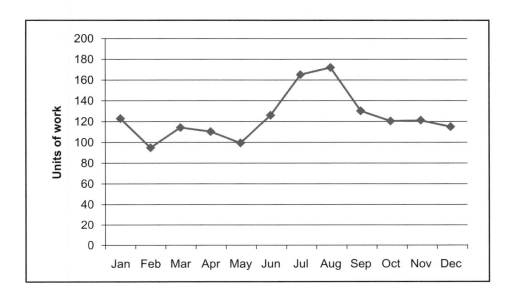

individual, team or department to a particular user profile to understand their impact on resources rather than spending the effort to consider them individually.

Table 8.1 shows how PBAs could be codified.

†Table 8.1 Codifying Patterns of Business Activity

PBA No. 45F Activities	Activity levels High	3	2	1	Low	N/A
Interact with customers remotely (frequency)			✗			
Interact with customers on site (frequency)				✗		
Archive or handle customer information			✗			
Process sensitive information (privacy)						✗
Generate confidential information						✗
Provide technical support (frequency)	✗					

(Continued)

Table 8.1 *(Continued)*

PBA No. 45F Activities	Activity levels High	3	2	1	Low	N/A
Seek technical assistance				✗		
Network bandwidth requirements		✗				
Data storage requirements (volume)		✗				
Tolerance for delay in service response			✗			
Seasonal variations in activity				✗		
Print documents and images			✗			
Mailing of documents using third party systems			✗			
Process transactions with wireless mobile device				✗		
Email using wireless device					✗	
Access work systems during domestic travel				✗		
Access work systems during overseas travel					✗	

USER PROFILES

User profiles should be based on the roles and responsibilities in an organisation. In this way, each user profile can be assigned to one or more PBA, as shown in Table 8.2.

You will notice that applications and processes can also be profiled in the same way as users. This approach allows patterns and profiles to be matched in order to understand and manage customer demand more easily and accurately.

THE BENEFITS OF DEMAND MANAGEMENT

Once the Demand Management process has understood demand fluctuations and applied controls to limit peak demand, Capacity Management becomes more effective in planning capacity, reducing unnecessary spend and acquiring resources more cost-effectively. As a result, service levels improve and the business gains increased confidence in IT's ability to meet both its present and future requirements.

†Table 8.2 Profile – PBA mapping

User profile	Applicable Pattern of Business Activity (PBA)	PBA code
Senior executive (UP1)	Moderate travel – domestic and overseas; highly sensitive information; zero latency on Service Requests; high need for technical assistance; need to be highly available to the business	45F 45A 35D
Highly mobile executive (UP2)	Extensive travel – domestic and overseas; sensitive information; low latency on Service Requests; moderate need for technical assistance; high customer contact; need to be highly available to customers	45A 35D 22A
Office-based staff (UP3)	Office-based administrative staff; low travel – domestic; medium latency on Service Requests; low need for technical assistance; full-featured desktop needs; moderate customer contact; high volume of paperwork; need to be highly productive during work hours	22A 14B 3A
Payment processing system (UP4)	Business system; high volume; transaction-based; high security needs; low latency on Service Requests; low seasonal variation; mailing of documents by postal service; automatic customer notification; under regulatory compliance; need for low unit costs; need to be highly secure and transparent (audit control)	12F
Customer assistance process (UP5)	Business process; moderate volume; transaction-based; moderate security needs; very low latency on service requests; medium seasonal variation; mailing of replacement parts by express; automatic customer notification; need to be highly responsive to customers	24G 10G

RELATIONSHIPS WITH OTHER SERVICE MANAGEMENT PROCESSES

Capacity Management

Demand Management is a key contributor to Capacity Management because it helps understand the nature of demand on resources and can reduce the capacity requirements by smoothing out peaks in demand.

Service Portfolio Management, Service Catalogue Management

Codifying patterns of business demand and user profiles can contribute to Service Portfolio and Service Catalogue Management by helping to align services to particular business needs and requirements.

Financial Management

Financial Management can contribute to Demand Management by assisting with financial uplifts and discounts to influence and smooth demand across peaks and troughs.

ROLES

Only large IT operations are likely to have a Demand Manager. It is more likely that the Demand Management activity will be undertaken by the Capacity Manager.

METRICS

There are no standard metrics associated with this process, but we offer some suggestions below:

- The peak : average load ratio (should reduce over time with effective demand management).

- The percentage of users who have been profiled.

- For a given period (e.g. one year) the amount of spend avoided through demand management.

- The percentage of services in the Service Catalogue that have been validated against user profiles and PBAs.

TEST QUESTIONS FOR CHAPTER 8

SL 10
SS 11, SS 12

9 SERVICE PORTFOLIO MANAGEMENT (SS 5.3)

INTRODUCTION

Although not strictly part of the Foundation level, it is nevertheless useful to have an understanding and awareness of the Service Portfolio, a key part of which is the Service Catalogue.

The Service Portfolio, which gives a management-level view of all IT services as they move through the Service Lifecycle, is a critical management system in ITIL v3. It has three parts:

- The Service Pipeline that holds information on services that are under development.
- The Service Catalogue that holds details of all services either already in production or ready to move into production.
- Retired Services that have been discontinued from operational use.

The Service Portfolio therefore provides a complete picture of all services under development for future delivery, services in production and services that have come to the end of their productive life. It is the foundation for managing the full Lifecycle for all services in terms of their business requirements, the business case for investment, the financial and other resources required for service development and operation, the risks associated with the development and operation of the service and, where relevant, how the service will be priced.

The IT service provider, in conjunction with the business, will identify a number of opportunities for investment in new or changed IT services. Before any of these opportunities are transformed into a service, important decisions must be made about the value of the new services to the business, the capacity of the IT service provider and the marketplace to deliver the service, and the relative priority of the proposed service in comparison with other potential investments. In other words, the organisation will need answers to questions such as:

- Why should we invest in this service rather than something else?
- What value will it deliver to the business?
- What will it cost to deliver the service solution and can we afford it?
- Do we have the resources and capabilities to deliver it?

- How does this investment fit with our broader strategy?
- What are the dependencies with other investments in progress or under consideration?
- What are the risks?
- Is the return on the investment acceptable in terms of investment cost, risks and timescale?

GOALS, PURPOSE AND OBJECTIVES

The goal of Service Portfolio Management (SPM) is to ensure that decisions to invest in IT services are sound and are fully aligned with the needs and priorities of the business. Once a decision is made to invest, the investment must be managed through its lifecycle, and SPM's goal here is to ensure that the investment delivers optimum value to the organisation. As a management support system, the Service Portfolio enables the organisation to answer strategic questions about its services, customers and pricing, as well as helping it set priorities and plan resource allocation.

An objective of SPM is to ensure there is an effective methodology for the evaluation of potential investments. Once an investment has been agreed, the purpose of SPM is to ensure that the investment is managed effectively throughout its lifecycle. Among other things this is about ensuring proper governance arrangements are in place, that investments and their business case are reassessed against changing conditions both within and outside the organisation and that the realisation of benefits is properly managed.

The objectives of SPM are:

- to develop and maintain a Service Portfolio that provides a complete picture of all services including their status;
- to establish conditions and requirements for inclusion of new services in the Service Portfolio;
- to ensure a Service Catalogue is developed and managed as part of the Portfolio, and agree the rules for transferring services to the Service Catalogue as they move into Transition and out of the Catalogue and as they move into retirement;
- to ensure the Service Portfolio meets the functional and performance requirements of its users and that its performance, availability and security meet agreed requirements;
- to ensure that management reports are produced in line with agreed reporting requirements.

SERVICE PORTFOLIO COMPONENTS

The Service Portfolio contains information about services across the entire lifecycle, providing information on the status of services as they move from concept through requirement specification, approval, design, transition into live operation and eventual retirement. The information held on each service develops and changes as it moves through the lifecycle. In the early part of the lifecycle, there will be little more than a description of the proposed service with details of the value proposition, business sponsors and other basic details. As we move through the lifecycle, requirements will be specified and either incorporated or cross-referenced. The business case will be included along with funding details, priorities and risks. Offerings and packages, costs and prices will be added once designed and agreed.

By the time the service is ready for operational delivery, the full content of the Service Portfolio should include:

- †"Service name;
- Service description;
- Service status;
- Service classification and criticality;
- applications used;
- data and/or data schema used;
- business processes supported;
- business owners;
- business users;
- IT owners;
- Service warranty level, SLA and SLR references;
- supporting services;
- supporting resources;
- dependent services;
- supporting OLAs, contracts and agreements;
- Service costs;
- Service charges (if applicable);
- Service revenue (if applicable);
- Service metrics."

In order to manage and understand the information, the Service Portfolio is separated conceptually, and often physically, into three separate components:

- The Service Pipeline, which covers services that have not yet moved into operation.
- Retired Services, which includes information on services that have been taken out of operational use and for which it is considered of value to retain the information about them.

- In between these are services that are operational and delivering to the customer. These services are covered by the Service Catalogue, which is described in more detail in Chapter 10 (see page 67) on Service Catalogue Management.

The structure of the Service Portfolio is illustrated in Figure 9.1.

Figure 9.1 The Service Portfolio (Source: OGC ITIL Service Strategy ISBN 978-0-113310-45-6)

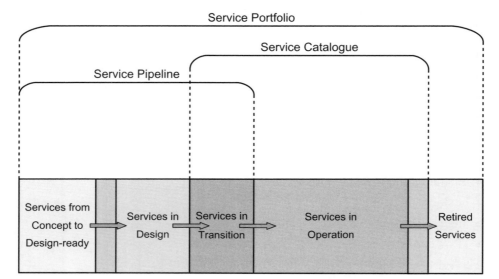

From a broader perspective, the Service Portfolio is best included as a part of the IT service provider's Service Knowledge Management System.

The Service Pipeline
The Service Pipeline holds details of all services that are not yet ready for transition into production. It gives IT service provider management a complete view of their plans for new and changing services and it is a measure of the IT provider's vision for, and confidence in, the future. It reflects the IT provider's service strategy.

The Service Catalogue
The Service Catalogue contains information about IT services that are currently in production or are about to go through Service Transition into production. It is therefore a measure of the IT service provider's current capacity, capability and confidence to deliver. The Service Catalogue is the part of the Service Portfolio that is available to customers and is written in language suitable for this purpose.

Retired Services
Services eventually come to the end of their useful life, perhaps because they are no longer relevant to the customer's needs or because they are no longer

cost-effective. There is no point continuing with a service that is not wanted or is uneconomical to run, unless there is an alternative justification for its retention.

Information about retired services should be retained as part of the IT service provider's Service Knowledge Management System for as long as such information is likely to be useful. In some circumstances, a retired service may become operationally viable and be taken out of retirement.

KEY ACTIVITIES

Service Portfolio Management is about how decisions are made to include new services and the continual review of existing services in the Service Portfolio. This is best described as a cyclic process that moves around the Define–Analyse–Approve–Charter loop illustrated in Figure 9.2.

Figure 9.2 The Service Portfolio Management Cycle (Source: OGC ITIL Service Strategy ISBN 978-0-113310-45-6)

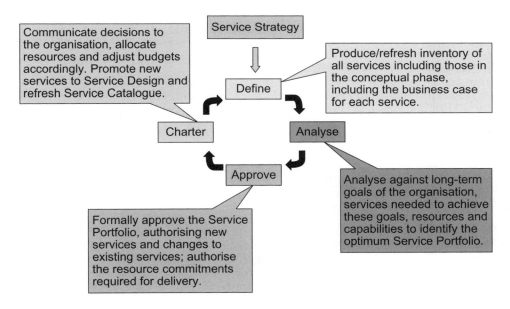

RENEWING THE PORTFOLIO

As circumstances change (e.g. changes in the economic outlook, changes in raw material prices or labour costs, marketplace changes etc.) decisions made on the content of the Service Portfolio will need to be reassessed. Part of Service Portfolio Management must therefore involve monitoring the commercial, social, economic and political environment to identify events that should trigger a reassessment of the Service Portfolio.

RELATIONSHIPS WITH OTHER SERVICE MANAGEMENT PROCESSES

Its importance throughout the Lifecycle, and its value to all other processes and functions, means that the Service Portfolio is described as the 'spine' that links the different Lifecycle stages together.

Business Relationship Management
Service Portfolio Management is a critical management system supporting the way the IT service provider works in conjunction with the business to ensure that IT adds optimum value. Managing the Service Portfolio requires full collaboration with the business and this means involvement from Business Relationship Management.

Financial Management
One of the key relationships for Service Portfolio Management is with Financial Management. The contribution from Financial Management is concerned with business case development, assessment of investment opportunities, comparative evaluation of different service options, the evaluation of financial risks and the determination of service value. All these are central to decisions about what should be included in the Service Portfolio or removed from it.

Financial Management is also responsible for ensuring that funding is available to support the delivery of the Service Portfolio and for ensuring budget allocations align with it.

Service Catalogue Management
Since the Service Portfolio includes the Service Catalogue there needs to be a close relationship between Service Portfolio Management and Service Catalogue Management. The information in both elements of the Service Portfolio must be consistent.

Supplier Management
Supplier Management ensures that all supporting services and their details and relationships are accurately reflected within the Service Portfolio and that the Service Portfolio is consistent with the Supplier and Contracts Database. Supplier Management will draw on information in the Service Portfolio as a basis for negotiating Underpinning Contracts.

Other processes
The Service Level Management process depends heavily on the content and quality of the Service Portfolio, especially the Service Catalogue.

Capacity Management has an input into the Service Portfolio to ensure that new technologies are given due consideration in service planning. The Service Portfolio is a key input to Capacity Management.

The construction and maintenance of the Service Portfolio requires input from IT Operations Management and Technical and Applications Management to ensure the Service Portfolio is accurate and achievable.

TEST QUESTIONS FOR CHAPTER 9

SS 02, SS 03

10 SERVICE CATALOGUE MANAGEMENT (SD 4.1)

INTRODUCTION

Service Catalogue Management provides a basis for customer-focused management of IT service delivery, which helps ensure that IT service offerings are aligned with the needs of the business. It does this by providing clear and consistent information on services in a language that the customers will understand and in a format that customers will want to use, thus enabling a constructive dialogue about IT services where all parties have a common understanding of what is being discussed. Where a Business Service Catalogue is in place, the process of ordering standard services is simplified and made more efficient because what is being offered is clear, the terms and conditions for its provision are clear and there is a simple and consistent self-service mechanism in place for obtaining it.

Service Catalogue Management, through the production and maintenance of the Technical Service Catalogue, provides a source of technical information that enables the IT service provider to manage services more effectively.

Information in the Service Catalogue enables a better understanding of how the delivery of IT services impacts the business as well as the risks and vulnerabilities that require to be managed by the IT service provider. This provides Service Level Management with a source of information for reporting to customers on performance, costs and other service issues and provides Supplier Management with a sound basis for contract negotiation with suppliers.

Integrating the Service Catalogue with the Configuration Management Database (CMDB) provides a mechanism for linking the outward-looking, business-focused aspects of service provision with the internal, technically focused aspects of Service Management.

GOALS, PURPOSE AND OBJECTIVES

Keeping the Service Catalogue up to date, accurate and complete does not happen by accident. It needs to be managed. In ITIL, the goal of the Service Catalogue Management process is to ensure that an up-to-date Service Catalogue is developed and maintained.

The purpose of Service Catalogue Management is to create and maintain a Service Catalogue of all services currently delivered or ready to be delivered by the IT service provider. Service Catalogue Management must ensure that the Service Catalogue meets the agreed functionality, usability, accessibility, availability and performance requirements of all those who need to use it.

The objectives of Service Catalogue Management are:

- to obtain an agreement with all key stakeholders, especially the customers, on the definition of a service;

- to design, develop and maintain the Service Catalogue and its contents as part of the overall Service Portfolio;

- to agree, in conjunction with Service Portfolio Management, on the interface between the Service Catalogue and the Service Pipeline;

- to liaise with Service Level Management and Business Relationship Management to ensure the information contained in the Service Catalogue is accurate, up to date and fit for purpose;

- to liaise with the business, Security Management, IT Service Continuity Management and other processes to ensure the content of the Business Service Catalogue is aligned with the business and its processes;

- to liaise with Configuration Management, support teams, Application Management and suppliers to ensure that information on Configuration Items (CIs), interfaces and dependencies within the Technical Service Catalogue is accurate and up to date;

- to maintain the Service Catalogue under strict change control and ensure by effective document version management that only current versions of the Service Catalogue are in use.

SCOPE

The provision and management of the Service Catalogue is in itself a service delivered by the IT service provider, and as such should encompass all the elements of a service including any SLAs between IT and the customers who use it.

In broad terms, Service Catalogue Management has two elements:

- The initial design and development of the Service Catalogue: its content and structure, its relationship with the remainder of the Service Portfolio, in particular the transfer of services from the Service Pipeline, the relationship with the Configuration Management Database, the processes, accountabilities and responsibilities for keeping it up to date, audit, etc.

- The ongoing management of the Service Catalogue: managing the information in the Service Catalogue to keep it up to date, complete and accurate as the business and technical environment change, coordinating with changes to the rest of Service Portfolio and the Configuration Management Database, managing availability, security and performance.

KEY ACTIVITIES

Service Catalogue design

The Service Catalogue, a key part of the Service Portfolio, is a central source of information about the services delivered or about to be delivered by the IT service provider.

The Service Catalogue is a subset of the Service Portfolio, the contents of which are described in Chapter 9. However, because it is customer facing, the Service Catalogue must include information that is important and of direct interest to the customer. This will include information such as:

- details of Service and product offerings;
- availability;
- support services;
- support arrangements;
- key policies;
- terms and conditions;
- Service Level Agreements;
- charges and prices;
- ordering and cancellation;
- key future plans (e.g. where there are existing plans to phase out, replace or change a service).

The Service Catalogue as a whole serves two purposes. First, it provides information on services to the customers of the IT service provider in a way that enables the customer to understand and make decisions about the services it uses or might wish to use. Second, it is a primary source of information for the IT service provider on the services it offers to its customers.

In many organisations, this dual purpose is reflected in the structure of the Service Catalogue, which is divided into two main parts: a Business Service Catalogue, which describes services in terms that are helpful and useful to the business, and a Technical Service Catalogue, which describes services in terms that are useful and helpful to the IT side.

Where the Service Catalogue is designed in this way, the Business Service Catalogue is the part that is made available to the customer. The Technical Service Catalogue may be shared with customers, but it is primarily intended for use internally by the IT service provider.

The Business Service Catalogue

As a primary vehicle for communications between the IT service provider and its customers, the Business Service Catalogue should be as easy to use as any good mail order catalogue. The Business Service Catalogue will serve its purpose best if it meets its users' requirements, and this means engaging with the user community in requirement gathering and design. If the Business Service Catalogue does meet the customers' needs, they will be unlikely to use it. Among other things, it is important that there is a common understanding of what the word 'Service' means.

What is often a source of confusion is that what the customer sees as a single service is most likely to be seen by the IT service provider as a mix of services, with a core service underpinned by supporting services.

EXAMPLE

The Payroll service, which the customer regards as a single service, relies on a whole host of supporting services such as PC support and server support, the network infrastructure, the corporate email service, to name but a few. Then there are printing services, security services and accommodation services. Payslips, sorted into mail-sort or walk-sort sequence, may be transported from the data centre's print facility to the finance department by an internal courier service.

The actual information included in the Business Service Catalogue will vary from organisation to organisation, but most will contain information similar to that shown in Figure 10.1.

The design of the Business Service Catalogue is always a balance between too much and too little information. There is sometimes a tendency to include information because it might be useful. The key point is to remember who is intended to use it. Some customers may have the time to plough through hundreds of pages of fine detail, but most will have neither the time nor the inclination to do so. The answer is to be brief and to the point, avoid jargon and acronyms and aim for ease of comprehension rather than trying to impress the customer with technical brilliance.

The Technical Service Catalogue

This part of the Service Catalogue holds details of Services from an IT perspective, including a service description in IT terms along with details of the key components or Configuration Items (CIs) that make up the service and the relationship between them. It describes in technical terms the supporting services listed in the Business Service Catalogue and explains the interrelationships and interdependencies between them. It should also include, if only by cross reference, details of relevant Operational Level Agreements (OLAs) and Underpinning Contracts (UCs). It will ideally include information on key personnel who are either responsible for or provide some kind of technical authority in respect of the service. The Technical Service Catalogue is neither intended for nor usually made available to customers.

Figure 10.1 Example Business Service Catalogue

Service Name:			Service: S001 Ref	S002	S003	S004
Short Description: Cross reference to detailed description ⇨			Service: Type			
Manager Responsible: Contact Details:	Support Contact: Contact Details:	Business Owner: Contact Details:				
Service Ordering Details: Link to online order form (if applicable) ⇨						
Service Charges/Tariff (if applicable):						
Business Unit #1 using Service:	Business Owner:	Contact Details:	Business Impact and Priority:	SLA ref:		
Business Unit #2 using Service:	Business Owner:	Contact Details:	Business Impact and Priority:	SLA ref:		
Business Unit #3 using Service:	Business Owner:	Contact Details:	Business Impact and Priority:	SLA ref:		
Supporting Service: #1	Name and brief description			Catalogue Cross ref ⇨		
Supporting Service: #2	Name and brief description			Catalogue Cross ref ⇨		
Supporting Service: #3 etc	Name and brief description			Catalogue Cross ref ⇨		
Customer Requirements: e.g. Information input; desktop hardware and operating software;						
Standard, Optional and Excluded Items;						
Performance: Service Hours; Key performance targets; Business Continuity arrangements; etc.						
Special Conditions: e.g. Security (link to Security Policy ⇨)						

As with the Business Service Catalogue, it is easy to put too much detail into the Technical Service Catalogue. The important point in its design is to have a clear understanding of how the Technical Service Catalogue will be put to use, remembering that more information generally means a higher maintenance and management cost. Listing all the technical staff who support a service might have some use, but people come and go, change roles, get promoted and so on, and this kind of detail easily gets out of date.

ROLES

The Service Catalogue Manager's responsibilities include ensuring that:

- all services in operation and new services moving into transition are correctly recorded in the Service Catalogue;

- retired services are removed from the Service Catalogue at the appropriate time;
- the Service Catalogue is maintained to be accurate, complete and up to date;
- the Service Catalogue continues to serve the needs of those who need to use it.

RELATIONSHIPS WITH OTHER SERVICE MANAGEMENT PROCESSES

Service Portfolio Management

The Service Catalogue is part of the Service Portfolio that contains information about services that are currently delivered by the IT service provider or are ready to move into transition to live operation. In other words, they are services at the stage in their Service Lifecycle where they will be of direct interest to customers.

Service Catalogue Management and Service Portfolio Management must work together to agree when and how services in the Service Pipeline will transfer into the Service Catalogue. This requires monitoring the status of the service through Service Design to be ready to update the Service Catalogue when the service is ready for Transition to live operation. There will be similar considerations when the service is ready to be retired from live operation.

Configuration Management

In organisations with a comprehensive Configuration Management Database (CMDB), all parts of the Service Catalogue should be an integrated part of the CMDB, which would otherwise hold duplicate information on CIs and relationships already in the Service Catalogue. If services are each defined as a CI, as part of a hierarchy of services, it is possible to relate incidents and changes to services affected. It also provides information to Capacity and Availability Management and assists Service Continuity Management perform Business Impact Analysis. It also provides a basis for service monitoring and reporting.

In organisations without a complete CMDB, the production of the Service Catalogue can be a good starting point for its development.

Financial Management

The Service Catalogue provides Financial Management with the information required on service demand for modelling, decision-making and control. It not only enables improved budgeting and planning, but also supports comparative benchmarking against other providers.

It must be remembered that customers expect that all services in the Business Service Catalogue are available for use and so, as soon as a service has moved into the Service Catalogue, it must be made available to customers who demand it. Due diligence is necessary to ensure that the service is a complete product that can be fully supported. This includes technical feasibility, financial viability and operational capability. Financial Management has a clear role in this activity.

TEST QUESTIONS FOR CHAPTER 10

SD 01, SD 23

11 SERVICE LEVEL MANAGEMENT (SD 4.2)

INTRODUCTION

Service Level Management (SLM) exists to ensure that services fully align with the needs of the business and meet the customers' requirements for functionality, availability and performance. The goal is to ensure that levels of service are negotiated and agreed with customers and all services are delivered to the agreed service levels defined in terms of agreed performance indicators. SLM must also ensure that services are continually improved where improvements are required by the customer and can be justified in terms of their cost.

SLM is the steward of the relationship between the IT service provider and its customers and is accountable to the user for the services delivered.

The principal activities of SLM are:

- to develop and negotiate SLAs with customers;
- to ensure SLAs are underpinned by internal (OLAs) and external (UCs) agreements that support the achievement of agreed service levels;
- to act as a bridge between the IT service provider and the business;
- to manage and maintain positive, constructive relationships with the customer. As the primary interface between IT and the business, it must be kept up to date with all relevant developments.

SLM helps IT become more professional, consistent and productive in its relationship with customers, creating and keeping open effective lines of communication. It ensures IT focuses on what matters most to the customer and the business and helps IT to deliver better value for money.

It ensures services are aligned to the needs of the business, providing a clear basis for the delivery of services including the definition of roles and responsibilities for both sides, provides measurable and achievable targets for service delivery, helps build a better mutual understanding and helps improve customer satisfaction with IT services.

GOALS, PURPOSE AND OBJECTIVES

Service Level Management exists to ensure that services fully align with the needs of the business and meet the customers' requirements for functionality, availability and performance. The goal is to ensure that levels of service are negotiated and agreed with customers and all services are delivered to the agreed service levels defined in terms of agreed performance indicators. SLM must also ensure that services are continually improved where improvements are required by the customer and can be justified in terms of their cost.

SLM is vital to Continual Service Improvement (CSI). SLM's goal is to maintain and improve IT service quality by a continuing process of agreeing, monitoring and reporting on IT service achievements and initiating corrective action where there is a business case for doing so and the business agrees that action should be taken. SLM supports the Seven-step Improvement Process because SLM determines what is to be measured, monitored and reported. It works with the business and customers to agree new requirements and identify service improvement opportunities and priorities. This information and the activities it drives are an important part of CSI.

The purpose of the SLM process is to ensure that all delivered services are monitored and measured against the agreed levels of service and that the results, expressed in accordance with the customers' needs, are reported regularly to the business and customers.

The objectives of SLM are:

- to build and maintain effective, productive relationships with customers;
- to define and agree with customers the required levels of IT services in a way that customers understand;
- to manage the performance of services to ensure agreed levels are achieved and that customers are happy with what they receive;
- to ensure systems are in place to improve continually service levels if the organisation wants it and the cost is justified and affordable.

BASIC CONCEPTS

Service Level Management provides a bridge between the IT service provider and the Business, operating as a focal point for customers and the business in their dealings with the IT service provider. Through regular contact and communication, SLM must represent the IT service provider to the Business, and the Business to the IT service provider. From its central position, SLM is able to build strong and effective relationships between the IT service provider and the business customers, managing their expectations and ensuring that delivered services meet or exceed those expectations.

Service Level Requirements
The needs of the business, expressed in terms the business understands, are documented as Service Level Requirements (SLRs), which contain a definition of the services the customers need, including key performance and availability targets. The SLRs will be translated by the IT service provider into Service

Specifications, which define how the IT provider will make the services available, including the use of third-party providers.

SERVICE LEVEL AGREEMENTS

Where one party delivers services to another, it is a good idea to have some kind of agreement setting out the basis on which the service is provided. Such agreements would normally contain, among other things, a description of what is to be provided, the key performance indicators, the way the service is to be charged for (where relevant) and the responsibilities of each of the parties. In ITIL SLM, the agreements between the internal IT service provider and the business customers that it supports are known as Service Level Agreements (SLAs) and it is through SLAs that SLM manages the relationship between itself and its customers.

SERVICE LEVEL AGREEMENT

ITIL defines a Service Level Agreement (SLA) as an agreement between an IT service provider and a customer. The SLA describes the IT service, records service level targets, and specifies the responsibilities for the IT service provider and the customer. A single SLA may cover multiple IT services or multiple customers.

In order to be effective, the SLA must be a written document signed off by all parties affected by it. SLAs are important so they will rarely be agreed without negotiation between the IT service provider and the customer, beginning with a Statement of Intent that sets out the terms, conditions and targets to be agreed. It has to be in a language that both sides will understand, and this means in the language of the customer and not the technical language or jargon of the provider. The SLA defines (in language that has meaning to the customer) precisely what is to be delivered and when and where it is to be delivered. It also defines the standard of quality to be delivered, usually in terms of performance and availability. It will define the responsibilities of both the service provider and the customer. This is important. It makes little sense for a service provider to commit to deliver a service without making it clear what is expected of the customer.

The SLA will include contact details, what should happen if something goes wrong, the way any disputes should be handled, any provisions for redress, the mechanism for getting the SLA changed if necessary and the period over which the agreement will stand unless otherwise changed by agreement. If the service is to be charged for, then the way charges are to be determined and the arrangements for invoicing should be included. Charges may also be included in a separate document, the Tariff, referenced in the SLA.

It is common in IT for individual services to be shared by a number of customers, and individual customers will use a range of services. This means that there is a choice in designing SLAs: they can be customer-based, where an SLA covers a range of services delivered to a particular customer; or they can be service-based, where a common SLA covers all customers of a given service.

Customer-based SLAs

A customer-based SLA is an agreement with a specific customer or customer group covering all the IT services they use. For example, a local authority education department might have a single agreement embracing payroll, school administration, human resources, purchasing, financial management systems, and so on. In some ways, this simplifies the relationship between IT and the customer, putting the customer's perspective to the fore. On the other hand, customer-based SLAs are complex and often difficult to agree and manage. Additionally, customers may be disappointed that the same service levels available to them, for common services such as email, for example, cannot be tailored to their specific needs.

Service-based SLAs

A service-based SLA is an agreement with all the customers of a specific service. An example might be the organisation's intranet service. This kind of agreement makes good sense where all customers are offered the same level of service, but becomes complicated when this is not the case. Sometimes, different levels of service are inevitable (e.g. where remote users have to rely on low-speed communications). Alternatively, customers may simply demand choice. For example, some organisations will offer a PC support service with identical terms and conditions for all users, but others may offer different levels of service according to what the customer is prepared to pay. Using banded levels of service (e.g. bronze, silver and gold support levels) is a very common way of simplifying this problem. Another issue with service-based SLAs is who signs on behalf of the customer and who represent them. Having user groups with elected representatives or spokespersons is one solution.

Multi-level SLAs

Some organisations choose a multi-level SLA approach, where elements of services common to all customers are covered by a corporate-level SLA. Issues relating to a particular customer or customer group, no matter what the service, are then covered by a customer-level SLA and all issues relating to a specific service for the customer or customer group are covered by a service-specific SLA.

The SLA for a service must be based on realistic, achievable targets (e.g. for performance and availability), and the achievement of these targets depends on the performance of the internal and external services that underpin the delivery of the main service. Putting it another way, SLAs must reflect the levels of service actually being delivered or that can be delivered. They are about what can be done rather than what we would like to be done. If a customer requires a different level of service, this would normally be dealt with by raising a Service Level Requirement.

In order for SLM to be confident about the achievement of its SLA targets, it must have specific agreements with the internal and external providers. These agreements fall into two distinct types:

- Underpinning Contracts (UCs);
- Operational Level Agreements (OLAs).

Both should be negotiated, agreed and in place before a commitment is made to the relevant SLA.

EXAMPLE

A local authority used the multi-level structure shown in Figure 11.1 for its Finance Department.

Figure 11.1 Multi-level SLAs (Source: OGC ITIL Service Design ISBN 978-0-113310-47-0)

Corporate SLAs: E.g. Corporate email service, Intranet

Customer-based SLA covering common service features:
E.g. Hours of operation; availability; security; reliability; support services etc. for:
General financial system, payroll, Council Tax etc.

Service-specific SLA:
E.g. Payslip production and printing

E.g. Council Tax Bill production

Underpinning Contracts

Where an external supplier provides services that underpin the delivery of an IT service, it is essential that the provisions of the contract with the external supplier are consistent with the targets built into any SLA that depends on the external supplier. SLM must avoid making commitments in SLAs that cannot be guaranteed because the Underpinning Contract with an external supplier offers a lower standard. For example, it would make little sense for SLM to base an SLA availability target on a projected server availability of 99.9 per cent when the support and maintenance contract for the server guarantees no better than 98 per cent. It is the responsibility of SLM to ensure consistency, seeking to renegotiate UCs where contractual commitments fall short of customer needs.

The ongoing relationship between the IT service provider and its suppliers is covered in Chapter 12 (on page 83) on Supplier Management, but it is important to recognise here that UCs must always be kept in line with the needs of the business. This means that as business requirements change, the IT service provider must ensure that UCs are renegotiated or replaced, if cost-effective to do so, to ensure they continue to serve the business.

Operational Level Agreements

Many organisations find it helpful to have written agreements between different parts of the IT service provider that specify the performance targets that each part is able and prepared to underwrite. These agreements, which are known as Operational Level Agreements (OLAs), enable SLM to have confidence in the SLAs they negotiate with customers. They are not formal contracts, and need not be written in the style of formal contractual documents, but they will make clear what should be expected of a particular section of the IT service provider.

OPERATIONAL LEVEL AGREEMENT

An Operational Level Agreement (OLA) is an agreement between an IT service provider and another part of the same organisation. An OLA supports the IT service provider's delivery of IT services to the customers. The OLA defines the goods or services to be provided and the responsibilities of both parties.

EXAMPLE

The delivery of service at the user's desk may depend on the availability of a working PC, and the PC Support service will be required to commit to a level of support that guarantees that a faulty PC will either be fixed, re-imaged or replaced within a set timescale.

Managing Service Levels

Putting SLAs in place with consistent UCs and OLAs achieves nothing unless performance against the SLAs is measured, monitored and reported and appropriate actions are taken to maintain and continually improve service delivery. The ongoing responsibilities of SLM are concerned with maintaining a constructive and positive relationship with its customers, measuring and monitoring performance against SLAs, reporting and reviewing performance with the customer, dealing with changing requirements and seeking to improve continually service levels where this is cost-effective. This is not a one-sided relationship, however. SLM also has a responsibility to help its customers and the business make the most effective use of IT and to meet their obligations included in SLAs.

Reports to customers and users should be in a format that is easy to follow. SLA Monitoring Charts (SLAM) are often used (sometimes referred to as a 'RAG' report based on the use of the colours red, amber and green to indicate SLA breach, warning or met, respectively). An example is shown in Figure 11.2.

SLM has responsibility for regularly reporting to the customer on performance, but will rely on other Service Management processes for the information: the Service Desk will report on the number of Incidents handled and their performance in dealing with them; Availability Management will report on Availability; Capacity Management will report on any capacity issues; and so on.

Figure 11.2 An example SLAM Chart (Source: based on OGC ITIL Continual Service Improvement ISBN 978-0-113310-49-4)

Time period / Target no.	1	2	3	4	5	6	7	8	9	10	11	12
1												
2			▨	▨	▨	■	■				■	
3											■	
4												
5		■										

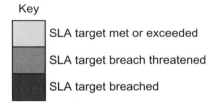

Key

☐ SLA target met or exceeded

▨ SLA target breach threatened

■ SLA target breached

SLA Review Meetings

Regular meetings with customers are a central part of SLM. They are not just an opportunity to report on and review performance, although this is one of the key issues. It is fundamentally about building and maintaining the relationship. Review meetings are a forum for exchanging information about issues of concern, such as the need for user training or worrying trends in performance or workload. They provide an opportunity for both the IT service provider and the customer to share their plans for future change: the business may be planning an expansion in usage; there may be relevant proposals in the Forward Schedule of Changes; IT may be planning to replace key service components or to introduce new service management elements. These meetings are a means to ensure that both sides have a common understanding and that there are no difficult surprises to manage.

Continual Service Improvement is a fundamental goal of Service Management. A key objective of the regular review meetings is to identify and agree service improvements and incorporate them into the Service Improvement Plan and Service Quality Plan as part of the Continual Improvement Stage of the Service Lifecycle.

SERVICE IMPROVEMENT PLAN (SIP)

A formal Plan to implement improvements to a Process or IT Service.

> Service Improvement Plans (SIPs) are about finding and implementing ways to restore or improve service quality. They should cover all relevant services, processes and activities, and address related priorities, costs, impacts and risks. A SIP will often involve a range of initiatives (e.g. covering internal IT processes, customer training and behaviour, and third-party services, and so on).

METRICS

Metrics can be used to assess both the effectiveness of the SLM process in delivering services to the standards agreed and the extent to which SLM is successful in managing the interface with the business.

Under the first heading, useful quantitative performance indicators would include:

- the frequency and severity of service breaches;
- the frequency and severity of threatened service breaches (near misses);
- the frequency and severity of breaches and threatened breaches resulting from UCs;
- the frequency and severity of breaches and threatened breaches resulting from OLAs;
- the number and percentage of SLA targets met;
- customer satisfaction with the process in relation to managing levels of service.

Measures under the second heading would include:

- the number and percentage of services with up-to-date SLAs;
- the frequency of service review meetings;
- the frequency of agreed reports delivered on time.

It is also important to assess customers' views on how useful the process is to them. This can be addressed through surveys, but often a more telling indication can be obtained from the level of customer representation at review meetings, the extent to which representatives change from one meeting to the next and the quality of contribution to meetings. All of these are useful pointers to how people really feel about the process.

Metrics can also be put in place to assess the efficiency and effectiveness of the SLM process. For example:

- The costs and time required to generate new and agree new SLAs.
- The costs of monitoring and reporting on SLA achievements.
- The cost of monitoring and reporting of SLAs.

- The time required for developing and agreeing SLAs.
- The percentage of services covered by SLAs.
- The percentage of SLAs reviewed by their review dates.
- The number of SLAs found to be unsatisfactory and needing to be corrected.

ROLES

The key role in SLM is the Service Level Manager, who has responsibility for directing and managing the SLM process. The Service Level Manager will have responsibility for the SLA framework and structure and for the overall relationship between the IT service provider and its customers and with the business. The SLM will have overall responsibility and accountability for the success of the SLM process.

In a smaller organisation, the Service Level Manager is likely to be involved personally in developing, negotiating, agreeing and reporting on individual SLAs, in negotiating OLAs and liaising with Supplier Management in relation to UCs in order to ensure that these are aligned with the agreed service level targets. In a larger organisation, some of these roles will be delegated to Service Level Management staff.

The Service Owner is a critical SLM role with responsibility for ensuring that a specified service or group of services are delivered to the agreed service levels and has responsibility for Continual Service Improvement and managing change for his or her services. The Service Owner represents the service within the organisation, ensuring the information in the Service Catalogue is correct and acts as an escalation point for major Incidents and a focus for service improvement. The Service Owner has a role in defining service targets, will participate in service review meetings with the business and with IT and takes part in SLA and OLA negotiations.

Although not part of SLM, it is important to mention Business Relationship Management (BRM) in this context. In common with SLM, BRM is responsible for maintaining an effective relationship with the business and business managers. BRM is tasked to ensure the IT service provider is meeting the overall needs of the business and consequently has a role in Service Portfolio Management. For SLM, meeting service level targets is a measure of how well the IT service provider meets the needs of the business.

Given that there is so much common ground between SLM and BRM, these roles are often combined to bring the main streams of relationship management together.

The Reporting Analyst is a CSI key role that is not strictly part of SLM. Nevertheless, the Reporting Analyst, who reviews and analyses data to assess end-to-end service achievement, identifying positive or negative trends, will often work closely with SLM.

RELATIONSHIPS WITH OTHER SERVICE MANAGEMENT PROCESSES

Service Level Management interacts with and to an extent depends on all other Service Management processes. Some of these relationships are more important than others, but SLM cannot deliver to its fullest potential unless all SM processes are fully implemented and effective.

Service Desk and Incident Management

There are key relationships with the Service Desk and Incident Management, which, in seeking to restore service as quickly as possible following an Incident, directly underpin the delivery of the service levels to which SLM has committed on behalf of the IT provider.

Problem Management

Problem Management has a clear role in dealing, both reactively and proactively, with Problems that might give rise to Incidents that undermine the delivery of the service.

Change management

Effective change management is clearly critical to maintaining service levels because badly managed and poorly planned change can lead to disruption of services and failure to achieve against SLAs.

Release Management

Sound Release Management minimises service disruption, ensures releases are deployed at times that suit the customer and minimises incidents due to releases that are either poorly managed or ill-conceived.

Other Processes

All processes will report to SLM on issues, opportunities and performance, thereby supporting SLM in its reviews with customers.

Availability Management, Capacity Management and Service Continuity Management are concerned with ensuring that services continue to deliver the service levels included in the relevant SLAs. SLM, as the primary contact with the customer, will provide information on required service levels and on upcoming changes to the business. In return, these processes will report to SLM on performance and make proposals for service improvement.

TEST QUESTIONS FOR CHAPTER 11

SD 08, SD 09, SD 10, SD 11, SD 12, SD 19, SD 21, SD 22
CSI 08
A 5, A 10

12 SUPPLIER MANAGEMENT (SD 4.7)

INTRODUCTION

Few IT services today are delivered in totality by the IT service provider. For example, services relying on networks for delivery are likely to depend on a telecommunications provider for links between geographically dispersed sites; hardware maintenance will usually be in the hands of a third-party supplier; commercial software packages will be supported and maintained by external suppliers, often, but not always, the software vendor.

As discussed under Service Level Management, the relationship between these external providers and the IT service provider is in part defined by Underpinning Contracts between the IT service provider and the third-party suppliers responsible for supporting services. However, Supplier Management, which seeks to ensure that suppliers and their services are managed in such a way that the continuing quality and good value for money of IT services is ensured, is about much more than the one-off negotiation of a support contract.

SUPPLIER

A third party responsible for supplying goods or services that are required to deliver IT services.

Supplier Management is all about getting the best from suppliers in order to ensure the delivery of services meet agreed service level targets at optimal cost. It is about getting good value for money from suppliers. It recognises that there is more to a supplier relationship than the contract, seeing the relationship as a continuing and dynamic asset that not only serves the needs of today, but also helps the IT service provider respond to new challenges and risks as the commercial, technological and social environment changes around it. It recognises the need for Continual Service Improvement and the value of productive relationships as a platform for achieving higher service quality or better value for money or both of these things.

GOALS, PURPOSE AND OBJECTIVES

The goal of Supplier Management is to manage suppliers and the services they deliver in order to ensure the organisation gets the best value from each supplier throughout the lifecycle of the relationship with the supplier. Given the complexity of modern IT service, it is common for individual services to be provided through a mix of internal and external suppliers. Supplier Management has to manage the complexity of relationships with external suppliers in such a way that they all pull in the same direction and, in doing so, deliver services that underpin the service level targets enshrined in SLAs at a cost that represents best value for the organisation. A key goal for Supplier Management is to ensure that the optimum value is achieved from the relationship with a supplier, and this rarely means squeezing suppliers until they have no more to offer. The goals of Supplier Management are also about the longer term. The old confrontational Supplier Management approaches are hopefully outdated. Supplier Management today has to be about building long-term relationships, ideally built around shared risk and reward models, where success in the relationship is a mutual goal.

This does not mean that the relationship between the organisation and its suppliers is casual. A key purpose of Supplier Management is to ensure that effective contracts are in place, ensuring that the supplier delivers according to the terms, conditions and delivery targets contained within the contract. What is understood by an effective contract is crucial. An effective contract is not about driving the price down to a point where the supplier cannot sustain delivery or needs to claw back revenue by holding the organisation to ransom over essential contract variations.

EXAMPLE

One public sector organisation squeezed a key supplier on price to a point where everyone should have realised that service delivery would be at risk. Unfortunately, the organisation continued to congratulate its hard negotiating tactics until the inevitable happened. The whole thing ended up in court with both sides blaming the other. Irrespective of the outcome of the court case, the IT service collapsed and the organisation was left to manage the mess.

The main objectives of Supplier Management are:

- to develop and maintain a supplier policy;
- to establish and manage constructive relationships with suppliers;
- to negotiate and agree contracts with suppliers that align with the needs of the business and manage these contracts through their lifecycle;
- to ensure, in collaboration with SLM, that contracts that underpin the delivery of other services are aligned with the targets contained in SLRs and SLAs;
- to manage suppler performance to ensure they deliver good value for money;
- to develop and maintain a supporting Supplier and Contract Database (SCD).

SCOPE

The scope of Supplier Management covers the management of all suppliers to the IT service provider. In practice, this does not mean that all suppliers should be given equal attention. Some will have a lesser role in the delivery of IT services, those that provide minor services or commodity items that can be easily sourced elsewhere. Some will have a much greater impact on the IT service provider, and these suppliers require more proactive management and attention, especially where their failure to deliver can have a profound effect on the ability of the IT service provider to deliver services.

GENERAL PRINCIPLES

Supplier Management is, of course, about negotiating contracts that are consistent with the needs of the business and that support the achievement of targets in the relevant SLAs. It is also about managing the longer-term relationship with suppliers and their continuing performance. It requires positive management throughout the contract lifecycle, monitoring delivery and performance to identify and deal with issues and potential problems before they occur. It involves the renegotiation, renewal and even the termination of contracts as the needs of the business change. It involves monitoring the extent to which contracts continue to deliver good value for money as the marketplace and technological options change over time and this in turn means maintaining a comprehensive base of information about the marketplace and the suppliers that populate it.

In order to benefit fully from the relationship with a supplier, the IT service provider must have a clear understanding of where it wants to be. It needs to understand and articulate its own long-term goals in the context of the business it serves, and to define the services it must design and develop in order to achieve these goals. An analysis of its own resources and capabilities against the resources and capabilities needed to deliver these services will identify areas where external assistance may be required, and this analysis, along with an analysis of risks, will provide a foundation for the development of new or changing relationships with suppliers.

KEY ACTIVITIES

The Supplier Management process should include the following key activities:

- The development, implementation and management of a supplier policy.
- The categorisation of suppliers and contracts and associated risk assessment.
- Supplier evaluation and selection.
- Contract negotiation and agreement.
- Development and maintenance of standard terms and conditions.
- Dispute management and resolution.
- Development and maintenance of a Supplier and Contract Database (SCD).

85

THE SUPPLIER AND CONTRACT DATABASE

The Supplier Management process is governed by the IT service provider's supplier policy and strategy. These determine how the organisation will use external suppliers and the rules of engagement when it does so. It should define how suppliers should be selected and how relationships should be managed. In the public sector, for example, the rules for procurement from the private sector are enshrined in legislation in most countries and these rules should be incorporated into supplier policy.

In common with other SM processes, sound Supplier Management depends on the effective management of information. In Supplier Management, the key information base is the Supplier and Contract Database (SCD), which will hold information on all suppliers and contracts, and on the goods and services provided by each supplier. The SCD is best implemented as a part of the Configuration Management System (CMS), itself part of the IT provider's Service Knowledge Management System (SKMS). The integration of the SCD with the CMS enables suppliers and contracts to be linked to services, CIs and other service elements that depend on the supplier contract, enabling better risk and impact assessment and management reporting. The information in the SCD will also be included for reference in the Service Portfolio and Service Catalogue.

The SCD is used to manage suppliers and contracts throughout the contract lifecycle, providing information to, and being updated from, the key Supplier Management activities. It holds details of suppliers, including key contacts along with contract details including renewal and termination dates.

ROLES

Managing the relationship with a supplier should be the responsibility of a specific person from the IT service provider, the Supplier Manager, although this person may manage the relationship with a number of suppliers. The time and effort allocated to the management of a given supplier and the level at which this is managed within the IT service supplier's organisation should reflect the importance of the supplier to the IT service provider's business. A supplier of minor services will generally need less attention than does a supplier with strategic importance across a range of services. For suppliers in the latter category it is good practice to adopt an open management approach based on mutual trust, where each side shares its plans with the other. This enables both sides to prepare for new challenges based on an understanding of the needs, pressures and priorities of the other partner.

This approach generally has more potential for generating value in the relationship than the traditional confrontational approach, as the supplier becomes more involved in helping the IT service provider to deliver benefit to the business. The objectives are shared risk and reward rather than blame and animosity.

The Supplier Manager's responsibilities include:

- maintaining a comprehensive SCD;
- ensuring contracts align with the business and offer good value for money;
- ensuring all suppliers and contracts offer an acceptable level of risk to the enterprise;
- managing supplier performance to ensure contractual obligations are met;
- managing contracts throughout their lifecycle, including all changes and variations.

RELATIONSHIPS WITH OTHER SERVICE MANAGEMENT PROCESSES

Service Level Management
SLM in relation to the alignment of UCs with SLA and SLR targets, includes the renegotiation of UCs, where possible, to improve performance or reduce service costs and the investigation of breaches and near breaches of SLR and SLA targets because of unsatisfactory performance. Supplier Management will also advise or liaise with SLM in relation to planned contract terminations and key supplier events such as failure, mergers and takeovers. Supplier Management is also a source of information on third-party service costs, which will feed through into IT charges if relevant.

Other Service Management Processes
Relationships between Supplier Management and other SM processes include those with:

- Information Security Management (ISM) to ensure suppliers understand and comply with IT security policy and specific security requirements in their dealings with the organisation;
- Service Portfolio Management and Service Catalogue Management to ensure that all details of suppliers, contracts and third-party services are accurately recorded and kept up to date. If these details are held with the CMDB, there will be a similar interface with CMS;
- IT Service Continuity Management (ITSCM) in relation to contracts held for business continuity services. ITSCM may also contribute to the risk assessment of suppliers by sharing the outcome of Business Impact Analysis (BIA);
- Financial Management to ensure there are adequate finances to cover contractual commitments and for Supplier Management to feed information into Financial Management for budget development;
- CSI functions in relation to Supplier Service Improvement Plans, which may underpin the achievement of service improvement targets;

- Service Strategy processes in relation to Supplier Policy and Strategy development and the more general formulation of IT strategy;

- Service Design in relation to the options for using third-party suppliers to deliver proposed services or to underpin their delivery.

In practice, it is also important for Supplier Management to work closely with business management, finance, procurement and legal services to ensure contracts are managed effectively throughout their lifecycle.

TEST QUESTIONS FOR CHAPTER 12

SD 02, SD 15, SD 18
A 15

13 CAPACITY MANAGEMENT (SD 4.3)

INTRODUCTION

The Capacity Management process is responsible for all activities related to the provision of adequate and cost-effective capacity. The scope also includes performance management.

Capacity and performance are tightly linked because although service levels are usually expressed in terms of performance (e.g. response time, throughput rate etc.), when resources run short of capacity, performance suffers.

EXAMPLE

A good analogy is a supermarket's ability to serve its customers in a reasonable time. In order to allow shoppers to checkout without having to queue for a long time, there is a continual need to balance the number of checkout staff with the number of shoppers.

The Capacity Management process is mainly a proactive one because it is driven by future business need. Therefore the earlier that capacity and performance are considered in the Service Lifecycle, the greater the degree of confidence that a service will be able to meet the required service levels when it is transitioned into operation.

The main challenge for Capacity Management is to predict the demand on resources to be able to provide enough capacity to meet service levels on an ongoing basis.

EXAMPLE

In the supermarket analogy, this means estimating the number of shoppers over the day and perhaps how many items they will buy and then scheduling staff working hours and breaks to minimise queuing.

In IT terms, this means gathering information about business plans, assessing the impact on services and underpinning resources and then buying or upgrading resources (or selling or downgrading resources if demand is falling) in time to avoid either insufficient capacity and missed service levels or excess capacity and unnecessary cost. For this reason, the Capacity Management process is sometimes more memorably summarised as 'Having the right IT capacity in the right place at the right time and at the right cost.'

Without forward planning, achieving this balance is not possible because reacting to capacity shortfalls takes time. It takes time to gain approval to purchase, to physically acquire the capacity and then install and configure it. In the meantime, performance suffers and the business is impacted. Equally, without forward planning, capacity shortfalls may need to be tackled urgently. In such situations, there is a potential for panic buying. It is unlikely that urgent purchases are made in the most cost-effective manner.

GOALS, PURPOSE AND OBJECTIVES

In simple terms, the goal of the Capacity Management process is to ensure that there are sufficient IT resources to satisfy the current and future needs of the business. This is a two-part balancing act:

- **Supply versus demand:** Sufficient resources must be available to meet the business demand and maintain service levels. This can be helped by influencing demand (through the Demand Management process) to make the most effective use of resources and by tuning and optimising current resources.
- **Costs versus resources:** Spend on resources must be justified by business need and resources must be used efficiently. This can be helped by considering the cost benefits of newer technology.

The purpose of the process is to provide a focal point and management responsibility for all capacity and performance-related activities in respect of both resources and services.

The primary objectives of the process are as follows:

- Produce and maintain a Capacity Plan, assessing the impact of changes on the plan and on the performance of services and resources.
- Contribute to meeting service levels by managing the capacity and performance of services and resources.
- Provide advice and guidance on all capacity and performance-related activities, assist with the diagnosis and resolution of related Incidents and Problems and propose proactive performance improvements where these are cost-justifiable.

THE CAPACITY PLAN

The Capacity Plan is a key output of the process because it predicts and costs the impact of new and changing business plans on the current IT environment.

This provides IT management with a reliable forecast to support decisions necessary to maintain service stability and achieve the balances described in the Introduction to this chapter. The plan is usually produced annually and synchronised to IT financial planning. Updates may be routinely produced once or twice a year or in response to unexpected changes and new requirements.

The accuracy of the plan relies on the level of understanding of the utilisation and capacity of the components supporting the services and the ability to predict their impact on service performance when the demand on them changes. This in turn is dependent on accurate configuration information and the ability to model the interaction between components and workload.

Some organisations base their plan on a simple extrapolation of current usage with little or no reference to business activities or plans. However, this has been likened to steering a car by looking out of the back window. What has happened in the past is not necessarily a useful guide to what might happen in the future.

THE THREE SUB-PROCESSES OF CAPACITY MANAGEMENT

Capacity Management has three sub-processes to reflect the different activities needed to prepare the Capacity Plan. Each of these requires different skills which in larger organisations might be undertaken by different people. Figure 13.1 shows how the sub-processes fit together and their contribution to the Capacity Management process.

Business Capacity Management
The Business Capacity Management sub-process analyses the Patterns of Business Activity (PBAs) coming from Demand Management. These PBAs show both the volume of work and how this volume fluctuates over time. Business Capacity Management then gathers information about new business activities such as launching a new product, relocating a department or opening a new facility. This may be provided directly from business managers to the Capacity Management team or may come from the Service Level Packages produced for the Service Portfolio. Superimposing forecasts of new activities on top of patterns of current usage helps this sub-process to provide Service Capacity Management with an accurate projection of changing business activities over time.

Service Capacity Management
Service Capacity Management seeks to correlate business activity and service usage. For example, a call centre's usage of the Customer Relationship Management (CRM) service is probably dependent on the number of customers, how often they call and what information they require. The relationship between these factors and CRM service usage can be mapped or modelled so that the impact of business activity changes can be predicted in terms of service performance (e.g. transaction response times) over time.

Component Capacity Management
When Service Capacity Management identifies that service levels will fall below target, Component Capacity Management is the sub-process responsible for

Figure 13.1 Capacity Management sub-processes (Source: OGC ITIL Service Design ISBN 978-0-113310-47-0)

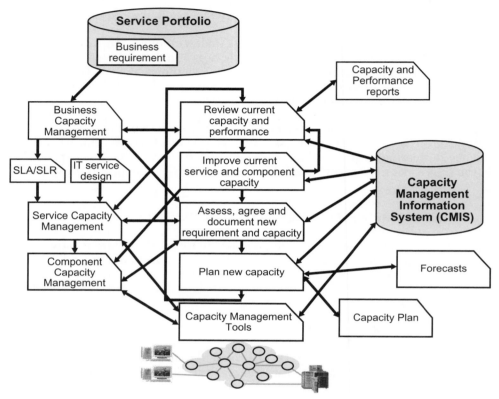

identifying the necessary changes to the technical infrastructure to maintain service levels. To be effective fully, configuration information is necessary to understand which components (configuration items) support which services. The utilisation of these components should be continually monitored against their capacity and, ideally, an alert generated when a threshold is reached that could cause service levels to be missed.

RELATIONSHIPS WITH OTHER SERVICE MANAGEMENT PROCESSES

Capacity Management has a close relationship with many of the other processes. These are detailed below.

Financial Management
Capacity Management contributes to Financial Management predominantly via the Capacity Plan. The Capacity Plan describes and financially quantifies the resources required to deliver the committed level of service. Where there is a need to acquire new resources, Capacity Management predicts how much additional

resource will be required and at what point in time. This allows Financial Management to budget for the cost of the new resources. During the budget year, as new resources are needed, Capacity Management will be instrumental in providing the justification for the actual purchase in terms of size, time and cost.

Service Level Management

The feedback that the Capacity Manager receives from business representatives in respect of their business plans and forecasts needs to be considered with the service level requirements gathered by the Service Level Manager. Capacity Management must therefore take into consideration the service level requirements when forecasting the resources needed to support new and growing services. The relationship works both ways, however. When the Service Level Manager is discussing service level requirements with the business, the capacity and performance requirements are costed by Capacity Management so that the business can make an informed decision regarding the balance between performance and cost. This is the control mechanism that prevents the business from asking for or demanding ever increasing levels of performance from the IT systems.

Demand Management

Demand Management works closely with and supports Capacity Management in several ways:

- By helping to understand Patterns of Business Activity and user profiles, Demand Management helps Capacity Management more accurately predict and plan for the consumption of resources for new users.

- By finding ways to smooth out peak loads, Demand Management helps Capacity Management make the most cost-effective use of existing resources and helps to defer the purchase of new resources.

- During times of peak load, Demand Management can dynamically throttle usage to maintain service levels, for example by restricting the number of concurrent users of an online system to protect response times.

IT Service Continuity Management

Capacity Management contributes to the Service Continuity Management process by sharing plans and modelling output to help ensure that the alternative facilities provided by Service Continuity Management remain in line with the live environment and can continue to provide contingency in the event of being invoked.

Change and Release Management

The introduction of new resources to maintain appropriate levels of capacity and performance is managed through both Change Management and Release and Deployment Management. These processes manage the impact of the change on other CIs. Likewise, Capacity Management supports Change Management by looking at the capacity and performance implications of the planned change and ensuring adequate capacity exists to accommodate subsequent deployment of the corresponding release.

Service Asset and Configuration Management

Service Asset and Configuration Management provides the information about CI status, specification and relationships that is clearly vital to Capacity Management activities such as modelling, planning and forecasting.

Availability Management

Capacity Management supports Availability Management because a shortage of capacity in a resource or service can impact availability.

Problem Management

Capacity Management obviously supports Incident and Problem Management where issues are capacity related.

ROLES

The Capacity Manager is responsible for the process. However, the scope is broad and may therefore be split between two or more capacity analysts, where one is responsible for maintaining a dialogue with business representatives and the Service Level Manager to identify new and changing business requirements, and another is likely to fulfil the more technical role of analysing the current and predicted load on performance levels (e.g. through modelling techniques).

METRICS

The following metrics can be used to confirm the effectiveness of the process in providing the appropriate level of resources:

- The number of SLA breaches (or loss of user time) caused through inadequate capacity (e.g. performance below target due to lack of capacity).
- The number of Incidents resulting from a lack of capacity or poor performance.

The following metrics can be used in respect of properly fulfilling the planning role:

- The number of unplanned purchases required to provide adequate capacity or performance.
- The percentage accuracy of actual versus planned spend as given in the Capacity Plan.
- The percentage of over capacity (by resource type or CI).
- The number of new or changed services implemented without capacity or performance-related issues.
- The actual business demand as a percentage of forecast demand.

The following metric can be used in respect of monitoring performance:

- The percentage of CIs monitored for performance.

TEST QUESTIONS FOR CHAPTER 13

SD 12

14 AVAILABILITY MANAGEMENT (SD 4.4.1 AND 4.4.4)

INTRODUCTION

The availability of IT services is the most basic requirement in any organisation. Since organisations are often so dependent on their IT services for so many business functions, if the IT service isn't available, the business of the organisation effectively stops. Availability Management is primarily a proactive process with a primary purpose of cost-effectively meeting the availability requirements the business has of its IT services both now and in the future.

If an organisation has any doubts about the need for investing in Availability Management, consider the impact of being without vital business functions that rely on the availability of IT services. Financially, the cost of service downtime can be measured in terms of lost user time as follows:

number of incidents × average outage duration × average number of users affected × average employment cost per user

EXAMPLE

Forty Incidents a week with an average outage of 40 minutes each, affecting on average 40 users at an employment cost of €40k each, incurs lost user time equivalent to more than €1.2 million per annum.

However, even the cost of lost user time can be small compared with the lost opportunity cost or consequential loss of not being able to trade during this downtime. There are obviously other industry sectors such as health care and security where the impact of losing key IT services is far more significant than a financial loss.

Availability Management can be extremely effective in identifying and eliminating potential causes of lost availability and in a commercial organisation it will undoubtedly save more money than it costs.

GOALS, PURPOSE AND OBJECTIVES

The goal of Availability Management is to ensure that service availability matches business needs cost-effectively.

The purpose of the process is to provide a focal point and management responsibility for all availability-related activities in respect of both resources and services.

The primary objectives for the process are:

- to prepare and maintain the Availability Plan;
- to monitor availability levels and the status of resources and services to identify potential and actual availability issues and prevent or minimise any consequent business interruptions;
- to manage the availability of services and resources to meet agreed service levels;
- to assist with the investigation and resolution of availability-related Incidents and Problems;
- to assess the impact of changes on availability levels and plans;
- to proactively improve availability where the cost is justified.

HOW COMPONENT AVAILABILITY AFFECTS SERVICE AVAILABILITY

In order to understand the potential for the failure of an IT service, it is first necessary to identify the components or configuration items on which the service depends. Clearly, for the service to be available, all the components that contribute to the hosting and delivery of the service must be available. In a simple model where each component is connected in series (i.e. one behind the other), the availability of the service is the product of the availability of the components on which it runs.

EXAMPLE

If three components are required to deliver a service and each has an availability of 98.0 per cent, the availability of the service is

$$98.0\% \times 98.0\% \times 98.0\% = 94.1\%.$$

This equates to a figure of 1 hour, 25 minutes a day.

Availability Management, as a proactive process, learns of business requirements from the Service Level Manager and then seeks to ensure that services and the components on which they depend are capable of meeting this requirement. Designing-in availability to new services is always more cost-effective than making changes after the service is deployed, so Availability Management needs to be actively involved at the design stage. The two most effective ways to design-in the required level of availability are to select components with an adequate specification and to design the systems to reduce the dependency on individual components.

EXAMPLE

When two identical components are put in parallel, as shown in Figure 14.1, the service only fails if both components fail.

Figure 14.1 Components in parallel

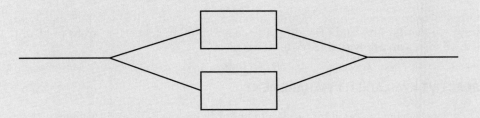

Therefore if each component in this example has an availability of 98.0 per cent, then the availability of the service is

$$1 - [(1 - 0.98) \times (1 - 0.98)] = 99.96\%.$$

Applying this design to our earlier example, three components each with a parallel back up having the same availability generates an overall service availability of

$$99.96\% \times 99.96\% \times 99.96\% = 99.88\%$$

instead of 94.1% or less than 2 minutes per day and a fifty-fold improvement.

In this way, single points of failure can be eliminated and the end-to-end availability improved.

Other methods for improving the availability of services include the use of fault tolerant components and systems that mask the effect of a component failure or allow one or more components to be taken out of service (e.g. for maintenance or replacement).

PROACTIVE AVAILABILITY MANAGEMENT TECHNIQUES

There are a number of techniques used by Availability Management that look to prevent service outages by identifying and eliminating the sources of service failures. One of these is the Availability Plan, wherein Availability Management identifies and costs the requirements for new and upgraded resources necessary to deliver the required levels of availability. The Availability Plan will also include an assessment of the risks of service interruption and failure and appropriate actions necessary to mitigate those risks.

Risk analysis and management are important across IT Service Management, especially in Processes and activities that concern service availability. These include Availability Management, Security Management and IT Services Continuity Management, which is covered in the next chapter where a fuller discussion of risk analysis and management is included.

Another technique is to assess the impact of Requests For Change (RFCs) to understand their potential to interrupt services and find ways to prevent this occurring.

Other proactive techniques include advising on cost-effective new technology to improve availability and providing advice and guidance to other areas of IT and the business on all availability-related aspects.

REACTIVE AVAILABILITY MANAGEMENT

On a reactive basis, Availability Management helps Incident and Problem Management to diagnose and resolve availability-related Incidents and Problems. Of course, the understanding gained from the resolution of such problems can often contribute to proactive initiatives to prevent similar occurrences in the future.

Availability Management also monitors, measures, reports and reviews service and component availability to ensure that service levels continue to be met and respond to any outages or potential service level breaches. In this respect, there is a link to the Event Management process.

RELATIONSHIPS WITH OTHER SERVICE MANAGEMENT PROCESSES

Service Asset and Configuration Management
Availability Management is heavily reliant on Service Asset and Configuration Management to identify the components used in delivering a service, their relationship with one another and their technical specifications.

IT Service Continuity Management
Availability Management is closely related to IT Service Continuity Management because invoking a continuity plan is simply another form of maintaining the availability of services in extreme situations. Both processes need to identify vital business functions and use risk management techniques to define appropriate responses.

Capacity Management
Availability Management is supported by Capacity Management because a shortage of capacity in a resource or service can impact availability.

Access Management and Information Security Management
Access Management and Information Security Management are both concerned with preventing unauthorised access and permitting authorised access.

Availability of a service depends on the ability of the user to access the service and negotiate the security controls according to their authority.

Change Management and Release and Deployment Management
Change Management as well as Release and Deployment Management must ensure that Availability Management is aware of planned changes and their potential to impact on the availability of services.

Service Level Management
Availability Management supports Service Level Management by managing the IT resources to meet cost-effectively agreed service levels and by contributing to the design of new and changed services to ensure the appropriate levels of availability are built-in.

Event, Incident and Problem Management
Reactively, Availability Management takes feeds from Event Management to warn of actual and impending failures and supports Incident and Problem Management in the diagnosis and resolution of availability-related Incidents and Problems.

ROLES

The Availability Manager is responsible for ensuring that the goals and objectives of the process are met. Responsibilities include:

- ensuring Service Levels in respect of availability are met for all current and new services;

- responding to availability-related Incidents and Problems;

- ensuring that appropriate CIs and services are monitored for availability through Event Management;

- specifying appropriate levels of component reliability, maintainability and serviceability;

- reporting availability performance against service levels;

- creating and maintaining the Availability Plan;

- the continual improvement of the Availability Management process;

- cost-justifying availability requirements with Financial Management;

- attending Change Advisory Board (CAB) meetings as required and assessing requests for change for their impact on availability.

METRICS

There are a number of measures used to assess and report the performance of a service or component in respect of it being available.

Availability is defined as the ability of a service or component to perform its required function when needed. It is usually calculated as a percentage:

$$\text{percentage availability} = \frac{\text{agreed service time} - \text{downtime}}{\text{agreed service time}} \times 100\%$$

(N.b. Downtime outside agreed service time is not included.)

Reliability is a measure of how long a service or component can perform its required function without interruption. It is usually calculated in one of two ways:

$$\text{mean time between system incidents (MTBSI)} = \frac{\text{available time}}{\text{number of breaks}}$$

$$\text{mean time between failures (MTBF)} = \frac{\text{available time} - \text{total downtime}}{\text{number of breaks}}$$

Maintainability is a measure of how quickly a service or component can be restored to its working state after a failure. It is usually calculated as:

$$\text{mean time to restore service (MTRS)} = \frac{\text{total downtime}}{\text{number of breaks}}$$

(N.b. Availability, reliability and maintainability measures all need to include a time interval, typically hours.)

Serviceability is a measure of a third-party provider's ability to meet their contracted support commitments in terms of availability, reliability and maintainability.

Each of these measures is subject to scrutiny and appropriate actions by Availability Management in order to minimise interruptions to services and service outages both proactively and reactively. The extent to which a service is vital to the business will determine the level of availability and resilience applied. Those business functions considered very important are known as Vital Business Functions (VBFs) and it is these on which Availability Management will be most focused.

In relation to the expanded Incident lifecycle, the following metrics are useful:

- Incident response time;
- Incident repair time;
- Incident recovery time;
- Incident restoration time;
- Incident resolution time.

KEY PERFORMANCE INDICATORS

In addition to the specific measures above, Availability Management can use a range of Key Performance Indicators (KPIs) to demonstrate continual improvement:

- Percentage reduction in service unavailability;
- Percentage increase in service reliability;
- Percentage improvement in end-to-end availability;
- Percentage reduction in the number of service breaks;
- Percentage reduction in lost user time due to unavailability of services;
- Percentage reduction in third-party contract breaches of availability service levels.

TEST QUESTIONS FOR CHAPTER 14

SD 05, SD 13, SD 16, SD 20

15 IT SERVICE CONTINUITY MANAGEMENT (SD 4.5)

INTRODUCTION

Most organisations' dependency on their IT systems is such that the loss of key applications or infrastructure could cause the company to fail within days if not earlier. Because of this, organisations need to plan how they will recover their key systems within an appropriate timescale in the event of a failure. This is the focus of the IT Service Continuity Management (ITSCM) process.

Organisations can of course suffer from the loss of systems other than IT systems and should therefore have a general Business Continuity Plan that protects against any eventuality that could threaten its vital business functions (VBFs). ITSCM should therefore support and align with the organisation's Business Continuity Management (BCM) process where this exists.

GOAL, PURPOSE AND OBJECTIVES

The goal of ITSCM is to support Business Continuity Management by ensuring that the IT resources, systems and services can be reinstated within agreed timescales in the event of a major incident.

The purpose of the process is to create and maintain the facilities and recovery capabilities needed to support this goal.

The objectives of the process are:

- to create and maintain the IT Service Continuity Plans and recovery plans;
- to carry out regular Business Impact Analysis (BIA) exercises to ensure that the plans remain aligned with changing business requirements;
- to carry out regular Risk Analysis and Management exercises to determine the potential for failure and identify and implement appropriate responses that meet agreed business continuity targets;
- to assess the impact of changes and take appropriate action to continue to provide the required level of protection;
- to ensure that the appropriate third-party contracts and agreements are in place and kept up to date to maintain the continuity and recovery plans;

- to proactively enhance recovery capabilities where it is cost-effective to do so;
- to provide advice and guidance on continuity and recovery-related issues.

KEY ACTIVITIES

The Service Continuity Management Lifecycle
Establishing and maintaining ITSCM is a cyclical process that ensures continued alignment with Business Continuity plans and business priorities. This process is shown in Figure 15.1.

Figure 15.1 ITSCM process (Source: OGC ITIL Service Design ISBN 978-0-113310-47-0)

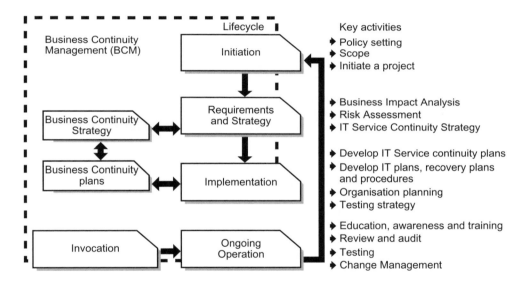

The first two steps, Initiation and then Requirements and Strategy, mainly relate to BCM. ITSCM begins with producing an ITSCM strategy to underpin the BCM strategy. The ITSCM strategy must ensure that cost-effective plans exist to recover IT services and any required IT infrastructure necessary to maintain VBFs.

The situation is more complex where some or all of the IT services are outsourced to another organisation. In this case, the ITSCM Manager must ensure that the outsourcer's continuity and recovery plans meet the objectives and timescales of the business.

Business Impact Analysis
Business Impact Analysis (BIA) is the activity performed by ITSCM, often together with Availability Management, that works with the business to understand the impact on the organisation of suffering degraded service or losing

an IT service or component. The analysis will identify business functions that are critical to the success of the organisation (VBFs) and it is these functions that ITSCM must protect from the impact of an IT failure. The business will define the recovery requirement for these functions that ITSCM must address through its IT continuity plans. Over time, the importance of business functions can change and new ones appear, so ITSCM must undertake regular BIA exercises and feed the results back into the continuity plans to ensure they remain appropriate and up to date.

Risk Analysis and Management

The first step in protecting VBFs is to understand their dependency on the IT services and infrastructure. This information can be discovered from the Configuration Management System. Next, ITSCM must consider a number of factors:

- What could cause a service or component to fail? Examples can include fire, flood and security breaches in addition to simple mechanical or electrical failure.

- What is the likelihood of this happening? In other words, what are the chances that each of the events defined above could occur?

- What is the impact of such an occurrence? If one of the events did occur, what effect would this have on the business? This might be expressed in terms of the impact on its reputation, its customers, its finances or its legal or compliance requirements, for example.

The outcome of these considerations will determine the appropriate actions ITSCM has to take to mitigate the risks adequately and cost-effectively. Typically, the greater the likelihood of failure and the greater the impact, the greater the level of protection needed and the greater the justification for the necessary expense.

The above underlines the importance of risk analysis and management to ITSCM.

RISK

A possible event that could cause harm or loss, or affect the ability to achieve Objectives. A Risk is measured by the probability of a Threat, the Vulnerability of the Asset to that Threat, and the Impact it would have if it occurred.

The first stage of risk analysis and management is to identify potential threats to an asset or service, estimate the probability that the threat might materialise, assess how vulnerable the asset or service is to these threats and to assess the impact should the threat materialise. For example, as identified above, flood is one example of a threat that might be relevant to an asset such as a data centre. We would determine the probability that the centre might be flooded, assess the vulnerability of the data centre to flooding and the impact on the organisation if it did flood. Putting all these together would give us a measure of risk.

The second part of risk management is doing something about the risks identified. Generally, we can do a number of things about risks:

- Some risks can just be accepted and provision made in case the worst happens. If we cannot insure our data centre because it sits in a flood plain, we may decide to hold a contingency fund in case it does flood.

- We can avoid or eliminate the risk; for example, we can eliminate the risk to our data centre by deciding to go back to manual processing. This is not always a practical solution.

- We can transfer the risk to somebody else, for example by taking out insurance or by outsourcing the data centre and disaster recovery.

- We can reduce the risk by reducing the probability of the threat or by reducing the severity if the risk materialises. For our data centre we might move it to the top of a hill to reduce the probability of a flood or reduce the impact of a flood by replacing under floor cables with fibre optics.

In many cases, the response to risk will be a combination of all or some of these options, with a balance being established between the business' tolerance to risks and the cost of countermeasures.

A key issue for IT Service Management, and ITSCM in particular, is to have some way of analysing and managing risk, and the best and safest approach is to use a tried and tested framework that covers all aspects of risk identification and management. Management of Risk (M_o_R®), a part of the Best Practice Guidance portfolio published by the Office of Government Commerce, is a recommended framework.

RELATIONSHIPS WITH OTHER SERVICE MANAGEMENT PROCESSES

Availability Management
There is clearly an overlap between the ITSCM process and the Availability Management process. The distinction is that Availability Management is primarily concerned with maintaining the availability of VBFs, whereas ITSCM provides contingency in the event of a failure that either Availability Management could not prevent or from which IT could not quickly recover.

Change Management
Changes need to be assessed for their impact on continuity plans and consequent changes incorporated into the change planning. The Continuity Plan itself is subject to change control.

Service Level Management
Service Level Management will provide advice on the definition of VBFs and the expectations of the business with regard to the permissible time delays in the restoration of services.

Capacity Management

Capacity Management helps to ensure adequate resources are available to accommodate services after the Continuity Plan is invoked and that agreed service levels can be maintained in this situation.

Asset and Configuration Management

Configuration Management maintains records of recovery CIs, their status and specification.

Information Security Management

The potential for a security breach to cause a major Incident means that Information Security Management contributes to the BIA and Risk Analysis activities.

ROLES

The IT Service Continuity Manager is responsible for ensuring that the objectives of the process are met. Their activities therefore include:

- undertaking BIA and risk management exercises for both existing and new services;
- implementing and maintaining the ITSCM process and continuity strategy and maintaining the alignment with business continuity planning;
- preparing and maintaining the continuity and recovery plans and ensuring that these continue to support the organisation's Business Continuity Strategy and plans;
- regularly testing the plans for effectiveness, reviewing the results and taking action to overcome any identified deficiencies;
- ensuring that any personnel who have a role in transitioning from one location to another are fully trained and aware of their responsibilities;
- managing third-party suppliers of recovery equipment and facilities to maintain the integrity of the continuity and recovery plans;
- attending Change Advisory Board (CAB) meetings as required and assessing changes for their impact on the plans and updating the plans accordingly;
- managing the continuity plan during invocation and restoring the service back to the primary or other designated facility.

METRICS

Metrics that can be used to measure the performance of the ITSCM service and process in respect of the effectiveness and preparedness of the organisation are as follows:

- The number of services not covered by the continuity and recovery plans (that should be covered).

- The number of issues identified in the last continuity test that remain to be addressed.
- The number of errors found in an audit of the information in lists of key people, their responsibilities and contact details.

TEST QUESTIONS FOR CHAPTER 15

SD 14
A 14

16 INFORMATION SECURITY MANAGEMENT AND ACCESS MANAGEMENT (SD 4.6, SO 4.5)

INTRODUCTION

The security of data and information is of vital importance to any organisation and it is therefore a business decision as to what information should be protected and to what level. The business's approach to the protection and use of data should be contained in a security policy to which everyone in the organisation should have access and the contents of which everyone should be aware. The system in place to enforce the security policy and ensure that the business's IT security objectives are met is known as the Information Security Management System (ISMS). Information Security Management supports corporate governance by ensuring that information security risks are properly managed.

Information Security Management and Access Management are separate processes in ITIL in different parts of the Service Lifecycle but are covered together in this chapter because of their common purpose.

GOALS, PURPOSE AND OBJECTIVES

The two processes, Information Security Management and Access Management have a common goal in that both are concerned with making sure that only the right people get to see information, but Information Security Management, which is a fundamental part of the governance framework, has a much broader remit.

The goal of the Information Security Management process is to make sure that IT security is consistent with business security, ensuring that information security is effectively managed in all service and Service Management activities and that information resources have effective stewardship and are properly used. This includes the identification and management of information security risks.

The purpose of Information Security Management is primarily to be a focal point for the management of all activities concerned with information security. This is not just about protecting information resources today. It is about putting in place, maintaining and enforcing an effective Information Security Policy. It is about understanding how the business will develop, anticipating the risks it will face, articulating how legislation and regulation will affect security requirements and making sure that Information Security Management is able to meet these challenges of the future.

The objective of Information Security Management is to ensure an effective Information Security Policy is in place and enforced through effective, documented security controls that apply not only to in-house employees, but also to suppliers and others who have business/contact with the organisation. It must ensure that any security breaches are managed promptly and effectively, and that risks are identified and documented and lessons are learned accordingly.

Access Management is concerned with the management of people's rights of access to information, and as such has common purpose not only with Information Security Management, but also with Availability Management, giving practical effect to the policies and requirements of both processes. Its goal is to ensure that the confidentiality, integrity and availability of information are effectively managed across the organisation. Data and information must not only be protected against unauthorised access and the possibility of it being stolen or changed. It must also be readily available to those who are authorised to access it.

A key part of Access Management is the management of people's rights to access information and services. People who have the right, in terms of business policy and need, to access information should have that right implemented through access controls. These rights must be consistent with relevant legislation such as data protection legislation, and must be kept under review and changed or revoked when a person's status changes within the organisation, or when a material risk is identified.

EXAMPLE

A doctor needs access to a patient's notes to help diagnose the possible cause of an illness and prescribe the appropriate remedy, but the confidentiality of these notes needs to be protected against access by unauthorised users. However, the patient may have a legal right to reserve access to certain information to specified individuals (e.g. HIV status, abortions, mental illness and so on).

In order for access rights to have proper effect and value, Access Management must ensure that people can be properly identified: that each person has a unique identity to which their rights can be attached and to which activities, legitimate or otherwise, can be traced. Identity management is critical to effective Access Management, preventing, for example one person from pretending to be another and hijacking their rights to access and change information or, some would say even more importantly, to create new information. Organisations must take action to manage circumstance where access controls may be bypassed, for example where software developers require access to live systems during Incident Management.

EXAMPLE

In one organisation, access to payroll information was very tightly controlled, but software developers fixing faults in what was a very old piece of software had full access to all parts of the system, with the ability to access, change and create records.

The security objective of an organisation is usually considered to be met when the availability, confidentiality, integrity and authenticity and non-repudiation are under control. These are defined below:

- **Availability:** Information is accessible and usable when required and the host systems can resist attacks and recover from or prevent failures.

- †"**Confidentiality:** Information is observed by or disclosed only to those who have a right to know."

- **Integrity:** Information is complete, accurate and protected against unauthorised modification.

- †"**Authenticity:** Authenticity concerns the correct labelling or attribution of information to prevent, for example, the originator of an email making it appear that the email came from another person. Authenticity is about ensuring that business transactions, as well as information exchanges between enterprises or with partners, can be trusted."

- †"**Non-repudiation:** The mechanism that prevents the originator of a transaction falsely denying that they originated it or prevents the receiver falsely denying having received it."

THE INFORMATION SECURITY POLICY

The Information Security Policy should support and be aligned to the business security policy. It should include policies covering the use of IT assets, email, the internet, important documents, remote access, access by third parties (such as suppliers) and asset disposal. In addition, it defines the approach to resetting passwords, maintaining anti-virus controls and classifying information. These policies should be available to all customers and users as well as to IT staff, and compliance to the policy should be referenced in all internal agreements and external contracts. The policy should be reviewed and revised on at least an annual basis.

THE INFORMATION SECURITY MANAGEMENT SYSTEM

The Information Security Management System (ISMS – also referred to as the Security Framework) helps establish a cost-effective security programme to support business objectives. Figure 16.1 shows an example framework widely used and based on the ISO 27001 standard that gives the five stages of the ISMS and the scope of each stage.

The objective of the ISMS is to ensure that appropriate controls, tools and procedures are established to support the Information Security Policy.

ACCESS MANAGEMENT

Access Management is the process of controlling access to data and information to ensure that authorised users have timely access while preventing access by

Figure 16.1 ISMS framework (Source: OGC ITIL Service Design ISBN 978-0-113310-47-0)

unauthorised users. The Access Management process may be the responsibility of a dedicated function but is usually carried out by all Technical and Application Management functions.

If the Service Desk is operating as the single point of contact, it is usual that it should receive any Service Requests for new or changed access rights and may also be authorised by the owner of the security policy to grant these rights. Typically this occurs when a new person joins the organisation or a new supplier is engaged, but it may also occur when someone moves from one department to another or changes role. Access rights should be withdrawn when someone leaves the organisation.

The Access Management process should include monitoring access to secure information so that in the event of a security-related incident arising, the cause can be traced and any security risks discovered can be removed. Monitoring will also identify unauthorised access attempts and instances of password errors as indications of possible security threats.

FACILITIES MANAGEMENT – THE CONTROL OF PHYSICAL ACCESS

Information Security Management defines the access control policy, and identifies the necessary physical security measures and who should have access to which site (e.g. the data centre). Facilities Management is responsible for enforcing this policy. The major components of physical access control are:

- the installation, maintenance and management of physical access security controls such as locks and barriers and surveillance equipment;

- monitoring of physical access to protected areas;

- physical security staffing;

- maintenance of floor plans showing areas of restricted access and the relevant security controls.

One of the most common means of breaching physical security is by 'social engineering': a rather grandiose term that usually refers simply to talking your way into a secure facility (e.g. by posing as a legitimate contractor, posing as someone else or simply following a legitimate person through an open door). For this reason, security access must not only be controlled appropriately but also continually monitored so that such breaches can be detected and security controls improved.

RELATIONSHIPS WITH OTHER SERVICE MANAGEMENT PROCESSES

To one extent or another, all other processes interface with Security Management.

Availability Management
Information Security and Access Management are key contributors to Availability Management because without the right level of protection, the availability and integrity of data and systems is compromised.

Service Desk
The Service Desk usually has the authority to respond to requests for changes to access rights and passwords and therefore contributes to the operational management of security.

Other Processes
Other process interfaces are with:

- Incident and Problem Management (response to and resolution of security-related issues);

- IT Service Continuity Management (a design consideration and a risk during testing);

- Change Management (impact assessment on security controls);

- Configuration Management (assistance with security classification for CIs);

- Capacity Management (when introducing new technology);

- Supplier Management (to ensure maintenance of security controls for operational activities carried out by third parties).

ROLES

The IT Security Manager is responsible for defining the Information Security Policy and establishing the ISMS. Once these are in place, it is the IT Security Manager's job to ensure that all the proper controls are in place, people are aware of the policy and their responsibilities and that the security system is functioning correctly. The IT Security Manager is the focal point for all security issues.

Service Operation teams are responsible for conducting day-to-day activities to manage operational security. It is important that these roles are kept separate from those of Security Management to prevent a conflict of interest. Operation roles include:

- policing and reporting;
- providing technical support and assistance;
- managing security controls;
- screening and vetting individuals;
- providing training and awareness;
- ensuring that security controls are appropriately referenced in operational documentation.

The Facilities Manager is responsible for physical security at an organisation's sites and computer facilities.

METRICS

Security Management metrics are needed to ensure that the organisation can meet both internal and external security requirements found in SLAs, contracts, legislation and governance. Metrics that can be used for this purpose include:

- the number of security-related Incidents per unit of time;
- the percentage of security-related Incidents that impacted services or users;
- the number of security audit issues and risks identified;
- the percentage of security audit issues and risks resolved;
- the number of changes and releases backed-out because of security issues;
- the average time to install security patches.

TEST QUESTIONS FOR CHAPTER 16

SD 14, SD 24, SD 25
SO 04, SO 10, SO 16, SO 20
A 18

17   KNOWLEDGE MANAGEMENT   (ST 4.7)

INTRODUCTION

The ability to deliver quality services is directly influenced by the people involved in the delivery, especially by their understanding of situations, possible response options, and the consequences and benefits of those options (i.e. by their knowledge). This applies across all phases of the Lifecycle.

Incidents which actually relate to a common underlying problem may present themselves with different symptoms. It is unrealistic to expect that all Service Desk staff will have the same knowledge about the relationship between possible symptoms and the cause, and hence automatically offer a suitable response. Being able to store and correlate information about such things and present the shared knowledge back to the Service Desk staff will enable them to be more effective.

Typically, Knowledge Management is displayed within the
Data → Information → Knowledge → Wisdom (DIKW) model
as illustrated in Figure 17.1 and where the terms are defined as:

- **Data:** Discrete set of facts.
- **Information:** Data set in context.
- **Knowledge:** Uses information, but includes an extra dimension derived from experience.
- **Wisdom:** Uses knowledge to make correct decisions and judgements.

It is unrealistic to expect every individual to have a deep and broad range of knowledge, but it is possible to record, store and make data, information and knowledge available to people.

GOALS, PURPOSE AND OBJECTIVES

The purpose of Knowledge Management is to ensure that the right person has the right knowledge at the right time to enable them to make sensible decisions about courses of action.

Figure 17.1 The DIKW model (Source: OGC ITIL Continual Service Improvement ISBN 978-0-113310-49-4)

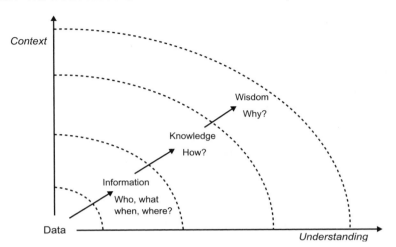

The objectives are to provide:

- more efficient services with improved quality, increased satisfaction and reduced cost;

- a clear and common understanding of the value provided by services and how that value is realised;

- relevant information on usage, resource consumption, constraints and difficulties that is always available.

KEY ACTIVITIES

The key activities of Knowledge Management are to gather, analyse, store and share knowledge and information within an organisation. To this end, an organisation needs to implement a Service Knowledge Management System (SKMS), as represented in a basic form in Figure 17.2.

The SKMS is a set of tools and databases that are used to manage knowledge and information. It includes the Configuration Management System, as well as other tools and databases. The SKMS stores, manages, updates and presents all information that an IT service provider needs to manage the full lifecycle of IT services.

The SKMS is underpinned by the Configuration Management System (CMS), the Configuration Management Databases (CMDB) and other Service Management databases. In its wider context it also holds knowledge from other sources such as:

- the experience of technical staff;

- records of peripheral matters of interest (e.g. weather, user numbers and behaviours, market conditions);

Figure 17.2 Service Knowledge Management System (Source: OGC ITIL Service Transition ISBN 978-0-113310-48-7)

- suppliers and partner requirements, abilities and skills;
- user skill levels (e.g. use of PCs or the internet).

ACTIVITIES, METHODS AND TECHNIQUES

An overall Knowledge Management Strategy is required, including how to identify, capture, and maintain knowledge and the underpinning data. It is also necessary to consider knowledge transfer (i.e. retrieving and sharing knowledge in order to solve problems), and support dynamic learning, strategic planning and decision-making. Evaluation and improvement is important as with other Service Management processes. We must measure the use made of the data, evaluate its usefulness and identify improvements.

CHALLENGES

Establishing effective Knowledge Management can be very challenging. Making incorrect choices in certain areas can lead, at the extremes, to paralysis by data overload or information which is so sparse as to be useless. It is essential that all data sources are trustworthy, accurate and up to date, as is the case for Configuration Management data. Key aspects are:

- understanding what knowledge is necessary to support the decisions that must be made;
- understanding which conditions need to be monitored (changing external and internal circumstances, ranging from end-user demand, legal requirements through to weather forecasts);
- the cost of capturing and maintaining data, and the value that data may bring, bearing in mind the negative impact of data overload on effective knowledge transfer;
- intellectual property rights and copyright issues;
- ensuring that information is not easily open to misinterpretation.

KEY METRICS

The key metrics indicating success are found in the wider Service Management sphere:

- Reduced time and effort required to support and maintain services.
- Reduced time to find information for diagnosing and fixing Incidents and Problems.
- Changes and releases implemented in timely manner.
- Reduced dependency on personnel for knowledge.
- Fewer errors made because available information was not used.

RELATIONSHIPS WITH OTHER SERVICE MANAGEMENT PROCESSES

Almost by definition, Knowledge Management interfaces with all the other Service Management processes, but it also interfaces with everyone within the business, and suppliers, customers and external sources of information.

ROLES

The Knowledge Manager's responsibilities include:

- ensuring that the service provider is able to gather, analyse, store and share knowledge and information;
- improving efficiency by reducing the need to rediscover knowledge.

TEST QUESTIONS FOR CHAPTER 17

ST 02, ST 04, ST 07, ST 08

18 SERVICE ASSET AND CONFIGURATION MANAGEMENT (ST 4.3)

INTRODUCTION

Organisations invest huge amounts of money in IT equipment and ancillary resources, which are assets of the organisation. Accordingly, we need to maintain information about those assets in terms of their source, value, location, who controls them etc. This is Asset Management.

Configuration Management goes beyond this in providing us with information about the relationships that exist between the various components. This is essential to effective service management solutions since this information underpins all of the other processes particularly Incident, Problem, Availability and Change Management.

When a change is proposed, comprehensive configuration information enables the rapid and accurate assessment of the impact of the change on services and components. Similarly, calls to the Service Desk can be simplified if the agent can automatically see what services and systems the caller uses.

GOALS, PURPOSE AND OBJECTIVES

The purpose of Service Asset and Configuration Management (SACM) is to:

- identify and control all items of interest;
- manage and protect the integrity of assets.

The objective of SACM is to define and control the components of services and infrastructure, and to maintain accurate configuration information on the historical, current and planned states of these components, services and infrastructure.

Asset Management covers service assets across the whole Service Lifecycle. It provides a complete inventory of assets and records who is responsible for their control. It includes full lifecycle management of IT and service assets, from the point of acquisition through maintenance to disposal.

Configuration Management provides a configuration model of the services, assets and infrastructure by recording the relationships between service assets and Configuration Items. It ensures that components are identified, baselined and maintained, and that changes to them are controlled. The scope covers interfaces to internal and external service providers where there are assets and Configuration Items that need to be controlled (e.g. shared assets).

SACM optimises the performance of service assets and configurations and therefore improves the overall performance of the service, and minimises the costs and risks caused by poorly managed assets (e.g. service outages, fines, incorrect licence fees and failed audits).

BASIC CONCEPTS

All of the information that we are interested in will be held in a repository known as the Configuration Management System (CMS) as a series of Configuration Item (CI) records, each of which has descriptive information (known as Attributes) including relationship data to other CIs. The CMS will typically consist of one or more Configuration Management Databases (CMDBs). Historically, there has often been confusion about this aspect, with many organisations striving to develop a single physical CMDB when it is the logical concept of a repository, the CMS, which is important.

CONFIGURATION ITEM

A Configuration Item (CI) is any component that needs to be managed in order to deliver an IT service. Information about each CI is recorded in a configuration record within the Configuration Management System and is maintained throughout its lifecycle by Configuration Management. CIs are under the control of Change Management. CIs typically include IT services, hardware, software, buildings, people and formal documentation such as process documentation and SLAs.

CIs should be selected using established selection criteria, grouped, classified and identified in such a way that they are manageable and traceable throughout the Service Lifecycle.

One of the most challenging aspects of establishing effective Configuration Management is defining the most appropriate level at which CIs are defined. A balance must be struck between having sufficient information to be truly useful and the effort that is involved in collecting and maintaining the information.

Representing the components and their relationships pictorially can help greatly in reaching an understanding of what is required.

CONFIGURATION MODEL

A Configuration Model is a model of the services, assets and the infrastructure that includes relationships between CIs, enabling other processes to access valuable information (e.g. assessing the impact of Incidents, Problems and proposed changes; planning and designing new or changed services and their release and deployment; optimising asset utilisation and costs).

An example of a Configuration Model is shown in Figure 18.1.

Figure 18.1 Example of a logical Configuration Model (Source: OGC ITIL Service Transition ISBN 978-0-113310-48-7)

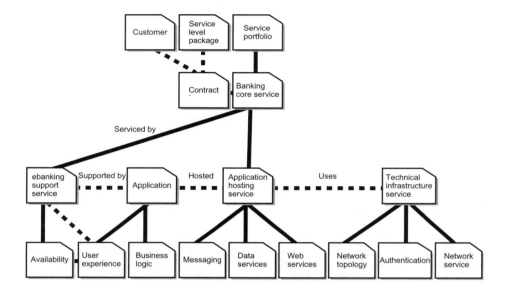

CONFIGURATION MANAGEMENT SYSTEM

A Configuration Management System (CMS) is a set of tools and databases used to manage an IT service provider's configuration data. The CMS also includes information about Incidents, Problems, known errors, changes and releases, and may contain data about employees, suppliers, locations, business units, customers and users. The CMS includes tools for collecting, storing, managing, updating and presenting data about all CIs and their relationships. The CMS is maintained by Configuration Management and is used by all IT Service Management processes.

CONFIGURATION MANAGEMENT DATABASE

A Configuration Management Database (CMDB) stores configuration records containing Attributes of CIs and their relationships. A CMS may include one or more CMDBs.

DEFINITIVE MEDIA LIBRARY

A Definitive Media Library (DML) is one or more locations in which the definitive and approved versions of all software CIs are securely stored. The DML may also contain associated CIs such as licences and documentation. The DML is a single logical storage area even if there are multiple locations. All software in the DML is under the control of Change and Release Management and is recorded in the Configuration Management System. Only software from the DML is acceptable for use in a release. See Figure 18.2.

Figure 18.2 Relationship between CMDB and DML (Source: OGC ITIL Service Transition ISBN 978-0-113310-48-7)

The CMS contains information about the logical software components, while the DML is a secure library which contains the definitive authorised versions of software approved for live use within the organisation, regardless of their source. The CMS and DML are used together in the building of a Release prior to Deployment, as illustrated in Figure 18.2.

Software held in the DML will have passed quality assurance tests, demonstrating its integrity and its freedom from viruses. DML software can be trusted. As said above, the DML stores definitive versions irrespective of source and essential documentation. It therefore holds not only in-house developed software but also third party/purchased software, along with licence documents or evidence of licences purchased.

The DML must be secure, in terms of preventing unauthorised access, in terms of SACM controlling what comes into and goes out of the store and, critically, in terms of the physical security and safety of its contents in the event of fire, flood and so on.

CONFIGURATION BASELINE

A Configuration Baseline is the configuration of a service, product or infrastructure that has been formally reviewed and agreed on, which thereafter serves as the basis for further activities and can be changed only through formal change procedures. A configuration baseline can be used to checkpoint a service development milestone, as a basis for future builds and changes, to assemble components for a change or release and to provide the basis for a configuration audit or back-out.

ACTIVITIES

The key activities of SACM are illustrated in Figure 18.3 and are:

Figure 18.3 Configuration activities (Source: OGC ITIL Service Transition ISBN 978-0-113310-48-7)

- **management and planning:** defining the level of Configuration Management required for a service or a change project;

- **configuration identification:** defining CI types and groupings, naming conventions etc.;

- **configuration control:** ensuring there are adequate mechanisms to control CIs while maintaining a record of all changes to ensure no mismatch with the physical world;

- **status accounting and reporting:** maintaining the status of CIs as they progress through their discrete states (e.g. Development, Approved, Live, Withdrawn);

- **verification and audit:** checking that the physical CIs exist, records in the CMS match the real world, and that documentation is accurate;

- **information management:** back-up copies of the CMS should be taken regularly and securely stored. It is advisable for one copy to be stored at a remote location for use in the event of a disaster.

CHALLENGES

Service Asset and Configuration Management can be one of the most difficult disciplines to introduce. Although it underpins virtually every aspect of Service Management, it is perceived as having little direct value itself. The following challenges are very common:

- Persuading technical support staff of the value of SACM because they may see it as a hindrance.

- Funding of SACM, because it is not visible to the business.

- Over-engineering and collecting too much data: getting the balance between what can be recorded and what needs to be.

- The CMS can become out of date as CIs are moved or changes are made. An out-of-date CMS is actually very dangerous since incorrect decisions can be made on the basis of the information.

KEY METRICS

Most of the metrics that indicate successful Configuration Management are actually seen in other processes. Some of the key ones are:

- the ratio of used licences to paid for licences (this should be close to 1 : 1);

- accuracy in budgets and charges for the assets used by each customer or business unit;

- the percentage reduction in business impact of outages and Incidents caused by poor Asset and Configuration Management;

- the reduction in the use of unauthorised hardware and software, and in non-standard and variant builds that increase complexity, support costs and risk to the business services.

RELATIONSHIPS WITH OTHER SERVICE MANAGEMENT PROCESSES

SACM underpins virtually every other Service Management process as we have already seen. The most significant relationships are:

- Change Management: identifying the impact of proposed changes;

- Financial Management: capturing key financial information;

- IT Service Continuity Management: providing awareness of assets the business depends on and controlling key spare assets and software;

- Incident and Problem Management: providing and maintaining key diagnostic information and maintaining and providing data to the Service Desk;

- Availability Management: supporting detection of points of failure.

ROLES

- Service Asset Manager: manages the lifecycle of assets.

- Configuration Manager: manages the lifecycle and relationships of all CIs.

- Configuration Analyst: analyses/proposes scope of asset and configuration processes; undertakes process activities.

- Configuration Administrator/Librarian: controls the receipt, identification, storage and withdrawal of all supported CIs (content control).

- CMS/Tools Administrator: monitors the performance and capacity of Asset and Configuration Management systems and recommends improvement opportunities (technical control).

TEST QUESTIONS FOR CHAPTER 18

ST 05, ST 09, ST 16, ST 24, ST 25
A 19

19 CHANGE MANAGEMENT (ST 4.2)

INTRODUCTION

It is often said that the only constant is change. Accordingly, change must be embraced as an essential and natural aspect of any environment, but poorly managed changes can cause chaos within an organisation. Indeed, poorly managed changes are often the major cause of Incidents. Not only does this cause disruption to the users, it also leads to rework that is frequently more difficult to achieve than getting it correct originally.

EXAMPLE

A major airline suffered several days of upheaval and embarrassment after their reservation system crashed and customers were unable to execute many transactions. The cause was traced to an inadequately tested change to the system. The loss, both financial and reputational, was substantial.

However, a Change Management process should not be viewed as a bureaucratic inhibitor that makes changes difficult to introduce. Rather it should be an enabler to allow the right changes to proceed as smoothly as possible regardless of their scale or complexity.

Historically, many organisations have had change control mechanisms in place, but these have often been fragmented and divergent in aspects such as assessment and authorisation. To be truly effective, a common, holistic approach to handling change is required.

GOALS, PURPOSE AND OBJECTIVES

The goal of Change Management is to ensure that IT and the business can be aligned and can be kept aligned with optimal efficiency and minimal disruption, re-work and risk by means of the consistent and effective management of the necessary changes needed to maintain alignment.

The purpose of the Change Management process is to ensure that all changes are managed through standard methods and procedures that ensure changes are effective, on time, meet their specified requirements and are properly recorded in the Configuration Management System.

The objective of Change Management is to ensure that all changes are recorded and then evaluated, authorised, prioritised, planned, tested, implemented, documented and reviewed in a controlled manner.

The scope of Change Management covers changes to service assets and Configuration Items across the whole Service Lifecycle. The process addresses all service changes at all levels: strategic, tactical and operational. Hence, although Change Management is described in the Service Transition volume, many changes will occur at an operational level and be relatively small in nature.

SERVICE CHANGE

Service Change is the addition, modification or removal of anything that could affect IT services. The scope should include all IT services, CIs, processes, documentation etc.

Organisations can choose whether requests are raised by specific roles or groups only, or whether anyone within the organisation can do so.

BASIC CONCEPTS

A change request is a formal communication requesting a change to one or more CIs. Different types of change may require different types of change request, each with specific forms and procedures (e.g. for impact assessment and change authorisation). The change types are shown in the Table 19.1.

Table 19.1 Example types of request by Service Lifecycle stage

Types of change	Procedures	SS	SD	ST	SO	CSI
Service portfolio change: New portfolio item Scope, business case or baseline changes Pipeline	Service Change Management	✓				

(Continued)

Table 19.1 *(Continued)*

Types of change	Procedures	SS	SD	ST	SO	CSI
Service or service definition change: 　To existing or planned 　　attributes 　Service design 　Service improvement	Service Change Management	✓	✓	✓	✓	✓
Project proposal: 　Business change 　No impact on service 　　or design baseline	Project Change Management procedure		✓	✓		✓
User access request	User Access procedure				✓	
Operational activity: 　Tuning 　H/W reboot 　Planned maintenance	Local procedure				✓	

A Request for Change (RFC) is a formal request for a change which may be submitted via a paper form or electronically through a service management tool. Most tools will ensure that complete information is provided, and automatically add some data such as identifiers and dates. This will avoid wasted time.

Changes are categorised into the following change types:

- **Normal:** A change that goes through the full assessment, authorisation and implementation stages.
- **Standard:** A pre-approved change that is low risk, relatively common and follows a procedure or work instruction (e.g. a password reset or the provision of a standard PC to a new employee). RFCs are not always required to implement a standard change, and they may be logged and tracked using a different mechanism (e.g. through the Request Fulfilment process). Often operational maintenance changes are treated as standard changes.

- **Emergency:** Reserved only for highly critical changes that must be introduced as soon as possible (e.g. changes needed to restore failed high-availability services or widespread service failure, or changes that will prevent such a failure from imminently occurring). The Change Management process normally has a specific procedure for handling emergency changes.

The Change Authority is the person or persons who will authorise specific changes to take place. Organisations can decide who will be responsible for authorising different types of change and, in the interests of operational efficiency, will often devolve this authority to the Change Management team or operational staff. It is vital that the designated Change Authority has the appropriate knowledge and skills to be able to make such decisions. Modern tools will allow electronic approvals, with definable defaults that ensure changes are progressed in a timely manner.

The Change Advisory Board (CAB) is a group of people that advises the Change Manager in the assessment, prioritisation and scheduling of changes. The CAB is made up of representatives from all relevant areas within the IT service provider, the business and third parties. The key factor is that all parties who have a view on a particular change should be represented. Membership of the CAB is therefore likely to be dynamic, even within a single meeting.

Meetings may involve face-to-face contact or be conducted by telephone or online. Depending on choices made within the organisation, meetings may be held at different times and intervals as demand dictates. CAB members assess both business and technical perspectives of proposed changes.

For emergency changes there may not be time to convene the full CAB, so it is necessary to identify a smaller group with authority to make emergency decisions (i.e. an Emergency Change Advisory Board (ECAB)).

Change procedures should specify how the composition of the CAB and ECAB will be determined in each instance.

No change should be approved without there being a Remediation Plan (i.e. what to do if the change is unsuccessful). Where possible, a back-out plan should be provided to recover the organisation to its original, or another, known state should the change fail. This might involve reloading a baselined set of configuration items, revisiting the change itself or, if the failure is severe, invoking the organisation's business continuity plan. It should be recognised that not all changes can be backed out, so the Remediation Plan must cover what to do in such situations. Only by considering the remediation options available prior to instigating a change, and establishing that the remediation is viable, can the risk of the proposed change be determined and the appropriate decisions taken.

The Change Schedule lists all approved changes and planned implementation dates. It becomes an important audit trail to support Incident/Problem Management among other processes.

A Change Process model is a repeatable way of dealing with a particular type of change. It sets out specific defined steps that are followed for a specific type of change. Standard and Emergency changes are typical examples that might be handled this way. Support tools can be used to automate the handling, management, reporting and escalation of the process. The Change Process model includes:

- steps to handle the change including handling issues and unexpected events;
- the chronological order to take the steps, with any dependences or co-processing defined;
- responsibilities (who should do what);
- timescales and thresholds for completion of the actions;
- escalation procedures (who should be contacted and when).

ACTIVITIES

The key activities of Change Management as a discipline are:

- planning and controlling change;
- understanding the impact of change;
- change decision-making and change authorisation;
- change and release scheduling;
- communication with stakeholders;
- ensuring that there are remediation plans;
- measurement and control;
- management reporting;
- continual improvement.

Figure 19.1 illustrates the process flow of a Normal change.

Typical activities in managing individual changes are:

- to create and record the RFC: the change is raised by the individual or organisational group that requires the change;
- to assess and evaluate the change:
  - to establish who should be involved in the assessment and authorisation;
  - to assess and evaluate the business justification, impact, cost, benefits and risk of changes (see the 'Seven Rs' below).
- to authorise the change if appropriate;
- to communicate the decision to all stakeholders, in particular the initiator of the RFC;
- to coordinate change implementation;
- to review (i.e. evaluate the success or otherwise of the change and any lessons learned) and close the RFC.

Figure 19.1 Normal change flow (Source: based on OGC ITIL Service Transition ISBN 978-0-113310-48-7)

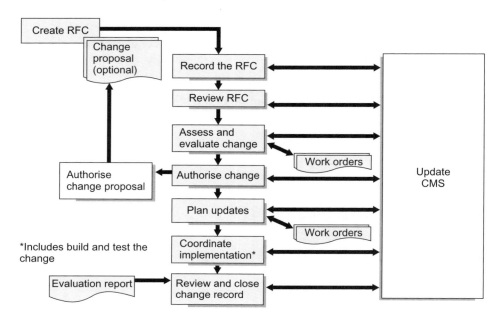

†"Every change should be assessed for impact. The following questions (often referred to as the Seven Rs of Change Management) must be answered for all changes:

- Who RAISED the change?
- What is the REASON for the change?
- What is the RETURN required from the change?
- What are the RISKS involved in the change?
- What RESOURCES are required to deliver the change?
- Who is RESPONSIBLE for the build, test and implementation of the change?
- What is the RELATIONSHIP between this change and other changes?"

This information is needed to ensure an accurate impact assessment is completed, and that the balance of risk and benefit to the live service is well understood. Without this information, the change may fail to deliver all the possible or expected business benefits or have an unexpected, detrimental effect on the live service. Examples abound of Operations teams implementing a change to the underlying infrastructure at the same time that a change is made to an application; usually with catastrophic results.

CHALLENGES

In trying to establish effective Change Management, the following challenges are commonly encountered:

- Inaccurate configuration details leading to poor evaluation and higher risk of change failure.
- The process is defined in, or perceived as, an over-bureaucratic way that hinders effective operation of IT and its services.
- People bypass the process (especially if it is seen to be bureaucratic).
- Too many changes are treated as emergencies.
- Accountability for changes isn't clearly defined leading to poor quality and compliance.
- Striking the right balance between stable production and being responsive to business needs.

KEY METRICS

These are the measures that indicate successful, or at least improving, Change Management:

- Increasing number of implemented changes meeting the customer's agreed requirements.
- A reduction in the number of disruptions to services, defects and rework caused by 'poor' changes
- A reduction in the number of unauthorised changes.
- A reduction in the number and percentage of unplanned changes and emergency fixes.
- An increasing change success rate (percentage of changes deemed successful at review/number of RFCs approved).
- A reduction in the percentage of incidents attributable to changes.

RELATIONSHIPS WITH OTHER SERVICE MANAGEMENT PROCESSES

Interfaces with Change Management include:

Organisational level processes

- Integration with business change processes to ensure change issues, aims and impacts are exchanged.

- Programme and project management need to align to service change.
- Sourcing and partnering require effective Change Management to manage relationships.

Asset and Configuration Management

- Enables change impact assessment and tracking of change workflow.
- CMS may identify related CIs affected by a change but not included in the original request.

Problem Management

- Changes are often required to implement workaround and fix known errors.

IT Service Continuity Management

- IT Service Continuity Plans need to be updated via Change Management.

Security Management

- Changes required by security are under Change Management.

Capacity and Demand Management

- Capacity Management needs to assess impact of changes on capacity.
- Changes required by Capacity Management are under Change Management.

ROLES

The prime role is that of the Change Manager, whose responsibilities include:

- managing the quality, review, assessment and approval of RFCs;
- chairing the CAB;
- acting as key liaison between initiators and approvers of changes.

TEST QUESTIONS FOR CHAPTER 19

ST 06, ST 10, ST 11, ST 12, ST 13, ST 15, ST 18, ST 19, ST 21, ST 22, ST 23
SO 14
A 2

20 RELEASE AND DEPLOYMENT MANAGEMENT (ST 4.4)

INTRODUCTION

Once a new or changed service has been developed, we need to get it into the live environment, activate it and provide support while it beds down. Most commonly, people think about releasing new versions of software, but the concept applies equally to hardware and other components such as documentation. Indeed, major upgrades or new services will frequently involve combinations of all elements.

In the past, many issues were caused by Development simply passing control to Operations in a 'clean-break' move. Release and Deployment Management is concerned with making this a more phased and controlled process, including a period of Early Life Support to ensure that everything is working as it should and can be used by the business.

Effective Release and Deployment processes require close interaction between Development and Operations, preventing the 'throwing it over the wall' syndrome so prevalent in the past.

GOALS, PURPOSE AND OBJECTIVES

There must be clear plans that enable the business to align its activities with them and everyone must be satisfied with the mechanisms used.

The goal of Release and Deployment Management is to build, test and deliver new or changed services successfully into the production environment and use within required timescales and with minimal disruption to existing services.

The purpose is to ensure that consistent and integral release packages are deployed in line with agreed policy and with plans agreed with the customers and stakeholders, and that this takes place under full and effective control. Any associated business and business process changes, including training and skills transfer, must be managed to take place in a timescale that is aligned with the release timetable.

The objective is to ensure that there are clear consistent plans that everyone understands and follows, that releases are managed efficiently and effectively through to deployment and use and that the new service and supporting systems are capable of being operated successfully and deliver the agreed service requirements (Utility and Warranty).

The scope of Release and Deployment Management includes the processes, systems and functions required to package, build, test and deploy a release into production in accordance with the Service Design Package (SDP). This includes handover to the Service Operation lifecycle stage.

Effective Release and Deployment Management adds value by ensuring that customers and users can use the new or changed service in a way that supports the business, and by delivering change faster and at optimum cost and minimal risk. Well-planned and well-implemented release and deployment can make a significant difference to an organisation's service costs by minimising troubleshooting and rework.

BASIC CONCEPTS

The two constituent aspects of the process are Release and Deployment.

RELEASE

A Release is a collection of hardware, software, documents, processes or other components required to implement one or more approved Changes to IT services. The contents of each Release are managed, tested and deployed as a single entity.

DEPLOYMENT

Deployment is the activity responsible for the movement of new or changed hardware, software, documentation, process etc. to the Live Environment.

A fundamental concept is that of a Release Unit (i.e. the components of a service that are normally released together). A Release Unit typically includes sufficient components to perform a useful function. For example, one Release Unit might be a desktop PC, including hardware, software, licences, documentation etc. There might be standardised units for different roles or departments, or the desktop might be customised for each new recruit (where each instance is a separate Release Unit). Another Release Unit might be a complete application, including IT Operations procedures and user training.

It is possible that a Release will consist of more than one Release Unit. A Release Package is one or more Release Units that are required to implement a new or changed service.

A Release Policy should be defined as part of the management control over releases. In fact, it is unlikely that an organisation will have a single Release Policy; it is more likely to have several, each covering one or more services. Each Policy should cover Identification, Roles and Responsibilities, expected frequency, change acceptance criteria, automation, configuration verification, entry and exit criteria through phases, and handover from Early Life Support to Operations.

ACTIVITIES, METHODS AND TECHNIQUES

Figure 20.1 shows the basic steps in the Release and Deployment process.

Figure 20.1 Basic Release and Deployment Process steps (Source: OGC ITIL Service Transition ISBN 978-0-113310-48-7)

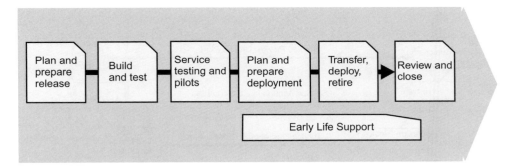

- **Planning:** Select the most appropriate Release and Deployment plans, and agree them with customers and stakeholders. Define the entry and exit criteria for each step in the process.
- **Build and test:** Assemble and integrate the release components.
- **Service testing and pilots:** Test service requirements and operational requirements using the most appropriate method for the release.
- **Plan and prepare for deployment:** Ensure everything is ready.
- **Deploy service and supporting processes:** Include the required user and technical training.
- **Retire/decommission any unused assets:** Remove hardware and software that is no longer required.
- **Verify deployment:** Check that users, Service Operations, other staff and stakeholders are capable of using or operating the service; identify any issues and take any necessary corrective action.

A frequent cause of new or changed services failing is that the necessary training is not provided or that there is insufficient checking to ensure that users can take advantage of new or changed features. Hence, once a new or changed service has been deployed into the production environment, Service Transition may provide Early Life Support for a limited period of time to ensure that everything has bedded-in correctly and that the service is being used as intended. During Early

Life Support the service levels and monitoring thresholds will be reviewed and additional resources may be provided for Incident and Problem Management.

One approach to testing used by the Release and Deployment Management and the Service Validation and Testing processes is the Service V-model (see Figure 20.2). This provides a framework to organise the levels of Configuration Items to be managed through the lifecycle and the associated validation and testing activities to be undertaken. The left-hand side of the V represents the specifications of the service requirements down to a detailed service design. The right-hand side focuses on the validation and testing activities that are performed against each of the specifications defined on the left.

Figure 20.2 An example Service V-model (Source: OGC ITIL Service Transition ISBN 978-0-113310-48-7)

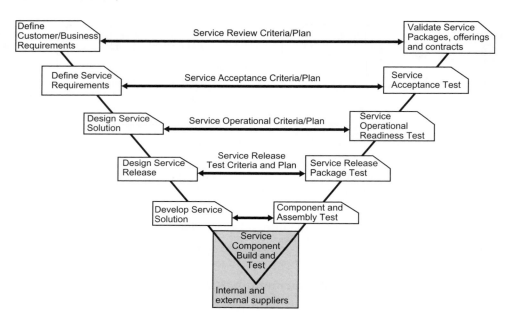

Different approaches are available when making the actual deployment. Deployments can either be 'Big bang' (i.e. all at once) or phased (i.e. deployed to users in stages and at different times). A release can be 'pushed', whereby the service component is deployed from the centre and pushed out to the target, or 'pulled', where users are free to initiate the deployment when required.

CHALLENGES

The challenges that organisations will face when defining the right policies and implementing effective Release and Deployment include:

- establishing standard performance metrics for all transitions;
- dealing with inaccurate project or supplier delivery dates;
- understanding all the stakeholder perspectives;
- understanding the risks;
- taking a pragmatic approach to the challenges of delivery.

KEY METRICS

The following are some of the key metrics for assessing the effectiveness of the solution:

- The variance in service performance against that required by customers (should be minimal and reducing).
- The number of Incidents recorded against the service (should be low and reducing).
- Increased customer and user satisfaction with the services delivered.
- Reduced customer dissatisfaction caused by poorly tested and deployed services.
- Reduced Incidents and Problems in deployment and production.
- Reduced discrepancies between the registered data in the CMS and the real world.

RELATIONSHIPS WITH OTHER SERVICE MANAGEMENT PROCESSES

The key interfaces include:

Change Management
All releases are driven by an authorised RFC.

Configuration Management
Providing input for the components during the build and updating during the various phases of the release and deployment.

Incident Management
Particularly during Early Life Support when extra attention and resources may be required.

IT Service Continuity Management
Continuity plans must be updated to reflect the new or changed service.

Capacity Management
New resources may be required or loads on existing ones changed.

ROLES

The Release Packaging and Design Manager's responsibilities include:

- establishing the final release configuration and building the final release;
- testing the release and publishing known errors and workarounds.

The Deployment Manager's responsibilities include:

- planning, scheduling and controlling the movement of Releases to test in live environments;
- ensuring that the integrity of the live environment is protected and that the correct components are released.

TEST QUESTIONS FOR CHAPTER 20

ST 01, ST 14, ST 20
A 7

21 THE SERVICE DESK (SO 6.2)

INTRODUCTION

The Service Desk is a Function and not a Process. A Function is a defined group of people who carry out a process or processes. The Service Desk conducts a number of processes, in particular Incident Management and Request Fulfilment.

The Service Desk is made up of a group of staff trained to deal with service events. Service Desk staff will have access to the necessary tools to manage these events.

For most IT users within an organisation, the Service Desk will be their only contact with the IT Department. Therefore, the impression made by the Service Desk in the handling of events will have a large influence on how the IT Department as a whole is viewed within that organisation.

The Service Desk should be the single point of contact for IT users within an organisation. The size and structure of a Service Desk will be driven by the size and structure of the organisation it supports. The number and skills of the IT user community and their geographical spread are factors.

The Service Desk is the single point of contact for all IT users wishing to log an Incident, report an event, initiate a change request, make a Service Request or raise a query regarding any of the services that the IT Department provides.

GOALS, PURPOSE AND OBJECTIVES

The main objectives of the Service Desk are to restore service as quickly as possible (Incident Management) and to fulfil Service Requests efficiently and effectively (Request Fulfilment).

BASIC CONCEPTS

Methods of contacting the Service Desk
Traditionally, most IT users have contacted their Service Desk via telephone. However, there are various methods of making contact with a Service Desk:

- Telephone;
- Web interface;

- Automated alert;
- Email;
- Pager;
- Personal contact.

Single point of contact

It is very important that the Service Desk is the single point of contact for IT users within an organisation. Without a single point of contact, there is no control and ownership throughout the management of Incidents, Service Requests and queries.

It is the Service Desk which owns Incidents throughout their lifecycle. It does not matter who is working on the Incident, the ownership remains with the Service Desk. The Service Desk will receive and log Incidents or Service Request details. They will undertake first-line investigation and diagnosis with escalation if Incidents or Service Requests are not resolved.

The existence of the single point of contact can be reinforced by advertising the sole Service Desk number or email address as widely as possible.

Service Desk structures

The Service Desk can be structured in a number of ways. The structure should be driven by the nature of the business supported. Factors such as user skill profile and geographical location of users will influence the structure.

Service Desk structures are defined below.

Local Service Desk: Local Service Desks are situated adjacent to the users that they support. Frequently, this means that they are in the same building or on the same site as the people who contact them.

The advantages of such a structure are visibility of the Service Desk function and easy communication links. However, there are disadvantages such as the risk of Incidents not being prioritised in line with business impact because users are able to physically appear at the Service Desk and request/demand action. Another potential disadvantage is that Service Desk staff are not used as efficiently as they would be under other Service Desk structures because they are 'fixed' in one place supporting local users.

Good reasons for adopting a Local Service Desk structure include time zone restrictions, language issues, the requirement to support a specialist group of users needing specialist support or the requirement to support specific services which again require specialist support. There may even be arguments for having a local Service Desk adjacent to and available to key users. Such key users may be important functionally, in that they undertake processes critical to the business of the organisation or hierarchically in that are at a senior level. (N.b. seniority should not drive the prioritisation of an Incident. Incidents should always be prioritised on the basis of business impact and urgency.)

Centralised Service Desk: Typically, organisations have moved away from Local Service Desks to adopting a centralised Service Desk. Efficiency and cost-effectiveness are the reasons for this. Economies of scale can be exploited by having all of the organisation's Service Desk staff in one physical location. By adopting a single telephone number, calls from anywhere in the organisation will be directed to the centralised Service Desk. It should not matter to the user where their call is dealt with; their only interest ought to be the way in which the call is handled.

Virtual Service Desk: From the user's point of view, the response they receive from a virtual Service Desk will be the same as the one they receive from a centralised Service Desk. However, the persons who operate a virtual Service Desk can be in a number of different locations. By utilising a single universal tool, users are able to obtain a service which is the same regardless of their location or the location of the responding Service Desk staff.

One advantage of such a structure is that it allows far greater staff flexibility. Staff may be able to work from home or organisations may be able to be more efficient by using offshore working by some or all of the Service Desk staff. There is, however, a risk that service quality lacks consistency and this is something that needs to be managed via metrics designed to measure the quality of service from the various locations.

Follow the Sun: Organisations with sites around the world may find it more efficient to switch between two or three Service Desks during a 24-hour period. For example, the Service Desk based in Singapore would take all the incoming calls for eight hours prior to switching to the Madrid Service Desk. Madrid would be the Service Desk through normal European working hours before switching to Chicago. After another eight hours, Chicago would switch back to Singapore and so on.

The advantage of this approach is that it makes it possible for Service Desk staff to work a normal shift without the need for overtime and additional payments.

A 'Follow the Sun' approach relies on good handovers between the sites. Language can be an issue and it is crucial that information from users is recorded in a central tool in such a way that it is understood wherever it is picked up.

Specialised Service Desk Groups: Within Service Desks it is possible to put together specialist groups who perhaps look after one particular high profile or complex service. Where this happens, calls can be routed to the specialist group via the telephony with an option being given to the caller to divert to the group.

KEY ACTIVITIES

The key activity undertaken by the Service Desk is to manage Incidents and Events as effectively and as efficiently as possible. In order to facilitate this, Service Desk staff need to have certain skills. It is the application of these skills, along with the use of an appropriate toolset, that allows the Service Desk to be effective and efficient.

Skills required by Service Desk staff

Staff should be recruited with the skills listed below. Ongoing training is required to ensure that these skills are being translated into an effective service and to ensure that the quality of that service is consistent. Service Desk staff should be:

- customer focused;
- business aware;
- service aware;
- technology aware;
- articulate.

They should have:

- good interpersonal skills;
- the ability to translate the user description into an Incident narrative.

Training will be needed on:

- the processes used by the Service Desk;
- using the tool and relevant technology;
- problem-solving skills (if this is within their scope).

SERVICE DESK METRICS

Metrics should be put in place to measure the performance of the Service Desk. While call volumes are important to indicate required staffing levels, they are not a measure of Service Desk performance or something that the Service Desk can necessarily control.

Metrics include:

- the average time to resolve an Incident (where the incident is resolved by the Service Desk and not subject to functional escalation);
- the percentage of calls resolved during the first call;
- the average time to escalate an Incident (this can then be compared with the relevant SLA);
- the average cost of calls (calls will be different, but this figure is useful for planning and assessing long-term trends).

RELATIONSHIPS WITH OTHER SERVICE MANAGEMENT PROCESSES

The Service Desk undertakes a number of Service Management processes, primarily Incident Management and Request Fulfilment. There will also be links to many other processes. Service Level Management provides the targets for Incident and Request handling. Change Management will provide details of forthcoming changes allowing the Service Desk to plan, train and roster staff accordingly.

ROLES

There are potentially a number of roles to be fulfilled on a Service Desk. These include:

- Service Desk Manager;
- Service Desk Supervisor;
- Service Desk Analyst;
- Super User.

The mix of roles will be determined by the size of the organisation being supported and the type of support being provided.

CHALLENGES

Challenges facing Service Desks include:

- recruiting, training and retaining staff with the appropriate skills;
- procuring, utilising and maximising the performance of an appropriate Service Desk tool;
- ensuring that the Service Desk is the single point of contact;
- ensuring that the Service Desk is not bypassed;
- obtaining meaningful Customer Satisfaction data.

TEST QUESTIONS FOR CHAPTER 21

SO 15
SF 02, SF 03, SF 06
A 1

22 REQUEST FULFILMENT (SO 4.3.1, 4.3.4)

INTRODUCTION

Request Fulfilment is the Process that carries out Service Requests from users. It covers Standard Change requests, requests for information and complaints. From a Service Desk point of view, the process of Request Fulfilment tends to cover all the calls that are not Incidents. Password resets and queries about obtaining additional software are some of the higher volume requests.

Requests are usually high in volume, but low risk and low cost. A separate distinct process is in place to avoid confusion with the Incident handling that the Service Desk is also undertaking.

GOALS, PURPOSE AND OBJECTIVES

The objective of the process is to action the Service Requests effectively and efficiently. Request Fulfilment allows Users to obtain information and complete Standard Changes as quickly as possible.

SERVICE REQUEST

A Service Request is a request from a user for information, for advice, for a Standard Change or for access to an IT Service.

STANDARD CHANGE

A Standard Change is a pre-approved Change that is low risk, relatively common and follows a Procedure or Work Instruction.

KEY ACTIVITIES

Request Fulfilment should be made as simple as possible. Unlike Incidents, Requests ought to be predictable and planned for. It will depend on the size and scale of an organisation whether Requests are handled through the same logging system as Incidents. For organisations with a large number of Requests, a separate logging and progressing system may be appropriate.

The key role of Request Fulfilment is to handle a large number of Requests efficiently and to avoid any bureaucratic bottlenecks. Users will be frustrated if a legitimate Request or query cannot be efficiently handled and responded to. A holistic view of the situation can be taken by handling all the Requests in one place, allowing training needs, communication gaps and requirements for Standard Changes to be identified.

REQUEST MODELS

Where high volumes of the same or similar requests are expected, a process model can be defined to standardise the activities to be undertaken. Adoption of Request models will streamline the process and allow greater volumes to be processed.

RELATIONSHIPS WITH OTHER SERVICE MANAGEMENT PROCESSES

Financial Management
There needs to be a strong link between Financial Management and Request Fulfilment to ensure that volumes, workload and use of resources are fully understood.

Change Management
Where the Request model relates to a Standard Change, there will have been the necessary approval from Change Management which will have taken into account the Financial Management issues.

TEST QUESTIONS FOR CHAPTER 22

SO 09

23   INCIDENT MANAGEMENT   (SO 4.2)

INTRODUCTION

Incident Management is the Process for dealing with all Incidents. These may be Incidents where service is being disrupted or Incidents where service has not yet been disrupted.

The value of Incident Management to the business is that resources are allocated to minimising and mitigating the impact of Incidents and service unavailability in line with business priorities. Lower levels of Incidents and quicker resolution times will enable the services to run as intended.

During the handling of Incidents, the Service Desk may be able to identify improvements in both business and technical processes. The Service Desk often has a unique position within organisations in that its staff can take a holistic view of how the organisation operates, allowing good practice to be propagated and bad practice to be eradicated.

GOALS, PURPOSE AND OBJECTIVES

The main goal of the Incident Management process is to restore normal service operation as quickly as possible and to minimise the adverse impact on business operations.

BASIC CONCEPTS

INCIDENT

An Incident is an unplanned interruption to an IT service or reduction in the quality of an IT service. Failure of a Configuration Item that has not yet impacted service is also an Incident.

146

- **Timescales:** Timescales for Incident handling and triggers for escalation must be agreed and documented in the SLA. Performance against SLA can then be measured and reported. Tools can be configured to enable automated escalation in accordance with the agreed timescales.

- **Incident Models:** The adoption of Incident Models is a method of standardising and automating, if possible, the approach to groups of similar Incidents. An Incident Model is a defined set of steps to be undertaken. Incident Model details can be input into the Incident handling tool(s).

- **Major Incidents:** Different organisations will have different definitions for what constitutes a Major Incident. For some organisations, the trigger for 'calling' a Major Incident is when a certain number of users have been impacted. For other organisations, the trigger may be the actual or potential financial loss from the loss of service. If the actual or potential financial loss is over a certain amount, the Incident becomes Major. For some business areas in some industries, there may be risk of injury or loss of life if particular services are not available. Again, this may be the trigger for the Incident becoming Major. Reputational damage to the organisation can be another trigger.

Larger organisations may have dedicated Major Incident Management teams available 24/7 who take control of Incidents that have been designated Major. One of the important roles that Major Incident Managers undertake is to protect those (frequently IT Operations Management, Technical Management and Application Management staff) who are trying to restore service from the communication demands being made on them. During a Major Incident, there will be many demands and requests for updates which need to be managed. Major Incident Management teams will have established routes for communication and escalation (both functional and hierarchical).

A Major Incident Management process is similar to the Incident Management process, but is progressed with greater urgency and with higher profile within the organisation. Activities undertaken must still be logged, but the focus is on restoring the service as quickly as possible with the minimum of disruption.

KEY ACTIVITIES

Incident Management process flow
The Incident Management process flow is illustrated in Figure 23.1 and contains the following steps:

- **Inputs to the process:** Incidents can be detected and reported in various ways. Users will call the Service Desk to report Incidents. Technical staff may log Incidents or email details of an Incident they have identified to the Service Desk. Increasingly Incidents are raised via web interfaces. The Event Management process will also report Incidents by monitoring.

- **Incident identification:** Work to understand and resolve Incidents cannot start until an Incident has been identified. For this reason, monitoring of the components that make up key services is essential. Incidents can be identified in various ways by users, technical staff and by monitoring.

Figure 23.1 Incident Management process flow (Source: OGC ITIL Service Operation
ISBN 978-0-113310-46-3)

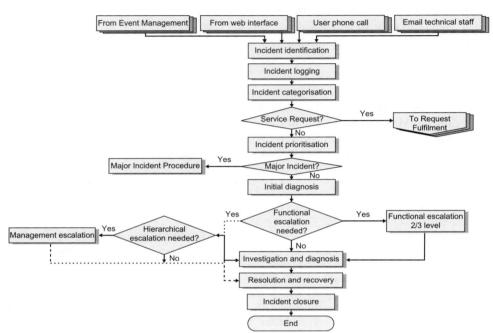

- **Incident logging:** All Incidents must be logged with the date and time being
  recorded. At this stage, the information required to manage the Incident will
  be logged. This will include a unique reference number, a description of
  symptoms, the Service or CI impacted, the impact, its urgency, and the name
  of person raising the Incident or the method of raising the Incident.

- **Incident categorisation:** A suitable categorisation code will be allocated.
  For example, this may be hardware or software with sub-codes for lower level
  categorisation. Accurate categorisation is important because it will allow
  useful metrics to be gathered highlighting areas of the infrastructure where
  Incidents are occurring.

- **Incident prioritisation:** The priority of an Incident is based on the impact
  and the urgency. Impact is the 'pain' to the business. Impact may relate to the
  number of users impacted, the potential financial loss to the organisation, the
  risk of breach of regulatory or legislative rules or, for some services, the risk of
  loss of life. Urgency relates to how quickly the business requires the Incident
  to be resolved.

Table 23.1 illustrates a simplistic priority coding system.

Target resolution times will have been allocated to each Priority level. These will
have been agreed with the business and recorded in the SLA.

Table 23.1 A simplistic Incident priority coding system

		Impact		
		High	Medium	Low
	High	Priority 1	Priority 2	Priority 3
Urgency	Medium	Priority 2	Priority 3	Priority 4
	Low	Priority 3	Priority 4	Priority 5

- **Initial diagnosis:** If the Incident has been raised by a call to the Service Desk, then it will be the Service Desk who conduct the initial diagnosis, usually while the user is still on the telephone. The availability of diagnostic scripts will help as will the ability to match against Problems and Known Errors. The CMDB may also be consulted at this stage.

- **Incident escalation:** Escalation may be functional or hierarchical.

  - Functional escalation occurs when the Service Desk is not able to resolve the Incident or where the Incident has not been resolved within the target resolution time. The Service Desk will involve second-level support, which has more specific technical knowledge. Further functional escalation may occur through the lifecycle of the Incident to third-level support, which may be part of the organisation or third parties such as suppliers. It is important to remember that the ownership of an Incident always remains with the Service Desk regardless of which other support areas are working on a resolution.

  - Hierarchical escalation raises the profile of a specific Incident within the IT organisation and also within business areas. More senior IT staff are able to provide focus and resources, but ownership of the Incident will be retained by the Service Desk. Organisations will have triggers that indicate when hierarchical escalation is required. This may be for all 'Priority 1' Incidents or when Incidents of a certain priority have not been resolved with a target timescale. The triggers for escalation will be recorded in the relevant SLA and ought to be highlighted by the support tool in use. The Service Desk will keep the user informed of all functional or hierarchical escalations that occur during the lifecycle of an Incident and at the same time the Incident record will be updated.

- **Investigation and diagnosis:** In this phase of the Incident lifecycle, work is undertaken by the Service Desk or support areas to understand what has to be done in order to restore service. This is often the most time-consuming part of the process although it can be speeded up using diagnostic scripts and by reference to other Incidents and Problems as well as Known Error databases.

- **Resolution and recovery:** The investigation and diagnosis phase will arrive at a resolution. This needs to be applied and then testing needs to take place to ensure that the Incident has been resolved and service restored. There may be a time lag between a fix being applied and the service running normally again (e.g. there may be a backlog of processing to catch up on). On other occasions, it may not be possible to ascertain whether the fix has worked for a period of time (e.g. if the original issue was with a month-end process). Regardless of where the resolution has been put in place or who was involved, the Incident should be passed back to the Service Desk for closure.

- **Incident closure:** Only the Service Desk should close Incidents. They need the user's agreement that the Incident has been resolved. All Incident documentation will have to be completed prior to closure and a closure category allocated to allow meaningful metrics to be produced. User satisfaction surveys ought to be conducted for an agreed (in the SLA) percentage of Incidents. These user satisfaction surveys can be undertaken via telephone, email or web interface.

RELATIONSHIPS WITH OTHER SERVICE MANAGEMENT PROCESSES

Incident Management is closely linked to Problem Management with one or more Incidents being caused by a Problem. There is also a strong link with Change Management. Changes are often implemented to resolve an Incident or a number of Incidents and, unfortunately, Changes that do not do exactly what they were intended to do may cause Incidents. Configuration Management provides the information needed to manage Incidents. Service Level Management will provide the target resolution times together with escalation criteria.

METRICS

Useful Incident metrics include:

- the percentage of Incidents resolved within SLA;
- the average cost of an Incident;
- the average cost of a Major Incident;
- the percentage of Incidents that are Major.

Additionally, from a staffing point of view, it is important to know the volume of both Incidents and Major Incidents. On their own, these metrics do not necessarily give a measure of effectiveness or efficiency, but they are important in understanding the scale of the issues being raised.

ROLES

The Incident Manager is responsible for the effectiveness and efficiency of the Incident Management process. First-line support is conducted by the Service

Desk with second- and third-line support being provided by technical teams either internal to the organisation or via third parties.

CHALLENGES

Difference between Incident and Problem Management
There is a very real difference between Incident Management and Problem Management. Incident Management is solely focused on restoring service as quickly as possible while Problem Management's aim is to understand and tackle the root cause. This can lead to tension between the two processes.

Other Challenges

- Early detection of Incidents (preferably before service is impacted).
- Persuading and explaining to all users that all Incidents must be logged via the Service Desk. Awareness campaigns are particularly useful in this area.

TEST QUESTIONS FOR CHAPTER 23

SF 01
SO 05, SO 08, SO 13, SO 17
TA 03
A 16, A 20

24   PROBLEM MANAGEMENT   (SO 4.4)

INTRODUCTION

Problem Management is responsible for the management of all Problems in the IT infrastructure. The process includes root cause analysis and arriving at the resolution of Problems. Problem Management remains responsible until resolutions are implemented via Change Management and Release Management.

Problem Management provides value to an organisation by avoiding, reducing and mitigating the adverse business impact of Problems. This allows services to be more available and to be more robust.

GOALS, PURPOSE AND OBJECTIVES

The objectives of Problem Management are:

- to prevent Problems and resulting Incidents from occurring;
- to stop repeat Incidents happening;
- to mitigate and reduce the adverse impact of Incidents that cannot be prevented.

BASIC CONCEPTS

PROBLEM

A Problem is the cause of one or more Incidents.

Problem Models
A Problem Model is a similar idea to that of an Incident Model. Problem Models provide a standardised approach to tackling Problems.

Difference between reactive and proactive
There are two parts of Problem Management. Reactive Problem Management responds to Incidents and Problems that occur. The proactive side of Problem

Management is concerned with preventing Incidents and Problems occurring. Proactive Problem Management is often triggered by Continual Service Improvement.

A good analogy is to consider a Fire Service. Any Fire Service is going to be involved in fighting fires. This is the reactive part of their role. All Fire Services are also involved in fire prevention by raising public awareness and the installation and testing of smoke alarms and sensors. This is the proactive side. Problem Management should have a similar split, ensuring that resources are involved in longer-term Problem prevention as well as the here and now reactive response to Problems and Incidents. It is often difficult to release resources to the proactive side, especially when the reactive demands are high, but it is proactive Problem prevention that allows organisations to become more mature in their Service Management.

KEY ACTIVITIES

The Problem Management process flow

Figure 24.1 Problem Management process flow (Source: OGC ITIL Service Operation ISBN 978-0-113310-46-3)

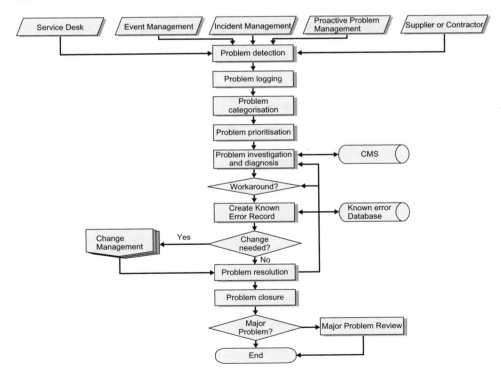

The Problem Management process flow is illustrated in Figure 24.1 and contains the following steps:

- **Inputs to the process:** The inputs to Problem Management can come from a number of sources. These include Incident Management, Event Management and the Service Desk. Additionally, proactive Problem Management may identify Problems. Suppliers and other processes such as Release Management, Capacity Management and Availability Management may also become aware of Problems.

- **Problem detection:** Problems can be detected in many ways. The Service Desk may believe that one or more Incidents are being caused by a particular Problem. Second-line support areas may identify a Problem when conducting Incident handling. Problems can also be detected automatically by the Service Management tools in use. Proactive Problem Management will identify problems often before any Incidents occur. Likewise, other processes such as Release Management and Availability Management will become aware of Problems.

- **Problem logging:** It is crucial that the full details of the Problem are recorded. This will allow analysis to take place and will enable comparisons to be made between Problems. All Incidents caused by the Problem should be linked to the Problem record allowing the scope and scale of the impact to be ascertained easily. The date and the time that all Problems are logged must be recorded within the Problem record.

- **Problem categorisation:** It is important to categorise Problems and it is recommended that the same system is used as adopted by the Incident Management process for any particular organisation. Correct and meaningful categorisation will allow helpful metrics to be produced and enable proactive Problem Management to identify areas to concentrate on.

- **Problem prioritisation:** Problems should be prioritised in the same way as Incidents. Table 24.1 shows a simplistic Problem priority coding system.

Table 24.1 A simplistic Problem priority coding system

		Impact		
		High	Medium	Low
	High	Priority 1	Priority 2	Priority 3
Urgency	Medium	Priority 2	Priority 3	Priority 4
	Low	Priority 3	Priority 4	Priority 5

Target Problem resolution times will have been allocated to each Priority level. These will have been agreed with the business and recorded in the SLA. One factor that will feed into the impact and urgency of Problems is the rate of reoccurrence.

- **Problem investigation and diagnosis:** The aim of the investigation and diagnosis phase is to ascertain the root cause of the Problem. The priority allocated to the Problem should drive the number of resources working on the investigation and diagnosis. Priority should be reassessed during the lifetime of the Problem to ensure that it remains correct.

There are various problem-solving techniques that can be employed to aid the diagnosis of Problems. These include:

- **Kepner and Tregoe:** A logical approach to problem-solving starting with defining and then describing the problem. Possible causes are established, and then probable causes tested and finally the true cause is verified.

- **Chronological Analysis:** This approach sets out all the things that have happened in a timeline. This makes it clearer to see what has happened and allows focus on the critical part of the timeline.

- **Brainstorming:** Gathering together the key individuals involved with a Problem in one place and mapping out all possible causes (and potential corrective activity). Such sessions should be under the control of the Problem Manager.

- **Pain Value Analysis:** This technique is useful for identifying which Problems should be tackled in which order. Pain to a business can be defined in a number of different ways, for example the number of users impacted or potential financial loss. Pain Value Analysis provides a framework for deciding which Problems are actually hurting the organisation most, allowing resources to be allocated where they are most needed.

- **Pareto Analysis:** The Pareto Principle is often referred to as the '80–20 Rule'. The rule states that for many events, roughly 80 per cent of the effects come from only 20 per cent of the causes. This rule can be used in Problem Management to target those causes (Problems) that are causing most of the Incidents.

- **Workarounds:** Sometimes before permanent fixes can be found, workarounds are identified. This often takes place during the Problem investigation and diagnosis phase. Workarounds are ways of restoring service that can be used without understanding the root cause. An obvious and frequently used example is the user who finds that their screen has 'frozen'. There could be any number of causes, but the first step, which quite often resolves the issue, is usually to turn off the PC and then turn it back on again.

Problem Records must remain open when a workaround has been identified and the workaround should be detailed in the Problem record. Permanent fixes should still be progressed. However, there may be reasons why workarounds remain in place for some time. These reasons include:

- a permanent fix is too risky;
- a permanent fix is too costly;
- the business impact of the Problem is not significant enough to justify further diagnosis at this time;
- the Problem will be permanently fixed by a new Release that is currently being planned.

- **Raising a Known Error Record:** The Known Error Database is an important source of information for the Service Desk and Support groups handling Incidents and Problems. A Known Error Record should be raised when the diagnosis has been completed and especially when a workaround has been identified.

KNOWN ERROR

A Known Error is a Problem that has a documented root cause and a workaround. Known Errors are created and managed throughout their lifecycle by Problem Management. Known Errors may also be identified by Development or Suppliers.

- **Problem resolution:** Once a permanent fix has been identified, it should be implemented as soon as possible. However, there may be good reasons why this is not possible. The reasons are similar to the reasons why organisations live with workarounds and include cost and risk. Additionally, an immediate fix may require a service outage which is not justifiable in the short term. A Request For Change (RFC) should be raised and progressed for any required Change identified.

- **Problem closure:** Problem Records should be closed once a Change has successfully been applied. It is important that the Problem Record stays open until it is certain that the Problem has been resolved. Checking that the Problem has been resolved should be undertaken via testing. It may take some time to ensure that a fix has been successful, for example it may be the next time a particular process is used such as end of day, end of month, end of quarter, year-end or end of tax year.

- **Major Problem Review:** Whenever a Major Problem has occurred, a Major Problem Review should be undertaken. Each organisation will have its own definition of a Major Problem based on the impact and urgency. It is crucial that these reviews look at lessons learnt rather than becoming 'allocation of blame' sessions. The output from a Major Problem Review ought to include what went well, what went badly, what could be done better in the future, how could the Problem have been prevented and how could the impact of the Problem have been reduced.

RELATIONSHIPS WITH OTHER SERVICE MANAGEMENT PROCESSES

There are very close connections between Problem Management and Incident Management. Also, Problem Management needs to work closely with the Service Transition processes of Change Management, Configuration Management and Release and Deployment Management.

Information about Problems and Known Errors will come from processes such as Availability Management, Capacity Management and IT Service Continuity Management. The proactive side of Problem Management has a close relationship with Continual Service Improvement. Financial Management and Service Level Management provide some of the cost and service guidelines to which Problem Management adheres.

METRICS

Metrics should be put in place to measure the effectiveness and the efficiency of the Problem Management process. Metrics should include:

- the percentage of Problems resolved within the timescales set out in the SLA;
- the average cost of resolving a Problem;
- the percentage of Major Problems where Major Problem Reviews have been carried out;
- the percentage of actions from completed Major Problem Reviews that have been completed;
- the number of Known Errors identified.

The actual number of Problems identified during a period is useful to give an indication of the scale of issues and the resources required, but on its own it is not a measure of the effectiveness or efficiency of the process.

ROLES

The key role is that of Problem Manager. The Problem Manager is responsible for Problem Management within the organisation. Larger organisations will have teams of Problem Managers. It is important that the Problem Manager can call on staff from a wide variety of support groups when tackling Problems.

CHALLENGES

Incident Management focuses on restoring service as quickly as possible while Problem Management is concerned with ascertaining and removing the root cause of one or more Incidents.

The two processes work closely together. However, there can at times be a tension between the Incident Management and Problem Management processes. Often the Problem investigation and diagnosis phase can be time-consuming.

If Incident Management has a quick workaround to restore service, they will want to use it. This may not aid Problem Management which needs to understand the root cause. Problem Management may require an outage or to take a 'dump' of data which again may be at odds with Incident Management striving to get the service back running as soon as possible.

Other challenges include:

- ensuring that the Incident and Problem tools are compatible and communicate with each other;
- understanding the real business impact of Problems.

TEST QUESTIONS FOR CHAPTER 24

SO 02, SO 06, SO 12, SO 13, SO 18

25 IT OPERATIONS MANAGEMENT
(6.4.1), (6.4.2)

INTRODUCTION

IT Operations Management is a Function and not a Process. It is responsible for operating the organisation's IT infrastructure and applications on a day-to-day basis. The IT infrastructure and applications underpin the organisation's services.

GOALS, PURPOSE AND OBJECTIVES

Delivery of stable service with unavailability minimised is the main goal.

IT Operations Management is the function that ensures that all the organisation's IT infrastructure and applications are managed and maintained on a day-to-day basis in order to deliver the agreed levels of service.

KEY ACTIVITIES

IT Operations Management is made up of two parts:

- **Operations Control:** Responsible for carrying out the day-to-day operational activities. This includes monitoring the IT infrastructure and applications and responding to Events, Incidents and Problems. More specifically tasks include Job Scheduling, Backup and Restore, Console Management, Print and Output Management as well as undertaking maintenance activities for Technical Management teams and Application Management teams.

- **Facilities Management:** Responsible for the day-to-day management of the physical IT environment. This typically would include responsibility for the data centre, server rooms as well as recovery rooms and sites. The power supply and back-up power supply would also be in scope. If any part of the physical IT environment is outsourced, then the Facilities Management arm of IT Operations Management would be responsible for day-to-day management of the contract and the relationship with the supplier.

It is important that IT Operations Management is involved at the right time throughout the Service Management lifecycle and in the right way. More specifically:

- **Service Strategy:** IT Operations Management will have an in-depth understanding of how current technology is used to deliver existing services. This understanding, together with an awareness of new and emerging technologies, allows IT Operations Management to have a meaningful input to the Strategy phase of the Service Management lifecycle. It is crucial that those responsible for Strategy use the knowledge that is available about how services are actually delivered on a day-to-day basis.

- **Service Design:** Carrying out the activities set out in the Service Design phase is the responsibility of IT Operations Management. Therefore, it is important that IT Operations Management has the ability to input to this phase.

- **Service Transition:** Testing is an area of Service Transition where you would expect IT Operations Management to be involved heavily. IT Operations staff have the knowledge and understanding of the live environment, which allows them to ensure testing is correctly designed and executed. It may well be IT Operations staff, under direction from Service Transition, who physically introduce Releases to the live environment and monitor their progress.

- **Service Operation:** This is the fundamental task of IT Operations Management. They maintain and monitor the components (infrastructure and applications) that underpin the services and react in a timely fashion to Events, Incidents and Problems identified.

- **Continual Service Improvement:** Staff from IT Operations Management will always be looking for ways to improve the services and boost efficiency and effectiveness.

RELATIONSHIPS WITH OTHER SERVICE MANAGEMENT FUNCTIONS

There may be overlaps between IT Operations Management and both Technical Management and Application Management. IT Operations Management is a distinct function but it is usual for teams from both Application Management and Technical Management to be part of this function.

Technical Management is responsible for the IT infrastructure while Application Management is responsible for applications. Technical Management has the same responsibilities for the IT infrastructure as Application Management has for applications.

TEST QUESTIONS FOR CHAPTER 25

SF 05

26 EVENT MANAGEMENT (SO 4.1.4)

INTRODUCTION

Event Management monitors all events throughout the organisation's IT infrastructure and applications to ensure normal operation. Event Management handles normal messages as well as being there to detect, escalate and react to exceptions.

The Event Management process is responsible for managing Events throughout their lifecycle.

EVENT MANAGEMENT

The Process responsible for managing Events throughout their lifecycle. Event Management is one of the main Activities of IT Operations.

EVENT

An Event can be defined as any detectable or discernable occurrence that has significance for the management of the IT infrastructure or the delivery of IT service and evaluation of the impact a deviation may cause to the services. Events are typically notifications created by an IT service, Configuration Item or monitoring tool.

Events can be split into three types:

- **Informational:** Such as notification of a scheduled job finishing or a user accessing an application.
- **Warning:** Including indications that utilisation of a particular CI has reached a certain percentage of capacity.
- **Exception:** Such as unauthorised software detected or a capacity threshold has been breached.

Event Management can be used by any part of Service Management where there is a requirement to monitor and control an activity, as long as the monitoring and control can be automated. Event Management requires the ability to raise automated alerts. If alerts cannot be raised, then only monitoring is taking place. Event Management is much more proactive than monitoring.

ALERT

An Alert is defined as a warning that a threshold has been reached, something has changed or a failure has occurred.

GOALS, PURPOSE AND OBJECTIVES

Event Management is the Service Operation process responsible for ensuring that the infrastructure, applications and security that underpin IT Services are proactively monitored with alerts being put in place and acted on.

KEY ACTIVITIES

Event Management follows a process similar to Incident Management with the following stages:

- Event occurs;
- Event notification;
- Event detection;
- Event filtering;
- Significance of Events decision;
- Event correlation;
- Trigger;
- Response selection;
- Review actions;
- Close Event.

The above stages of the process should ideally be automated within the selected tool(s), but manual intervention may be required at times.

The sooner Events are detected, the sooner they can be tackled. For example, for a service that is required to be available from 7.00 a.m., it is desirable to have a number of alerts in place to indicate if any of the components required to provide that service are not available at a time prior to 7.00 a.m..

RELATIONSHIPS WITH OTHER SERVICE MANAGEMENT PROCESSES

Incident Management
There is a close relationship between Event Management and Incident Management. The processes are similar and some Events will be triggers for the Incident Management process. Proactive Event Management will reduce the number of Incidents because exceptions will be identified before Incidents occur.

Other Processes
Many areas of Service Management will identify areas that they want to control and monitor. Configuration Management and Capacity Management will have a number of requirements for Event Management.

TEST QUESTIONS FOR CHAPTER 26

SO 01, SO 03, SO 11, SO 19, SO 25

27 APPLICATION MANAGEMENT (SO 6.5.1, 6.5.2)

INTRODUCTION

Application Management is a Function and not a Process. It will manage applications through the totality of their lifecycle. This starts with the first business 'idea' and completes when the application is no longer required. Application Management is involved in the design, testing and continual improvement of applications and the services that the applications support.

An application is any software program or programs that support a business process. Such applications, in conjunction with data, hardware, middleware and the operating system, make up the IT infrastructure that supports a service. It is not unusual for large organisations with a diverse set of services to have a high number of Application teams. These teams may be grouped together depending on the type(s) of technology used in the applications that they support.

The applications may be developed in-house or they may be bought in. Bought in applications will need varying degrees of customisation prior to release. For those teams responsible for bought-in applications, managing the ongoing relationship with the supplier (in conjunction with Supplier Management) is important.

Application Management teams manage and support applications on a day-to-day basis. For example, they will usually be the functional escalation route used by the Service Desk when an Incident or Problem has been logged and categorised against their application.

GOALS, PURPOSE AND OBJECTIVES

Application Management has two objectives:

- Custodian of technical knowledge and expertise relating to the managing of applications. Application Management makes certain that the required technical knowledge to design, test, operate and continually improve applications is available.

- Provider of the actual resources to facilitate all phases of the Service Lifecycle, ensuring that staff are adequately trained and effective. It is often important for staff who are to be deployed in Service Operations to have been involved in the Service Design and the Service Transition activities for a particular application.

KEY ACTIVITIES

Application Management has to be involved throughout the Service Management lifecycle. It is important that Application Management is involved at the right time and in the right way. More specifically:

- **Service Strategy:** High-level requirements are the outputs of this phase. The decision-making criteria relating to whether applications are developed in-house or are bought in (and customised as necessary) are of particular relevance to Applications Management. Application Management will have the knowledge and experience to be able to input to this decision.

- **Service Design:** How applications are to be designed and subsequently managed is established during the Service Design phase. Application Management will have an understanding of how similar applications are presently managed, and will provide information and views during the Service Design phase.

- **Service Transition:** Application Management will be included in testing and in ensuring that the testing process is appropriate and robust. Knowledge held within the Application Management teams on the applications and how they interface with each other and with the technical infrastructure will be used to help draw up test scripts. Known Errors may be identified at this stage. The Known Errors may be eradicated or, after a cost and risk assessment, be allowed into the live environment with Problem Management and the Known Error Database being updated.

- **Service Operation:** Application Management will typically be available to respond to support requests for the applications for which they are responsible. It is common for Application Management teams to undertake operational activities as part of the IT Operations Management function. Application Management teams provide second-line support and are available for functional escalation relating to Events, Incidents and Problems.

- **Continual Service Improvement:** The performance of applications which make up or underpin a service will be constantly monitored. Improvements will be identified and considered from the point of view of cost and urgency. For applications that have been bought in, close liaison is required with the supplier to ensure that the organisation is aware of possible enhancements that may be considered for implementation.

RELATIONSHIPS WITH OTHER SERVICE MANAGEMENT PROCESSES

IT Operation Management, Technical Management
There may be overlaps between Application Management and both IT Operations Management and Technical Management. Application Management is responsible for the applications while Technical Management is responsible for the IT infrastructure. Application Management has the same responsibilities for the applications as Technical Management has for the IT infrastructure.

IT Operations Management is a distinct function, but it is usual for teams from both Application Management and Technical Management to be part of this function.

28 TECHNICAL MANAGEMENT (SO 6.3.1, 6.3.2)

INTRODUCTION

Technical Management is not a Process, it is a Function that provides the resources and ensures that knowledge of the relevant technologies is kept up to date.

How technical teams are managed will vary from organisation to organisation depending on scale and the blends of technologies used.

Technical Management covers all the teams or areas that support the delivery and management of the IT infrastructure through the provision of technical knowledge and expertise. This includes teams such as Networks, Mainframe, Middleware, Desktop, Server and Database.

GOALS, PURPOSE AND OBJECTIVES

Technical Management has two objectives:

- Custodian of technical knowledge and expertise relating to the IT infrastructure of the organisation. Technical Management makes certain that the required technical knowledge to design, test, operate and continually improve IT services is available.
- Provider of the actual resources to facilitate all phases of the Service Lifecycle, ensuring that staff are adequately trained and effective. It is often important for staff who are to be deployed in Service Operations to have been involved in the Service Design and the Service Transition activities for a particular service.

KEY ACTIVITIES

Technical Management has to be involved throughout the Service Management lifecycle. It is important that Technical Management is involved at the right time and in the right way. More specifically:

- **Service Strategy:** The knowledge and expertise required to manage and operate the IT infrastructure will be identified in the Service Strategy phase of the Service Management lifecycle. Technical Management teams will have an important input to the agreement on standards for technical architecture.

- **Service Design:** During the Service Design phase, Technical Management teams will provide expertise on the IT infrastructure and will make suggestions for how new parts of the infrastructure can be managed at an operational level.

- **Service Transition:** Technical Management will be included in testing and in ensuring that the testing process is appropriate and robust. The knowledge held within the Technical Management teams of the technical infrastructure and how it interfaces with the applications will be used to help draw up test scripts.

- **Service Operation:** It is common for Technical Management teams to undertake operational activities as part of the IT Operations Management function. Technical Management teams provide second-line support and are available for functional escalation relating to Events, Incidents and Problems.

- **Continual Service Improvement:** The performance of the IT infrastructure components that underpin a service will be constantly monitored. Improvements will be identified and considered from the point of view of cost and urgency. For IT infrastructure that has been bought in, close liaison is required with the supplier to ensure that the organisation is aware of possible enhancements and that these are considered for implementation.

RELATIONSHIPS WITH OTHER SERVICE MANAGEMENT FUNCTIONS

IT Operations Management, Application Management
There may be overlaps between Technical Management and both IT Operations Management and Application Management. Technical Management is responsible for the IT infrastructure while Application Management is responsible for applications. Technical Management has the same responsibilities for the IT infrastructure as Application Management has for applications.

IT Operations Management is a distinct function but it is usual for teams from both Application Management and Technical Management to be part of this function.

29 THE SEVEN-STEP IMPROVEMENT PROCESS (CSI 4.1)

GOALS, PURPOSE AND OBJECTIVES

The objectives of the Seven-step Improvement Process are to:

- define a set of measures that are relevant to business requirements and which will support the identification of effective improvement opportunities;
- adopt a structured approach to gathering, processing and analysing the measurement data in order to identify improvement opportunities;
- communicate those improvement opportunities so that appropriate decisions can be taken about actions.

The Seven-step Improvement Process is fundamental in supporting CSI and operates across the entire Service Lifecycle. It focuses on identifying improvement opportunities, not only for the processes and services, but also for the disciplines implemented as part of each of the Lifecycle stages, including the discipline of CSI itself.

Value is created by ensuring that the services and the mechanisms for delivering those services continue to align with and meet business requirements, and by identifying opportunities for continual improvement.

ACTIVITIES, METHODS AND TECHNIQUES

Figure 29.1 illustrates the process steps. Note that the unnumbered eighth box provides the guiding information that informs all decisions.

ROLES

Everybody within the organisation has a role to play in continual improvement. The key role that is essential to the effective implementation of this process is the CSI Manager.

This is role of real responsibility and either needs to have the appropriate seniority and authority or have clear and unambiguous senior support. Responsibilities include:

- developing the CSI domain;

- communicating the vision of CSI across the organisation;

- working with the Service Owners and Service Level Manager to define the monitoring requirements, identify and prioritise improvement opportunities and establish Service Improvement Plans (SIPs);

- identifying frameworks, models and standards that will support CSI activities;

- ensuring that activities are coordinated throughout the entire Service Lifecycle;

- presenting improvement recommendations to senior management.

There is also likely to be an analyst who will be responsible for gathering and manipulating data, and presenting it in the desired formats.

Figure 29.1 The Seven-step Improvement Process (Source: OGC ITIL Continual Service Improvement ISBN 978-0-113310-49-4)

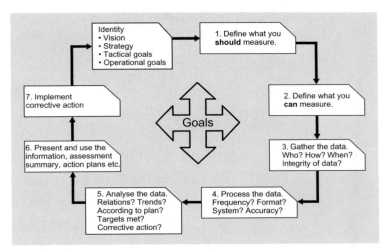

Table 29.1 The Seven-step Improvement Process

Step 1	Define what you **should** measure	Take into account vision, strategy, goals and objectives to determine what to measure. These measurements should enable the provider to demonstrate value to the business by linking back through to key business drivers.

(Continued)

Table 29.1 *(Continued)*

Step 2	Define what you **can** measure	There may be a gap between the capabilities of current tools and mechanisms to provide the necessary information. If the desired data really cannot be gathered or if the cost is prohibitive, the measures in Step 1 may need to be revisited.
Step 3	Gather the data	Use monitoring to gather the data. Monitoring may be either automatic or manual. Extra care needs to be taken to ensure that manually gathered data is accurate and consistent.
Step 4	Process the data	Convert the data gathered into the required format for the audience. This can be seen as turning data into information.
Step 5	Analyse the data	Transform the information into knowledge. Develop an understanding of the real meaning of identified patterns and trends, by querying the results to understand its intrinsic value.
Step 6	Present and use the information	Communicate the information at the right level of detail for the audience and in a format that is understandable, provides value and will support informed decisionmaking.
Step 7	Implement corrective action	Use the knowledge gained to make the necessary changes throughout the lifecycle.

SECTION 4:
MEASUREMENT AND METRICS, AND THE DEMING CYCLE

30 MEASUREMENT AND METRICS

INTRODUCTION

While measurement and metrics are neither Processes nor Functions, this chapter earns its place here because it is difficult to overestimate their importance.

Measurement is a prerequisite to improvement. Put simply, if you can't measure something, you can't improve it or show that it has improved. The reason for this is that to make an improvement, you have to identify that something has gone wrong or not happened and then understand why. Only then can you diagnose the root cause and apply a change to eliminate it, preventing the same thing from happening again and thereby improving performance.

There are other reasons for measurement:

- To demonstrate that an operation or service has performed according to requirements or specification. An example of this would be the publication of a train company's performance against its service levels for the timetable (i.e. the percentage of trains that arrived on time).

- To prove to a stakeholder that they received what they commissioned and for which they might have paid (e.g. an independent audit of the performance of a third-party sales company engaged to generate new sales from a call centre).

- To compare the performance of one operation or service against another, as in a benchmark.

- To establish a baseline that represents the present situation and from which to demonstrate a variation in the future (e.g. the share price of a new company on the day it goes public and trading in shares starts is a baseline).

These examples show that measurements are justified for reasons other than improvement. However, only when used to create improvement can they tangibly increase value for an organisation and its customers. It is for this reason that measurements and metrics as a topic is included within the Continual Service Improvement part of the Service Lifecycle.

KEY PERFORMANCE INDICATORS AND METRICS

There is often confusion concerning the differences between Key Performance Indicators (KPIs) and metrics. Here are ITIL's definitions:

METRIC

Something that is measured and reported to help manage a Process, IT Service or Activity.

KEY PERFORMANCE INDICATOR

Only the most important metrics are defined as KPIs. KPIs should be selected to ensure that Efficiency, Effectiveness and Cost-Effectiveness are all managed.

To expand slightly on these definitions, the following view of KPIs is helpful: 'Metrics are used to help an organisation define and evaluate how successful it is, typically in terms of making progress towards its long-term organisational goals.'

In summary therefore, a KPI is simply a more important metric because it references goals rather than just performance. As such, there are typically fewer KPIs than metrics and we often find that KPIs are expressed in terms of two or more metrics. For example, 'Number of incidents reported' and 'Number of incidents resolved by the Service Desk' are both metrics, but 'Percentage of incidents resolved by the Service Desk' expresses the latter as a proportion of the former to produce a meaningful measure of quality or KPI for a customer.

Three types of metric

ITIL recognises three distinct types of metric in support of Continual Service Improvement:

- **Technology metrics:** These metrics are associated with components such as 'Mean time between failures'. These metrics are only usually used internally to understand the capability of the technology components on which a service depends to remain in service.

- **Process metrics:** These are typically used to measure the quality, performance, value and compliance of a Service Management Process as a way of identifying improvement opportunities. An example is 'Percentage of failed changes'. These metrics are used to ensure that the processes are conforming to documented procedures.

- **Service metrics:** These are used to measure and report on an end-to-end service, for example 'Percentage availability of the web service in the last month'. These are the metrics that are used in performance reports provided to customers.

In summary, measurements and metrics are focused on the key attributes of performance, compliance, quality and value.

Baselines

Baselines have two purposes:

- To provide a reference point against which to demonstrate future improvement.

- To measure the health of an operation or process to see if it requires attention.

Baselines can and should be established at strategic, tactical and operation levels. Initially, baseline measures may be difficult to compile and of questionable accuracy. However, the data is still valuable as a focus for improvement potential.

Critical Success Factors

Critical success factors (CSFs) identify areas that are critical to the success of the enterprise and, as such, they tend to be high level and few in number. For example, the involvement of the business could be a CSF for IT Service. CSI might have senior management involvement or commitment as a CSF. Improved IT service quality could be a sensible CSF for IT Service Management. We might see clearly defined roles and responsibilities as a CSF in any organisation.

For CSFs to be more than just a vague concept there has to be some way of measuring them: a way of calibrating our performance against the things that are most important to our business; that define our success or failure. To achieve this we need to break down each CSF into things that we can measure and that will help us assess how well we are doing. We need something we can measure that will give us a characteristic or a numerical value that will tell us whether our goals are being achieved.

Earlier, we described Key Performance Indicators (KPIs) as important because they reference goals rather than just performance. This discussion of CSFs shows how organisational goals, Critical Success Factors, KPIs and metrics are interrelated in our performance management and improvement framework.

Baselines tell us where we started from, or where we were the last time we checked, whereas goals, CSFs and KPIs tell us where we are going and if we have arrived, or at least if we are still going in the right direction.

USING METRICS AND KPIS TO IMPROVE PERFORMANCE

It is not the aim of this book to provide formal guidance on the use of measurement in IT Service Management. Many books have been written on the subject and the ITIL Foundation syllabus does not require the candidate to achieve such expertise. However, some guidance on constructing meaningful measures and reports is useful in order to help you establish a measurement framework that you can use for performance improvement and in which you have confidence in its integrity and value.

Measures should always encourage the correct behaviour. Measures that give incentive to productivity without a corresponding quality measure usually don't do this.

EXAMPLE

Having a target for 'Number of calls handled per Service Desk analyst per day' will only encourage analysts to shorten calls, typically to the detriment of the caller. In a real-life example, one member of a sales team promoting a new product consistently sold more products than her colleagues. However, when management monitored the calls to understand the secret of her success, they were horrified to hear that she was promising full refunds if the buyer was in any way unhappy. She achieved the highest sales but also created the highest refund levels, except she wasn't measured against refunds!

Measures should be meaningful to those receiving the performance reports. It may be easy for IT to report 'Mean time between system incidents' or perhaps 'Percentage availability of service X', but the service recipient may only be interested in or understand the number and duration of outages and, more importantly, what the service provider is doing to prevent future outages.

Measures should be unambiguous. For example, Service Desks are increasingly recognising the importance of using 'First-line resolution rate' as a KPI. This is entirely appropriate, provided it is properly measured. However, there are significant variations in the way this KPI is measured that make it very hard to compare across organisations or establish a target value. Most organisations measure first-line resolution rate by dividing the total number of logged calls by the number of logged calls resolved by the Service Desk without escalation, expressed as a percentage. The simplest reason for variations is because contacts to the Service Desk can be broadly divided into Incidents, Service Requests (including password resets) and information requests. Incidents are much harder to fix at first line than either of the others. Therefore by failing to separate out the incidents from the requests, the first-line resolution rate will vary according to the mix of contact types as well as the performance of the Service Desk, making the measure meaningless.

A further distortion of measurement occurs with variations against the period over which a measure is taken. Put simply, the longer the period, the easier it is to meet the target. For example, if the target availability of a service is expressed as 99 per cent, it is easier to meet this over a monthly period than a weekly or daily period. Either is valid, but each organisation needs to decide which is most applicable.

METRICS IN REPORTS

Focus on the exceptions. Where you are reporting measures internally, rather than to a customer, report the exceptions rather than the conformance. For example, if 200 changes were implemented last month and four failed, instead of reporting a 98 per cent success rate and patting each other on the back, report that there were four failures. These represent the improvement opportunity and provide a focus for action.

KPIs and metrics should therefore be constructed in a way that all parties to the agreement understand and accept as an accurate measure of performance. When comparing or benchmarking such measures, ensure that the values against which you compare are constructed on the same basis: they often aren't!

When constructing performance reports do not rely solely on charts or numeric tables but use both together for a full picture. Charts are useful for showing trends and exceptions but are often manipulated to create a specific perception, for example by starting the y-axis at a value other than zero to increase apparent variations, or by excluding exceptions to better define a pattern. Numbers show absolute values and generally have higher integrity, but are less useful for showing trends.

Most recipients of reports focus on exceptions, so where there is an exception, it is the responsibility of the report creator to explain the cause. Where the exception is undesirable, the explanation should include the actions taken to prevent future exceptions. The combination of charts, numbers and explanations in a report will always provide more value than a report missing any one of these.

TEST QUESTIONS FOR CHAPTER 30

CSI 05, CSI 06, CSI 07, CSI 10

31 THE DEMING CYCLE (CSI 3.6, 5.5)

INTRODUCTION

Many organisations attempt Service Improvement through 'Big bang' implementations and by the utilisation of large projects. This may be appropriate, but often small iterative step improvements to a service or process can be more efficient and less risky.

The Deming Cycle was introduced by W. Edwards Deming as a method for quality improvement. If processes are in place, they can be measured. Changes can be made to those process and the impact of the changes assessed via further measurement. This enables ongoing measurable improvement.

Figure 31.1 The Deming Cycle (Source: OGC ITIL Continual Service Improvement ISBN 978-0-113310-49-4)

Over time the step improvements enable the service or process to become more mature. After each phase of Plan, Do, Check, Act, there is a period of consolidation to enable new improvements to 'bed-in' and to ensure that they are doing what they were intended to do.

GOALS, PURPOSE AND OBJECTIVES

The goal is Continual Service Improvement. This relates to the services provided by the organisation and also to the processes used to deliver those services. The Deming Cycle may be used to improve, for example, an online ordering service or the Service Level Management process within an organisation.

KEY ACTIVITIES

- **Plan:** Planning the Improvements. Measures for success are agreed. Gap analysis is undertaken and a plan produced to close the gap through a series of step improvements.

- **Do:** Implementation of Improvements. A project is instigated and conducted to implementation to close the gaps identified in the Plan phase. The project may include a number of step changes to improve a service or process.

- **Check:** Monitoring, Measuring and Reviewing. The results of the implemented improvements are compared with the measures for success identified and ratified in the Plan phase.

- **Act:** Improvements implemented. The improvements that have been identified are fully implemented.

Figure 31.2 The Deming Cycle: adapted for CSI (Source: based on OGC ITIL Continual Service Improvement ISBN 978-0-113310-49-4)

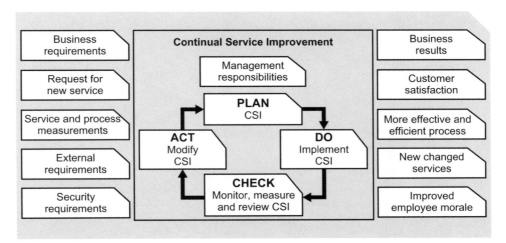

RELATIONSHIPS WITH OTHER SERVICE MANAGEMENT PROCESSES

The Deming Cycle can be used in order to improve any of the Service Management processes.

TEST QUESTIONS FOR CHAPTER 31

CSI 03
A 17

APPENDIX
Exam Techniques

INTRODUCTION

Sitting any sort of test or exam is stressful, but candidates should remember that the Foundation level exam is testing their basic understanding of the subject and terminology. It is a stepping-stone to more advanced training and qualifications and is designed to be passable by the vast majority of candidates.

There are a number of techniques and hints to keep in mind when sitting the Foundation exam. Using these techniques and hints should enable candidates to maximise their scores. There is, of course, no substitute for a having a good knowledge of the topics included in the syllabus.

TECHNIQUES

Before taking the exam, make sure that you are as prepared and relaxed as possible: visit the facilities, have a drink, try to get comfortable. When you start the exam adopt a methodical approach to ensure that you don't miss questions, and, if time permits, check your answers.

- There are 40 questions, so you have about 90 seconds for each. This doesn't sound like much time, but it is. In reality, many questions will take you much less time than this.
- Read each question carefully.
- Answer with only one option per question. There is only one right answer.
- There will only ever be four options: A, B, C or D. Ensure no other options are selected on your answer grid.
- Answer the straightforward questions first and return to more complex ones, or ones that you are unsure of, later.
- If you think you have found an obvious right answer, sense-check that all the other options are wrong.
- Although good practice says they shouldn't be used, watch for negatives in questions. For example, 'Which of the following is NOT an advantage of implementing etc.?'

- Answer all the questions. Don't leave blanks on the answer grid.
- When tackling questions that you are unsure of, try the following:

  - Try to eliminate some of the options.
  - See if there are any clues in another question.
  - In the final resort, take an educated guess.

- Take care in changing an answer. Unless it is clearly wrong (e.g. because you misread the question initially) your first instinct is often proven right.

Points to remember:

- There is no negative marking (i.e. marks are not deducted for wrong answers).
- There aren't any trick questions; the objective is to test your knowledge and understanding.

INDEX